Sultans, Shamans, and Saints

Sultans, Shamans, and Saints

Islam and Muslims in Southeast Asia

Howard M. Federspiel

University of Hawai'i Press
Honolulu

LIBRARY OF CONGRESS CATALOGING-IN-PUBLICATION DATA
Federspiel, Howard M.
  Sultans, shamans, and saints : Islam and Muslims in
Southeast Asia / Howard M. Federspiel.
      p. cm.
  Includes bibliographical references and index.
  ISBN-13: 978-0-8248-3052-6 (hardcover : alk. paper)
  ISBN-10: 0-8248-3052-0 (hardcover : alk. paper)
  1. Islam—South Asia—History. 2. Muslims—South Asia—
History. I. Title.
BP63.A37F43 2007
297.0959—dc22

                                2006024209

University of Hawai'i Press books are printed on acid-free
paper and meet the guidelines for permanence and durability
of the Council on Library Resources.

Designed by University of Hawai'i Press production staff
Printed by The Maple-Vail Book Manufacturing Group

To my family:

Johanna, the matriarch;

my daughter, Karen, and her two children, Steven and Kara;

my son, Karl, his wife, Irene, and their daughter, Kasandra

When, ultimately, you gaze through the veils to how
    things really are,
With great wonder you will say, again and again,
"This is truly not what we thought it was!"

—RUMI, *Mathnawi*

Contents

Maps

Preface

Foreign names, places, and terminology present a particular challenge to readers who are not yet familiar with Southeast Asia. The difficulties arise principally from the facts that several different languages operate in the region, and that two additional languages from outside the region—Arabic and Sanskrit—bring in a large number of loanwords. Moreover, names change over time, so that spellings for one era are not always the same for another period. The following guidelines have been used to clarify some underlying principles.

First, personal names are given in the form in which they appear in the language the person himself uses. Thus, a Malay will use Ahmad; an Acehnese may use Achmad; and an Arab will use Ahmad. Muhammad is common in Arabic, but is often spelt Mohammad in Malay. Moreover, Indonesians use surnames, but Malays do not, so that entries in the Bibliography note that difference. Hence it is Akiro, yusuf in Indonesian, but yusuf Akiro in Malay practice. The Malays observe such name usage in Malaysia, Singapore, Brunei, Thailand, Cambodia, and Vietnam.

Second, association names are rendered in English translation, followed immediately by any acronym, with the original language words in parenthesis; for example, Islamic Union–Persis (Persatuan Islam).

Third, place-names use the spelling on international maps, which generally follow local spellings. So I have used Makkah (Mecca) and Madinah (Medina) for the holy cities in Arabia, and Melaka (Malacca) for the historical port in the Straits of Melaka.

Political names for territories sometimes change over time. Ceylon became Sri Lanka. Khmer became Cambodia, but for a time in the 1970s was Kampuchea. The most illustrative case was Ayuthia, which became Siam, which then became Thailand. When such a name changes from one era to another in the text, a short statement is made noting the new form.

Fourth, books and manuscripts are given in English translation followed by the original foreign-language title in parenthesis. An example is "Story of the Crown of Kings" *(Syair Taj al-Muluk)*.

Five, religious terms are given in English when possible, but local usage of the word is given in parentheses. The original term is further defined in the glossary at the end of the book. An example is "prompting at the grave side" *(talqin)*.

Finally, all names, places, and terms rendered in Arabic or Arabic script employ the transliteration system used by the cataloging service of the U.S. Library of Congress. This system extends to older Malay texts written in Arabic script. Consequently, it spells the name for a member of the Islamic religion Muslim, no longer Moslem, as was common before the 1960s. Also, it is Qur'an, not Koran, as was once common. As a scripture well known in English-speaking areas, Qur'an is treated like other holy books, as, say, the Bible. The ancillary scripture, the Traditions *(Hadith)*, is treated in the same manner.

The maps used in this volume were designed by the author especially for the study.

The following library collections were used in the preparation of this text. I would like to express my thanks for the assistance of numerous staff and administrators during my work at various institutions: the Ohio University Library; the Ohio State University Library system; the graduate library at the University of Michigan and the rare books collection; Duke University Library; Cornell University Library; Winthrop University Library; the Library of Congress system, particularly the Orientalia and rare books sections; the U.S. State Department library; the Foreign Service Institute library; the graduate library and the library of the Institute of Islamic Studies at McGill University in Canada; the Leiden University collection; the General Archives of the Netherlands; the Library of the School of African and Oriental Studies; the British General Library; the library of Southeast Asian Studies; the Singapore General Library; the Islamic Library (Kuala Lumpur); the special collection of Muslim Council (MUIS) in Singapore; the University of Malaya Library; the Indonesian Museum Library (Jakarta); the Islamic Library (Yogyakarta); the North Sumatran Council of Islamic Scholars Library (Medan); and the Bandung Institute of Technology Library.

I also wish to thank diplomatic officials and governmental officials for their assistance at the Indonesian Embassy, the Thai Embassy, the Malaysian Embassy, the Saudi Arabian Embassy, and the Republic of the Philippines Embassy all in Washington, DC; the American Embassy in Indonesia and the American Embassy in Brunei Darussalam; the Ministry of Education in Brunei Darussalam; the Department of Religious Affairs in Indonesia; the Office of Islamic Affairs in the Prime Minister's Office in Malaysia; and the Islamic Council officials in Singapore. I also received assistance for some parts of this work from the U.S. Fulbright Commission, the National Endowment for the Humanities, Winthrop University, Ohio State University at Newark, and the Association for Asian Studies.

I am indebted to Kent Mulliner and Raymond Scupin for reviewing the original manuscript, and they have my deep appreciation. Finally, I wish to express my gratitude to a number of colleagues who listened to my research efforts and encouraged me over the years: the late John S. Thomson, Ruth T. McVey, Lian The Mulliner, John MacDougall, A. Uner Turgay, Donald Weatherbee, and Donald McCloud.

Introduction

It is not enough to simply identify and analyse Islamic tradition in its historical form, as some sort of static body of knowledge. Islamic tradition, rather, forms a continuous stream of consciousness, which has been evolving over the centuries, and which continues to evolve in the present.

On a Sunday evening, when returning from a day at Brastagi, a mountain retreat in the interior of North Sumatra, one would have seen two meaningful phenomena unfolding. The first consisted of heavy activity at the fruit and vegetable assembly points in hilltop villages, where agriculturalists brought their products for delivery to the markets on the coast, particularly to Singapore. There was a hubbub as goods were unloaded from local conveyances into small trucks, which then drove with breathtaking speed down the precipitous mountain roads to the port at Belawan, whence small boats moved the goods rapidly on to their destinations at Medan, Singapore, or perhaps to some Malaysian port across the Straits of Melaka. This perpetual scene was testimony to a vigorous local trade vital to all the parties in the region—Christians, animists, Buddhists, and Muslims. The production, movement, and ultimate use of these agricultural products involved all types of people, and as is so often the case with open trade, religious affiliation was not much of a factor, although the multicultural aspects of the regional society were manifest.

The second phenomenon revolved around the bus stops where city workers waited for their ride back to Medan to begin the new workweek after too brief visits to their rural family homes. The closer to the city and the later it was, the more people were on the move. It was a prosperous time, and people looked forward to their week in the city, so the atmosphere was upbeat and friendly. The buses, small and large, disgorged these people into the southern sections of the city, where they milled around the shops, eating stalls, and mosques, talking with friends and relaxing as darkness fell and they enjoyed the final hours of the weekend. If one's timing was right, the call to prayer issued from numerous loudspeakers, after which many of the men and some of the women moved toward the lighted places of worship to begin their ablutions and prayers. The mosques on the main road revealed to the traveler worshipers in long lines and undulating patterns as they stood, knelt, and prostrated themselves in the prescribed motions of Muslim worship. The entire scene—trade, travel, small pleasures, and worship—could be seen to provide a brief sketch of civilization at a normal, unspectacular time and place. Significantly, religion was integral to the portrait and natural to it without undue notice or effort exerted on the part of the believers. Islam was not born in Southeast Asia, but it became an important element in the region, almost as if it had been created for the role it fulfilled.

This book is a study of Islam and Muslims in Southeast Asia, a non-Arabic setting. In it, Islam is recognized as the religion that has been practiced by large numbers of people since the seventh century A.D. It was established by a religious and political figure named Muhammad, who lived, preached, and undertook to deliver a message he understood as a command from God to create a community of believers. That religion went on to become an identifying characteristic for a civilization that extended from the Iberian Peninsula in the west to the borders of India in the ninth and tenth centuries; and its creed, tenets, ceremonies, beliefs, and practices were given an orthodox framework by numerous scholars, rulers, and religious activists. By the fifteenth century it had split into two sizeable communities, the Sunnis and the Shi'ahs. It had also established jurisprudential schools and a number of mystical orders that crisscrossed the various regions where the followers of Islam lived and worked. Islam throughout its history has been a religion, a way of life, and a definer of culture and civilization. A Muslim is an adherent of Islam who identifies with the religion and lives in general accordance with the values and tenets both of the religion and of the civilization that has emerged to represent Islam. Here I use both terms, "Islam" and "Muslim," in that wide civilizational sense, but do not exclude the narrower meaning of simple religious identification.

Today in Southeast Asia the principal religions are Islam, with more than two hundred million followers; Buddhism, with slightly more than two hundred million adherents; and several other religions with significant numbers of worshipers. Buddhism, both the Mahayana and Theravada sects, dominates the mainland north of the Eighth Parallel—that is, Burma, Thailand, and the Indochina states. Islam, almost entirely the Sunni sect, dominates the area south of that line—namely, southern Thailand, Malaysia, Indonesia, Brunei, and the southern Philippines. Christianity has groups of followers throughout the region; most are Catholics, but some areas of Protestant strength predominate in the northern and central Philippines, several areas of Indonesia, and parts of South Vietnam. Hinduism is prominent on the island of Bali and has a limited number of followers among Indian settlers throughout the region. Taoism, Confucianism, and several other Chinese religiocultural value systems have been adopted throughout the area by the overseas Chinese. Finally, shamanism and animism persist alongside the other religious systems nearly everywhere in Southeast Asia, but clearly prevail in several regions, notably West Irian, interior Kalimantan (Borneo), and the highland areas of Indochina.

It is postulated that an Islamic zone of Southeast Asia has existed historically that crosses political and geographic boundaries of the region. It consists of the territory, just mentioned, where the Sunni Muslims are located. The "Muslim Zone" serves as a true cultural area, and attempts will be made to include material here that shows this to be true. The zone was never united politically, and in the twentieth century it has been divided politically among eight distinct nation-states. Neither has it ever been consolidated culturally; a wide variety of customs exist within the territory, including significant differences within areas of the zone itself. Linguistically it is not unified either, Malay and Javanese being the two major languages and several other languages serving as regional vehicles. Ethnically there are considerable differences, although Malays and Javanese dominate, but Bugis, Minangs, Bantamese, and Chams have been prominent as well. Finally, a few Muslim activists, both historically and in the present, have "imagined" the zone as a common unit, but the concept has never been a political consideration in the public mind. The only phenomenon common in the region is the adherence of large portions of the population to common religious institutions, teachings, and values. It is only in the form of religious identification, therefore, that this very diverse group of people exhibit some commonality.

This study operates on the basis of two premises: (1) Islam is a dynamic religion that has been adapted to time and place by its followers and (2) Islam in any region can be measured for orthodoxy, not simply against the Middle East, but against the general norms of Islam throughout the world. Consequently, I shall examine Islam in Southeast Asia in terms of four large periods: the time of Islam's arrival (up to 1300); the first flowering of Islamic identity (1300 to 1800); the era of imperialism (1800 to 1950); and that of independent nation-states (1950 to 2000). I selected these four eras only after much consideration of historical factors across the Muslim Zone. While they are not altogether satisfactory when considered from the viewpoint of political developments in one area or another, as an overall division of time the four periods offer a nice compromise that allows for discussion of cross-zone events without too much awkwardness. For general convenience, the study concludes with the end of the twentieth century. Events occurring after that time frame as yet lack historical and cultural

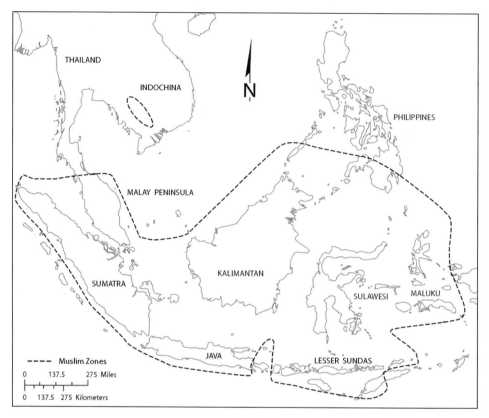

1. The Muslim Zone

context for any thorough analysis, so no attempt has been made to cover those events, except in casual reference.

The study does not use a single methodological approach, but comes closest perhaps to the "historical-periods' comparison" of G. Bergsträsser in his 1930 study of Islamic jurisprudence. He maintained that a long-lasting social institution could be properly analyzed by examining key facets of that institution at several different historical points to ascertain whether change was taking place and how the institution was responding to the changing context of history itself. For example, the place of the mosque in Islamic society could be examined in 1800, 1900, and 2000, and a comparison made about the differences among the three descriptions. Ideally, insight about the importance of the mosque over a two-century span would emerge. Bergsträsser had precisely that idea in mind, but would examine several other facets of Islam to accompany the mosque examination in order to give a broader view of the evolution of Islam over time. My cross-disciplinary examination of Islam at four different periods in Southeast Asian history probably approximates what Bergsträsser intended.[1]

Consequently, in each era a common set of points will be examined. Each chapter will begin with a explanation of Southeast Asian developments in a wider Asian world, followed by an examination of the ethnic groups, political events, customs and cultures, religious factors, and art forms that were apparent at the time. A conclusion and a list of key readings for further investigation is provided for each chapter. A general conclusion at the end of the entire study reviews the major Islamic institutions of Southeast Asia and their meaning to Southeast Asia historically and contemporaneously.

This work is not intended to be a "history," although a historical framework has been adopted for purposes of presentation; rather, it is a study that traverses many fields and disciplines. This must be so, because, as already observed, Muslims do not consider Islam a religion in the Western meaning of the term, but rather a particular manifestation that has shaped and influenced wide areas of human life and social institutions beyond the confines of what is often regarded as religion. Thus, we must necessarily examine it in a wider context of a variety of human experiences.

General Background Readings

Andaya, Barbara Watson, and Leonard Y. 1982. *A History of Malaysia*. A composite history of the territories that constitute Malaysia, giving both overall themes and sufficient detail.

Denny, Frederick M. 1986. *An Introduction to Islam*. A description of the terms, rites, and prominent groups in Islam.

Hodgson, Marshall G. S. 1958–1959. *The Venture of Islam*. 3 vols. An overarching history of the Islamic regions of the world, showing the legacy of Islam as it developed in the central Islamic world.

Holt, P. M., Ann K. S. Lambton, and Bernard Lewis, eds. 1970. *Cambridge History of Islam*. 4 vols. A history of classical Islamic civilizations, with later development of Islam outside of the Middle East.

Miller, Terry E., and Sean William, eds. 1998. *The Garland Encyclopedia of World Music: Southeast Asia*. The musical tradition of Southeast Asia related to custom, religion, and various other influences.

Ricklefs, M. C. 1981. *A History of Modern Indonesia*. A history of the Indonesian nation in which several of the regional traditions are drawn together to form a composite whole.

Saunders, Graham. 1994. *A History of Brunei*. A straightforward rendition of the Brunean attempt to create and sustain a history separate from that of its neighbors.

Steinberg, David J., ed. 1987. *In Search of Southeast Asia.* An overview of the modern nation-states of Southeast Asia, emphasizing their effort to attain independence and develop as independent cultures.

Tarling, Nicholas, ed. 1992. *Cambridge History of Southeast Asia.* 2 vols. An overview of Southeast Asian cultures and their unification into the modern nation-states of the region.

1 Muslim Wayfarers (600 A.D.–1300)

There is an island from which one continually hears the noise of drums, flutes, lutes and all sorts of musical instruments, a sound soft and agreeable, and at the same time dancing steps and clapping of hands. If one listens carefully one can distinguish all the sounds without confusion. Sailors who visit these regions say that the Antichrist lives here.

General Context

The Greater Asian Setting

A convenient way of beginning a study of Islam in Southeast Asia is to focus on the sea routes that crossed the Indian Ocean and, in one sense, tied the various civilizations of Asia to one another. Those sea routes, with the Indian Ocean as their center, allowed ships from as far west as the Red Sea to cross the northern stretches of the ocean, which fronted much of the Middle East and the Indian subcontinent, past Ceylon, through the Malay-Indonesian world as far as China to the East. There were also side routes from the Middle East to the eastern coast of Africa, in the Far East from China to the ports of Korea and Japan, and in Southeast Asia from the western part of the Indonesian archipelago to the eastern islands of that chain. These routes were long-lasting, having originated in rudimentary form long before the rise of recorded history in any of the regions affected (Map 2).

Many scholars from both East and West regarded the sea routes as the linkage between the primary civilizations of Asia—that is, the Islamic world, Brahman India, and Middle-Kingdom China—when all three were at the height of their development and influence between the seventh and eighteenth centuries.[1] It is worth summarizing these civilizations and their relationship to one another at this early point in our discussion, since they played such a key role in the development of Islam in Southeast Asia.

The Middle East was dominated by Islamic civilization. Islam had its beginnings in the frontier area of the Arabian Peninsula, peripheral to two major civilizations of the day. To the northwest lay the Byzantine Empire (527–1453), successor to the Roman and Greek civilization of the Mediterranean, while to the northeast was the Sassanid Empire (227–637), which succeeded not only the Medes and Persians, but much of Mesopotamian civilization as well. The religion received its scripture through a prophet,

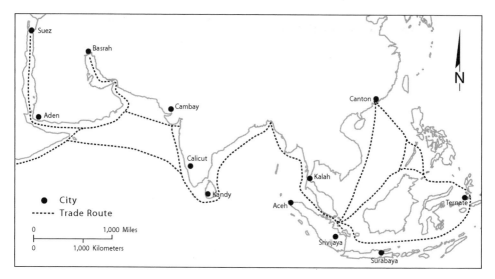

2. The Trade Routes

Muhammad, who had his ministry at Makkah (Mecca) and Madinah (Medina) in Arabia, and began to develop an Islamic community before his death in 632. The main principles of Islam consisted of belief in a single god, Allah, who created and sustained all things. Allah had sent prophets at various times with the message of how to worship him properly, how humans should deal with one another appropriately, and how humans should act as proper stewards of the world about them. The message sent through Muhammad was called the Qurʾan, that is, the "Recitation." Muslims were obliged to follow the "pillars of Islam" which consisted of confessing that Allah was the only god and that Muhammad was His messenger, performing the ritual five prayers each day, fasting during the daylight hours of the month of Ramadan, giving a portion of one's wealth to the poor, and undertaking a pilgrimage to the holy city of Makkah once during a lifetime. Islam proclaimed that there were angels, other prophets before Muhammad, scriptures that preceded the Qurʾan, that God as creator determined all things, and that there would be a Day of Judgment when all humans would account for their deeds and misdeeds. There were important concepts in Islam, such as the "doctrine of oneness" *(tawhid)*, according to which all things, all concepts, and all of life tended toward unity in God, and a "sacred law" *(shariʾah)* laid out by God as His unchanging standards of justice, which humans should strive to fulfill. After his death Muhammad's status was elevated to that of a guide for Muslims, which led to the codification of the record of his words and acts, known as the "Traditions" *(Hadith)*, which ultimately was considered a second scripture subordinate to but explanatory of the Qurʾan. Later legalist schools were established that took the principles found in the Qurʾan and the Traditions and turned them into a "jurisprudential law" (*fiqh*). Many Muslims held that this derived jurisprudence was an indication, a reflection, or the actual rendition of God's immutable and transcendent law. Others stated that jurisprudence was important simply as a guide to good behavior. Finally, Islamic mysticism (*tasawwuf*) became important, in which a metaphysical union was sought between the human mystic and God through the medium of esoteric exercises.

Under the early patriarchs immediately after Muhammad's death, Muslim armies utterly vanquished Sassanid political power in the area now known as Iran and Iraq, and assumed control of large portions of the Byzantine area in Egypt and along the eastern Mediterranean litoral. Under the Umayyad kingdom (656–750) and the Abbasid Empire (750–1256), Islam began to develop a distinctive culture, drawing on cultural elements unique to itself but incorporating large portions of Sassanid and Byzantine ways as well as elements from Indian civilization further to the east. Islam became a civilization in its own right, with a unique political form, an important literature, a fully developed economy, and social institutions, especially in the ninth and tenth centuries. So, for much of the era discussed in this chapter, Islam as a religion, as a culture, and as a civilization was undergoing its own early development. Importantly, it was not until the end of the twelfth century in the person of al-Ghazali (d. 1111) that the basic theological issues were resolved to a point that a religious orthodoxy was fully defined, even though the other components of the civilization—politics, economy, and literature—had reached a high level of maturity two centuries earlier.

The introduction of new peoples to Islam was rapid in the seventh and eighth centuries, adding Persians, Egyptians, Circassians, Turks, and numerous other Middle Eastern and North African peoples to the original Arab population. By the end of the era Islam was also extending itself into new regions in the Sahel, the steppe territory of Africa south of the Sahara, and into the Balkans. It also inherited sea and land routes to eastern Asia from the Sassanians, so that Arabs and Persians, now as Muslims, moved along those trade corridors as traders and adventurers.

As for India in this time frame, it was experiencing the continuation of a civilization developed earlier under the Maurya (322–185 B.C.E) and Gupta (320–647 C.E.) dynasties, when most of India came under control of a single political authority and was generally uniform in culture. The caste system, which had been fashioned and solidified earlier, gave regularity to Indian society, while the three great religious traditions—Hinduism, Mahayana Buddhism, and Jainism—spread through society and defined Indian spiritual goals. However, the period under discussion saw India in a decentralized condition politically, with local dynasties dividing control of Indic territory. At the same time, culturally there was commonality throughout the subcontinent that reflected the civilization developed earlier. During this period Indian travel and trade to Southeast Asia was heavy and transported Indian civilization to Southeast Asia, where it dominated local states emerging at the time. The influence of Brahmans at the court of Southeast Asian princes, the probable use of Indian workers and craftsmen in building architectural structures, and the presence of some Indian colonists have led historians of Southeast Asia to speak of an "Indian era." Mostly, however, it was not Indian presence that was historically important, for it was small and diffuse, but the influence of Indian religion, thought, and culture that determined the region's Indic tone.

Northern Asia was dominated by the great empire of China, which had already established its own unique civilization, particularly during the early and late Han dynasties (206 B.C.E.–222 C.E.), when the values of Confucianism set the standards for political life and general family values. Alongside these fundamental values, the religious notions of Taoism, a local religious system, and later Buddhism coming from India, gave spiritual identity to most of the Chinese population. Over the next thousand years this became the most sophisticated political system of its time, with political control resting at the local level with a gentry class and at the universal level with the court of the emperor, assisted by an able civil service recruited through a system of examinations. This empire was not only politically sophisticated, but also well developed in the arts and literature, and possessed a sense of cultural identification with the general population. It was a high civilization according to most measures, and its rulers, intellectuals, and people considered their existing culture superior, even though general knowledge of other civilizations was limited. Its economic system was highly developed, particularly with the rise of the silk industry and the production of fine pottery that drew merchants from elsewhere to bargain for these products and many others that the Chinese civilization was able to produce. At times its own merchants went abroad, traveling throughout Asian waters as far as India, but Korean, Japanese, and Southeast Asian commerce was more common to them. China established a tribute system, whereby local rulers in Southeast Asia recognized the Chinese emperor as their overlord, in order to bind those states to China politically and economically.

The three Asian civilizations were distinct from one another in the development of their language, social institutions, and historical dynamics, but they were inevitably products of the world era in which they existed, and they had much in common with one another. Economically and technologically they were at similar stages of development, so that the contacts they had with one another were pursued to their common advantage, and the lively trade that ensued made it possible for high-quality goods to circulate throughout the three regions. Land routes through central Asia allowed some contact, but the sea routes seem to have offered the best means for the trading of economic goods among the three civilizations. Cultural elements were invariably passed along the route as well.

The trade routes to Southeast Asia in the pre-European era provide a clear picture of the fundamentals that operated in this time frame. Terminal ports in the Middle East changed as time progressed, with south Arabian ports such as Aden and Oman alternating in influence with the Persian Gulf ports al-Ubadullah, Basrah, Siraf, and Kish. When the Sassanid Empire and the Abbasid Empire (750–1258) were strong, the Persian Gulf was the site of primary shipping, and when Egypt rose under the Mamelukes (1250–1517), the south Arabian ports were more prominent. At the other end of the sea routes, in China, the southern ports vied with one another for importance under the Tang (618–907) and Sung (960–1279) dynasties, with Canton, Amoy, and Zaitun the primary location of ports. In South Asia, coastal Gujerat, the Malabar Coast, and Ceylon had prominent ports. Kandy on Ceylon was always important, while Cambay in the Gujerat was also well used during this era. In Southeast Asia the first leading port for international Asian trade was Kalah, apparently located at Kedah on the southwestern side of the Malayan Peninsula, replaced by Srivijaya near present-day Palembang on the southern end of Sumatra, and later still by several sites along the eastern Malayan Peninsula coast in the northern Pahang and Trengganu areas.[2]

The goods shipped along this trade route were varied. The Middle East produced glass, ceramics, and rugs; India, cotton textiles and metalwork; and China, silk and ceramics; while Southeast Asia was the source of special woods, metals, camphor, and spices. The methods of collecting and preparing these goods varied according to the civilization involved, but generally there was a division of labor among producers, collectors, and processors, so that international trading was a specialty in itself. Likewise, the financial arrangements differed, with capital to support the enterprises being raised or provided by rulers, state agencies, individuals, and combines, according to time and place. For example, Arab shipping usually was in the hands of private combines, which made ships' captains little more than paid employees, but great profit was made by the owners when voyages were successful. In China, state agencies controlled shipping and sponsored some trading ventures, often dictating the conditions of such activity in order to give the state ventures an upper hand over private Chinese efforts. In India, producers often manufactured goods according to foreign specification and received set payment, usually ahead of time, to meet production quotas and schedules. There was considerable variety in the financial, shipping, and production arrangements.

International trading activities were undertaken by many peoples along the routes, with the range of each group differing substantially. The Persians, and later the Arabs, were active all along the sea routes, being the primary long-distance haulers; they will be discussed further in the next section. Chinese traders were prominent in trade in Southeast Asia and went as far as India on occasion, and perhaps as far as the Middle East a few times. Indian traders were evident in Southeast Asia, with some presence in East Asia and the Middle East. Southeast Asian traders visited India regularly and China on occasion, but were less prominent than other groups in those two places. Sometimes traders used their own ships, and at other times they shipped their goods in the vessels of peoples more familiar with particular regions or with cheap cargo space to rent. Leased ship space was common between Southeast Asia and China, where large Chinese vessels frequently transported the goods of the Arabs and Persians in both directions because of the carrying capacity of those ships.

The chief feature of all ports was the harbor where ships laid up and warehouses were located. Local rulers established weighing facilities and custom sheds. Frequently there was a residential quarter where port-service personnel lived and merchants rented or owned houses while sojourning, as they engaged in negotiating new cargoes or waited for favorable winds. This was particularly important in the Southeast Asian region, where winds changed with the seasons and especially with the onset of the monsoon rains, so that travel to and from Southeast Asia was regulated by those winds. The local rulers exacted a tax for use of a port and, in exchange, provided officials and regulations for the port's order and proper operation. In the Malay regions a member of the local ruler's council of state, usually the chief minister, had overall charge of trade and was the point of contact between the port officials and the court. Ports provided regulations, such as the maritime laws of Melaka, which were generalized codes about conduct aboard ship and in port, the buying and selling of goods, and taxation in the ports.

Often the traders resident in such international ports were accorded special jurisdiction by the ruler separate from that granted to other parts of the realm—obviously because of the profitable excise taxes such ports brought into court coffers and the problems of regulating people of other cultures who were constantly on the move. Consequently, ports were permitted many of their own public facilities and forms of entertainment, while sojourners were allowed to live under their own rules of personal behavior. In the Muslim community usually this was the Shafiʿi jurisprudential code, also used along the Indian Ocean periphery. The port populations were under the direct supervision of one or more harbormasters, often recruited from among the foreign merchants themselves. These harbormasters kept order with the help of a small detachment of "police," decided disputes among merchants, and represented the community to the chief minister and, sometimes, to the royal courts of the country.

The brisk traffic that took place among these ports entailed the passage of people and ideas throughout the region. Hence, in Southeast Asia there were a large number of spare men from outside the area, due to shipwreck, desertion, or just search for adventure. Apparently, a large number of these outsiders were Muslim, at least in the fifteenth to seventeenth centuries (later they were joined by Europeans) and were a source of mercenary manpower for various armies. Religious scholars moved easily along this lifeline as well. For example, at Samudra on the northern coast of Sumatra, religious scholars arrived regularly from India, Persia, and Arabia. Pilgrims to religious shrines moved between ports, many traveling toward Ceylon to visit the shrine at Adam's Foot and others going all the way to the Red Sea and Arabia to visit the holy cities of Makkah and Madinah on pilgrimage. Religious literature also flowed along the shipping lanes, finding acceptance at a large number of places along the entire route. Textual analysis indicates that considerable amounts of literature from the Middle East entered Southeast Asia through India.[3] It would seem that some Arabic writings from southern Arabia and Basrah went directly to Southeast Asia as well.

The sea routes enabled many merchants and their financial backers to become wealthy. But the routes were hazardous because of navigational hazards and calamities such as storms and piracy. These factors caused many potentially profitable voyages to suffer financial disaster. Piracy was probably the most serious danger, and it existed along the entire international trade route from the Middle East to China. It was usually perpetrated by freebooters, but sometimes privateers were sponsored by local states along the routes and victimized only those traders who refused to make financial arrangements with them by entering their ports and paying excise taxes on their cargoes. Piracy enjoyed considerable success and was apparently so common that many of the notable travelers of this era recorded interest in the practice, reporting only a sense of minor discomfort to their travel arrangements.[4]

The sea routes were on the periphery of the three civilizations, not at their centers, and were connected to the major cities of the interior by overland or river routes, where they melded with the extensive internal trade networks in each civilization. This location—to the side, as it were—was important historically because it was not central, and none of the dominant political powers regarded it as a path of attack on the other civilizations, nor did any Asian political power seek to usurp the entire route for economic gain, as the Europeans attempted to do later. Consequently there was ample freedom of movement, though at considerable risk, for merchants to move along the route for economic reasons, although obviously the major Asian powers often had to be assuaged or their permission sought in order to operate in particular sectors of the route.

At times, of course, the major political states did assert some power over the portion of the sea routes closest to them, but mostly for the suppression of piracy rather than for any great regulation of the types of goods involved in the trade. The Abbasids in the tenth century used a small fleet to patrol the route between the Persian Gulf and the western coast of India, while the Chinese in the South China Sea in the tenth century, and the Mamelukes in the Arabian Sea in the twelfth century, did the same. Also, there were some attempts by local political forces along the trade routes to control them for their own benefit and to build political power from the proceeds of that trade. The classic case was Srivijaya (670–1025), whose political control extended through many parts of maritime Southeast Asia. The Chola kingdom (907–1310) in the early eleventh century is a later example. Located astride the sea routes in the southern Indian and the Ceylon area, the Chola rulers used a navy to eliminate local trade rivals, enforced their rule on many ports in the area between Sri Lanka and Sumatra, and imposed taxes on shipping throughout the region.

None of these political attempts to dominate sections of the sea routes caused much dislocation, primarily because those powers were interested in expanding trade rather than curtailing it, although the rise and fall of affluent groups along the route were influential in the promotion or restraint of trade. However, the political stability of the major civilizations the trade routes served and their economic affluence apparently did act as a stimulus or a brake on trade, as might be expected.

In Southeast Asia the trade routes crisscrossed the region. Chinese trade moved through the South China Sea, the eastern Indonesian archipelago, along the north coast of Sumatra, and to southern Sumatra for jungle and seashore products. The traders of the northern Javanese ports moved out to the eastern islands to bring back spices, particularly nutmeg and cloves. The peoples of the eastern archipelago, in turn, took spices to Java and visited the Lesser Sundas as well, bringing back grain for its food-poor islands. In the Malay Straits area, pepper and jungle products were the staples of trade, and the merchants from the west—Indians, Arabo-Indians, Arabs, and eventually Europeans—traded heavily there. Southeast Asians were gatherers, traders, and importers of goods. Patani was a center of the ironwood trade; the eastern reaches of Sumatra had abundant seashore products; Aceh and Banten were centers of pepper production; and Maluku had spices. All Southeast Asia wanted lacquerware and silk from China and cotton cloth from India, as well as products from within the Southeast Asian region itself, particularly foodstuffs, which were crucially short in some areas. Here the Magindanaoan and central Javanese areas were important in furnishing abundant rice. In general, maritime Southeast Asia was an important, and in some ways vital, part of the entire international trade routes of the era.

The Southeast Asian Setting

In this era there were five important migratory movements that affected the Southeast Asian region. The first involved the peoples along the trade routes—Persians, Arabs, Indians, and Chinese—who came and went according to the shipping seasons, with several ports in the Southeast Asian region serving as their destination points. As we have already seen, these four peoples made an impact on Southeast Asia through buying, selling, and trading goods. They provided local rulers with a significant source of revenue from taxes on goods and control of the local buying and selling of goods, and they attracted other local groups who tried to seize their wealth through piracy. This traffic of people was to be an important factor in the spread of Islam in the region.

The second migration consisted of Chinese moving south into the Red River delta (Vietnam) and Sinicizing that area, which was to have a long-term historical influence, but one that was peripheral to the considerations of any study on Islam. The third population shift involved Indian migration to Southeast Asia, which was highly important to the development of small, self-sufficient states that in turn led to a specific Southeast Asian cultural identity. This cultural identity, later discussed separately, acted as a precursor to Islamization. The fourth population movement consisted of the Mongols' invasion of parts of Southeast Asia, which, though short-lived, disrupted political control, particularly in the mainland Indochina area. In insular Southeast Asia, the Mongols further weakened an already fading Majapahit kingdom on Java and cleared the way for Muslim states to begin to emerge. The fifth movement, also occurring near the end of the era, was the migration of Thai groups from the southern borders of China into the areas now known as Thailand, which marked the rise of non-Indian peoples in the formation of the states in the region. The Thai, with their new religion, Theravada Buddhism, acted as a block against the spread of Islam into the Indochina area, of course an important factor, though in a negative way.

The most significant political feature of the era was the building of small states in the region, many of which were the foundation of national states that were to emerge a few centuries later. Usually these small states formed where a series of political entities had sprung up around some geographical feature and the dominance of prominent leaders. The main examples were centered in northern Indochina in the Red River delta (Vietnam), immediately south in the central highlands (Champa), further south on the Mekong River (Angkor), still further west on the Irrawaddy River

(Pagan), on the southern part of the island of Sumatra (Srivijaya), and in the eastern part of the island of Java (Mataram). Except in Vietnam where Chinese influence was prevalent, the new states were under the strong cultural influence of Indian civilization.

Hinduism and then Mahayana Buddhism were the major religions of the period, although local religious rites and beliefs based on preexisting animism continued to flourish outside the royal courts. Sanskrit was the language of the courts and religious abbeys, and intellectual concepts came from India. Rulers installed governments, using Brahman models from northern India, including the concept of the ruler as divinely blessed. Structures were erected at first honoring Hinduism and, later, Buddhism. The shrines at Angkor Wat in Indochina and at Borobudur in central Java remain world-famous today; both were built by branches of the highly influential Sailendra dynasty, with its origins in India. By the end of the era, a shift occurred, and Indian influence began to recede, mostly the result of a decline in prestige of the Indian elite and the emergence of local ethnic groups such as the Thai and the Javanese. Theravada Buddhism began to replace other forms of religion on mainland Southeast Asia, and China under the Mongols launched a series of punitive raids throughout the region that shook the political leadership and set the stage for a new era of state building with assumptions different from what had gone before. Islam was to constitute an important ingredient in this new construction, but that was to come later.

For our purposes in discussing Islam during this era, only a small sector of Southeast Asia was directly relevant, while other parts were indirectly important for contextual reasons. Of most moment were the sea-route approaches in the Indian Ocean, several coastal landfalls on the Malayan Peninsula, on Sumatra, on the northern coast of Borneo/Kalimantan, and on the eastern coast of Indochina, as well as in the southern ports of China. The Muslim Arabs, Persians, and Indians did visit these places, but apparently *only* visited, leaving but a few traces of their considerable travel through the region. In fact, Southeast Asia appeared to be of only incidental importance to the progress of Islam during this era; the neighboring areas of the Indian Ocean to the west and southern China to the north were far more significant. Both historical and anthropological contemporary records provide some clues to the status and position of Muslims in those areas. Southeast Asia proper was an area only traversed by Muslims, or useful for supporting their trading activity, as when they had to use local ports for indirect trade with China at times when its own ports were closed to foreigners.

On the northern tip of Sumatra there were important stops on the international trade routes. At this time they were small Muslim enclaves existing next to a population that was not yet converted and may have been hostile to Islam, regarding it as an intrusive culture and religion. Apparently there was warfare between the Muslims and the surrounding peoples, although it is difficult to ascertain which side was the usual aggressor. It may have been the Muslim rulers attempting to convert the "pagan" population, but we know little about the actual state of relationships between the port population and the peoples in the hinterland. From tombs that existed in northern Sumatra, that exhibit styles common to Gujerat in western India, it is apparent that the merchants from the Indian Ocean were an important factor in the conversion of those states to Islam.

People and Their Activities

Important Ethnic Groups

Aside from the Indian group, which has already been discussed, the most important groups in the region for the purposes of this study were the Persians and the Arabs. Local peoples in the Indian Ocean areas, on Sumatra, in the Champa region, and in southern China were peripherally important.

The Persians were the first group of Middle Easterners to use the trade routes extensively, beginning probably in the age of ancient Greece, and they continued to constitute the majority of the trading groups during this period, although there appears to have been a steady growth in the number of Arabs. With the rise of Islam in the seventh century, there was conversion to Islam among these traders, as there was with the general populations in their home countries. However, one should be careful about ascribing too great a commitment to Islam among this group in the early years after Islam came to dominate the Middle East. A prayer used on the shipping lanes recognized Allah and His mercy, but centered mostly on Muhammad as the Prophet of God and asked for his intercession.[5] In general, the prayer fell short of expressing the formulas common to standard Muslim prayers of the classical Islamic period, indicating perhaps that the crews who used this prayer were only superficially converted. However, with time this group of Muslims become the carriers of the religion and its attendant culture, and in this early period they brought that faith and outlook to the Indian Ocean territories and to the southern China area through the establishment of their colonies. Therefore, they constituted the most significant group for our consideration during this period.

Local populations were important to this discussion insofar as they reacted to the trade conducted by the Persians and Arabs. There were three general ways this could be done. First, some groups attempted to become participants in international trade, undertaking ventures beyond Southeast Asia, particularly to India, but sometimes to China. Second, some were important in regional trade, providing local goods to foreign traders and selling the goods they brought to the general Southeast Asian population.

Third, still other groups attempted to profit from the great amount of materials at the disposal of the traders by organizing piracy against them. Srivijaya offers a case in point concerning the first two methods of participation. This kingdom, located on the southern end of Sumatra, helped to organize the economic system along rivers that was to remain a vital part of the economic system of the region for several centuries thereafter. In that system, landing places and markets at key junctions on rivers were used as trading centers where traders from the coast gathered the products of the interior and prepared them for purchase by other merchants downstream and, ultimately, by foreign traders, either at the mouth of a river or some nearby port. The gold of west-central Sumatra, found in the interior, was brought out by way of rivers and the traders on them. Other products were gathered in this way as well.

Srivijaya also attempted to organize the key ports that handled transit of ships in and out of the region and sometimes were used for transshipment of goods, as at Kalah and at Srivijaya itself. Finally, with their own ships, Sriyijayan merchants participated in trade, sending expeditions elsewhere in Southeast Asia and sometimes traveling as far as South Asia or China. Piracy, on the other hand, was never centralized, and pirates were known to be active along the entire route from the Middle East to China. Occasionally some regional power would seek to suppress piracy as a means of keeping the very lucrative trade routes functioning.

Conversion to Islam

Conversion to Islam occurred initially among the Arabs and Persians at the ports of the Middle East as that religion spread its influence midway in the seventh century. Conversion among this group was not instantaneous, and was probably still taking place into the eighth century, if it paralleled the rate of conversion elsewhere in the Middle East. Thereafter Arab—and perhaps Persian—colonies were established along the trade routes, which led to intermarriage and the subsequent conversion of some of the families that provided the women married by Arab and Persian merchants. Also, perhaps other nearby peoples who had contact and interaction with the Arab colonies converted as an indication of close association with traders. This appears to be the case in some island areas of the Indian Ocean and in Southeast Asia itself, with the Indian Ocean sites receiving this historical impetus first. Conversion to Islam of some local people apparently occurred in the southern Chinese port cities at this time, the propagators being associated with the Arab trade enterprises in those cities. Southeast Asian conversions took place later than in the Indian Ocean and China, at Ferlac on Sumatra, in east Java, and in the Champa region of Indochina, in the twelfth and thirteenth centuries. In the 1960s one group of Indonesian Muslims interested in the historical record of their community asserted, on the basis of an unsubstantiated Arabic manuscript, that Islam arrived in Aceh in northern Sumatra as early as the seventh century, and that the impetus came directly from the Arab world. This interpretation, however, did not educe great credit among other scholars, who held that Arab colonies in Southeast Asia were established at a later date.

The expulsion of over a hundred thousand foreign traders from South China during a peasant rebellion against the Tang dynasty in 878 prompted a number of Arab and Persian traders to establish a colony on the west coast of the Malay Peninsula at Kalah. It is reasoned by several scholars that those colonists probably reestablished many of the institutions from the Chinese ports, which reflected Muslim commercial law, weights, and officials.[6] There may well have been other cases of Arab settlement late in the period under study, but convincing proof has not come forward to us on this matter. In any case, the peoples on the Indian Ocean approaches seem to have undergone considerable conversion during this period, precisely because the Arabs dominated the trade in that region and established many colonies along the west Indian coast and at some sites in Africa. In essence, the western Indian Ocean became an Arab economic region and Islam was important in the colonies that the Arabs established.

There seems to have been only a slow adoption of Islam among local populations in the Indian Ocean basin and in Southeast Asia, probably because the Muslim traders were not missionaries but people devoted to economic enterprise. Their early trading endeavors were merely trips back and forth, with little time for staying in a particular place and affecting the people there with their culture and religion. In such enterprises it was not in the interest of the merchants to emphasize religion, but rather to tolerate whatever customs, religious activities, and other mores they encountered, even while holding their own beliefs and practices dear.

Where Muslims did settle, as in the Indian Ocean periphery, their association with Islam manifested itself in the families they started from marriage with local women. Islam's teachings were readily apparent in those new communities, and they quickly built the institutions necessary to support the full practice of the religion. In the records of travelers there are references to prayer, fasting, and the celebration of the two 'Id celebrations marking the end of the fasting month and the rite of sacrifice during the pilgrimage season. Mosques were built in some port cities and Muslims who died there were buried with Muslim grave markers, sometimes bearing religious inscriptions. At one site at Phan-rang on the central Vietnamese coast, a Muslim colony existed with a trader-guild organization headed by the traditional overseer of the marketplace and his assistant; such guild organizations were probably common in other Arab colonies as well, reflecting the institutions common to the trading occupation. Religious judges apparently carried out their administration of justice with some knowledge of proper religious injunctions for such cases. Again at Phan-rang, a special code regarding taxation and settlements of debts was apparently in use, reflecting Muslim trading principles common at the time.[7] There also appear to have been small Arab settlements, perhaps trading outposts, at the Javanese ports of Tuban, Gresik, and Surabaya around 850, but the first Muslim gravestones there were dated in the eleventh century, and no others until the twelfth century, so permanent settlement seems unlikely.

Personalities of importance were mostly Arab merchants and other travelers, none having any particularly strong association with religion that would indicate they were leading figures in the establishment of Islam in the Southeast Asian region. As far as doctrine goes, we know from inscriptions on tombstones of Muslims from this era that the Qur'an was highly regarded, as some of the epitaphs used prominent verses from it, emphasizing the role of God as "merciful," "compassionate," and "ever-forgiving." Furthermore, God was acknowledged to be the creator of all that existed and was termed the "master of the Day of Judgment," again references to terminology used in the Qur'an. Muhammad was regarded as the emissary of God. These were all standard teachings of Islam in the Middle East of the time. One tombstone called for blessings on the family of the Prophet, apparently indicating a tendency toward Shi'ism, but the expression could have been used by a Sunni before the split with Shi'ism became pronounced. In general there is enough evidence to suggest that the early Muslims in Southeast Asia were committed to their religion and carried Islam's institutions with them as part of their identification and lifestyle. We have little evidence beyond those simple associations.[8]

Finally, a word needs to be said about the theories of Islamization that have caused the writing of many treatises addressing the problem of how Islam arrived in Southeast Asia and the peoples who were responsible for bringing it there. Several Dutch scholars concluded that the Gujeratis were the primary carriers of Islam; S. Q. Fatimi argued that it was the Bengalis; and Majul asserted that it was the Chinese who were the important intermediaries. D. W. J. Drewes showed the importance of interpreting myth and legend in making an analysis, and Naguib al-Attas analyzed the early Islamic manuscripts to show how philological evidence could lend its support to a reconstruction. Anthony Johns indicated the important role of the Islamic mystics in the conversions, while Th. Pigeaud and H. J. de Graaf showed the importance of the north coastal region of Java to the process. C. Berg drew on the Old Javanese chronicles to reveal the early contacts of Muslims with east Java. Suffice it to mention that the assembly of evidence for the reconstruction of what occurred has involved many scholars, and they have made great headway with the task. In this chapter some of their evidence has already been presented and even more of it will be in the next. I shall, however, avoid a full discussion of their debates with one another as peripheral to the purpose of this book; it would add pages without yielding much more insight than is already provided by drawing on their findings.[9]

Conclusion

This first era was merely introductory with respect to Islam in Southeast Asia; it has largely focused on a traveling population visiting key locations, which barely intruded on the societies it encountered. Only a few converts to Islam were made, and there is no evidence of Islamic culture emerging anywhere or of Islam having had any notable impact outside the Arab and Persians communities. At most, only a few thousand converts were made within the territorial zone we associate with Southeast Asia, and those were connected directly to traveling Muslim groups. Obviously, the number of converts was greater in the Indian Ocean periphery, and even for a time in the southern Chinese ports. The new Muslim societies in the Indian Ocean region were not disrupted, while those in China received a setback when Chinese xenophobia caused some groups to move against Muslim traders and their Chinese converts. When Islamic conversion did begin among the local population of Southeast Asia proper, it appears to have been on northern Sumatra, the first landfalls experienced by traders using the sea lanes connecting South Asia and the Middle East.

Key Readings

Forbes, Andrew D. W. 1981. "Southern Arabia and the Islamicization of the Central Indian Ocean Archipelagos." A study of Arab merchants in the Indian Ocean periphery and the establishment of Arab colonies.

Huzayyin, S. A. 1942. *Arabia and the Far East.* Summaries of the major Chinese, Arabic, and Indian sources available on the trade routes and evidence of the passage of Muslim traders along those routes.

Majul, C. A. 1962. "Theories on the Introduction and Expansion of Islam in Malaysia." A review of the major scholarly interpretations of Islam's arrival in Southeast Asia.

Labib, Subhi J. 1981. "Die islamische Expansion und das Piratenwesen im Indischen Ozean." A description of the trade routes in the pre-European era and how the various political powers both sought to fight against endemic piracy or encouraged it for their own purposes.

Tibbetts, G. R. 1975. "Early Muslim Traders in South-East Asia." Summaries of the chief Arabic sources concerning early Southeast Asian travel.

2 The Emergence of a Hybrid Muslim Culture (1300–1800)

> The king is poor, proud and beggarly, he never fails of visiting
> stranger merchants . . . and, according to custom, he must have
> a present. When the stranger returns the visit, . . . he must make
> him a present, otherwise he thinks due respect is not paid to
> him, and in return of those presents his Majesty will honor the
> stranger with a seat near his sacred person.

General Context

The Indian Ocean Trade Routes

In this era the sea routes continued to link the civilizations of Asia, although there was fluctuation in their use. The downfall of the Sung dynasty in China and the Abbasids in the Middle East curtailed trade, while the rise of the Ming in China, the Dehli Sultanate in India, and the Il-Khanid Mongols in the Middle East strengthened trade route usage. Despite this fluctuation, the trade routes developed considerably during this period and were a greater international economic and cultural asset than they had been earlier. Now, the Muslims also continued to use them—incidentally, for their first purpose was trade—for the conversion of the population they encountered.

Muslims were important participants in the trade between China, India, and the spice islands with the Arabo-Persian world early in this era. At Calicut on the Malabar coast, for example, the Muslims took on board goods for every place"[1] and that "at every monsoon ten or fifteen of these ships sailed" for the Red Sea, Aden, and Makkah. In addition to this important role as long-range carriers, other "Moors" were prominent among those merchants, playing an intermediary role in the region, moving goods from one point in South and Southeast Asia to another. At Bengal, for example, there were "Arabs, Persians, . . . and Indians as well as Chinese" and these merchants sailed to the Coromandel Coast, Malacca, Sumatra, Pegu, Cambaya, and Ceylon."[2] There was Muslim presence at other locations as well. Sixteenth-century Banten in west Java was a thriving port and a center of the pepper trade, with "Arabs, Guzeratis, Malabars, Bengalis, and Melakans," taking part.[3] At the important "spice island" of Tidore the foreign community handled most of the island's trade and acted as an intermediary between the indigenous spice harvesters and the outside world.

The major port cities had similarities throughout the maritime regions of the Indian Ocean, Southeast Asia, and South China, especially in regard to facilities and the institutions that served travelers and merchants. Each port, of course, differed according to the culture within which it was located and the size and purpose of the port itself. Several, like Cambay in Gujerat, Calicut on the Malabar Coast, Melaka on the Malay Peninsula, and, later, Aceh on Sumatra, were major transshipment ports with extensive facilities, sizeable port populations, and elaborate rules of conduct. Others were secondary ports where goods were gathered and bartered, such as Bengal in India, Pegu in Burma, Ternate and Tidore in the eastern Indonesian archipelago, and Banten, Giri, and Gresik on Java. At those places facilities were less extensive, but the foreign populations were still sizeable, and considerable concern was shown the interests of merchants. There also were stopover ports, resupply ports, and assorted minor ports where facilities and amenities varied considerably, usually by happenstance.

Melaka was the most renowned port of the era, since it was the major transshipment site between East and West because the seasonal shifts in the wind made it a natural meeting place for merchants from East Asia and those from the West. Merchants making the India–China trip could wait out the changes in the wind before proceeding with the second half of their voyage in either direction. Ships arriving from India or China could sell their cargoes at Melaka to someone proceeding farther along the route. The gathering trade of Southeast Asia intended for the West, such as spices, and for China, such as birds' nests and shark fins, were assembled at Melaka for shipment to their destinations. The points of origin and destination for the traders was very wide, including the Indian subcontinent, the eastern coast of present-day Indochina, China, and Japan, and Southeast Asia, from Burma through the Indonesian islands to the Philippines.

Midway in the era, European traders arrived and affected the nature and extent of the trade system. The Portuguese came first in the very early sixteenth century, followed by the Spanish later in the century, with both groups aggressively challenging other traders and the manner in which the goods of Asia were controlled and allotted. The Portuguese attempted to control key ports across the Indian Ocean litoral—Hormuz, Surat, Goa, and Melaka—as a means of redirecting the local trade toward Portuguese-controlled ports, a goal that was not realized to the extent the Portuguese thought it would be but was nevertheless significant. They also tried to monopolize spices in Maluku, but that venture was not very successful. In particular, they were unable to supplant the existing trading system, which simply shifted to Aceh, Brunei, Patani, and Bantem when the Portuguese took Melaka in 1511. Nonetheless, the Portuguese were able to use Melaka and several other ports as gathering places for their own trade and as staging areas for Catholic missionary efforts in the eastern Indonesian archipelago.

In addition, the Portuguese entered into the politics of South and Southeast Asia, siding at times with particular rulers against others and assisting their chosen allies with arms, manpower, and funds with the aim of shaping the political environment to their advantage. Even before the arrival of the Dutch in the seventeenth century, however, the Portuguese venture went into decline, and after defeat by Dutch Company forces, was reduced to controlling only a part of the island of Timor in the Lesser Sunda Islands, Macao in southern China, and Goa in India.

The Spanish, second on the scene and arriving from the Pacific, established their base of operations around 1565 in an archipelago they named the Philippines and, in competition with the Portuguese, attempted to control important sources of materials, especially spices in Maluku. Unsuccessful there against Portuguese competition, they were able to promote Manila as a trading site with private Chinese merchants. The Spanish were active in proselytizing local peoples to Christianity and introducing Spanish culture so that, in a relatively short period, they gained political authority from Luzon south through the Visayas. Since they claimed territory that had earlier been under the influence of Muslim principalities in Brunei, the Sulu Islands, and Mindanao, there was considerable hostility to their presence. Sporadic fighting between the Spanish and their southern Muslim neighbors persisted to the end of the nineteenth century.

In the seventeenth century, the French, English, and Dutch arrived and challenged the Portuguese and Spanish; the Spanish were essentially driven back to their base in the Philippines and the Portuguese reduced to minor players thereafter. In the eighteenth century, the Dutch, operating through a single company, the United East Indies Company (VOC) with heavily armed ships, managed to achieve a monopoly of some spices in the eastern islands. They also took over several strategic ports—particularly Sunda Kelapa on Java, renamed Batavia—and deflected armed resistance against them by several local states both on land and sea. By the end of the era the Dutch were the major political power and had coerced most local states into signing agreements that recognized the Dutch Company as the dominant economic player, to the detriment of everyone else. The international trading system that had existed at the beginning of the era suffered considerable dislocation by the Europeans, and particularly by the Dutch, who essentially created a new system of moving goods while the older international trading system went into sharp decline.

The Greater Asian Setting

In the Middle East there was notable political and cultural change in the period from the fifteenth to nineteenth centuries. In the Islamic West (i.e., Spain and the Maghreb), Muslims were edged out of the Iberian Peninsula by Spanish and Portuguese Christian states by 1500, and the center of that illustrious but fragile civilization moved to Morocco, where its political power converged around rural strongholds controlled by warrior-mystics. In the Islamic East, the political center moved westward from Baghdad into the Anatolian region with the rise of the Ottoman Empire, which settled itself at Constantinople, renamed Istanbul, in 1453. Ottoman rulers claimed the caliphate and used that institution to proclaim their capital the political and religious center of the Islamic world. There they developed an illustrious court, an elaborate central administration, and effective military and naval forces

Conquest of Egypt gave the Ottomans a stake in the ports and shipping at the southern end of the Red Sea and along the southern coast of Arabia. The Ottomans responded to Portuguese actions against Muslim shipping and ports in the Indian Ocean in the early years of the sixteenth century by sending a naval force to drive them from Diu on the south Indian coast. The commander of the Ottoman expedition asked Indian and Southeast Asian Muslims for cooperation in that endeavor, but he received no direct assistance and there was little coordination in the struggle against the Portuguese. Ottoman defeat on that occasion released freebooters into Southeast Asia, where they became mercenaries in several armies of the region. A second expedition was sent by the Ottomans to assist the Acehnese against the Portuguese in 1565, but the main fleet was diverted to Yemen to put down a rising against Ottoman authority. Nonetheless, two ships did reach Aceh, carrying foundry workers with cannon-making capabilities and military specialists with innovative military skills, such as sapping and use of trenches. This was the only direct relationship of a Muslim political entity in the central Islamic world with a Southeast Asian Muslim state until the twentieth century.

Earlier in the twelfth century the renowned al-Ghazali, one of the describers of Sunni orthodoxy, formulated concepts whereby Islamic mysticism, regarded up to that time as undisciplined and even heretical by the religious establishment, was made compatible with beliefs and practices recognized in Sunni Islam. Consequently many learned Muslims acquainted themselves with the new religious science and became practicing adepts. In the following century Ibn ʿArabi (d. 1240) formulated a theosophic mysticism that regarded sensory experience as the true source of religious knowledge, particularly concerning the nature of God. This assertion was accepted by many religious scholars of the time and was spread by mystical orders, which also adopted a host of practices and beliefs that were not accepted by most Sunni Muslim leaders. One important aspect of mysticism was that it could be used as a tool in missionary efforts because of its structure of local cells, which relied on an adept to organize new members into a mystical order. This sort of proselytization was used in Africa south of the Sahara, in central Asia, in India, and in Southeast Asia.

While the culture of the Islamic lands continued to diversify, many commonalities persisted. First, Arabic continued to be the language of Islamic worship, scholarship, and mystical practice. Education, whether by private tutors or in the schools that appeared in this era, recognized the study of Arabic as the master science, the key to opening the mysteries of the Islamic religion. Its status was shown by use of the Arabic script in writing other languages. Swahili, Malay, and Urdu all adopted Arabic syllabaries during this era. Second, popular religious cults that had sprung up in the ʿAbbasid period stressing saint worship, extrasensory knowledge, and healing assumed importance throughout the Islamic world. Mystic adepts participated in this popular religion much more than did traditional scholars, even though the latter were usually tolerant of such practices. Finally, throughout the Islamic world some common tenets of Muslim law were observed, such as marriage and divorce, inheritance, celebration of Muslim festivals, and dietary regulations. These facets of religious life were often combined with local practices, which made it possible to adhere to Islamic injunctions while maintaining local mores. Accommodation on both sides was the norm.

South Asia continued to be predominantly Hindu, but during this era Islam was introduced through the invasions of Afghans and Mongols from the northwest, which changed the character of political rule and the manifestations of culture. The takeover began with the raids by Afghan princes on the Deccan plain in the twelfth and thirteenth centuries, followed by the establishment of political power by the Lodi kings and the sultanate of Delhi in the thirteenth and fourteenth centuries. Following these two fragile kingdoms, the Mughal Empire, beginning in 1525 and ending in the seventeenth century, built a more substantial political base among Muslims and Hindus that gave it a claim to being specifically Indian even if Muslim in religious identification. It was the approximate equivalent of the Ottoman Empire in the Middle East in political accomplishment, and probably was superior in cultural achievements. Importantly, the Mughal Empire controlled the coastal regions of most of India, so it remained tied to the international trade routes that are such an important part of our discussion. Because it was the Muslim political entity closest to Southeast Asia, there has been speculation that it exerted an influence on the development of Southeast Asian Islam. However, while its impact was considerable, it was only one of several Muslim areas having influence there, literature being a particular case in point.

In China, the Ming dynasty appeared in the mid-fourteenth century and emphasized Confucianism as the ideology of the state and the regulator of society even while allowing Buddhism and Taoism considerable freedom. During this period the major features of the classical Chinese state appeared: a strong, sometimes despotic emperor, a court system marked by intrigue among the eunuchs serving the imperial household, the examination system as the way to advancement in the civil service system, and local rule through the gentry. The Ming dynasty was a salutary period in Chinese history, possessing a high degree of culture. In particular, pottery became a developed art form, with lacquers and special paints creating a product that was in high demand in China and abroad. The regime was tolerant of Islam and entrusted some Muslims with important state positions; it is surmised that one ruler may have actually been a Muslim himself.

Chinese involvement with the region to its south was significant for a time. The tribute system was given new emphasis, and efforts were made, sometimes with military and naval pressure, to bring the rulers of the primary states in Southeast Asia to China in order to recognize the Ming emperor as their superior. International trade was encouraged and the ports of southern China were opened for that purpose, while Chinese ships were also allowed to travel abroad. In the most expansive policy ever demonstrated by Chinese rulers, a fleet for the southern ocean was formed and sent on several expeditions between 1405 and 1433 to promote Chinese interests and make the sea lanes safe for trading. Under the command of a Muslim Chinese admiral, Cheng-Ho (commanded 1405 to 1433), the fleet was manned by many Chinese Muslims who used the opportunity to convert some of the population of the territories they visited and, more often, to favor local Muslim groups over their non-Muslim adversaries. Around 1435 the Ming rulers decided that overseas trade was no longer in the interests of China, disbanded the fleet, and placed limits on Chinese trading abroad, which, however, still permitted contact with several nearby states in Southeast Asia by private Chinese traders.

The Southeast Asian Setting

On mainland Southeast Asia the formation of states continued with expansion in the Irrawaddy Basin, where Pegu, Martaban, and other states vied with Pagan for supremacy. The Mekong region operated as a second locus of political power, where Khmer influence expanded throughout most of the era and then began to contract near the end of the age. The Red River state of Vietnam came under the influence of Chinese culture, particularly its examination system and Confucian ethics. The Thais strengthened their kingdom, centered at Bangkok, and began an expansion that brought them into conflict with the Burmese kingdoms to the west and the Khmers in the east. The Champa kingdom was eliminated as a political entity by southern Vietnamese and Khmer rulers as they expanded their own control in the region. Outside of Vietnam, which identified with Mahayana Buddhism, most other populations adopted Theravada Buddhism.

Among these states the Thai kingdom at Bangkok, known as Ayuthia, had the most influence on the area that we refer to as the Muslim Zone. The rulers of Ayuthia sought territorial expansion in many directions and had little difficulty in asserting general control over the lightly populated states on the Malay Peninsula. However, the distance from the capital to those Malay states was too great to permit actual integration into the Ayuthian political or cultural system, so feudal overlordship was established in which the rulers to the south periodically recognized the Ayuthian ruler as suzerain. This was done by sending, every three years, a dish made of gold and silver as a symbol of that relationship.

In insular Southeast Asia the most marked political development was the fall of the Javanese state of Majapahit (1294–1478), which earlier had extended its control to vital points in the southern Philippines, in the Straits of Melaka, and on the Malayan Peninsula. For a time it was the dominant political power in a part of the zone earlier occupied by Srivijaya, but without the same depth of commercial activity to buttress its political control. While fashioning a fairly wide political dominion, it was unsuccessful in sustaining the political will or developing sufficient military/naval strength to allow it to consolidate its holdings. It steadily shed its non-Javanese possessions in the fifteenth century and ultimately lost its political hold in Java to a series of small political states with active ports located on the northern and eastern coasts of Java late in the century. These states challenged Majapahit for political control, and when its ruling elite proved incapable of response, Majapahit disintegrated. The loss of the sole regional power opened the way for a sudden decentralization of political control, with small states vying with one another for control of parts of the region. Melaka, Aceh, Johore, Brunei, and Banten in the west were the most prominent, while in the east principalities at Ternate, Tidore, and Makassar rose in importance.

People and Their Activities

Important Ethnic Groups
In transregional trade non-Southeast Asian groups continued to be important, particularly the Chinese, Indians, and Arabs, as they had been in the previous era. Their dominance was apparent at Melaka, where they converged in large numbers with such wealthy cargoes that each was given a harbormaster. From among the traders in Southeast Asia only the Javanese were afforded this degree of deference. Chinese traders were prominent in

most of the ports of the emerging Muslim Zone, sometimes staying for lengthy periods of time and even forming liaisons with local women, so that in some ports their descendants became important in the local communities. By the seventeenth century, immigration had been occurring long enough that the Chinese community consisted of both immigrants and locally born Chinese, with the latter group often a mixed race, and sometimes Muslim. There was a long-standing practice of the Malay courtier class at Palembang, including the royal family, of marrying the daughters of wealthy Chinese merchants and insisting that they become Muslim. This wealthy Chinese group provided the contacts to promote trade with China, strengthening the affluence of the courtiers.

The Indian groups diminished because of the fading of Brahmanism and the dwindling use of Sanskrit as a language of importance, particularly as conversion from Buddhism to Islam occurred. However, Indian merchants were still regarded as consequential, continuing to conduct a large part of the international trade of the region. There was some shift toward Indians from the southern areas, and many of this group were in fact descendants of mixed marriages between Arab traders and Indian women over the previous hundred years. While some Arabs still visited Southeast Asia as traders, it was the Arabo-Indian group that was more prominent and, as Muslims, the members of this group became the conduit through which Islam was transported to the Southeast Asian region—sometimes directly and sometimes by transporting Muslim activists *(da'i)* bent on making conversions to Islam. The last of the foreign groups, the Arabs, continued to be important even though their numbers were small. A "noble" *(sayyid)* community of Hadrami Arabs appeared in the early part of the eighteenth century and took up trading activity that linked the various Hadrami communities in Southeast Asia. Several hundred settled in Palembang during this period, and, because of their high status as claimed descendants of the Prophet Muhammad, some gained entry into the nobility through marriage, even to the royal family. All were exempt from tolls and customs.

Among local populations, the Malays and the Javanese both rose in importance during this era. The Javanese had been significant earlier, and their reputation as overlords of several key territories in insular Southeast Asia gave them continuing influence, even after those overseas holdings were lost. Of equal import was the availability of abundant rice from inland Java and the need for that commodity in many places of the region, especially at Melaka and in Maluku. There were an estimated three million Javanese in 1650, and Javanese society was sophisticated, possessing a hereditary aristocracy at its head, an influential administrative class, a prominent business community, and a general society of agriculturalists, craftsmen, and artisans in metal work and wood working. There was also a sizeable subsociety centering on religious villages, where teachers and holy men became persons of respect and importance.

The second group, the Malays, continued an earlier migratory movement from the southern Sumatran region into the Straits of Melaka basin and dominated the eastern coast of Sumatra, some of the southwestern coast of the Malay Peninsula, and the islands between. The migration moved also along the coast of northern Borneo and into Annam and Khmer in Indochina, where the Malays associated with and mixed with the Cham population, which moved from the central highlands to those areas in this time frame. It is reasoned that much of the Malay migration northward was on the part of aristocratic families seeking adventure and new fortunes, especially as the Srivijayan realm disintegrated and opportunities within it dwindled. Apparently these families became rulers in the Straits region, as we shall see at Melaka, but in other areas as well. Many of the local people—the so-called river people and sea people—became Malays by accepting the language of their new overlords, becoming their vassals, and, later, when it arrived, accepting the religion of Islam. Eventually language, custom, and religious traits marked them as Malays.

Local Malay dynasties often settled around places that were later to develop into ports. In time, many of them became meeting places of local and foreign traders, supplying rulers with excess funds to expand their realms and force nearby shipping to pay excise taxes. Several of these maritime states became influential in the region—Pasai, Melaka, Patani, and Brunei in particular—and they developed as centers of culture and administration. It was also mentioned earlier that Malays were one of the several groups prominent in both piracy and local trading. During this era both enterprises continued to be associated with them.

On Sumatra the Minangs, Bataks, and, later, the Achenese were major players. The Minangs represented an interior, tightly organized society that accepted Islam. Their high regard for women was common to most Sumatran groups, but their social institutions went further in assigning all wealth residing in capital assets to the female side of the family and building a society that reflected this high status. This agricultural and strictly regulated society produced a prosperous region in the highlands of west Sumatra with a decentralized political system that was to endure for several centuries. An overflow population from this society, consisting almost entirely of young men, moved about in the Straits areas and into the Sulu Sea basin. Most traveled as adventurers, tradesmen, or sellers of handicrafts in a circular migration, but some settled in the regions of their travels, married women there, and became part of local communities. The most significant migrations of Minangs occurred just to the north of Melaka on the Malay Peninsula in the sixteenth century and in eastern Sumatra in the early seventeenth century. In all the places they entered Minangs were known as pious believers in Islam, as learned and moral people, and as good traders and businessmen. Some of these adventurers found their way into the administration and military services of the Malay states. An early Muslim ruler in Sulu, for example, was a Minang.

In the southern Philippine Islands chain lived several groups consisting of people from the same racial stock as the Malays to the west. They were divided into numerous groupings, with two branches—the Magindanao and the Iranum—prevalent during this era. The Magindanao settled along the Pulangi River valley, which gave them an advantage over the groups inland and, through shrewd alliances, built an important imperium for the region in the seventeenth century. The Iranum peoples spread along the southwest coast of Mindanao and into the interior. A volcanic eruption in the mid-eighteenth century destroyed their agricultural base, which forced them to the southwest, some of them turning to piracy and slave taking as a means of living. Many eventually relocated onto islands in the Sulu Sea, the islands of the Melaka Straits, and the northwest coast of Kalimantan. In the last thirty-five years of the eighteenth century and on into the nineteenth century, they were a scourge to shipping and to coastal settlements from the Melaka Straits to Maluku. The central Philippines was one of their favorite targets for gathering slaves; they carried away thousands of Christian Visayans from that region and distributed them across the Muslim Zone.

On Sulawesi there were several important ethnic confederations that had strong local and regional governments capable of resisting the families that sought to gain control over the region. In the sixteenth century an alliance between the existing confederal states of Talloq and Gowa created the state of Makassar, which was a case of an inland group with abundant agricultural products uniting with a coastal group with a major harbor. Using the profits from trade, especially the usage fees on the "free" port that it operated, the new rulers were able to extend their control throughout the nearby islands, establishing a new trading system. It became a strong rival to the Dutch system in the seventeenth century and ultimately was defeated by the Dutch, the port passing into Dutch hands by the Treaty of Bongaya of 1667.

Near Makassar were another people, the Bugis, sea nomads who used small ships to sail throughout maritime Southeast Asia in the effort to establish their own trade network and gained importance in the eighteenth century. Particularly after the rise of the Dutch, the Bugis operated a subsidiary economic system that concentrated on gathering small amounts of goods from isolated territories, an activity that would have been an unprofitable operation for the Dutch. They also dealt in contraband, such as European weapons, bootleg spices, and slaves, and they also continued to make contact with the international trading system of Muslim Indian merchants who operated out of Aceh and several other ports in the eighteenth century. As we shall see, Bugis ultimately found the unsettled conditions in the Straits of Melaka to be to their advantage, and a number of settlers went there in the eighteenth century, where their leaders became rulers or corulers of several states.

A very elemental society existed on Ambon during this time period, with societal groupings or tribes centering on ancestral descent and a common territory. In some areas these tribes formed confederations, as occurred in northern Hitu in the late fifteenth century, with its center at Hitu Lama. At Hitu there was overall recognition of four confederal rulers who were important figures throughout the sixteenth and seventeenth centuries, each with his own color—black, red, yellow, and green—as symbols of authority. Islam entered the Ambon area in the last quarter of the fifteenth century, brought there by merchants who settled along the coastline, primarily from Tuban on the north coast of Java; but groups away from the coastal cities kept their strong animistic and shamanistic religious forms. Even among the groups converted to Islam many traditional customs were retained, particularly the ceremonial dances, the recognition of a holy tree, and the acknowledgment of long-standing ritual at marriages.

In the Banda Islands there was no overall ruler on Lontara and the other islands of the chain in the early sixteenth century; rather, political authority was found in petty chiefs who had charge of villages of people and were obeyed out of respect and tradition. The Bandanese were noted shipbuilders, capable of building good-sized crafts that enabled Bandanese merchants to extend their trade as far as Java and to the ports in the Straits of Melaka, where they sold spices for the foodstuffs and other goods needed at home.

A final ethnic group was the Chams, large portions of whom fled or were driven from central Vietnam, where the Champa Kingdom was destroyed by the military action of Vietnamese rulers from Hue and Hanoi. Cham refugees fled south into the Malay area and then migrated into the Annam, Khmer, and Ayuthian areas where they took up agriculture, small trading, and military service. In the Khmer region, the Cham settled generally in the areas controlled by the Malays, apparently because of similarities of language and custom. Ayuthian rulers used them as part of their mercenary military forces. In return they were permitted to settle in areas on the express condition that they provide manpower for military service. However, this sometimes created difficulties with the authority of the Khmer state. The Cham launched two significant revolts against the Khmer rulers in the sixteenth century.

Conversion to Islam

Research on court chronicles and tombstones has set the probable arrival times for Islam in various parts of Southeast Asia. The base date of 1292 is generally used for the entry of Islam at Perlak on Sumatra. Melaka was Islamized in 1445, Java in 1450, and Maluku in 1490. Then followed northern Borneo and the Philippines, beginning with Sulu in 1450 and Brunei and Magindanao in 1480. Undoubtedly these dates, mostly drawn from royal chronicles, record the conversions of principal rulers as criteria for dating. Probably Islamization of much of the port population occurred earlier, and the general population converted over time between the arrival of Muslims at the ports until after acceptance by the royal courts.[4]

Muslim and European travelers of the age vividly described the Islamic port culture of the Indian Ocean–Southeast Asian littoral. A Muslim traveler noted that the port cities of the Indian Ocean had places of Muslim learning and that Muslim law was followed in those courts. Samudera in northern Sumatra seems to have been regarded as an integral part of the Muslim world of that time. A European merchant indicated that Muslims dominated the port populations of Aceh, where the judge was an influential figure in matters of inheritance. When the partner of the merchant died, their joint trade goods were seized in accordance with the Islamic commercial law that a merchant's goods were forfeit when he died intestate. However, in a costly case, the merchant appealed to the port judge, who awarded the goods to him on the basis of his trade partnership with the deceased. A Portuguese traveler described Tidore's port as having its own mosque, its own judge, and its law based on Arab maritime law. Other references in his chronicles alluded to mosques in the larger towns, and even at a fishing village.[5]

The importance and influence of these Muslim port populations can be seen at several other places in maritime Southeast Asia. At Melaka in 1445, Tamil Muslim merchants were powerful enough that they were able to kill the infant ruler and install his half-brother, the son of a Tamil Muslim mother, apparently to promote Tamil Muslim interests, and possibly those of the port over non-port factions. At coastal Javanese cities, such as Demak and Giri/Gresik in the fifteenth century, Muslim trading communities were strong enough to remove officials appointed by the non-Muslim Majapahit kingdom and replace them with rulers of their own. But primarily, Islam in the ports was associated with merchants from elsewhere, with Southeast Asians Muslims being in a very distinct minority. That changed late in the sixteenth century, when some local groups became Muslim.

Muslim officials in the Chinese fleet, drawn largely from the province of Yunnan, were another group that undertook Islamic propagation in

Southeast Asia during this era. Those officials were part of the naval force or the naval shipyard operations that the Chinese fleet established on the northern coast of Java and at Champa. Chronicles at Ceribon recounted the efforts of these Muslim fleet mandarins to expand the number of converts to Islam in their areas of operation, and also to locate individuals capable of leading the local Islamic communities and to form Muslim militias.[6] As stated earlier, the Chinese officials also established mosques at many places, for example, at Semarang, Ceribon, Tuban, and at the mouth of the Brantas River near Surabaya. The chronicles noted, however, that with the withdrawal of the fleet to China midway in the sixteenth century, many of the mosques became temples for spirit worship among non-Muslim Chinese settlers.

The milieu of the royal courts was different from the culture of the ports, since courts usually had established ceremonies, established customary ways of doing things, and strong beliefs about the nature and ends of political control. While it might have been easy enough for a member of a royal court to become interested in Islam, it was probably very difficult to observe its practice, ceremony, and worship requirements given the strength of prevailing custom. At best, Islam might be introduced as a small cult, with members giving personal time to devotion but most of the time honoring court etiquette and custom. Equally, one might make a political conversion, as several rulers apparently did, for the purpose of attracting Muslim merchants to their ports. When conversion of a royal court occurred, the courtiers continued to operate within the context of their previous lives and protocol.

In one celebrated case, Islam arrived in the form of a foreign wife for the non-Muslim ruler of Majapahit on Java in the fifteenth century. She was allowed to practice her religion and to keep her Muslim retainers with her. Court chronicles related a story, most likely apocryphal, stating that the marriage produced twin boys, who eventually overthrew the Majapahit kingdom and established the succeeding Muslim kingdom of Demak. The story of the twins seems to have been contrived by a later Mataramese court writer to serve dynastic interests of that later period. It is likely that the Champa princess and her circle of Muslim retainers were used for political advantage by the Buddhist ruler of Majapahit to placate Muslim port populations who were restive under Majapahit rule. Alternative history suggests that the story was a misinterpretation of a historical incident when a Chinese diplomat to Majapahit brought along a Cham Muslim wife, who was later buried in a cemetery in East Java. All versions of the story indicate, however, that foreign Muslim personalities were able to live at some royal courts without suffering for their association with an "unofficial" religion.[7]

In other cases, Islam arrived via Muslim officials from abroad brought into the service of non-Muslim rulers who became influential enough to attract followers and persuade them to become Muslims themselves. In fact, state functionaries from abroad were highly trusted by some local rulers, such as those in Champa and Brunei, where they were sent on diplomatic missions to China to pay tribute to the emperor. At Makassar, according to legend, the ruler who first converted to Islam employed a retinue of religious scholars from different traditions who held discussions for the diversion of the crown prince in the period just before he became ruler. Supposedly, he became a Muslim on the basis of the arguments presented by the Muslim scholars. In other instances rulers at important ports decided to accept a close identity to the dominant group among the port population in order to improve their own power positions at court. This occurred at Perlak and Pasai on northern Sumatra in the late thirteenth century. At other times the change was accomplished through the diplomatic relationship of states where a ruler, wishing to gain economic advantage, married the daughter of a Muslim ruler elsewhere, converted to Islam himself, ordered his court to become Muslim, and then allowed religious propagandists into his territory to proselytize the population. This diplomatic transfer of Islam apparently occurred in Melaka when the ruler there married the daughter of the ruler of Muslim Pasai. In the mid-fourteenth century, the raja of Brunei married the daughter of the sultan of Johore, taking the name Muhammad I (r. 1363–1402) as evidence of his conversion.

The third stage of Islamization involved the general population outside of the ports and the courts. In the first instance, when a ruler became Muslim, his subjects usually followed suit, although certainly the conversion was nominal rather than substantive in the beginning. Apparently the conversion of the ruler did allow Muslim teachers and mystics passing through the ports to undertake the explanation of rites, practices, and behavior of Muslims, and in many cases to make the rationalizations for conversion to Islam. Islam terms such people "propagators" *(da'i)*. At Ternate in the Spice Islands, Islam made its way to the court when the ruler and his entourage became Muslim, followed by the ruler making a treaty with Gresik in northeast Java to send "teachers" to foster Islam among the general population. This stage marked the real acceptance of Islam in Southeast Asia, as it involved significant numbers of people and as it meant that Islam was no longer merely the religion of a foreign element or part of the ritual of the elite in the capital.

On occasion Muslim rulers employed "holy war" *(perang sabil)* to spread Islam, but usually such expeditions would have been undertaken for booty, territorial gain, and glory in any case. Several travelers of the era stated that at Pedie the king waged war against the heathen in the inland and converted them to Islam. One account went into considerable detail concerning the Acehnese campaigns into Gayo territory, where the term "holy war" was used extensively. In this way, Melaka converted the small states on the

Malay Peninsula and those on the east coast of Sumatra. Likewise, Aceh Islamized the adjacent Gayo lands and Minangkabau but exacted "heavy taxation" from the Bataks, who refused to convert. On Java, Demak spread Islam through conquest in southern Sumatra and western Java, except that the "holy war" was actually undertaken by militant mystic brotherhoods. In action reminiscent of Muslim Turkic mystics in the conquest of the Balkans and Muslim Indic mystics in the campaigns on the Deccan Plain of India, Javanese mystic masters at Gresik established centers of operation in north-central Java, launching a "holy war" against the Majapahit Empire. Establishing the new state of Demak on the ruins of Majapahit, religious activists exhorted further holy war to open new territory where they could work to convert populations to Islam. Even as late as the eighteenth century there were calls for the use of holy war to complete the conversion process in the zone.[8]

There was also the work of individual Muslim propagators working alone in isolated areas. Chronicles in the Sulu region provided an example of a propagator known only by the title "the honorable," who served as a healer and magician in the Sulu area while teaching those with whom he came in contact the rudiments of Islam. He arrived around 1380 and labored for over a decade, even building a mosque, but made only a few converts. This probably happened elsewhere as well, perhaps with the same limited impact.[9]

Travelers related that there was a movement toward Islam among the local populations of certain Southeast Asian areas they visited. One stated that mystic adepts from the Straits of Melaka and the Red Sea taught the inhabitants "short prayers (dhikr) and ceremonial forms" for use in mystic practice.[10] Some chiefs were converted, circumcised, and took Muslim names. Other travelers' reports stated that conversions were relatively easy to make, as the foreign Muslims were willing to take wives from the families of converts. At the same time, conversion was far from complete, as new Muslims usually continued to hold with earlier, non-Muslim practices and beliefs. In Maluku, for example, the sons of Muslims there inherited half their property according to Muslim law, while their nephews inherited the other half in accordance with the local customs in existence before Islam's arrival. Spanish records mentioned that Muslims from Borneo were operating on Luzon, but had not completed their work of conversion when the Spanish arrived.[11] One interpretation regarded the ruler's conversion as merely moving in conformity with a value shift in the population that he was forced to accept. Some conversion of the general population before that of the ruler undoubtedly did occur, but the efforts of Muslims already there, rulers and propagators, centered on the rulers, so that the propagators' work in the general population could be undertaken without political impediment.[12]

Conversion to Islam may have been precipitous in certain areas but was not a rapid process overall, actually taking a long time. As late as the eighteenth century an ethnological study of the island of Sumatra stated that, while Islam was firmly established in Aceh and Minangkabau, it was only beginning to affect Lampung in south Sumatra. Islam had "made considerable progress . . . and most villages have mosques in them: yet an attachment to the original superstitions of the country, induces them" to ignore much of that teaching for the animistic worship of the forefathers.[13]

These stages of Islam's entry into Southeast Asia were not clearly demarcated; that is, the ports were not totally Islamized throughout the region before conversion of the rulers began, and so on. Rather, the development was uneven and, whereas one area passed through the three stages quickly, in another place the process began later, and in still another area only the first or second stage was attained. For example, while Islam was still confined to the port culture on Java, at Melaka the courts and the hinterland already were Islamized. Despite this unevenness, however, there was a pattern to the development that moved generally from west to east. The entrepôt ports on Sumatra and the Malayan Peninsula were the first ones converted, followed by key ports on the major trade routes—Java, Ternate, Tidore—and then by the lesser ports on the secondary trade routes—on Kalimantan, at Sulu, and on Sulawesi. Rulers on the major trade routes were quicker to convert than those of the secondary routes and more interested in seeing the religion spread among their own population and among neighboring states. Some areas, such as interior Kalimantan, hardly were touched at all.

The spread of Islam was significant in the fifteenth century and reached its greatest activity in the sixteenth century. Although all observers were agreed on the increased rate of conversion to Islam in the sixteenth century, there were differences of opinion among them about why that growth occurred then. One theory advanced the notion that the Portuguese presence in Southeast Asia stimulated a race between Islam and Christianity to proselytize the area. Since the Portuguese were regarded as intruders and enemies of many groups in the region, Islam was able to act as a counterforce and became identified with indigenous interests. Hence, Islam was used as a rallying point against the Christian Portuguese and later the Dutch. Another viewpoint asserted that by the sixteenth century Islam was firmly established in the Malay–Indonesian world and had enough converts available to spread rapidly, as it did. According to this theory, Islam's spread in Southeast Asia began slowly in the early fourteenth century, increased its momentum in the fifteenth century, and dominated the sixteenth century. It was a natural and inevitable historical development largely unrelated to the Portuguese presence. Still another theory maintained that the Muslim effort was of such strength that conversion was inevitable, but still, the Portuguese capture of Melaka forced Muslim traders to use a variety of other ports, where they inevitably augmented the spread of Islam through the propagators that accompanied them on their travels.[14]

Three cases will illustrate the conversion process in west Sumatra, Mindanao, and Sulawesi, respectively. Regarding west Sumatra, in the second half of the sixteenth century Islam became established at Tiku, the leading Minang port on the west coast, apparently brought there by Indian Muslims from Gujerat. Muslim titles were used for port and administrative officials, and Islamic teachers were active among the population of the port. With the coming of Acehnese imperial governors to the ports of Ulakan and Pariaman on the coast later in the sixteenth century, these centers were opened to the Muslim traders. Local merchants at those two cities began converting to Islam as well, apparently because Islamic law allowed inheritance to be held by the merchants themselves rather than following the matrilineal customs of the surrounding area, where wealth was invested in assets, particularly land, and not normally available for venture capitalism. However, there was little proselytization outside these merchant groups to the end of the eighteenth century.

On the eastern side of Sumatra, the population centers of Kampar and Indragiri became client states of Melaka in the latter part of the sixteenth century, and their rulers accepted Islam as part of the political arrangements they made. This opened the way for penetration of Islam to the royal Minang court at Buo-Sumpur Kudus, where it became practical for the Minang rulers to use Muslim scribes and merchants to conduct regular commerce and administration with those newly Islamized courts. Ultimately the Minang rulers converted to Islam, but apparently as a means of tapping new sources of "power" and support for their governance; actual Muslim forms of rule common in the region did not occur. In the gold fields, again because of contact with outsider groups, in this case those involved with shipping, the villagers and merchants dealing with production and refining converted to Islam by the middle of the seventeenth century. Like the conversion of the royal court, it was a nominal association with Islam.

In the interior of west Sumatra, Islam became attached to village life when functionaries, formerly associated with shamanism and Brahmanism, converted to Islam. Such functionaries stood outside the ruling local councils and were important as recorders of life-cycle events—birth, death, house raisings, and great journeys—and oversaw the proper usage of custom. Also following the pattern of pre-Islamic religious practice, Muslim mystics established small religious cults in the living quarters of the men, who lived apart from the women and children. Muslim mystic brotherhoods replaced the Buddhist orders operating there earlier. In general, then, the initial contact of Islam with Minang society was often nominal and certainly subservient to Minang cultural norms.

In the case of Mindanao, legend maintained that Sharif Awliya (active 1460) and Sharif Maraja (active ca. 1500) were reputedly the first noted Muslims to visit Mindanao with the intent of converting the local population to Islam. Much more historical was the arrival of Sharif Muhammad Kabungsuwan (active ca. 1515) and his party of adventurers from Johore, who landed on the southwestern Mindanao coast in the first quarter of the sixteenth century. Kabungsuwan established himself as the Islamic ruler over all Muslims living in the neighborhood of the mouth of the Pulangi River, which was to become the center of Magindanao. Very early in his reign he held a great circumcision ceremony, convincing many of the male inhabitants of his new principality to enter Islam in that way, and was relatively successful in the effort. Then, with the assistance of the Sea People, he undertook warfare against neighboring peoples to bring them under his political control; conversion to Islam was encouraged among these new subjects.

In the case of Sulawesi, around 1618 the kingdoms of Gowa and Tallo combined to form the state of Makassar. Under Matoaya (r. 1590–1615?), Islam became the accepted religion of the royal court, and consequently the port populations of Muslims became influential in state operation and attitudes. Matoaya launched a series of naval raids against a wide range of territories stretching from the east coast of Kalimantan across Maluku and southward to the Lesser Sundas. These raids were known as the "Islamic wars," as ostensibly their purpose was to convert the peoples of the territory to Islam; but, significantly, the conquered areas were also brought into an economic union with Makassar. The rulers and populations of the defeated states were not forcibly converted to Islam, but the degree of resistance to the Makassarese forces and any refusal to consider Islam led to harsh terms of vassalage. Islamic propagators, mostly from Giri on Java, were sent to teach people the rudiments of religion and to establish Islamic institutions such as schools and retreats for mystics. Here is one of the clearest cases of proselytization being a primary policy of the state.

The Political Situation

Common Features
Interstate Relationships

Interstate relations in this period were feudal—that is, there was a system where lesser rulers with control over a sizeable population and territory owed allegiance to another, more politically powerful ruler. While having control over his own feudal establishment, the vassal owed him tribute and, usually, the furnishing of military or naval forces when called upon to supply them.

Early in the era the Chinese emperor was at the top of this hierarchy,

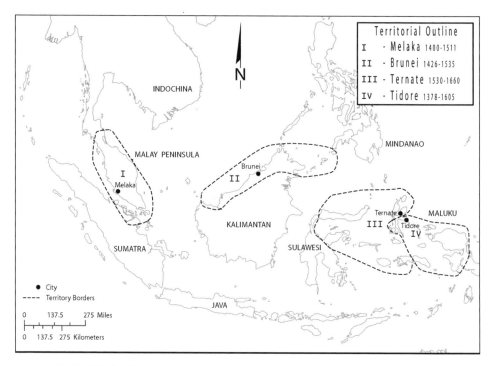

3. Earliest Muslim Kingdoms

and through trade, diplomatic persuasion, and sometimes military or naval coercion, various states were drawn into a subsidiary relationship with China. Rulers of the paramount states of Southeast Asia—Melaka, Brunei, the city-states of northeast Java—recognized Chinese great power status and received indications, through documents, diplomatic contacts, and sometimes other assistance, that such an arrangement existed. Vassal status with China carried with it few real feudal responsibilities, but rather only acknowledgment and some expensive gifts so that trade could be conducted. The Ming decision to discontinue the tribute system in the late fifteenth century, of course, removed the Chinese emperor as the apex of the vassalage system, except possibly for the Sulu area, which always sought a close relationship with the Chinese for trade and protection against the Spanish. In general, however, China was removed from the interstate equation after the sixteenth century.

There was some attempt on the part of Muslim rulers to align themselves with rulers in the central Islamic world, but few moved beyond incidental contact. The distance apparently was too great for the technology of the time. Several Southeast Asian Muslim rulers, such as those at Mataram, Banten, and Pasai, all contacted the ruler of Makkah to obtain certificates to rule and to use certain Muslim titles, but no continuing relationship was apparently sought. Aceh's attempts in the sixteenth century were more meaningful, however, for Achenese ambassadors apparently did go to Istanbul and were eventually able to meet with the Ottoman ruler and gain assistance from him for action against the Portuguese. It is difficult to ascertain whether the Acehnese rulers considered a vassal relationship to have been formed as a result of this diplomatic contact, even though the Ottomans apparently thought they did. Achenese rulers seem to have regarded their requests for aid as communication between two important leaders of relatively equal status. There was a suggestion of vassalage there, but hardly the reality.

A more interactive feudal relationship than in China or the central Islamic world existed in the relationship between the Thai kingdom of Ayuthia and the proto-states of the Malay Peninsula. Ayuthian attempts to include the lower part of the peninsula were successful for only a short while: Melaka defeated an Ayuthian military expedition to break the relationship, and Ayuthian attempts to include states in northern Sumatra were not successful. The northernmost Malay rulers on the Malay Peninsula in particular—in Kedah, Trengganu, Kelantan, and Patani—often willingly renewed their ties with Ayuthia as a defensive measure, for dynastic certification, and for trade. As with China, the non-Islamic nature of Ayuthia and its rulers was not a hindrance at this particular time, although later it was to assume importance among those Malays opposed to continued rule from the non-Muslim Thais. Throughout the Ayuthian region there was a great deal of fluidity, with vassals attempting constantly to narrow or lengthen the distance between them and the authority at Bangkok.

The second rung of the feudal arrangement was indigenous to the Muslim Zone of Southeast Asia itself. In the period immediately previous to this era, the Javanese kingdom of Majapahit had overlordship arrangements with Samudera-Pasai and Brunei, while the two vassals exercised political and economic influence in their own nearby areas, where they had their own system of local vassals. At the beginning of this era Melaka was powerful in the west over territories in the Straits of Melaka, on the east coast of Sumatra, and on the southern part of the Malay Peninsula. The widening Muslim Zone in the last half of the era brought changes in the political environment caused by the rise of new powers. Aceh, Johore, Makassar, Mataram, Ternate, and Tidore all acted as suzerains for nearby states, with most other principalities forced through military/naval action or diplomacy to become vassal states of these regional powers. In this time frame as well, the Portuguese and the Dutch became important on the political stage and through similar conquest and political pressure brought a number of states under their influence. Tradewise, the conditions were almost the same, namely, the "overlord" insisted that all trade pass through its port, with the vassal states allowed to participate in trade with the suzerain but seldom with outsiders.

By the seventeenth century there was a fairly extensive and sophisticated exchange of diplomatic officials among Asian states. Johore was known to have "ambassadors" at Aceh and in several of the north Javanese ports, and Makassar kept representatives in other ports as well. Chinese settlers in Palembang apparently served as consular officers in Palembang, assisting with the trade between the two states. After their arrival Europeans were included in the system. When the Portuguese controlled Melaka, for example, they maintained an ambassador at Aceh to discuss trade issues and act as a "lookout" regarding Acehnese intentions and the attitudes of other Europeans using Acehnese ports as a base of their operations. That emissary was accorded protection, even though Aceh and the Portuguese were usually on bad terms with one another. European traders frequently acted as emissaries from the rulers of their respective countries, thereby raising their status above that of mere merchants. The sultans were flattered by such emissaries and spent considerable effort in drafting messages for greeting European monarchs. Also, Aceh itself sent representatives to many other states and principalities in South and Southeast Asia, who proved useful in promoting alliances and even gaining allies for warfare, particularly against the Portuguese.

The Courts of the Rulers

The courts of rulers—whether suzerain or vassal—developed some common conceptions about the nature of governing and also about the importance of maintaining an elaborate court life. While differences with the earlier states in the region were evident, there was considerable carryover of institutions and style of court life from the pre-Muslim era. The most striking feature was the court used as the center of a sacred and magical system, where the ruler controlled symbols of authority while undertaking ceremonies and acts that were widely regarded as gathering and concentrating still more power in the court. The population of a principality owed its allegiance because the ruler constantly demonstrated that power to rule belonged to him through the magnificence of his court and its ceremonies, through his victories over others, and through his ability to stay in power. The term "sovereign" was used to connote this political control and relationship, and the term "disloyalty" to indicate actions that ran contrary to the ruler's sovereignty and/or challenged his right to hold power. The perception that the ruler was connected with divinity was transferred as well, except that in the case of the Muslim rulers the conception of "shadow of God on earth" replaced the earlier notion that the ruler was a superior human or a god undertaking an earthly existence. The "shadow of God" slogan owed its roots to the 'Abbasid Empire of the Golden Age of

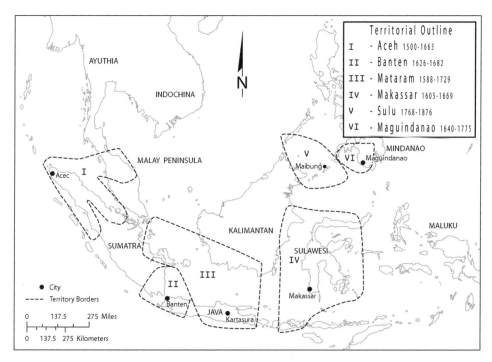

4. Later Muslim Kingdoms

Islam during which its caliphs insinuated that they were ordained by God to rule, although it was the Safavids (1501–1732) of Persia who used the actual title "shadow of God."

The symbols of sovereignty, that is, royal regalia, remained much as they had been prior to conversion to Islam. Consequently, great reverence was attached to the ceremonial sword, the umbrella, and the scepter, as well as a host of other royal relics. The court etiquette prominent in the old empires of Srivijaya and Majapahit continued to be prevalent and were only slightly modified by the inclusion of ritual pertinent to Islam. The symbols of sovereignty were not considered to be mere symbols, but real carriers of magic and power that could be used by their possessor when he deemed it necessary. A Spanish report noted the significance of royal paraphernalia at Ternate; when the ruler's son came aboard a visiting Spanish ship he carried with him some of the regalia—a scepter and several golden boxes containing water and betel.[15] Similarly, on Java great emphasis was placed on the symbols of sovereignty that had existed from before Islam's arrival in order that the Muslim kingdom of Demak be recognized as the logical successor to the non-Muslim Majapahit kingdom. For example, there was a "crown" of Majapahit—actually an elaborate hat—that was jealousy guarded as an heirloom. The staff of an early propagator of Islam on Java, Shaykh Maulana Ibrahim (d. 1419), was made a royal relic after it had been used by him as a magical wand to assist Muslim forces in defeating the Majapahit army. The Muslim Javanese ruler Senapati (r. 1575–1601) reportedly used the same staff in military operations that spread the kingdom of Demak to its greatest expansion in the sixteenth century. Islam did not discard the regalia already in place but assiduously added to them. It was an eclectic process, and Islam could not prevent the addition of new items even if their addition smacked of syncretism, or even heresy.

In addition, court life had an elaborate ritual and complicated etiquette that dominated a long procession of court ceremonies marking holidays, commemorations, arrivals and departures of important guests, and the elevation of courtiers to prominent positions. In general, the ritual and court etiquette existent prior to the arrival of Islam remained, but Islam made contributions to it over time, such as the inclusion of the important events of the Muslim year. Patterns of clothing, the use of colored umbrellas, and the carrying of certain implements such as the ceremonial knife, were all vital parts of the proceedings, with all factors being prescribed by custom. East Asian history at the time shows similar regulation of colors, umbrellas, and clothing in China, Korea, and Japan, indicating that this was a region-wide development. Sumptuous living, fine foods, and diverting amusements were emblems of the courts' affluence. Most of these celebrations involved the idle elite, who consisted of the royal family and courtiers, sojourners from other lands temporarily attached to the court, and clients of the royal family. Wives of the ruler and their retainers had an important place at these events, even if they came heavily veiled or were screened off from public view. Finally, there were numerous entertainers and retainers of the royal family, many of whom were slaves.

Furthermore, the model of court administrative structure from the Brahman period was retained, with the offices of state being organized around the principle of four great, eight lesser, sixteen smaller, and thirty-two inferior officers; and, at least initially, the assignment of "right" and "left" for protocol was continued. These organizational concepts, which had been highly important earlier, were used mainly for determining precedence at important ceremonies but had no great meaning otherwise. Regarding principal officers, the positions of "first minister" and the "interior minister" were almost always used; other positions were sometimes ceremonial and often had no incumbents. The first minister usually had control over the treasury, the general functioning of administration, and sometimes the operation of the justice system. The interior minister was usually the collector of port fees, in charge of ceremonies, and, sometimes, had responsibilities in the area of justice. Frequently a "fleet commander" was included as a minister, and the "heir apparent" often had a high advisory role, especially if there was a state council of leading officials to assist the ruler. There were regular ministers, such as the "treasurer," important administrators, such as the "harbormaster," along with other officials of various ranks. It is likely that, in the case of Java, the entire local government system was taken over from earlier Muslim states, and the local governing systems of the Malays likewise seem to have been in place earlier.[16] All these elements reflected preexisting patterns, but they were adjusted to a new environment, so that Islam was given a position of importance: Muslim holy men and schools were granted patronage, Muslim scholars appeared at court as advisers and sometimes as officials, and Islamic activists were supported in their efforts to convert and extend the dominion of Islam within the state itself, and often outside it.

Upon conversion to Islam most rulers took Arabic-Muslim names. The names Iskandar Muda, Harun Oedin, Mandarsjah, Agung, Hidajat, Said Oedin and Baab Oeddin, while showing some deterioration from their Middle Eastern origins, nonetheless were clearly Arabic and Islamic in their identification. Also, while Muslim rulers usually assumed Muslim titles, some maintained a number of non-Muslim ones as well. The Indic title of "raja" was commonly retained as the title for a state's ruler, but over time declined in importance and became the title of a secondary ruler, being replaced the Middle Eastern term "sultan." Initially, however, the "sultan" was reserved for only the primary raja in a particular area, and the use of the Islamic title indicated his status above the rest. In 1445 the third Melakan ruler, Muzaffar Shah (r. 1445–1459), took the title as an indication that he was committed to Islam, as his two predecessors had been Muslims in name only. During the fifteenth century there were only two other rulers in the region with that title, the rulers of Pasai and Bengal.[17]

The monopoly on the title of "sultan" seems to have been short-lived. Later, nearly all prominent Muslim rulers assumed that title, although it was less used in central Java than elsewhere. Further, when they issued coins, Muslim rulers often had the title "king" and the words confessing the faith of Islam inscribed on them, but not "raja" or "sultan." Still later, several of the rulers also took more prestigious Muslim titles—prestigious at least in the central Muslim world—of "commander of the faithful" and "successor of the Prophet." Like sultan, these terms became part of even lesser rulers' epithets and consequently lacked the authority and respect they commanded in the Middle East, where they were held by only an elect group of rulers.

At the same time, non-Muslim titles continued to have great prestige, even above that of the Muslim titles. In the Malay areas the term "He who is paramount" (Yang di Pertuan) was regarded as a title of considerable dignity; its equivalent on Java was "the illustrious" (Susuhunan). Other local titles, such as prince (pangeran) and lord (gusti), were used as well. The authority to use such titles came from a variety of sources. In some cases they were arbitrarily assumed and court chroniclers assisted by including them as legitimate in their accounts. As mentioned above, Muslim titles sometimes were obtained from the Middle East, such as from the Sharif of Mekkah, who, for an appropriate gift, would certify the right of a Muslim ruler in Southeast Asia to rule. At other times authority closer by, such as the emperor of China or the king of Ayuthia, assigned titles as a way of reinforcing their suzerainty over a Muslim vassal.

Court writers were also essential, for it was their task to weave plausible points of contact in the genealogies of ruling families and royal families, particularly those of bygone eras. Through a written "history" that traced a path of succession back to esteemed leaders of the past, it was believed that their power could be transferred to contemporary rulers. For instance, court writers used stratagems to tie Muslim Mataram with pre-Islamic Majapahit because Majapahit was highly regarded among the Javanese populace and the elite.[18] These writers also tied Melaka to the rulers of Srivijaya on Sumatra to make possible a Melakan claim over the Straits area. They sometimes claimed Middle Eastern antecedents for rulers. Again, court documents asserted that Alexander (Iskandar) the Great (r. 339–323 B.C.E.) was a predecessor of the rulers at Melaka and Aceh, claims that were intended to convey power from a faraway source that appealed to the literature of the time, which continued to tell of the great hero of Middle Eastern fame, celebrated even among Muslims.[19]

The armies of nearly every ruler in the region during this period, Muslim and non-Muslim, were usually composed of a mixture of fighting men raised by the chief vassals of a kingdom. Being short of labor themselves, these vassals frequently turned to mercenaries drawn from the many nationalities and peoples who moved along the trade routes. Here the port culture, with ships as links in the network, furnished the men, arms, and much of the equipment. When the Batak ruler marched against Aceh in the late sixteenth century, the Achenese ruler had in his army "Turks, Saracens, Malabars, Gujerates, Abyssinians and Lusons from Kalimantan."[20] There were also mercenary Muslim forces in Khmer, who alternated their loyalty between the Khmer king and the king of Ayuthia. Muslim commanders were sometimes placed in high offices, such as garrison commanders or even province chiefs. On the other hand, it was not only Muslims who were recruited as mercenaries; for example, the mercenary army of Melaka was composed mostly of non-Muslim Javanese and, later, European drifters became part of the available military labor pool. Finally, elite military units existed in some places, such as at Aceh, where the ruler had a special, highly trained guard, probably modeled on the elite infantry corps of the Ottomans.

Some women served as rulers of several Southeast Asian Muslim states.

The celebrated cases occurred in Aceh, Patani, and Jepara. Two of those rulers, Taj Alam (r. 1641–1675) at Aceh and Ratu Kali Nyamat (r. late sixteenth century) at Jepara, were spouses who assumed rule when their husbands died and no male contender was able to command enough respect to gain the position. Both of these women rulers were regarded as "strong" rulers. Taj Alam was devoted to refashioning the Acehnese state into a more humane system than had existed earlier, and Kali Nyamat continued her dynasty's policy of countering the Portuguese by bringing together a coalition of Muslim states to oppose them. The other cases, in Aceh (1675–1699) and Patani (1528–1624, 1707–1717), however, involved figurehead rulers so that non-royal administrators could govern their own spheres without interference from a strong ruler. In both places the women rulers were pampered but kept isolated so as to forestall action detrimental to the administrators. The admission of women to ruling positions may be accounted for by the esteemed status of women in most Southeast Asian societies, especially in the area of inheritance, where they had much to say about all matters, even if it was customary for men to be political leaders.

The Nature of Islamic States

Three basic social organizations undergirded the political systems of the Muslim Zone during this era. For convenience I shall refer to them as the "community model," the "vassal model," and the "hierarchy model." The community model was characterized by tight familial and clan organization. Customs and mores were usually well developed, highly cherished, and strongly defended. Local leaders and rulers emerged from that social organization who reflected the values of the community and decided important matters only with the near consensus of the community itself. Higher government emerged as the result of cooperation between communities, but leaders serving at this level were compelled to respect the general agreement of the communities they served. Taxation and service requirements were local, and higher levels of government had to rely on their own sources of income, which were usually limited. Islam had difficulty entering such political systems and usually had to append itself to social institutions to gain entrance, simply because rulers were not able to implement Islamic policies very well when they converted.

The vassal model emerged from loose, often migrant population groups without much social cohesion, living in isolated areas and lacking strong ties to larger ethnic groups. Here, community organization and custom developed around the importance of the ruler within that society. Higher government formed as a result of the attachment of local leaders to more powerful leaders, and they in turn were tied to still more powerful leaders at a higher level. The power of any individual ruler rested on the people he could organize to perform human activities—work, warfare, or social rites—and the position of a ruler in the hierarchy of rulers was not always important. A lesser vassal might be more powerful than a higher one because of wealth, organization, or other factors, and when this occurred the ruler with the economic advantage often acted independently. Feudal dues from land production and service requirements were common and strengthened the upper levels of rulers. As it developed, this form became identified with Islam, because the ruler used the titles and concepts in Islam to promote his authority. The concept of a special relationship between God and ruler was an important justification for having the authority to rule.

The hierarchy model was used in population groups where higher authority had been established for a considerable period of time and had been able to organize society in such a way that government was integral to it. Although local communities were regulated by local customs and local institutions were developed, the authority of higher rulers was regarded as important as well. In the fully developed model, allocations of land, people, and taxes were made by the principal ruler to courtiers, religious establishments, and others in return for tribute money, "presents," and services, usually labor and/or military duties. Appanage land was assigned to an official for the time he held his office, or to a courtier for the length of time during which he was supported by the sovereign of the court he served. When the official or courtier died or fell from favor the grant was withdrawn. Royal courts that had lasted for a long period of time and had centralized many aspects of government were instrumental in developing this model. When Islam arrived, rulers in this type of society regarded it as a source of more power to be used in ruling; but Islamic identity depended greatly on whether competing value systems existed. In Brunei, Islam succeeded quite well because the contending systems were based on custom and an elite identification with China, but on Java there was more difficulty because of the strong and pervading identification of the population and elite with Old Javanese civilization, with its ties to a strong hierarchy and Brahman forms.

The foremost Muslim states of this era all emerged from one of these three forms, but usually had transcended the societal underpinning to become an entity we shall call an "imperium." The imperium was an artificial creation of a unifying ruler, often using warfare or the threat of hostilities to bring diverse people and territories together for economic and political purposes. The existing arrangements of rule in each of the constituent parts—community, vassal, or hierarchy—were allowed to continue in general terms, but an imperial organization consisting of governors and their staffs was placed over particular population groups or regional centers to maintain order and to assure continued control of the ruler over the constituent unit. Usually there was an attempt to centralize certain functions, particularly trade, but armies and navies as well, so that power and wealth flowed toward the center. The usual key to the development of an imperium once it had come into existence was to have a source of income independent of the base from which the ruler arose. Sometimes that was the mining of precious metals, or rich agricultural land where taxes could be levied. In most cases, however, it came from having prosperous ports where excise taxes on the goods of passing merchants and the opportunity for trading ventures on a large scale offered a long-term supply of such funds. Wealth was crucial, and when it disappeared, as it did in Minangkabau when the gold fields ran out and in Aceh when the international trading system declined, any pretensions to becoming or remaining an imperium faded.

In part, the imperium reflected the values of the group from which it arose, but in all the cases discussed here the adoption of a strong Islamic monarch was regarded as pivotal to providing the status and instrumentalities capable of furthering the system. At this time in maritime Southeast Asia, Islamization was regarded as essential, for it promoted trade as a recognized and important part of human activity, it sanctified strong rulers as vice-regents of God, and it allowed preferred political units that were organized and devoted to the ends of religion. All-in-all, the indigenous political systems showed considerable variance, although European treaties tended to treat them as if there were no differences, which was one cause of misunderstanding and friction between the Europeans and local rulers.

The Growth of Muslim States

Melaka in the Straits of Melaka

The archetype of the vassal model that rose to become an imperium was Melaka. This state was important throughout the era, although its greatest period was during the fourteenth century. The first ruler, possibly a descendant of the Srivijayan dynasty and named Parameswara (r. to 1414), married a princess of Pasai circa 1400 and took the Arabic name Muhammad Iskandar Shah. The ruler's sons, who succeeded him consecutively to 1445, retained both Arabic and Sanskrit names, indicating that the Islamization at the royal court was nominal in nature.

The Islamic age of Melaka started with the Tamil Muslim insurrection of 1445, which made Muzaffar Shah, a secondary son of the former ruler by an Indian concubine, the new ruler. He embarked on an expansionist policy, which brought under its suzerainty most of the Malayan areas on the Malay Peninsula, east Sumatra, and the islands in the Straits, which centralized trade at Melaka. Using military and naval forces manned largely by mercenary Chinese, Ayuthia's control was broken, and diplomatic missions were sent to China to win and assure the Chinese emperor's recognition of Melaka's status as independent from both Majapahit and Ayuthia, the two dominant regional powers of the time.

The high age of the kingdom came with the reign of Mahmud (r. 1488–1511). The political system was fully developed by this juncture and became a model throughout the Malay region. At its apex was a sultan, who spent considerable time on state affairs, patronage of the arts and literature, and the diffusion of Islam, but also pursued a lavish lifestyle—hunting, feasting, and enjoying concubines. The rulers of Melaka possessed a pedigree that related them to the Srivijaya rulers of the sixth to thirteenth centuries and through them to the "two-horned" Iskandar, a reference to Alexander the Great. The legend of the first ruler's arrival in Melaka was carefully described in the state annals, and at several points in the chronicles a political arrangement was outlined in which the ruler promised in a public statement to look after the welfare of the people in return for their loyalty. It was also part of the understanding that the population was not to revolt against the ruler even if he inflicted evil upon them, as the only power that could remove the ruler for violations of that covenant was God.

The designated heir apparent, usually a brother or uncle of the ruler, held the title of deputy commander and was usually in charge of military affairs. When the ruler died, however, factions supported different contenders from the royal family, leading to great controversy and long periods of consolidation by the winner. Members of the royal family were free to continue to enjoy themselves insofar as the ruler was able and willing to give them stipends and appanages to support them; in the case of Melaka these were usually ample.

Prominent state officials from the wealthy class saw to the functioning of the state and its economy. The chief minister was in charge of the treasury, justice, and overall functioning of the administration. The legal and protocol official was responsible for the collection of port fees, court ceremonies, and receptions, and also served as prosecutor of criminal offenses. As in other nearby Malay entrepreneurial states, there was considerable effort on the part of leading "citizens" to gain wealth through investment in trading activities, and to use the status that came with that wealth to seek political office, contending with others from the same class. The leading personalities at any time were usually chosen by the ruler to become members of a state advisory council, where the members created factions that sought to enhance the prerogatives of their members and to undercut competing groups. There were four harbormasters who supervised the port. All of these officials usually engaged in trade activities themselves and benefited from the expansionist policy pursued by the state. The ordinary people were "lightly" taxed and, since labor was scarce, were treated fairly well by merchants and officials. In fact, nearly all the hard labor was done by "free" women, men and women in bondage for debt and crime, and male and female slaves taken in warfare or purchased from slavers who plied the Southeast Asian region. Bondage and slavery were important and well-established institutions, particularly since labor was in short supply and the prestige and power of important people was based on control of labor, free or forced.

Court life was an important feature of the Melakan state. Audiences and ceremonies were frequent, apparently well organized, and marked by color, pomp, and ceremony. The arrival of important trade officials with special missions, the receptions for emissaries from other rulers, the presentation of honors to local officials and champions, and receptions of delegations bringing wives for the ruler were all marked with elaborate ceremonies. Carefully clothed and groomed court officials appeared in their prescribed order during ceremonies, musicians played their instruments on cue, gifts were presented, and honors bestowed—all ceremonies undertaken with great regard for an intricate protocol and custom. Further, Melaka was a cultural center where Malay literature was developed and appreciated.

A code of laws identified with Melaka dealt with civil, criminal, and maritime matters. The laws were far-reaching, as they set the standards that were to be used in the harbor and on the seas under the jurisdiction of Melakan patrols when dealing with division of spoils, sailing regulations, rights of merchants under various conditions, and attack at sea. In this development of law not much concern was in evidence with the conceptual sacred law *(shar³iah)* that occurred later, but Muslim scholars and merchants were willing to introduce Islamic precepts when fitting, both to comply with religious principles and for the practical purpose of using a system of Muslim trade laws that had proven very practical elsewhere. Specific to law itself, Islamic legal principles appeared clearly in the sections on judicial procedure, commercial matters, marital relations, murder, theft, and apostasy. Still the laws and law codes that emerged were first of all reflective of the local customary law, which prescribed the greatest portion of principles, procedure, and punishments, while Islamic law fit into that custom and gave it underlying principle and direction.

Melaka fell to the Portuguese in 1511 after a short defense of the port city. It survived as the state of Johore, which was a leading regional power until the eighteenth century, first as an independent state and later as a client state of the Dutch Company. In modern times it has served as the historical antecedent for the twentieth-century state of Malaysia.

Ternate in Maluku

The Islamic state of Ternate offers an example of an imperium that developed out of the community model. In the Halmahera region four states—Ternate, Tidore, Bacan, and Gildo—originally vied among themselves for political mastery. Ternate became the leading power and extended its control over the other four neighboring islands of the Halmaheran chain, on Mindanao, on the northeast coast of Menado, and on the island of Sangir. It claimed authority, but did not always exercise it, over Ambon, Ceram, Buru, Bacan, and Moti to the south. Conversion to Islam began during the last part of the fifteenth century, brought by merchants from Ambon, probably many of them from the Muslim-Javanese colonies established by merchants from Tuban on the Javanese north coast. Conversions were made initially in the ports, followed by the nobility, while the general population's conversion was much slower and was far from complete in the beginning of the sixteenth century. Prior to the arrival of Islam there was an official designated as "guardian of the realm" *(imam sawahi)*, who attempted to limit the impact of Islam by maintaining preexisting customs. Eventually he lost his standing in matters of faith and was assigned to safekeeping of royal regalia.

The chief rulers in the Maluku region bore the title *kolano,* apparently a Javanese loanword derived from the Panji tales connected with the Hindu Ramayana pageants that were especially popular in the pre-Islamic era; the term "sultan" was used as well. The rulers were regarded as having superhuman status, so were attended by a great deal of pomp, ceremony, and deference. They were well clothed, had costly regalia, and the courtiers and retainers bowed and crawled in their presence. The ruler was assisted by a number of ministers and counselors drawn from the royal family, who exercised a great deal of power and influence through these positions. Because edible produce was in limited supply throughout the region, there was a royal quartermaster who collected foodstuffs from the various islands and distributed it among the nobility, royalty, and for ceremonies at the palace.

At Ternate local rulers were important. Certainly nobles shared in the export–import trade that supported much of the economic life of the royal court and the royal family, but their primary responsibility was the governing of districts, given them as appanages. They were assisted by subdistrict chiefs with long standing in the communities. There was also a council on which senior counselors chosen from among the subdistrict chiefs helped to set state policy. Over time their influence waned as the chief ministers of the realm gained status at council meetings.

There were two judges *(qadi),* supposedly trained in Islamic jurisprudence, but in practice the positions were filled by members of the royal family, who purchased them from the ruler. Since these royal jurists were usually not well versed in Islamic sciences, their rulings were made in accordance with common sense and the established custom of the region. In the latter half of the seventeenth century it was decided to fill one of the two positions with a prominent Muslim scholar not a member of the royal family, but there was no corresponding increase in the "Islamic" content of court decisions as a result of this appointment.

Ternate and its competitor states existed in a world where foreign traders operated and the gathering of spices was paramount. When the first Portuguese expedition to the Spice Islands arrived in 1511, a contract was made with Ternate whereby the ruler allowed the Portuguese a small trading settlement and agreed to a monopoly of locally grown cloves in exchange for high prices and military assistance when needed. The initial period of Portuguese presence was politically turbulent because Portuguese personnel meddled in Ternatan affairs, with the result that rulers were replaced on whim by Portuguese factions. In 1536 a more settled period began under the Portuguese administrator A. Galvão (governed 1536–1540), who curtailed Portuguese interference in local affairs, ensured general order, and promoted the Portuguese settlements as self-contained Catholic communities. Trade was generally good and the monopoly of cloves fairly effective.

The period beginning in 1539 constituted a third Portuguese period in which the monopoly of cloves was abandoned for open trade. Also, Francis Xavier (d. 1552) undertook missionary activities in this era that produced a large expansion of Christians in the local population, estimated to be as high as twenty thousand. But when Portuguese officials attempted to put forward a Christian as ruler of Ternate, there was a strong reaction from Muslim elements of the population.[21] Under Hairun (r. to 1570) and Baab Ullah (r. 1570–1583) there were efforts to limit, and then remove, missionary activity. The result was a reconversion of large numbers of Christians to Islam. The Portuguese were driven out, but in the seventeenth century the state came under Dutch Company control, effectively ending the independence of the state.

Mataram on Java

The archetype of the hierarchal model was Mataram, one of the most enduring of the Islamic states. It owed its original form to the legacy of the pre-Islamic kingdom of Majapahit and that of Demak, the first Muslim-Javanese kingdom immediately preceding Mataram. Majapahit, as a culmination of many Indianized states in east Java, had continued the development of a strong agricultural society providing the financial and popular underpinning that fortified the tradition of strong rule in the royal court, which dominated all levels of government. Demak, on the other hand, had been the main instrument of conversion to Islam in the area, promoting the work of renowned Islamic propagators *(wali sangha)* and bringing large groups of Javans under Muslim political control.

The Demak state broke up in the last half of the fifteenth century, and one of its successor rulers, Senapati (r. 1582–1601), conquered large parts of central Java, including Demak, and founded the state of Mataram. The dynasty through the first four rulers devoted considerable effort toward attaining military and naval power; and, while generally successful in becoming the leading state on the island, its political effectiveness was debilitated by the long warfare against the northeastern states, Surabaya and Madura in particular. The rulers, the royal family, the gentry, and large portions of the population were nominally Muslim. A more pietistic Islam could be found in the harbor cities of the north coast and among merchants and places where Islamic propagators settled and founded strong Muslim institutions, such as schools and lodges for mystics.

The first ruler of Mataram used the title *susuhunan,* meaning "illustrious," whose shortened form, *sunan,* had previously been used by spiritual leaders, particularly the famous propagators of Islam in the fourteenth century. The title was indigenous to Javanese culture and was an indicator of the allegiance of the court to the prevailing value system. However, there were some attempts to conform to Muslim practice in that the first ruler took the title of "sultan" in 1544, while the third ruler, Agung (r. 1624–1645), sent emissaries to Makkah in 1641 to obtain the special title "Sultan Abdullah Muhammad Maulana Matarani," which was granted to him by the ruler of Makkah. The Javanese title had greater popularity than did the Islamic designator.

The government was reflective of the earlier Brahman forms that had preceded Islam. There was a chief minister, chosen by the ruler, apparently at will, although usually from the royal family. Slightly lower in rank came a set of twelve court regents who headed important departments, such as justice, law enforcement, treasury, and care of the royal regalia; these officials were designated as commanding a specific number of warriors on either the "left" or the "right" of the battle formation, and they also sat on the left or the right in the reception areas of the palace. In addition, there was another group of officials with less definitive assignments who were required to be at court, and were occasionally given specific personal assignments by the ruler himself. There were harbormasters who spent part of their time at courts and part at the ports to assure that the ruler received an adequate share of the profits from the trade of the ports.

Justice also reflected the Brahman tradition and its adaptation to the Javanese environment. Laws of the state, covering most capital crimes and other violations against the ruler's authority, were exercised by the ruler himself. Sultan Agung passed general control of the court over to his chief religious official *(penghulu),* who presided with the assistance of a panel of religious advisers, but this was a short-lived innovation and religious officials later gave way to regular judges. Cases involving community law were handled at the local and regional levels, where territorial rulers tried the cases, using a wide variety of styles and procedures.

Outside of the capital there was an administration supposedly answerable to the ruler. The court appointed governors over some territories, such as the northeast ports, who administered them while their vassal rulers were at court at the behest of the Mataram ruler. Regional officials organized their own governments similarly to that of the sultan's royal court, with a first minister, twelve ministers, and a prosecutor. Below the governors were regents who had small courts and administrations of their own. At the local level there were village headmen, usually appointed by the official in control of the appanage land where the village was located. This system gave some autonomy to regional and local rulers, but not nearly as much as in the "vassal" states described earlier.

The role of Islam in administration was limited, but it was given prominence in some matters. A mosque was attached to the royal enclosure, and a leading court figure, called the superintendant *(penghulu)*, directed the other officials of the mosque. There was also a chief religious judge at court who supervised legalists *(mufti)* charged with undertaking review of matters brought to them by the ruler and other high officials for conformity with the principles of Islamic law. Among the early rulers only Sultan Agung actively promoted Islam as state policy, and that only occurred in the last decade of his long reign. His law code was developed at that time; it was an attempt to combine local custom and Muslim law, although it is usually regarded as short on Islamic content.

But alongside Islam there was acknowledgment that older values, from Java itself and from Indian culture, remained important. There was the widely held conception that spiritual "light" emanated from the ruler for the benefit of the entire realm. There was a belief that Nyah Rata Kidul, the goddess of the Southern Ocean, played a special role in the fate of Mataram. The Panji literature, with its Old Javanese theme of the returning "messiah" *(ratu adil)* was held in high esteem. Hindu and Brahman values regarding the place of the political system in the cosmos were regarded as relevant and given voice through the puppet shows depicting the Javanized version of the Indian epic *Mahabarata*. Also, great attention was given to the royal regalia, consisting of special weapons, clothing, and other articles, all of which were believed to have supernatural powers for use by the rulers that possessed them.

Later rulers of Mataram were not especially religious and their decisions did not promote Islamic identification. This was cause for concern among the Islamic functionaries in the capital. When the fourth ruler, Amangkurat I (r. 1646–1677), had a publicly known love affair with a wife of a high government official, religious officials were so outraged that they attempted to raid his palace. Royal retribution was severe: several thousand participants and their families were executed. There were also several rebellions in the countryside led by Muslim leaders shouting Islamic rallying cries; the rebellions were put down forcefully and the Muslim leaders severely punished. For example, in the reign of Sultan Agung, a rebellion occurred at Têmbayat where the legendary saint Sunan Bayat (active 1677) was buried. The rebels were all religious personalities associated with the gravesite and saw themselves as opposing a ruler who was less than ideal; their revolt was also put down with much loss of life among the rebels.

Chinese withdrawal from Southeast Asian affairs had occurred earlier than the rise of the Mataram dynasty, so that feudal relations with that country were no longer necessary or fashionable. Not surprisingly, given the "old" civilization that Mataram inherited and the amount of naval and military power it generated, its rulers regarded themselves as the liege of a large grouping of vassals, particularly in the eastern section of Java—Surabaya, Madura, Balambangan—but also on the neighboring islands of Kalimantan and the Lesser Sundas. Mataram rulers were wary of their officials in general and their vassals in particular, insisting that they and members of their families spend considerable time at the royal court to limit their scope of independence and keep them away from their own local sources of strength, which could be used to challenge Mataram's authority.

When the Dutch arrived, the ruler of Mataram regarded them as competitors and a threat. At particular times the rulers went to war against the Dutch, as Sultan Agung did in 1628 and 1629, and at others undertook military action against its outposts. On other occasions, however, when they needed Dutch assistance, as during the Surabaya war in the mid-1620s, and when the Makassarese threatened the northeast coast of Java in 1675, Mataram's rulers called on the Dutch for aid. Throughout the long relationship, which was to last into the twentieth century, and despite the growing power of the Dutch vis-à-vis the Mataram rulers, those rulers never regarded themselves as being the vassals of the Dutch, even though they eventually had to accept conditions that indicated such a relationship did exist.

In 1755 the kingdom was divided in two, with one realm continuing to center itself on Kartasura, later Surakarta, and the other on Yogyakarta. At that time control over the outlying districts to the north, east, and southeast had been lost, with the Dutch controlling everything along the north and east coasts, and only the eastern end of Java still disputed with Bali. Accordingly, the robust Mataram kingdom of the sixteenth century had shrunk to two small semi-independent principalities by the end of the eighteenth century.

Aceh on Sumatra

Aceh seems always to have been an imperium, although it may have originated with a small ethnic group, similar to the vassal model states explained earlier. The Acehnese state appears to have been an economic and political venture by a prominent family to use the gains from a centralized system and international trade to build a kingdom overarching the existing societal organization of the Acehnese region. Identification of the population with its rulers during its rise and heyday appears to have been a contributing factor to its success.

As a Muslim, the first ruler of the dynasty used a polyglot Malay-Arabic title, Sri Paduka Berpakat Rahim, which was a mixture of Indic, Malay, and Arab conceptions; all the rulers enjoyed the additional Muslim title of sultan. A few rulers were energetic and able to give attention to the building of the kingdom, such as Ri'ayat Syah al-Kahar (r. 1539–1571). Many other rulers exercised power poorly and were overthrown, such as five from 1579 to 1589 who were considered unsuitable by the merchant elite and either killed or otherwise removed. All rulers were assisted by a group of nobles, who formed a council to assist in setting state policy and served as key administrators, such as chief minister, harbormaster, and fleet commander. A chief religious judge apparently reviewed decrees, policies, and other state documents and letters to advise the ruler on the appropriateness of the contents of those documents from the Islamic perspective. Also, there were officials at the mosque near the palace that were apparently state-supported. At this particular point in time the governmental system resembled the Melakan sultanate, and the resemblance was probably deliberate.

A vassal system operated in the Acehnese area, with Aceh the chief suzerain. Much of the coastal areas of Sumatra and nearby islands, as well as some territory on the Malay Archipelago, were controlled either directly by governors, or through vassals. The vassal states resented Acehnese overlordship, because the trade system forced them to ship only to the chief port of Aceh, with the ruler determining the prices of goods and having first choice of whatever he wanted to buy at low prices. In general, vassals of Aceh were almost always restive, seeking opportunities for breaking free of its control, even though punitive expeditions against such vassals exacted severe retribution.

The Portuguese at Melaka were regarded as the archenemy and continual efforts were made to remove them from control of their port, always unsuccessfully. Several military and naval expeditions were sent against Melaka, but the Portuguese were able to repulse them all. However, efforts to construct a rival trading system to that of the Portuguese had some success. This centered on trading ventures that delivered pepper and other spices directly to the Red Sea in the mid-sixteenth century. This venture lasted for nearly thirty years, with five to twenty-three ships making the trip each year, underwritten with capital from Muslim merchants in Aceh and from the coastal areas of India. Eventually, Aceh simply became a replacement port for Melaka where Asian traders could undertake trade outside the Portuguese and, later, Dutch systems.

In a second period, one marked by royal absolutism, Iskandar Muda (r. 1607–1636) was the single ruler, although the next two rulers constituted an "aftermath" of the imperial period, when institutions and styles of leadership transformed into a decentralized political system with less interest in foreign aggrandizement. Court ritual was highly important, nearly everything involving the daily life of the ruler was set in ceremony, meaning that it was demanding in terms of personnel, money, and time. As well, the ruler was active in making laws, conducting legal administration, performing oversight of economically prosperous districts, sending forth foreign expeditions to add to the glory and size of the realm, holding discussions with religious officials on philosophical themes, and carrying on trade as the chief merchant of the realm. In general the Acehnese court regulated the market so that prices were high by insisting that foreign buyers purchase at least part of their cargo from the sultan's own supply or from other members of his court, always at exorbitant prices.

During this period of royal absolutism the central figure of the court was the ruler, called sultan, although Iskandar Muda used the grandiose title "crown of the world." The sultan received his investiture from the chief judge and through the homage of the chief nobles of the realm. He was surrounded by a panoply of retainers—some royal, some common, and some of indeterminate status—using titles developed during the mercantile period. Outside of the royal court there were three levels of administration: the village, headed by a chief and assisted by an Islamic prayer leader at the first rung; the district of several villages for common prayer, with a prayer leader and a judge at the second level; and the state, headed by a state chief and assisted by a higher-level judge at the top level. The state chiefs were recruited from people at the center who were personally loyal to the sultan and were installed as his retainers with documents containing the royal seal. These state chiefs were especially charged with meeting the tax burdens placed on a political unit and also with supplying the personnel needed for military campaigns. In addition to this territorial administration, there were commanders or governors assigned to oversee crucial areas of production or ports recently added to the Acehnese imperium. These governors were kept under the tight control of the Achenese ruler and replaced frequently to lessen corruption and to assure that the facilities they commanded were administered for the benefit of the ruler himself.

The ruler issued decrees that became part of the law enforced throughout the realm, but usually they were drafted by a council of nobles who assisted him and then reviewed by the chief religious judge. The ruler was usually not a judge himself, since special courts existed for that purpose, but when interested in a particular case, the ruler often did pass judgment. Some cases were tried according to Islamic law: for example, arms and legs were amputated for theft. In other cases, particularly where the sensibilities of the royal court were disturbed, punishments were often arbitrary and even capricious; several observers remarked on the severity of punishments meted out for trivial offenses.

In the imperial period the Portuguese were still regarded as an enemy, and in 1629 Iskandar Muda assembled an armada of five hundred ships, carrying nineteen thousand men and extensive artillery, with the intention of capturing Melaka and driving the Portuguese from the region. But the Acehnese suffered a decisive defeat, experiencing a staggering loss of ships, equipment, and men-at-arms. While Aceh continued to exist as a regional power for some time thereafter, it was no longer as powerful as it had been up to that point in history, and a slow dwindling of its overseas holdings began to occur from that time on.

The Muslim Community

Religious Elements
Islamic Specialists

This study will use the term "religious specialists" for people who were recognized as performing particular tasks for the Muslim community of believers, wherever they served in society. The specialists differed in each era, as we shall see later, but for this period, some of those people were prominent fulfilling official duties in the royal courts, others served as religious scholars in the general society, still others were attached to the mosque, some operated mystic cells or sects, and a good number were activists or propagators of religion responsible for the conversion of non-Muslims to Islam.

There were Islamic court specialists at all of the Muslim principalities in this era, although their influence differed according to the ruler they served. Many were true counselors, giving advice on matters of political and economic importance, particularly from the perspective of what might be expected from a Muslim ruler. Some of these personages were well traveled, sophisticated, and knowledgeable about the broader Muslim world, so they made ideal counselors. Al-Raniri (d. 1658), for example, was from the Gujerat, had studied under a Hadrami Arab teacher at Surat, lived in Aceh twice in his lifetime, and visited Makkah. At times some of these counselors were influential enough to promote an "Islamic agenda," as happened early in the era in Pasai and Demak, when both states undertook "holy wars" to fight non-Muslims and to spread Islam. At Johore these Muslim counselors dominated a naive ruler, conspiring with the regent to promote self-serving agendas and keeping the king entirely "ignorant of what was happening."[22] Such religious advisers existed in eighteenth-century Palembang as well, who were consulted on key state matters, including war.

There were Islamic justice officials of several ranks: chief judges, judges (qadi), and legalists (mufti). Their jurisdictions varied, some courts being assigned broad responsibilities, though at other times narrowed to include only family law and pious endowments. Many rulers conducted trials themselves, so that the role of the Muslim judges was curtailed or enhanced as a ruler's interest in judicial matters waxed and waned. Some of these legal officials translated legal studies from the Middle East or India and blended them with local custom to arrive at new variations of Islamic law.

Further, at the royal courts officials looked after some matters connected with worship and other matters of religious obligation. On Sulawesi in the seventeenth century, one ruler granted considerable authority to a religious official to oversee the functioning of mosques throughout the realm in order to promote strong identification with Islam and undercut local custom, which he regarded as a hindrance to the growth of royal authority. At Yogyakarta officials looked after the payment of the poor tax (zakat) to religious specialists and needy persons, while at Sulu there was an official in charge of the care of orphans. There were also officials at the palace mosque, sometimes many of the same people who served as judges and counselors, who "officiated" by leading prayers and giving sermons. In addition, there were religious teachers at court who gave lessons in some of the religious sciences, Qur'an studies, Arabic language, mystical practice, and law.

Finally, some royal courts, such as Aceh in the seventeenth century, had a number of scholars (ʿalim) forming an intellectual community for the pleasure and edification of the ruler. Meeting in council with the ruler, these notables discussed religious matters, instructed him and his courtiers in religious sciences, and posed interesting questions for the entertainment of the ruler. A similar intellectual community was also found at Palembang in the eighteenth century. Since training in Islam was difficult to attain, the positions of counselors, legal experts, and scholars were sometimes filled by foreigners, very often Arabs, and it was only in the eighteenth century that a trend began for hiring local scholars, often members of royal families. Many of these officials and specialists were supported by the ruler in some fashion, either by the bestowal of gifts, which seems to have been the method early in the era, or by the assignment of funds from the ruler's income, which was more common later.

There were also religious specialists, also known as scholars who did not identify with the royal courts but founded their own religious centers, sometimes regarding court life as antithetical to good Islamic practice. Panembahan Giri (active ca. 1500), the civil-religious ruler of Giri, justified a rebellion against Amangkurat I (r. 1645–1677) of Mataram in the 1670s on the charge that Amangkurat had betrayed Islam by making agreements with the Christian Dutch. The "living saint" at Tembayat opposed the royal

court of Mataram on several occasions, and the Minang activist Raja Ibrahim (d. 1678) rallied followers from Malay areas to oppose the Dutch at
Melaka. These early antiauthoritarian leaders started a practice, which was
to grow with time, of representing the local population who felt aggrieved
by excessive taxation, demands for corvee labor, or abuse from officials.
Some observers have regarded such observances as "anti-European," but
mostly they seem to have been directed against both indigenous and foreign rule regarded as oppressive.

Other scholars, often from the central Islamic world or India, provided
Islamic education to interested groups outside of the royal courts. Their
efforts were marked in this era by itinerant teaching, that is, giving instruction at a place until the local population lost interest and then moving on
to a new location, where the process was repeated. These scholars were part
of a larger movement into the area by Muslim propagators *(da'i)* who came
with the distinct intention of proselytizing. Some of these scholars eventually settled in an area and started schools, which attracted other foreign
scholars or local learners who became part of the new Islamic community
centered around the school.

Another group of religious specialists were found in the mosques. Early
in the era mosques were few, poorly built, and had little organization
attached to them, but by its end the numbers had increased and organization was more apparent. Sultan Agung of Mataram devised an elaborate
system of mosque specialists for his domains, although it is doubtful that it
became at all universal during his reign; accordingly, it is more appropriately discussed in the next chapter, when the system functioned more fully.
At Brunei there were three positions connected with mosque: the sermon
giver, the chief sermon giver, and the prayer leader, a local variation on the
standard offices of prayer leader *(imam)*, sermon reciter *(khatib)*, and prayer
caller *(bilal)* used after this era in nearly all non-Javanese areas. In general,
a small rice tax was set aside for the support of mosque specialists, although
the tax was usually voluntary and not large enough to support the mosque
personnel very well. Such positions were usually filled by the few men who
did go on the pilgrimage, along with men with some knowledge of the
Islamic sciences, learned formally in the few private schools that existed or
in private sessions with others in the mosque or mystical groups.

Still another group of religious specialists were mystics *(sufi)*, who were
also propagators. In the stories of conversion told in the Pasai and Malay
chronicles, such persons were heralded in a dream of a prominent ruler.
Immediately upon their arrival, the propagators proceeded to complete
the conversion of the ruler that had been begun in his dream. Although
mentioned only as single persons, and probably mythical and symbolic personalities at that, it is likely that this group was the real force behind the

mission of converting the local population, and was a mixed group of Arabs—"noble" Arabs *(sayyid)* were specifically mentioned—Indians of Arabic descent, and local activists organized by these overseas groups. Information about these activists is sparse in the early part of the era, but the case of Makassar in the seventeenth century provided an example of how such propagation worked in practice. Yusuf al-Makassari was a "master" in the Khalwatiyah mystical order, first at Makassar and later at Banten, where he trained "deputies" to expand outward from his own circle to found other circles of believers among the population that was only nominally Muslim. He was enormously successful in this endeavor and, after his death, a considerable number of his disciples returned to Makassar to continue his work there.

Included among the propagators of Islam were the "nine saints" *(wali sangha)* of Java, who were lionized in Javanese literature of the nineteenth century and given recognition by late-twentieth-century writers on "revivalism" as their predecessors. The "saints" appear to have been real people, but they were shrouded in legend that evolved about them, although tombs purported to be theirs were sites of veneration apparently before the eighteenth century. Maulana Malik Ibrahim (d. 1419) was active in the Gresik area; Sunan Ampel (d. 1478) propagated near Surabaya; Sunan Bonang (d. 1525) did his work at Tuban; Sunan Giri established a religious dynasty at Giri and converted the population in the Blambangan region; Sunan Drajat (active 1478) worked with the sick and orphans in eastern Java; Sunan Kalijaga (active 1543) used the classical Javanese theater as a proselytizing tool in the area around Demak; Sunan Kudus (active 1537) and Sunan Muria (active ca. 1540) worked at Kudus, where Sunan Muria used the classical Javanese orchestra and theater as instruments for conversion; and Sunan Gunung Jati converted the population to Islam in Banten and Ceribon, while establishing his own dynasties in both places. Several others were associated with the grouping in later legend, including Sitti Jenar (active ca. 1560), who was pronounced a heretic by the others and executed, and Raden Fattah (d. 1527), who became ruler of Demak.

The saints were credited with building several important mosques, establishing schools, training others to become propagators of Islam, and instructing innumerable Javans to worship and believe standard Sunni doctrine. For the most part those propagators appear to have been mystics who used established retreats and attracted disciples to join them and participate in the mystic rites that they established. Clearly they urged political leaders, especially the ruler of Demak, to expand his domains so that they could spread Islam within the captured territory, and they even helped to organize military forces for the ruler. Overall, they used a variety of approaches to further their propagating mission.

Education and Intellectual Centers

Aceh was an important way station for itinerant Muslim scholars traveling along the trade routes. As a consequence, education developed rapidly there, starting with classes in the mosque, called "the circle" because pupils sat in a circle with the teacher and memorized the Qur'an, studied the Arabic language, and were introduced to the various sciences of Islam. Such classes gradually were moved from the mosques to specially constructed schools located on the grounds of the mosques or nearby, which continued to use the "circle" for learning. Advanced schools then developed that specialized in the sciences of Islam, such as jurisprudence *(fiqh)*, theology *(kalam)*, and mystical knowledge *(tasawwuf)*. These advanced schools were headed by trained persons, initially from the Arabic world or India, and later by the people who were trained in the schools of the Muslim Zone itself.

The next advance in schooling occurred in west Sumatra, where Tuanku Burhanuddin (d. 1691), who studied in Aceh, returned home and started a school. He called the new institution a "general school" *(surau)*. On the beginning level these schools provided basic Islamic instruction —introduction to the Qur'an and the pillars of belief and practice—and on the upper level more advanced studies in the religious sciences were offered. These schools in west Sumatra were large, since they employed a number of teachers, operated in a complex of buildings, and enrolled several hundred students. This was to become the common model used in west Sumatra for the next three centuries.

On Java an institution known as the "Islamic boarding school" came into existence in the early sixteenth century at the main mosque in Demak, and a similar school was established at Tembayat. Later, under the Mataram rulers, the number of boarding schools was increased through the assistance of the ruler, who assigned land rent on specific pieces of property to their support. Lessons at such schools were given orally by the teachers to the students, often in verse for easy retention. Students took notes on the oral presentations and these were passed on from one generation of students to another. As well, there were times when Arabic-language materials were used, as in studying the structure and meaning of the Qur'an. In such study notations in Javanese were frequently made in the margins, sometimes merely translating the Arabic and, at other times noting reading pauses or points of grammar for the use of the student in recitation. In learning about Islamic obligations, a lengthy composition called the "Sixty" *(Sittin)* was often sung, because it was in verse and was regarded as a good way to capture the student's interest. This piece outlined religious duties, ceremonies, and obligations necessary for the believer.

A wide number of Islamic books from the central Islamic world were available for study in the seventeenth and eighteenth centuries in the boarding schools, although there was no indication that any one school used all of them. It was highly likely they were used at different places, and that the student who traveled extensively to get his education would eventually come across most of them. There were famous personalities among the writers of these texts. Al-Ghazali was outstanding as the great renovator of his age as well as being a leading mystic. Al-Jili was famous as a mystic. Al-Nawawi (d. 1277), al-Samarqandi (d. 938), and al-Sayuti were prolific writers on wide sections of the religious sciences and did much of the defining of Sunni orthodoxy for their time. The overall selection of these texts indicates a close relationship with the central Islamic world and attests to the fact that Sunni intellectual standards were the basis for formal Islamic learning in the Muslim schools of the zone.

The first significant center of learning, marked by the production of new writings by local scholars on Islamics, came into existence at Aceh in the seventeenth century. Significantly, the manuscripts produced there had an impact on the Malay language, on the development of literary forms, and on the substance of Islam itself. The first figure was Hamzah Fansuri (d. 1607?), a Malay who was a member of the Qadiriyah mystical order. He wrote mostly in Malay, but drew heavily on Arabic and Persian language terms in his writing. His most important poetical work was the *Lover's Drink (Syarab al-Asyiqin),* which used the "Persian-erotic" school of mystical writing, while *The Secret of the Gnostics (Asrar al-Arifin)* stressed the efforts of the mystic to find union with God. He used the images of the mystic as traveler and the perils of ocean traveling as symbolic of the difficulties of attaining spiritual union with God. Syamsuddin Sumatrani (d. 1630), his student, continued writing in the style and outlook of Hamzah, using both Malay and Arabic, but he laid emphasis on the seven grades of mystical achievement and the twenty attributes of God that were common beliefs among mystical writers of the time.

The third major scholar of the Acehnese school was Nuruddin al-Raniri, the most prolific and highly regarded author of the period. His writings upheld the importance of the Ashʿari school of theology—a cornerstone of Sunni orthodoxy—and stressed the necessity of following Muslim jurisprudence at the expense of local custom. Al-Raniri was probably the first of the religious teachers in the Malay-Indonesian world to place stress on that factor. In retrospect, his production of nearly fifty religious expositions constituted an intellectual high point for Southeast Asian Muslim scholarship that was not to be attained again until the twentieth century. Among them were a guide to proper worship in Islam titled *The Straight Path (Sirat al-Mustaqim),* a commentary on the Qurʾan, a set of Traditions of the Prophet, and a primer on mysticism. Abdul Rauf Singkili (d. 1693), the last major member of the Sumatran school, translated al-Baidawi's highly regarded commentary on the Qur'an into Malay.

The intellectual center for writing in Malay moved to Palembang in the late eighteenth and early nineteenth centuries, where a series of rulers there were patrons of religious scholars. There were three "giants" among this group of intellectuals. Syihabuddin (active 1740) focused on Islamic creeds, giving particular attention to the need of correct belief for mystic practitioners. Kemas Fakruddin (active 1769) rejected the "seven grades of being," the chief indicator of heterodoxy among Muslim mystics of the period. Shaykh Abdul Samad (d. 1788) was concerned about local practices that he believed fell outside of Islam, and he labeled those who venerated shrines of their ancestors as "pseudo-Muslims." He also rendered into Malay an abridged rendition of al-Ghazali's *The Revival of the Religious Science (Siyar as-Salikin ila 'Ibadah Rabb al-'Abidin)*. Several more writers were associated with this center, some of whom were anonymous. Among them was the writer of the *Book of a Thousand Questions (Kitab Sa-Ribu Mas'alah)*, which dealt with intricate questions of belief and curiosity and drew on Islamic cosmography and legend to provide answers to esoteric questions.

At Banjarmasin, Shaykh Arsyad al-Banjari (d. 1812) wrote a book on standard mysticism and a guide to Islamic law in the area of worship that drew heavily on al-Raniri. At Trengganu, Taj al-Din bin Ata' Allah al-Iskandari (d. unknown) also wrote a work on mysticism in Malay. In sum, scholarly efforts sought to correct practices regarded as falling outside of standard Sunni norms. Moreover, these scholars were not original, usually paraphrasing earlier Arab scholars and making their views known in the local Southeast Asian languages. But in doing that, they were consistent with historic Islamic scholarship, which always regarded reiteration and explanation of the accepted as the correct approach in matters of faith and religious teachings.

The Pillars of Islam

The "pillars of Islam" consist of the confession of faith in God, prayer, fasting in the month of Ramadan, giving alms, and undertaking the pilgrimage. To these we would add also the use of the Qur'an by the Muslim population. In the first two centuries of this era there are only passing references to these important practices of Islam in the various court chronicles of Southeast Asia. The confession of faith was mentioned in the three major chronicles as marking the entry into Islam of the rulers and others who converted. Significantly, circumcision of males was regarded as a necessary accompanying act to the confession. Five daily prayers were regarded as prescribed by the Prophet for believers, and the general population was admonished by one ruler to perform those prayers faithfully, with punishment for those who did not. The same ruler also supported the building of

mosques in all population centers having the required forty males necessary for the establishment of Friday worship. There were some references to
times of prayer as indicators of the time of day, implying that the practice
of praying was recognized, even if there were very few references to people
actually praying. Also, the month of Ramadan was mentioned as being
important, but no statement was made about the actual observance of the
fast during that month. However, the night of the twenty-seventh of Ramadan was regarded as important enough (without saying why) for the ruler
of Melaka to perform a ceremony in the palace mosque and to recite the
"required" prayers. The religious tax was commended to the people in one
place to consist of a certain amount of rice, presumably for the use of
mosque officials. Little mention was made of the pilgrimage, and the few
oblique references that did exist referred to religious personages by the
title *al-hajj* or to plans by several rulers to go on the pilgrimage, which
none in this era ever did. The Qur'an was regarded as the holiest of books
and as blessed, some general statements being made about the wisdom it
contained, without much specificity.

In the second two centuries of the era the portrait of Muslim performance of basic requirements was more pronounced than in the opening two
centuries. On Java written evidence existed in the form of tracts, pamphlets,
and manuals that efforts were made by some Muslim teachers and propagators *(da'i)* to introduce the standard legalistic teachings of Islam into the
lives of new converts. In particular prayer was stressed, but the other major
obligations of fasting, alms giving, and the pilgrimage were included as well.
Further, it was known that these Muslim propagators also attempted to tie
Hindu-Buddhistic religious practices into Islam and to forge a transition
from one to another, particularly in the Buddhist learning centers *(man-
dala)* that were absorbed into the standard Muslim boarding schools *(pesantren)* on Java. Accordingly, "contemplation" *(samadhi)* became ritual prayer
(salat), and other practices were found that could be transformed as well. At
Aceh guides to behavior detailed the procedures for prayer, fasting, giving
alms, and undertaking the pilgrimage, along with other matters. With the
stress on "orthodoxy" that occurred under Iskandar Thani (r. 1636–1641),
it is reasonable to assume that such details would have been given attention, even among the mystic cells that existed there.

In the final period covered in this era, the eighteenth century, the primary obligations of Islam were recognized as important by principal members of society, but the actual observation of such rites was sporadic among
Muslims at the royal courts and among the population. There were references to people who were pious and tried to fulfill the practices of Islam,
but they often appeared to have been foreign-born or were regarded as very
special people, such as devout mystics and learned scholars dedicated to
religion as a lifestyle.

Concerning prayer, in Perak chronicles provided a portrait of an ideal ruler, in which he would hear petitions from the people between the observances of the regular ritual of prayer throughout the day.[23] Some other rulers did try to encourage their subjects to participate in Friday worship and occasionally issued warnings via a public crier to be diligent in attendance; this act of encouragement indicates general shortcomings in the practice. Commentary by several observers reported that within the general population prayer was not popular nor frequent. In some places on Java there was only a single prayer in the evening, which consisted merely of the "confession of faith."

Fasting was recognized as a proper religious rite throughout the region, but its practice differed. In west Sumatra fasting was undertaken by some leaders for a short length of time, apparently without regard for the actual fasting month, during which they abstained from food, drink, and questionable recreations, such as gambling, while devoting themselves to prayer. During the fasting month a few people attempted to fast, but the rite was ignored for the remainder of the month among the general population. At Gresik, fasting was regarded as an important activity for the pious, and the standard was set that one day in ten throughout the year should be spent in such abstinence—namely, the entire month of Ramadan, six days in Shawal, and two days in the pilgrimage season. In general, all elements of the population at Gresik practiced fasting, although the elderly, those traveling, and women nursing infants were excused. Evening prayers were an important part of the observance.

The Yogyakarta royal court issued instructions about proper distribution of the poor tax to religious officials in various regions. Other than frequent mention of the rice contributions given to mosque specialists, sources are generally silent about the giving of alms.

The pilgrimage was performed, although the numbers were comparatively small. A court history related that one ruler regularly honored the returned pilgrims whom he knew about, and that another ruler sent a prince and several court retainers on the pilgrimage. The group departed from Penang on a Turkish ship that sailed to Jeddah, where they were quartered with people who had migrated earlier from Southeast Asia. After taking the "lesser pilgrimage," that is, visiting the Kaʾbah site out of season and visiting the tomb of the Prophet at Madinah and other well-known sites, the group went to Makkah to participate in the formal pilgrimage, and then returned to Johore.[24]

The Qurʾan was considered a holy symbol for taking oaths, and was also the object of study for many beginning students throughout the region. Performances by trained reciters were a source of enjoyment for many audiences, and some people were encouraged by pious rulers to take up the art. Also, the Qurʾan was referred to in the abstract as a source of all knowledge and as the place to find God's commands and admonitions. Accordingly, though a few scholars were conversant with its contents, usually its "laws" were abstracted and much commented upon in books of jurisprudence, which were studied instead of the Qur'an itself.

Religious Practice

Islamic mystical practice was an important expression of religion among Southeast Asian Muslims during the era. Earlier, other forms of mystical practice had been an important ingredient in the religious systems from India—both Hinduism and Buddhism—so the concept, the general approach to the practice, and even some of the methods of inducing mystical trances were already familiar. Muslim mystics often took over functioning Buddhist worship groups and, by substituting Arabic words and Muslim terms for the Sanskrit terms used earlier, brought the groups over to Islam. However, the process was not without problems, for converts to Islam through this approach had some difficulty jettisoning some of the earlier thinking regarded as "heretical" among pious Muslims.[25] A dispute over proper mystical belief developed among different groups of practitioners in the late sixteenth and early seventeenth centuries. That dispute took place at several sites in the Muslim Zone, but the main arena from about 1588 to 1636 was at the Acehnese royal court. In the early part of the era the thinking of the "unitarians" *(wujudiyah)* dominated, who followed the teachings of Ibn ʿArabi and al-Jili and regarded all creation—humans and the universe—as included within God Himself, on the assumption that everything had necessarily to be part of God so that the meaning of "Oneness" *(tawhid)* would not be violated. They also laid stress on the seven grades of experience the mystical "wayfarer" passed through on his way to achieve "unity" with God. The leaders of this trend in mystical Islamic thought were Hamzah Fansuri and Syamsuddin Sumatrani, already discussed. The "dualism" that was an intrinsic part of their message was common throughout the Muslim Zone and had many proponents on Java, where similar thinking had emerged from Hindu and Buddhist traditions.

A second generation of scholars arose in Aceh that challenged the unitarians by explaining that God consisted of a "core" and "emanations" from the core. The core was "pure God," unobtainable for humans, while creation—humans and universe—was part of the emanations, not part of the core. This made mystical imagery consistent with Islamic doctrine without violating the principle of "Oneness" or being guilty of the blasphemy of relating human action with God. These later scholars, led by al-Raniri, also insisted that mysticism could be correctly accomplished only in conjunction with full observance of Muslim law. Al-Raniri convinced the Achinese ruler to move against the unitarians and their sympathizers. The books of

Fansuri and Syamsuddin were publicly burned, and later there were arrests and executions of those who continued to follow the "heresy" of dualism.

Abdul Rauf Singkili succeeded al-Raniri as the chief religious authority in Aceh, and he immediately put an end to the open persecution of the unitarians, but spent much time preaching and convincing those still cleaving to the unitarian doctrines to abandon them for Shattariyah belief and practice, which he held was more in keeping with standard Sunni mystical teachings. He was fairly successful in that endeavor. His own formulations stressed that God was distinct from his creation, using the analogy of a hand and its shadow to show the relationship—God being the hand and creation the shadow. For the most part, however, the Muslim mystics of Southeast Asia, like those in other parts of the Muslim world, were not always very discerning about the issue, and the simpler views of dualism were often expressed by mystics all the way into the twenty-first century.

During the eighteenth century, mysticism remained strong and was considered the most important path to religious piety. A court history implied that there were considerable numbers of mystic masters, presumably with accompanying groups of mystic adepts, operating within the Riau region. Some of these were from southern Arabia, as they were referred to as "noble," and others were local scholars. It was observed that occasionally a mystic master would misunderstand his own experience and veer off into the dualistic heresy. A story is told of one such leader, who upset the entire Straits region with his blasphemy of associating himself with God and then assuming a conceit that expressed itself in the desire to become ruler of Johore. Although his aspirations to royalty were regarded as fanciful, he was once condemned to death for his extravagant religious claims, and finally was assassinated when the ruler regarded him as no longer able to be controlled.[26]

Local Customs and Islam
Shamans, Saints, and Amulets
Folk beliefs among the Malays at the time of Islam's arrival revolved around the role of the shaman *(bomoh* or *dukun)*, where two different characters were evident. One can differentiate between the healer and the sorcerer. The healer used a vast array of herbs, potions, massage, magic formulas, and various other devices to cure the great range of ailments and diseases that afflicted the population. The sorcerer, on the other hand, was a foreteller of auspicious and inauspicious occasions who could also cast spells and give advice on all manner of problems brought to him. These practitioners were in place when Islam arrived, and the new religion did not essentially change their roles, nor did its religious specialists really try to do so. However, Islam unwittingly gave these practitioners some new

material with which to work. Arabic expressions, particularly the key Islamic ones, such as "the confession" (shahadah), "the remembrance" (dhikr), the "opener" (bismillah) to the Qur'an, and the "magnificat" (takbir), were taken over as incantations, sometimes replacing but more often supplementing the Sanskrit expressions already in use.

The central concept with which the practitioners worked, however, was little changed. That concept centered on inner power (semangat)—the soul, spirit, or life force that each person, animal, and object had been allotted or had accumulated. The person himself was regarded as the container, or more properly the "sheath," that retained this inner power. The work of the folk practitioner was to repair or strengthen the sheath and to gather and concentrate power in it. Hence the curing of ailments or disease was not regarded as treatment, but rather as making it possible for the inner power to be retained properly so that it could overcome the body's affliction. There was no attack by pious Muslims on the practice of healing.

Aside from healers, however, there was widespread belief that certain people had access to magical power. People had great faith in the power of weapons, particularly swords; indeed, up to twelve years would often be spent awaiting the favorable moment in which to forge a weapon to capture that power. Shamans were also thought to have miraculously strong powers capable of conquering severe ailments and infirmities. Practitioners of magic were censured by many learned Muslims as dabbling in matters that belonged to either God or Satan (Iblis). In a particular case, an early Muslim ruler of Bone on Sulawesi forbade shamans to practice magic, although this prohibition gave way almost immediately because it was such an accepted part of community life.

Cults for worshiping ancestors revolving around graves and village markers had been an important part of village life prior to the arrival of Islam and continued to be so, although the force of ancestor worship was muted considerably. The rites enacted by such cults, particularly common in Javanese villages, used incantations drawn mostly from Old Javanese, but some Arabic terms began to be adopted as well; obviously the use of Arabic was a cultural attempt to obtain Islamic sanctification. However, at another level, some shrines were absorbed into the Islamic worship of saints that had been fully developed earlier in Middle Eastern Islam. A chosen place could be given new identity as the site of a Muslim saint, either by accepting a local belief that the saint was actually buried there or by beatifying known religious personages who had lived in the area. Indeed, Muslim holy men (wali), often mystic masters (shaykh) or simple hermits, were regarded as possessing "blessedness" (berkat), which made their graves desired sites for visitation and worship. Pilgrimages to such sites were common, on one level to commemorate the life and work of the saint himself, on another level to meditate, and on still another level to ask for the intercession of the saint in some matter of personal concern.

Arabic concepts used in the Middle East to honor prominent grave sites were adopted, such as the "sacred power" (keramat) and "blessedness" that could be gained by the visitors to those sites. The eighteenth-century scholar ʿAbd al-Samad labeled acts such as utilizing the magic of a shaman, using non-Islamic relics as amulets, and seeking blessings from shrines not a part of Islamic tradition as evidence of "polytheism" (shirk) and as forbidden by the teachings of Islam specifically. On the other hand, he did not include within this prohibition any of the similar powers claimed for objects of long-standing Muslim tradition, such as the water of the Zamzam well in Makkah or amulets containing Arab charms, which he was known to send to his correspondents in several parts of the Muslim Zone.[27]

Life-Cycle Events

References to life-cycle events were made casually in the chronicles that constituted the source for indigenous practices during the thirteenth and fourteenth centuries and were not fully descriptive of what actually occurred. By the fifteenth, sixteenth, and seventeenth centuries, there were enough observers from East and West that a fuller picture of these rites and practice emerged. In some places during this era childbirth was accompanied by a purification for the woman who had given birth, whereby she was placed over or near a fire for a period of time ranging between three and forty days, to drive out any lingering spirits and repair her body. It was observed that this procedure was uncomfortable and at times painful, as often the skin of the woman would become blistered and blackened. Apparently there was strong social pressure against large families, and the economic role of women as workers was important enough to limit the size of families; accordingly, contraception and abortion were considered acceptable.

In most places, children underwent a tonsure ceremony eight days after birth. Circumcision received more attention and seems to have been regarded as an important event, distinguishing the male believer from the unbeliever, and this procedure was performed immediately upon conversion. At Brunei, males were circumcised when they reached puberty, that is, around eleven or twelve years of age; their adult name was given at that time as well. The 1605 circumcision of a boy ruler in Banten was accompanied by an elaborate celebration at the grand assembly area of the palace, where music was played, jugglers and tumblers performed, nobles came to pay their respects, and gifts were given. It was observed in Mindanao that the circumcision of the prince was often an occasion for the cutting of all other boys of the same age. They were brought together, via a public announcement, about a week before the celebration, and the procedure performed on them at that time, leaving only the prince to be circumcised on the day of the celebration itself. When the rite was performed, the "priest" "takes hold of the Fore-skin with two Sticks, and with a pair of Scissors snips it off."[28] Female cutting was also practiced at this time, in which the tissue surrounding the clitoris was removed and a small cut made on the clitoris itself. This ceremony for females was also done at the onset of puberty and was performed privately, with only women involved and knowledgeable about it. The male rite was clearly prescribed by Islam; the female operation had only widespread custom to support it, but in Southeast Asia at this time it was still considered to be countenanced by Islam.

Early betrothal appears to have been a pattern in Muslim areas of the western region—that is, Aceh, Banten, Brunei, and Patani—occurring often when the girls reached puberty in the twelfth year, although marriage usually took place some three to four years later. A Spanish report on Brunei stated that at the bride's first marriage there was a large feast and that entertainment consisted mostly of cock fighting. However, prior to the feast the bride resided for eight days in a canopied area with a sleeping mat, where the women of the wedding party attended her during this period of waiting and preparation.[29]

At Aceh men tended to marry several women and gave one of them preference, with the children from that union recognized as his heirs. This arrangement did not include slave women and concubines, who were apparently treated before the law and in custom as personal retainers without individual legal standing. At marriage a bridegroom paid a sum of money or trade goods to the bride's parents and also gave the bride a lien on his estate to provide for her expenses connected with the marriage. At the same time, the estate of the woman was handed over to the husband, who managed it and held it in trust for as long as the marriage lasted. If the husband died during a marriage, the preferred wife had first claim on the husband's estate. In contrast, on Java monogamous marriages were the norm, as women were highly regarded because of their kinship relationships, control of property, and work opportunities, all of which gave them economic value. Here, the groom paid a substantial bride-price to enter a marriage and was expected to treat his wife well, lest she decide to end the marriage and demand total payment of the dower. In some places, such as at Patani, a system of temporary marriage was arranged for visiting merchants whereby a woman would operate a household and provide sexual services for a given sum of money over a period of time. The offspring of such a temporary union belonged to the woman and had no claim on the father.

Funerals were usually held within a day of death. Observers stated that the body of the deceased was wrapped in white cloth and quickly buried.

The mourners revisited the grave site for several days thereafter to prevent the deceased from "standing up" and causing difficulties for the living. References were also made to the use of the third, seventh, fortieth, and hundredth days after the burial for ritual meals as a means of celebrating the good deeds of the deceased and allowing him to enjoy the feasting as recompense for the honorable life he had led.[30] In all these life-cycle events the chief ingredient was usually local custom, although Islam played a supporting role in all of them.

Muslim Celebrations

The chronicles of the first two centuries of this era seldom mention the events of the Muslim calendar. However, there were statements that two major Islamic holidays existed, but no mention of their Arabic or Malay names. One was said to fall after the end of Ramadan and the other was a day of sacrifice, obviously referring to the two ʿId celebrations after the fasting month and during the pilgrimage season. By the sixteenth and seventeenth centuries, the references to Muslim celebrations and important days were much clearer, although full descriptions of these events were still sparse. Concerning the calendar itself, it is apparent from manuscript dating that the Javanese court scribes began converting Javanese time over to the Muslim calendar around 1625 and that the Muslim lunar year became prominent then, rather than the previous solar year of the Javanese calendar.

The major feast day of ʿId al-Fitr was well known throughout the region. The Acehenese ruler Iskandar Muda made the sighting of the new moon a royal court event, as it was used to mark a ceremony at which vassals presented tribute to the ruler. During the month he also celebrated the Night of Power *(layla al-qadar)* on the twenty-fifth of Ramadan with a very formal vigil; and at the end of the month, again with the sighting of the moon, he marked the end of fasting and called for the public to celebrate ʿId. On Java, from the time of Sultan Agung onward, this holiday was celebrated with a large public festival including a parade through the streets, with the ruler, his family, and his chief courtiers riding in pomp. This festival was conducted with royal style that had been evident in a major Buddhist holiday earlier, indicating that there was continuity in ceremony and celebration even if the religious meaning of the particular holiday had changed.

The birthday of the Prophet does not appear to have been as popular at this time as it was to become later, although some people did celebrate the occasion. On Java, Sultan Agung of Mataram made this an important event, requiring all important administrators to be in the capital on that day, probably bringing them under the ruler's influence. There was a large public fair as well.

ʿId al-ʿAdha was celebrated at most royal courts. Under the Mataram rulers this became an important holiday that involved a court ceremony and a public procession. At Aceh, particularly during the time of Iskandar Muda, it was celebrated with an elaborate festival, a prayer at the palace mosque, and a ceremony involving thousands of retainers, guards, officials, and service people. Afterward there was a ritual slaughtering of oxen and carabao, as called for in the guidelines of Islamic jurisprudence.

Cultural Development
Urban Design and Architecture

The layout of buildings and streets had been important in the preceding era when such arrangements were regarded as having sacred significance; some of that attitude seems to have continued, at least in the Javanese area. But the Malay cities, with their prominent ports, apparently arranged some things for utilitarian purposes. City quarters were often designated for, or perhaps came to be recognized as primarily inhabited by certain foreign groups, so there might be an Indian quarter, a Javanese quarter, and a Chinese quarter, for example. Likewise storage facilities, custom offices, and the harbormaster's place of business had to be at a central location; and finally, market areas had to be convenient for their users and of reasonable size. These considerations were generally apparent at Samudera-Pasai and at Melaka. A historical description of Melaka revealed the most accomplished of these urban arrangements: "The original population and the foreign traders from overseas all lived in separate residential districts. . . . North of the . . . river lay Upeh, the big commercial quarter, itself consisting of two separate districts, in one of which lived people who came from northwestern Asia, and in the other people from the East. . . . Since most of the merchants also had accommodation for selling their wares in front of their houses, the two districts of Upeh and Ilir, seen from the sea, stretched out along the coast like one long bazaar. As of old the Malay fisherfolk were housed in the district of Sabok in the marshy lands along the river. . . . The streets were wide, but in this town with its predominately wooden houses . . . the danger of fire was ever present."[31]

Architectural attainment was obvious in central Java. In 1746 Pakubuwana II transferred the Mataram capital from Kartasura to the the village of Sala, which he renamed Surakarta, and an entire new palace complex was constructed there between that year and 1790. The new palace was modeled after the mythical kingdom of Kahendran as portrayed in Vishnuite mythology. The new palace layout began with the planting of sacred *wringin* trees in the northern and southern assembly areas. When it was finished, the Kraton Kasunanan was enclosed by a great wall, six meters high and measuring 1,000 x 1,800 meters on the sides of the rectangle. It enclosed several residential villages inhabited by royal servants and administrators. Alongside the central building and courtyard complex was the royal palladium—a building holding the royal paraphernalia, heirlooms, and regalia—considered to be the repository of the symbols of power of the kingdom. Among them were "an ornamental bed: a set of statues of the legendary goddesses of Javanese mythology Dewi Sri and Dewi Sadana; the eternal flame of Ki Agung Sela; the sacred flower that bloomed as long as the king possessed the right to rule; the state regalia; and the symbols of state."[32]

The chronicles for the first centuries of the era mention that some Malay rulers promoted the building of mosques and prayer houses, attempting to establish such structures at all places where communal worship was incumbent on a community, that is, where there were forty adult males. There were also references to the existence of mosques in the royal compounds of rulers. The early Muslim builders used a square floor plan, built a wooden structure on top of an elevated, massive-stone foundation, used pointed roofs of two to five tiers, built a veranda onto the side or front of the structure, and surrounded the mosque with open space and, sometimes, a palisade. Minarets generally were not built, because the veranda served as the place where the call to prayer was given through the beating of a giant drum. The multiple-roofed mosque, sometimes known as the *mastika* style because the top roof bore that name, may have been popularized by Gai See Chang (active 1481), supervisor of the Chinese shipyards at Semarang. He reputedly built the great mosque at Demak, which was widely regarded as the prototype for this classical Southeast Asian mosque, even though others had been built before it in similar style. The prominent mosques of the period were the Sunan Ngampel Mosque in Surabaya, the Kampong Hulu Mosque in Melaka, and a mosque in Champa.

Despite general use of floral decoration in mosques in the central Islamic world at this time, in Southeast Asia studies show that some mosques used animal and even some human representation. In a few mosques, figures of monkeys, snakes, and birds transformed themselves across a design and flowed into the hair and curls of human beings on the other side. At the same time, some floral designs using local flowers and leaves similar to already existing art forms from pre-Islamic periods were prominent rather than those developed in the Middle East. Apparently, the early pulpit used by the sermon reciter to deliver the Friday sermon was a design common to Hindu places of worship and was associated with the conveyance of a god.

In the second part of this era, many of the same characteristics of mosques continued to exist. The mosques built on Java during this time frame reflected Hindu characteristics or the building style of ordinary structures designed to handle a damp, rainy climate. The minaret at the Kudus mosque and the gateways at several other mosques used a heavily ornamented facing and a ponderous structure resembling the *candi* shrines from the Indic period scattered through Java and other places in Southeast Asia. The "vernacular" mosque used the Southeast Asian high-pitched, thatched roofs necessary for water runoff.[33] Nearly all the mosques had more than one roof as had been the case with those built earlier, partly for style but also for the rainy weather. With minor variations, the form was common throughout the Muslim Zone, such as in Aceh at the Indera Puri Mosque, at Maluku at the Ternate Mosque, and on Kalimantan at the Pontianak Mosque. As in the earlier part of the era, minarets were not common, so the mosque at Kudus, mentioned above, was something of an exception.

Throughout the era the affluence of the Muslim Zone was apparent, as could be measured by its royal courts and leading cities. Obviously these were not copies of the Middle Eastern cities, with their "ring" arrangements and "city quarters," but they do show the importance of trade and the willingness of rulers to spend lavishly on public facilities, characteristics that marked the Middle Eastern region as well. As for mosques, they drew on Chinese architectural forms initially, but still met Islamic requirements of having washing facilities, large prayer halls, a pulpit, and a niche to indicate the direction of prayer—all basic requirements for worship.

Language

Until this era the languages of the Muslim Zone were mostly written in Indic syllabaries with an infusion of many Indian words and terms into their vocabularies. With the arrival of Islam, the Arabic syllabary replaced those derived from Sanskrit in many places, and Arabic words and expressions began to make an impact. Malay was the language that moved over to the new forms readily and was adapted by Arab and Indian traders as the lingua franca because so many of them were Muslims. In addition, at Melaka and in the states of Aceh, the Malay language gained acceptance at the courts of rulers and spread farther as the court language of those political entities. Particularly at Melaka the rise of a new literature in Malay gave the language heightened expression.

In areas where Malay was the popular language, several basic forms of literature developed during this time period. The simple *pantun* was very popular, as it was easy to use, with its four lines, rhymed *abab*, with a catchy phrase making up the first two lines. The second thought segments were not directly related, but could be subtly connected, contrasted, or in some other way express insightfulness. A large repertoire of *pantuns* was common in society, with many people adept at their use and at creating or adapting verses for needed situations. The "poem form" *(syair)* was rhymed in four-line lengths *aaaa*, dealt with a single subject or theme, and could be tailored to any length. In shorter length they often expressed mystical-erotic themes or the interplay of lovers, while in longer pieces they told stories of adventure and historical subjects. A second set of literature was found in the "guides" *(kitab)*, which were intended to assist those studying religious sciences, usually derived from Arabic with Malay commentaries; it was the common literature of a committed Muslim community. Related to this form was "refined" *(adab)* literature, which consisted of edifying tales concerning the prophet Muhammad, the revered personalities and saints of Islam, and Muslim heroes. The third set of literature revolved around the "story" *(hikayat)* and related to events, usually pertaining to important mythological or past occurrences that could become part of a story or history. All of these forms were common at royal courts.

On Java an extensive language, generally referred to as Old Javanese, had been prominent at court, where Brahman and Buddhist writers had helped to create an extensive literature reflecting a mind-set that was distinctively Javanese, although influenced by Vishnuite and Buddhistic values from India. The Javanese language was constructed around customary manners of performing ceremonies, carrying on polite discourse, and handling the general conduct of the court and society in general. The language of the court was influenced by Sanskrit, with idiom, verse meter, and style of speaking having made an impact on the Javanese language. This use of Sanskrit was much less influential away from court. With the advent of Islam there was a two-way borrowing, as Islam, with its Arabic terminology for concepts, confronted a civilization with its own Sanskrit terminology for many of those same concepts. Hence Javanese words came to be used for some matters while Arabic prevailed in other cases. During the first penetrations of Islam into Java, many Arabic-language texts were reviewed by local scholars and given interlinear glosses so that fairly detailed descriptions were available in Javanese for use by the local population. To make the reference work in the texts uncomplicated, the Javanese glosses were written in Arabic script so that both languages could read in the same direction (i.e., right to left).

During this period the large number of traders from Arabia, China, and India were active in Southeast Asia, mostly as wayfarers on their trips east and west along the international trade routes and as traders seeking to buy and sell goods within the Southeast Asian region. Among themselves they spoke their own languages, and at times they apparently developed some pidgin languages to promote simple trade, but these eventually gave way to the use of Malay, so these languages had limited usage. Chinese, however, does seem to have been important as a language on the north coast of Java, whereas Arabic was strong enough that it had an impact on Malay in most of the Malay-speaking region. Aside from its usage in the trading centers, Arabic found further development in its use as a holy language of Islam and as an intellectual language in places of Islamic learning. In the first instance, Arabic contributed conceptual terms to the areas of politics, religion, and science. Furthermore, Arabic names were assumed by the ruler and his courtiers to indicate their association with Islam. Some people used the title *sayyid* to claim ancestry extending back to Muhammad, apparently in order to enhance their position of authority; and "honored" was assigned to those who had passed on. Certainly Arabic did not entirely replace Sanskrit as the primary influence on the languages of the region, but at first it had a heavy impact on court and scholarly vocabularies—that is, on small, influential groups—and later a minor but important long-run influence on the development of Malay-Indonesian.

Literature

Foundation legends, originally transmitted orally but later written, were important in several places during the era. In the environs of Brunei there was a common myth, later given the title "Brunei Foundation Myth" *(Shaer Awang Semaun)*, which related that the first Brunei ruler had emerged from an egg that descended from heaven. The ruler then married a local tribal woman. The myth was interpreted in twentieth-century Brunei historiography as a reference to the first propagators of Islam arriving by sea and making contact with local pagan societies already residing in the area. In southern Sulawesi, the *I La Galigo* epic cycle related the adventures of the noble class and the values of chivalry they employed in their relationships with one another. The cycle began with creation and then detailed the adventures of a succession of heroes, including the "great travelers," who visited most areas in East Asia as well as heaven and the underworld. In central Mindanao, the *Darangan* contained maxims and anecdotes about the early development of the Maranao peoples before the arrival of Islam. *The Cindua Mato* from western Sumatra dealt with the importance of heritage and custom in Minang society. The tales it incorporated focused on the importance of women in Minang society and how the chief characters of the epic undid the violations against ideal society that mischief makers had unleashed. The discussion of Islam was slight, but indicated that Muslim ways had been accepted as part of Minang institutions and custom though certainly not central to the culture of that region. All these epics stressed the values of the peoples who invented them and remained important to the end of the twentieth century. All were essentially pre-Islamic in composition but later took on Islamic references as part of the acculturation process.

Court chronicles were common throughout the era and constituted a continuing genre throughout the region. *The Chronicles of the Kings of Pasai* was the oldest, its initial formation being in the late fourteenth century. *The Malay Annals* likewise was probably begun during the reign of the Melakan dynasty in the early sixteenth century, but appeared almost a century later in the successor kingdom of Johore. Interestingly, the opening chapters of *The Malay Annals* were a repetition of the *Chronicles of the Kings of Pasai*, used as an introduction to the stories concerning the Melakan rulers. Continuity was regarded as an important means of amassing spiritual power from the past, and that consideration may have been the reason for the retelling of the Pasai record. In the sixteenth century the *Kedah Annals (Hikayat Merang Mahawangsa)* appeared, and was reviled by scholars for inconsistencies in grammar, historical events, and sources. While it contains a list of Kedah's rulers, it is more important for its collection of stories from Indian, Arabic, and Malay sources. In the seventeenth century the *Mataram Chronicles* justified the first Mataram ruler's assumption of power and proclaimed his legitimacy to reign over the entire island of Java. The *Chronicles* was an updating of the earlier *Chronicles of Demak*, written during the reign of Panembahan Seda Krapyak (r. 1501–1613). These combined sets of Javan court histories formed the initial body that, with various additions over time, eventually came to be known by the collective title the *Javanese Chronicles.* In Aceh *The Garden of the Kings (Bustan al-Salatin)*, by al-Raniri, was a combination genealogy of the Acehnese rulers, history of the dynasty, and study of the administration of the sultanate, with anecdotal material drawn from other ages and times for comparative and entertainment purposes. It had few peers in the Southeast Asian Muslim Zone at that time. Important court chronicles were also written at Patani and Banjarmasin, begun sometime in the seventeenth century. They were hardly histories, in the sense that they did not record events accurately as chronicles did in the central Islamic world of the time.

In the Malay region, Islam did not have a strong local civilization with which to compete but still had to overcome the strong influence of Brahman India. In the fourteenth and fifteenth centuries, particularly at Melaka/Johore, an important Malay literature developed using the Arabic syllabary, but it was heavily imitative of non-Muslim values and story lines from India. Indian Hindu literature, particularly renditions of the great epics, remained popular, but an adaptation began in which Arabic terms and Islamic concepts were injected in some places while keeping the Indian storytelling intact. The *Story of the Victorious Pandawas* and the *Story of the Noble Rama* were noted examples of this transitional literature. As well, some of the popular literature of the Middle East and India made its way into the region at this time. *The Tale of Amir Hamzah*, popular throughout the Muslim world, was taken from a pre-Islamic Persian classic that had been rewritten to reflect classical Islamic civilization. The *Story of Yusuf* told the story of Yusuf and Zulaykha (Joseph and Potiphar's wife), found both in the Bible and the Qurʾan, has been a favorite theme of writers throughout Islamic history.

In the sixteenth century at Aceh and the Malay areas, the Indian epics underwent further adaptation to Muslim tastes. The Ramayana epic was rewritten with several important changes. References to the god Brahma became Allah, the story of Adam was included at the beginning, and generally "Islamic" coloring appeared throughout the work. But the genre was revised for a whole new series of poetic tales from Persian and Arabic sources as well. Impetus for this new trend was popularized by the work of Hamzah Fansuri and Abdul Rauf in Aceh, who were using the Persian quatrain *(rubai)*, in which the first, second, and fourth lines rhymed. Both wrote a large number of poems, all of them on religious themes, such as Hamzah's *Poem of Devotees (Syair Sidang Fakir)* and Abdul Rauf's *Poem of the Mystic Way (Syair Ma'arifat)*. Usually, however, the Malay verse form *(syair)* was used. While this form originally was used to spread the doctrine of the popular mystic outlook advocated by the "unitarians," it was also used in producing tales of fantasy, which were very popular as oral literature. These new poems told about the heroines Zubaidah and Bidasari and the heroes Badrul Zaman and Yatim Musa, probably drawn from Indic literature.

In the seventeenth century, literature in the Malay region began to reflect Middle Eastern themes, even though they may have come via India and were then translated into Malay. The *Story of the Crown of Kings (Syair Taj al-Muluk)*, originally a Persian work from Bokhara by Bukhari al-Jawhari (active in the sixteenth century) was indicative of such works; it even retained much of its Middle Eastern verse form, which used the Persian rhyming couplet *(mathnawi)*, the Persian quatrain, and Arabic lyric *(ghazal)* forms. It set forth a pantheistic view of God and the universe in a mystic context, but also offered advice for the "good ruler" and warned readers to beware of the perils awaiting humans on the Day of Judgment. In west Sumatra a Malay-language treatise titled *The Ultimate of Righteousness (Lubab al-Kifayah)*, by Jamaluddin (active early seventeenth century), became important as a standard text among Naqsyabandiyah mystic cells operating there; its popularity rested on its choice selections from earlier Naqsyabandiyah authors in the central Islamic world.

On Java the influence of Old Javanese culture remained strong throughout the era and colored the new literature that began to appear with the rise of Islamic states. At the time of Sultan Agung in the sixteenth century and immediately thereafter, tales were recited orally about the exploits of that ruler; later they were collected into a saga called *Legends of Sultan Agung*. Some tales were couched in allegory that revealed a dualistic—that is, mystical–realistic—relationship in culture and the universe, an outlook that had been common prior to the arrival of Islam. The *Baron Sakender Tales* were reflective of this genre; this particular set of stories was tied to the arrival of the Dutch and the impact they had on local culture, where the crassness of the intruders stood in marked contrast to the refinement of Javanese society. Later, but still in the same era, the *Song of the Golden House*, also ascribed to Sultan Agung, laid out a theory for governance wherein the ruler was viewed as leading his subjects beyond the normal life of humans to a greater appreciation of God.

Javanese literature in the seventeenth century concentrated on a retelling of Old Javanese tales in Indian meters, such as *Ethical Maxims (Niti Sastra)* and similar titles that outlined the "refined" behavior and high character esteemed at the royal court. In the northern coastal region similar works on ethics and refinement appeared that also included important principles of statecraft. An example was *Sacred Maxims (Niti Sruti)*, written by a central Javanese noble named Karang Gayam (active ca. 1580), which became important enough that it was studied at the Mataram court during the seventeenth century and later as representative of classical Javanese thinking.

A number of popular religious guides *(primbon)* appeared in Java during the early part of the era dealing with proper practice and belief concerning Islamic mysticism. All of them advocated practices that conformed with standard Sunni Muslim mysticism, with emphasis on beliefs about the nature of God, on using the "litany" *(ratib)* as prayer, and on performing certain other rites along with prayer, such as recitation of the "intention" *(niyah)* to set the stage for mystical effort. The works spoke out specifically against practices that could be construed as "pantheistic," that is, considering God and nature as one or separating nature from God; ideally, nature is part of God but God transcends nature. Manuscripts were prepared by Sunan Bonang, a fabled propagator of Islam in central Java, and by Shaykh Bari (active ca. 1520), which presented standard lessons of Islam in answer to questions from a hypothetical questioner, usually derived from the Muslim theologian al-Ghazali. This set of documents indicate that there was a segment of Javanese society, not connected with the royal courts but operative in general society, that was interested in putting aside pre-Islamic outlooks to concentrate on standard Sunni Islamic practices and values.

In the northern coastal region specifically, a genre developed that was known as "literature of the Prophet" *(anbiya)*, drawn from Malay and Arabo-Persian sources where it had been popular earlier. The first stories were probably those concerning the prophet Yusuf and his temptation by Zulaykha, as well as incidents in the life of Muhammad. This genre was aimed at fulfilling a heavy demand for popular devotional literature that could be read and recited by the rising number of new believers in that area of Java.

Java in the eighteenth century was a rich literary environment displaying the dual trends of Old Javanese themes and the newer ones of the Islamic world. Several reference books on old Javanese culture were produced as well as a popular literature, epitomized by *The Fantastic Sparrow Hawk*, a romance drawing on a hero from the Panji stories, written by the Kartasura chief minister Purbaya (in office 1728–1738). Also at Kartasura, the crown prince commissioned the preparation of the Centini manuscript, which drew together works from the "traveling student" genre *(santri lelana)*, a large body of descriptive materials in song, ballad, and historical formats dealing with the sights and wonders of Java. This particular manuscript told of a student-wanderer on Java who came to appreciate its Hindu and Islamic pasts in the forms of ruins, palaces, schools, natural environment, and human activity.

Middle Eastern and Malay literature had some popularity on Java at this time. Several poem cycles were important. The first was the *Amir Hamza Epic*, which had several key tales attached to it, such as the "Honored Prince," a tale of a quest for a renowned sword, and the "Princess Renganis" tale, which told the story of a romance between the Persian hero Amir Hamzah and a self-reliant princess. A "biography" was popular in West Java, titled *The Story of a Saint (Hikayat Seh)*, which outlined the life, miracles, and anecdotes concerning the famous Muslim mystic ʿAbd al-Qadir Jilani (d. 1166). There were also several stories of Muhammad's ascension to heaven, a popular theme throughout the Muslim world, and other anecdotes concerning the Prophet's life, such as *Muhammad's Shaving*, which told about how the Prophet shaved his head when he first understood that he was to be God's emissary.

While much of the court at Kartasura was concerned with Old Javanese themes, during the reign of Pakubuwono II, the grandmother of the ruler, one Ratu Pakubuwana (d. 1732), formed a cult about her grandson in which she portrayed him as the spiritual successor to Sultan Agung. Under her guidance the *Story of Sultan Iskandar* and several other tales received a new introduction in which the ruler, Pakubuwano II, was associated with the story as a descendant and given attributes equal to those of the heroes of the story, which included prayers for his success. The story presented an idealized model of the good and pious ruler, and was full of noble examples. It also dealt with the importance of mystical union between a ruler and his people on one level and between a ruler and God on another, a theme already explored in several other works dating all the way back to the reign of Sultan Agung in the sixteenth century. Al-Raniri would have labeled it as heretical.

At the royal court in Surakarta during most of the eighteenth century, the most prestigious writer was Jasadipura I (d. 1803), a long-lived, renowned court poet who was a prolific writer in several fields and the founder of a dynasty of important court poets that was to be prominent for well over a century. His influence on the development of the Javanese language was profound, because of his exquisite style and the breadth of his writings. In the highly regarded field of classical Javanese studies, he rewrote the Ramayana story with new titles, and in Islamic literature he wrote new versions of the Persian epics, particularly the *Romance of Amir Hamzah* and the *Crown of Kings (Serat Tadjusalatin)*, popular earlier in seventeenth-century Aceh. He also wrote an account of a mystic teacher brought before Pakubuwano II on charges of heresy, who was treated leniently because he had kept his heretical views to himself and thus had not infected society.

Drama

In the pre-Islamic era the Javanese shadow play developed using stories from the Indic *Mahabharata,* which reflected Hindu esthetics and morality. Its most sophisticated renditions were presented as entertainment at the courts of rulers, but it was popular in various forms in the general population. During the early Islamic period on Java, particularly at Demak, several of the famed nine propagators of Islam reputedly used the shadow puppet theater to introduce Islamic conceptions and values. To undertake this they had first to desacralize the Hindu tales by turning the plots and themes into mere entertainment having little to do with the value system they had embodied earlier. Once the propagators were successful in this transformation, they then substituted Muslim story lines, such as the tales of Amir Hamzah and Muhammad Hanafiah, for the Hindu sagas, with a corresponding change in the value system, in order to emphasize the fundamentals of Islam.

A similar development aimed at recasting Javanese drama into an Islamic context occurred in the north coastal cities of Java, where the myths and legends from classical Javanese were similarly reworked to include Islamic values. The effort took place in the seventeenth century, when there was an attempt to collect, classify, and correlate all the myths and legends from the Islamic and Javanese traditions. This produced the *Book of Tales (Serat Kanda),* which dealt with the conceptions underlying the characters in the Indian epics. The figure of Javanese folk-hero Semar was of particular interest, probably because he was popular among the segment of the people that still accorded Javanese mythology great respect. These works exhibited a subtle blending of Muslim elements into the Javanese stories and constituted essentially a new genre.[34]

Music and Dance

In the chronicles of the first two centuries of the era there were occasional references to musical instruments and their use. The gong was commonly found at most mosques, being used to summon the faithful to prayer at the proper times, particularly to the communal prayer on Friday. Likewise the gong was sounded in the royal compound to mark the onset of activities regarded as important. A number of other instruments were evident in the royal compound, notably drums of different kinds, long flutes *(srunei),* regular flutes *(niffiri),* clarinets, castanets *(cherachap),* trumpets, and violins *(hirbab kapachi).* Some, such as trumpets and drums, were used in public processions; others, for instance, drums and clarinets, were used to accompany a person to a ceremony honoring him. Most instruments comprised the orchestra considered necessary to conduct ceremonies at royal courts, such as the installation of a high official. Even a letter from a foreign prince was regarded as deserving a ceremony and was brought to the ruler with a procession complete with the music from a big drum, trumpet, and kettledrums. Dancers sometimes performed without accompanying music, but sang and danced in rhythm to those songs. Dancers were described as beautifully attired with jewelry hanging over their breasts and shoulders, and the dancing consisted of hand, arm, head, and body movements. The court ritual of Aceh called for the participation of drums, which played different fanfares for particular events.

During the seventeenth and eighteenth centuries in northern Java, especially in Ceribon, short songs *(suluk)* were sung at meetings of mystics, often accompanied by music and dancing. The songs dealt with mystic concepts and followed several different forms. Sometimes they were question-and-answer drills, and at times cryptic, permitting only the initiated to understand the import of the instructions given in the singing. The songs were imitative of those sung by the puppeteer at key intervals in a puppet performance in order to advance the action or present a particular point to the audience. In that sense there was a positive link with pre-Islamic practice in the region. At various places throughout the zone there were also "piercing" ceremonies *(dabus)*, in which dancers accompanied by a small group of musicians with drums, gongs, and stringed instruments would sing in praise of God and the Prophet. At the key moment in the performance, as some of the dancers reached the stage where they entered into a mystical trance, sharp instruments such as daggers, knives, and nails would be inserted into their skin without apparent injury to them. Other singing or chanting forms have already been mentioned, such as the songs recited in memory of the Prophet *(qasidah)*, often at the commemoration of his birthday, the performance of the "litany" *(ratib)* ceremony in which groups moved in swaying unison while reciting the name of God in an effort to induce a mystical trance, and the use of a similar but less organized chanting ceremony of the "remembrance" *(dhikr)*, also for trance inducement. These forms of worship that involved singing and chanting pervaded all parts of the Muslim Zone, being found in the Malay and Javanese world and at the eastern end of the zone among the Maranao in the southern Philippine Islands.

Art and Crafts

Two particular art forms were apparent in this time frame: illumination and calligraphy. A few examples of illumination from the Javanese courts were apparent in manuscripts prepared there during this era, but the technique was limited and had little connection per se with Islam. Calligraphy was apparently in greater use and had obviously been brought into Southeast Asia from the Islamic areas to the west along with the use of Arabic language, and particularly with the adoption of the Arabic script for writing Malay and other regional languages. Calligraphy was evident on some of the early tombs; that of Maulana Ibrahim at Gresik was most prominent, on which the sides of the graves and the entire headstone were covered with ornate Arabic calligraphy calling attention to the renowned propagator and giving praise to God and the Prophet of God. Other prominent tombstones of the era, while not as ornate, often used Arabic calligraphy to explain the vital statistics of the deceased and present a Qur'anic verse or one of the Islamic expressions of belief. But calligraphy was not limited to the cemetery; it filled an important niche in the courts of the rulers of the age, when letter writing was used by them for purposes of state. A letter from the ruler of Aceh, Alauddin Riayat Shah al-Mukamil (r. 1589–1604), to Queen Elizabeth I of England (r. 1558–1603) in 1601, still exists and is regarded as a prize example of the use of calligraphy in such letter writing. The Malay version, using Arabic script, was illuminated with geometric patterns, floral designs, and local foliage representations and comprises an exquisite example of the use of art by rulers of the age. In the eighteenth century calligraphy was used widely among rulers on their seals, which included their name and a religious expression to authenticate their positions as Muslim rulers. The tie to standard Muslim practices elsewhere was very close.

Metalwork, woodworking, and weaving were all well developed throughout the region and their products were part of the goods that were bartered with international and regional traders. Of particular note was the batik cloth industry on Java where a host of exquisite patterns in rich colors was developed, the lacquers applied to vases and furniture in the Palembang area, and the finely crafted metalwork of the Tausug peoples in the Sulu Archipelago. Generally speaking, these art forms were developed inside the environment of the cultures concerned, usually having pre-Islamic roots, and there was little to distinguish them as "Islamic" in the sense that they owed any special influence on their development to the Islamic culture that had accompanied the arrival of that religion from the Middle East and India. Two examples illuminate the issue. First, in the carving of decorative wooden screens, local floral patterns were used in preference to the stylized ones developed in the Middle East, although in some small circles the craftsmen of Southeast Asia might employ Arabic calligraphy, but that was not usual. Second, in the manufacture of the ceremonial dagger the metal of the blade near the hilt was shaped to give an approximation of Arabic expressions, such as the "confession of faith," but this was done as part of the magio-animistic rite of endowing the dagger with special power. So the connections with Islam were slight and problematical.

Conclusion

There were three substantial developments involving Islam in the Southeast Asian Muslim Zone in the thirteenth to eighteenth centuries. First, three standard political systems emerged during this era: the vassal system, the hierarchy system, and the community model. In the first two systems, the ruler was regarded as blessed by God, gathered power through lineage, magical court regalia, and connection with supernatural phenomena, was expected to be autocratic but paternalistic, and could not be dethroned unless God's blessing was removed. The vassal system had elements of consultation—from nobles, prominent business interests, and the clergy—inherent in it, while the hierarchy system was based on strong intermediate levels of control and a hereditary administrative class. In marked contrast, the community model saw local communities jealously guarding their own autonomy and forming weak hierarchal structures at administrative levels above the local communities. Rulers of states in this system were nominal, holding limited power and dependent on their own wits for income. In all three systems trade and entrepreneurship were highly regarded, and association with Islam and its proselytization was regarded as beneficial. In the first two groups the rulers and the elite advanced such policies for their own benefit, while in the decentralized model some important limits were placed on economic activity and proselytization to make both conform to existing mores and customs, enabling local control to remain paramount. When the "imperium" came into existence, an attempt was made to heighten Islamic identification, since it was recognized as allowing the ruler greater power in organizing the state and in shaping society to religious ends, even as the desire for power and glory were enhanced.

Second, the mores and customs of each area and locality were recognized as important and as constituting a living tradition to be protected and allowed great expression. Islam was expected to be molded to these customs, to contribute to the culture by helping to cleanse it of unworthy aspects, and to elevate custom with its own blessing and sanction. In part, Islam did just that; but in part it also began to question the underlying assumptions of some customs and traditions, causing some long-term erosion and open ruptures in those cultures. So, although Islam was expected to integrate with local custom, often it was local custom that adapted to Islam, so that a dynamic process was set in motion—one that was not altogether clear in its direction at this particular juncture. Many of these cultural accommodations were still being worked out in the next era, and the differences between Islam and custom became much more of an issue at that time.

Third, a literature developed incorporating Islamic themes and values that took their place alongside an older Indic literature, the two blending in part and creating a hybrid that was regarded as "Islamic" in tone. At the same time there was an infusion of religious literature that was reflective of the "orthodoxy" of Sunni Islam and in keeping with the standard literature of the broader Islamic world. One can be impressed by the considerable amount of writing in the Islamic field, especially by the eighteenth century. Overall, this period witnessed the conversion of a goodly section of the population to Islam and considerable consolidation through political, cultural, and literary institutions of that new religion. At the beginning of this era Islam had been a fragile entity, but by the end it was an essential part of the Southeast Asian scene, giving identity to most of the peoples living in the Muslim Zone.

Key Readings

Azra, Azyumardi. 1997. "Education, Law, Mysticism: Constructing Social Realities." A historical and social-scientific account of the development of Islamic institutions in Southeast Asia.

Barbosa, Duarte. 1967. *The Book of Duarte Barbosa.* 2 vols. The report of a Portuguese scribe concerning the local population of Southeast Asia.

Beaulieu. 1795. "Voyage to the East Indies." The observations of a French sea captain, particularly at Aceh.

Brown, C. C., trans. 1970. *Sejarah Melayu* or *Malay Annals.* A well-annotated edition of a classic court chronicle of several Malay-Muslim principalities.

Johns, Anthony H. 1957. "Malay Sufism as Illustrated in an Anonymous Collection of Seventeenth Century Tracts." An anthology of brief writings revealing the purposes and aims of mystical practice.

Jones, Russell. 1979. "Ten Conversion Myths from Indonesia." An outline and explanation of how conversion to Islam probably happened in Southeast Asia.

Kathirthamby-Wells, J. 1990. "Banten: A West Indian Port and Polity during the Sixteenth and Seventeenth Centuries." A historical reconstruction and explanation of a key port city, its identification with Islam, and its conflict with the Dutch Company.

Meilink-Roeloefz, M. A. P. 1962. *Asian Trade and European Influence in the Indonesian Archipelago between 1500 and about 1630.* A summary and reconstruction of trading relationships at the time of the arrival of the

Europeans and the impact they had on the international trading relationships.

Pigeaud, Th. G. Th. *The Literature of Java.* 1967–1970. 4 vols. A classification of Javanese literature and a summary of the various works placed in the categories that were developed for studying the important genres.

Pigeaud, Th. G. Th., and H. J. de Graaf. *Islamic States in Java, 1500–1700.* 1976. A summary of historical events and developments on Java, with references to other monographs containing fuller studies of shorter historical periods.

Ricklefs, M. C. *The Seen and Unseen World in Java 1726 to 1749.* A perceptive account of the role of Islamic religious belief in the events of a key period of Dutch–Javanese relations.

Winstedt, Richard O. *A History of Classical Malay Literature.* 1969. An analysis of Malay literature with good summaries of key literary writings.

3 The Emergence of New Muslim Institutions (1800 to 1945)

> The nobles all carry [ceremonial daggers] of the common
> serpentine form. Those that have the wavy lines on the blade
> are regarded as the most valuable. The handles are usually
> made of whale's teeth, nicely carved; and the scabbards are
> overlaid with gold. . . . They also wear a belt covered with large
> diamond-shaped plates of silver, on which are inscribed verses
> of the [Qur'an].

General Context

The Colonial Experience

The Napoleonic Wars at the end of the eighteenth and beginning of the
nineteenth centuries were a watershed for European influence and dominance in the Muslim Zone of Southeast Asia. In the eighteenth century the
Dutch Company dominated the entire area, with minor competition from
the Spanish and British, and occasional forays on the part of the Americans,
French, and other Europeans. The poor political position of the Dutch in
Europe during the Napoleonic Wars, however, gave Great Britain opportunity to change the political and trade environment to its advantage, which
was consolidated over the next century. At the same time, governance by
trading companies was replaced by administrative systems that organized
and ruled as governments did, effectively changing the very nature of the
European presence. That power was more pervasive, less tolerant of local
rights or lifestyles than the trading companies had been, and intruded itself
into nearly all the cultures of the Muslim Zone. The Muslim states that had
flourished earlier and survived during the previous era proved unable to
withstand this political change and continued to decline. Indigenous political and economic institutions were made subservient to European control,
at considerable loss to the local population. Refitting of those local institutions that could be adapted to the European system was imposed, and those
practices that stood in the new system's path were destroyed.

In this era the trade routes, per se, were no longer an important consideration in Southeast Asia Islam as they had been in earlier eras. That is
not to say the traditional trade routes ceased to exist, for they did continue
to be used, with European ships undertaking the principal role of long-dis-

tance hauling. Still, there was some minor shipping done by local merchants along the Middle East to China route, but it was of very limited importance. The Muslim trading communities of South Asia were severely and permanently harmed by the change, while those in Southeast Asia were forced into new roles as well. In Southeast Asia the traders had to adjust to a new economic system that drew on Western knowledge and technology to reorient their trade toward the products that would support the market needs of Europe.

As a result, economies emerged that were based on large-scale exploitation of natural resources that could be used in the world economy. Hence tea and coffee production, extraction of palm oil, mining of tin and other metals, production of lumber, and the raising of various grains, vegetables, and fruits became important. The theory of dual economies came into play in accordance to which a monetary system relating to the colonizer's economic sphere operated at one level of society, and a nonmonetary, barter-type economy continued to be used for large areas of local society not affected by international markets. The real impact of this dual system was greatly debated, but was certainly operative in many areas of colonial life throughout the world, and certainly in the Muslim Zone of Southeast Asia.

There was a steady growth of the colonial political infrastructure throughout the era, and all five colonial systems—Dutch, English, Spanish, American, and French—showed this growth. Actually this was an era of political consolidation throughout the world, with nation-states undergoing considerable centralization of political authority as communication, transportation, and technology revolutions made it possible to make decisions at the national level rather than at the local level, as had been the general rule earlier. Hence, in colonial areas the staffs of the colonial administrators took on more responsibility for decisions that had previously been made by local authorities, usually in the interest of commonality, but often out of a sense of moral superiority. In the first instance, much of the centralization had to do with creating an effective infrastructure to support the new colonial economies, but in time it extended to other important fields, such as health, justice, and education, although all of these areas could be linked to folkways, long-established custom, and religious tradition.

Although the Southeast Asian area was divided among several colonial powers, the development of Islam was relatively the same during this era. An amalgamation of religious and local cultural values had a certain sameness throughout the region. As well, in certain places, purist Islamic values begin to challenge that accommodation. In the final fifty years of the era, in particular, some Muslim groups sought to gain supremacy over those indigenous cultures and to change the overall perceptions of the population toward Islam and what they regarded as the proper obligations demanded by Islam. Finally, at the end of the colonial period both Islam and local culture came under the increasing influence of European cultural norms, and this called for still another accommodation that led to a further fractionalizing of indigenous elites.

The Greater Asian Setting

Asia fell under European influence during the nineteenth century, and that condition remained until the end of the era in 1950. With the disintegration of the Ottoman Empire between 1900 and 1924, the Middle East became a region of states dominated politically by Great Britian and France. Politically, however, there was no contact between these new states and the Islamic peoples of Southeast Asia; however, in the early twentieth century some political conceptions originating in the Middle East seem to have affected the Indonesian political scene, particularly the drives toward modernization under Mustafa Kemal Ataturk (governed 1923–1938) in Turkey and Reza Khan Pahlevi (governed 1923–1941) in Iran. Nationalist leaders of Indonesia were impressed by the development schemes of those two rulers and saw the pressure placed on Muslim behavior as crucial to change. The passage of pilgrims from Southeast Asia grew during this time span, expanding from thousands to tens of thousands by the end of the period. Students from Southeast Asia, already visiting the holy cities of Makkah and Madinah for the pilgrimage, continued to stay on for several years to study. Along with general knowledge of Islamic lore, some of these students also returned to Southeast Asia, bringing with them the ideologies of the Middle East, as in the case of Wahhabi thinking in the early nineteenth century and modernist Muslim thinking at the turn of the twentieth. Finally, migration, mostly circular, of Arabs to Southeast Asia continued, with people from the Hadhramaut being the most visible in this sustained trend. Instead of becoming part of the international trade system as their forebears had, these immigrants took part in local trade systems, acting as "middlemen" in the colonial economies that emerged. In those roles they served as collectors of goods produced by the indigenous population and transferred them to European trading companies. In general the Middle East remained important to Islamic development in Southeast Asia, but it was less for its economic relationship than for its religious and intellectual transference of ideas and education.

South Asia was transformed politically during this era by the disintegration of Muslim political control and the takeover by the British. The traditional Indian economic system was devastated by the British production of cheap cotton goods that flooded the Asian markets and destroyed the Indian weaving business. As a result of that development, the overseas trade that had rested so heavily on the sale of Indian textiles was placed in jeopardy, and local traders no longer had the preferred trade goods necessary to penetrate the markets of Southeast Asia. Small traders from southern

India, particularly among the Tamils, still journeyed out to Southeast Asia to take part in middleman roles in the colonial economic systems established by the English in the Malay region and the Dutch in the Indonesian archipelago. But this was a lesser role than what Indian merchants had enjoyed earlier. In the early twentieth century some intellectual currents, such as the thinking of Mirza Ghulam Ahmad (d. 1908) and Muhammad Iqbal (d. 1938), had some influence on Muslim and nationalist thought in Southeast Asia, particularly on Java. In general, however, Southeast Asian Muslims regarded Arabic writers as more relevant than those of the Indian subcontinent.

China ended its tributary relationships with Southeast Asian countries during the Ming period, as we saw in a previous chapter, and those rights were never restored. However, there was a continuing migration of Chinese to Southeast Asia, and large numbers of Chinese settled throughout the region, making them in time a significant portion of the population in the western Malaya Peninsula region, in the western Kalimantan region, and on the island of Java. Since few of them became Muslim, they became competitors of the Muslims in many ways, particularly in small trading and business communities. Finally, the experience of the Chinese Revolution in 1910 and the early republican stress on returning China to Chinese control after a long period of "foreign" (Manchu) rule was an inspiration to people in the Muslim Zone to form their own nationalist movements, particularly on Java and in West Sumatra.

Throughout the latter half of the nineteenth century and until the end of this era, the Japanese became more important in East Asia and attempted to compete with the European powers for control of China. It also fueled its new industrial economy by importing large amounts of raw materials from Southeast Asia, especially depending on the region for oil and rubber. The era ended, in fact, with the Japanese attempt to incorporate Southeast Asia into a Japanese-controlled region during World War II, but that attempt was eventually unsuccessful, as discussed later. Overall, the greater Asian region continued to have both a direct and an indirect impact on the development of Southeast Asia during this era, but it was significantly reduced from what it had been in the previous period.

The Southeast Asian Setting

At the beginning of the nineteenth century Southeast Asia consisted of two subregions: mainland Indochina and the Malay-Indonesian maritime region. They differed along three different lines. First, religiously, the mainland area was under the influence of Buddhism while the maritime region followed Islam. Second, the mainland area was marked by kingdoms dependent on agriculture and settled peoples for their basic livelihood, while in the maritime region people depended mostly on resource gathering and trade. Finally, the British and French took control of the mainland area, except for Siam (formerly Ayuthia), while the British, Dutch, Spanish, and Americans divided control over the maritime region. Siam came under the heavy influence of the French and British, meaning that, for all intents and purposes, the entire Southeast Asian region was under colonial influence of one sort or another. During this time frame the indigenous governments that did survive had control over only limited spheres of internal affairs, and their contact with other local leaders was circumscribed, with the responsibility for foreign affairs being assumed by the colonial powers. Consequently, in a political sense, Southeast Asia consisted of a series of enclaves where colonial officials dealt with one another, while the local rulers were given small, limited political roles and had little mutual contact. But, as we shall see in the coming discussion, these colonial systems were not entirely closed, although they certainly were restrictive. Influences from outside did pass into them, societies continued to develop within them, and nationalistic endeavor emerged from those areas in the same approximate time frames.

During the eighteenth century most areas of Southeast Asia came under the control or influence of the Dutch East Indies Company–VOC, which remained until the end of the century when the company went into bankruptcy. The Dutch government assumed control of some of the company's assets, but its influence throughout the Muslim Zone was limited. In the later part of the eighteenth century the British East Indies Company operated a port at Penang Island, off the western coast of the Malayan Peninsula, and located trading factories in southwest Sumatra at Bencoolen. The Philippines remained under Spanish control and asserted control over the southern islands in the late nineteenth century, and then was replaced by the Americans at the turn of the twentieth century. The French moved into Indochina in the mid-nineteenth century, setting up its headquarters in Hanoi with direct rule in a few places while establishing colonies and protectorates over the rest. Siam, later Thailand, continued to control a number of Malay-speaking territories in the southern part of its domains. Thus, the era was marked by considerable political change overall, with foreign rule continuing in most places.

People and Their Activities

Mid-twentieth-century scholarship held that the peoples of maritime Southeast Asia consisted of three major zones of population: the heavy wet-rice areas where the remnants of Hinduism prevailed, found primarily in central and east Java and on Bali; the coastal regions where trading and Islamic values were predominant; and the mountainous interiors of islands, consisting of pagan tribal groups engaging in dry agriculture. The wetland populations were settled in villages, had strong ties with their officials, and lived in accordance with their traditions. In the coastal regions a mixture of peoples existed in trading communities with some educational institutions and government infrastructure. Fishermen and agriculturalists surrounded the trading centers and supported them. The pagan tribal groups of the interior practiced shifting agriculture because the land they occupied was marginal, and their societies reflected strong kinship ties. Overall, however, there were considerable regional differences mostly affected by ethnic identity, which was very strong.[1]

There were two major population groups closely related to Islam during this era: the Malays and the Javanese. As stated in Chapter 2, the Malays occupied the Straits of Melaka Basin, the entire Malay Peninsula north through Patani, the coastal region of northern Borneo, with scattered villages in the Indochina region, particularly along the lower reaches of the Mekong. There were about five million Malays throughout the region at the turn of the twentieth century. Politically, they were a decentralized people, but they had common cultural characteristics and were good organizers, while economically they were generally dynamic. They wore similar clothing, had like customs, and identified with Islam as their common religion, practiced indifferently during this period but still a clear point of identification. They absorbed other local peoples they encountered in their great expansion, so that "river people" and "sea people" were integrated when the newcomers accepted the cultural standards, including conversion to Islam. Malays used mostly the vassal form of government outlined earlier, with historical Melaka serving as the ideal, except in Brunei, where a long-seated government had constructed a hierarchy system. When the European colonial system gained full control in the nineteenth century, most of the Malays were located in the British colonies, although some fell into the Dutch zone, the Thai sphere, and a small number under control of the French.

The Javanese were the most populous group. There were about three million in 1795, but early in the twentieth century their number had reached nearly thirty million, an enormous growth for one century. Dutch scholars of the period stated that the population contained two groups. The "red group" *(bongsa abangan)* regarded themselves as Muslims and observed some Islamic festivities but were not much concerned with its beliefs and practices. The "white group" *(bongsa poetihan)* attended religious schools and put the "orthodox" practices and beliefs of Sunni Islam into effect in their lives and society. The red group was overwhelmingly the larger of the two.[2] Looking at the situation from another perspective, however, the foregoing description of a dual attitude toward Islam was most characteristic of interior Java; the northern coastal area, known generally as the Pasisir, was much more influenced by Islam as a result of the rich trade that passed through the ports there and fortified the new religion with literature, teachers, and communication brought from the Islamic lands to the west.

Alongside these two major groups were smaller groups of considerable importance, such as the Minangs and the Acehnese on Sumatra; the Sundanese on Java; the Tausug, the Magindanao, and the Maranao in the Philippine region; the Makassarese and Bugis on Sulawesi; and the Cham in Thai-Indo China region. The Acehnese, numbered about 300,000 midway in the nineteenth century and the Minangs about 600,000 in the 1830s. These two groups have been described in the last chapter, and they remained much the same during this era. The Sundanese society of western Java borrowed heavily from Javanese civilization but contained elements of Malay influence as well. The inhabitants, nearly 2,500,000 in the middle of the nineteenth century, were Muslims, although those in the upland areas were nominal in their allegiance to Islam, with a strong influence remaining from earlier animism and Hindusim.[3]

In the Philippine region the most complex society was the Tausug, which incorporated large numbers of slaves taken from other places in Southeast Asia, and particularly from the Christian Visayas immediately to the north. The society and government were closely related to the Malay forms immediately to the west, but Islam was regarded as an important point of identification. Warfare with the Spanish was incessant, but the Spanish eventually brought the Tausug and other peoples under their political control. The Magindanao, with the closely related Iranum, were the major population grouping in southwest Mindanao, and were more culturally diverse than most of their Muslim neighbors because of close contacts with the Indonesian islands to the south. The Maranao were peoples settled around Lake Lanao and were divided into four major "divisions," all recognizing a common origin. Because no centralizing force ever existed in the Sulu-Mindanao region, disputes and feuds were not easily resolved and low-level warfare prevailed through much of the period, but it was not severe enough that it greatly harmed the agricultural economy. American census figures for the early twentieth century set the total population at 372,464, the great bulk of which constituted these three populations.[4]

On Sulawesi the two dominant groups were the Makassarese and the Bugis, both noted for establishing trade networks tying together local economies throughout Southeast Asia. Coexisting with the Makassarese were strong proponents of Islam, as noted in the last chapter, with a small but influential religious literature and rulers who sought to proselytize as part of their own mission of kingship. During the eighteenth and nineteenth centuries the Bugis established colonies to facilitate trade, especially in the Straits of Melaka, where they gained control over several Malay states and generally handled sea–shore gathering operations in the region. Through the political positions it gained, the rulers became strong patrons of Islamic learning. In the early twentieth century there were about 400,000 people belonging to these two groups.[5]

The Cham people continued to constitute a small but influential presence in Siam and Cambodia (formerly Khmer), with a small number in the Cochin China region. In all areas they were primarily agriculturalists and fisherfolk, but in the Siam and Cambodia area they were often found serving in the army and naval forces in disproportionate numbers. They tended in this period to intermix and identify with the Malay settlers migrating from Patani and Kelantan and relied on contacts in those Malay centers for cultural and educational assistance. There were perhaps 150,000 people in this grouping at the turn of the twentieth century.[6]

Finally, there were smaller groups whose influence was local, such as the sea people located throughout the entire region, the Samal of the Sulu Sea being the most notable. There were Ambonese and Molukans in the eastern Indonesian archipelago and the Bajaus and Ilanums in the Sulu-Mindanoan area who accepted Islam generally. Some groups of Dayaks, Kedayans, Dusun, and related peoples in Borneo/Kalimantan who came in contact with the Malays and other Islamic peoples converted to Islam as well, but most of them remained animists. As well, there were Chinese immigrants who converted in small groups, Indian immigrants—many of them Shi'ah—who migrated to the zone, and Arabs who were found throughout the region. These last three groups, prominent earlier as traders, now became investors, operated small businesses, or played the role of middlemen in distribution, often between colonial agents and the local population.

The Political Situation

The Dutch Colonial System

Beginning with the arrival of officials at the end of the Napoleonic Wars, a new Dutch colonial system was inaugurated that endured until the onset of the Japanese military period in 1942. Under this system, the government of the Netherlands at The Hague set the overall terms of administration and policy for the Netherlands East Indies and appointed a governor-general at the administrative capital in Batavia.

The political values at the beginning of the era were based on two factors: the evolution of colonial society and Dutch government intentions. The first value reflected the attitudes arising from the development of a racial society with four distinct groupings. The top group consisted of the Dutch administrators and settlers, regarded throughout the era as the colony's elite. Impressive amounts of government resources were expended on the creation and operation of an infrastructure that would serve them, such as schools, hospitals, housing areas, and entertainment facilities. Just

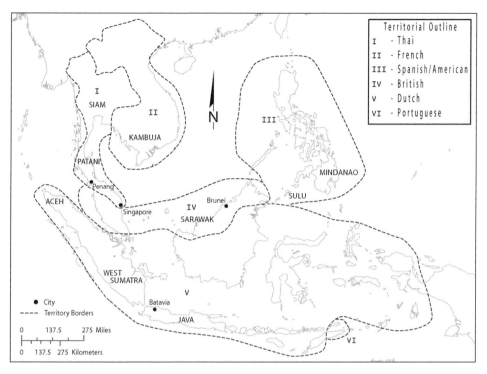

5. Colonial Holdings in Southeast Asia

below this level were the local officials and administrators, who constituted an elite in indigenous society and were given access to some facilities intended primarily for Europeans, such as the school system. Below these two elites were the Asian and Middle Eastern migrants—mostly Chinese, but also including Indians and Arabs—who served as economic middlemen between the Dutch and indigenous sectors. They were given considerable freedom to shape their own communities—using their own funds to do so —and to follow their own traditions. At the lowest place in society was the local population, largely rural, which worked in the native agricultural establishment. Members of the rural population served as workers on Dutch plantations and as laborers in the few industries that were established in the territory during this time period. Throughout the era this alignment of society was carefully regulated, so that the position of the Dutch settlers was strengthened, the new Indonesian elite pushed its way into the older traditional elite, and some agriculturalists moved to urban areas to take on new kinds of employment.

The first Dutch policy of significance occurred in the 1830s and was known as the Cultivation System; it called for forced deliveries of certain agricultural produce, usually coffee, sugar, and indigo. The deliveries of these products produced an enormous windfall in profits for the colonial administration, but the taxation system was applied in such a way that it heavily exploited the Javanese agriculturalists, leaving many unable to make the required deliveries and placing them deeply in debt. The Cultivation System was radically modified after 1850 when private plantations became the preferred method of agriculture production. Throughout the century as well, the village agriculturalist was subject to labor details—earlier as a condition of his membership in a particular village, later as a victim of exploitative work contracts.

A major policy shift occurred at the turn of the twentieth century when the Dutch colonial administration had consolidated its hold over the entire Indonesian archipelago. In the early years of the new century, a realignment of provinces created a system of local government councils to assist with local rule, which were filled mostly by Europeans but included some local members from the gentry class. In 1918 this system was extended to the "national" level with the creation of a "Peoples' Chamber" (Volksraad). The Peoples' Chamber was advisory to the governor-general, mostly appointed, and included only a small number of local members.

At the same time the "Ethical Policy" was adopted to compensate for the exploitive economic policies of the nineteenth century. The new approach aimed at more and better education, improvement of the economic condition of the local population, upgrading health and living conditions, and a number of other features. Surprisingly, the colonial administrators began a considerable transformation of the Indies in general to improve the living conditions of the local population that continued even after the end of the Ethical Policy. However, such activism was suspect among large sectors of the general population, who regarded Dutch policies as aimed at the destruction of their customary, cultural, and religious values.

Still another policy direction was taken by the Dutch when colonial administrators became convinced that customary law practiced in the village societies of the region offered clues to ethnic institutions, particularly regulation of village societies. Customary law was regarded as the living law of an area or region; the European scholars studying the phenomenon held that there were over nineteen major customary law zones in the Indies. There was a hope that this custom, heretofore an unwritten usage, could be codified and that the legal system of the Netherlands Indies could absorb it. Accompanying this conception was a corollary that related mostly to Islam, known as the "reception theory,"[7] which held that outside values and mores had to be integrated into the customary law of a region before they could be considered as "accepted" by its inhabitants. Indeed, only that accepted part of the outside value system was valid, and certainly not the original value system itself. The assertion was repeatedly made that Islam had been only partially "accepted" throughout the archipelago and that, accordingly, local Muslims responded only to their particular custom, not necessarily to the uncontested dictates of their religion.

The Islamic policy of the Dutch during the nineteenth century was crafted to keep Muslims under Dutch control and away from close association with Muslims elsewhere. There was fear that a strong Islamic identification, especially with those in the central Islamic world, would promote animosity against non-Muslim political control. Several bitter uprisings in Java, west Sumatra, and Banten during the nineteenth century confirmed this view, since Muslims returning from Makkah were leaders of those revolts. In particular, the pilgrimage was singled out as the institution that had the most pernicious effect on the population. Especially feared was the ideology of pan-Islamism, which advocated the overthrow of the colonial system throughout the Middle East and Asia as a precondition for the creation of a union of Muslim lands free of European occupation. Beginning in 1825, but perpetuated throughout the century until the advent of the new policy late in the century, an expensive pilgrim's pass had to be purchased for travelers to the Muslim holy land, and at times limits were placed on the total number of pilgrims allowed in a given year. As we shall see in the discussion on Singapore, Dutch efforts to limit the pilgrimage merely encouraged those interested in going to seek other ways of accomplishing it.

Dutch attitudes toward the pilgrimage changed near the beginning of the twentieth century. C. Snouck Hurgronje (d. 1936), the key adviser on the matter, argued that Indonesians who undertook the pilgrimage were not in Makkah long enough to be politicized, but that students who stayed for long periods of time were susceptible. His view was that those who undertook the pilgrimage saw it as fulfilling an important religious obligation, had necessarily to work long and hard to accrue the funds for such an undertaking, and usually were single-minded about it, regarding it as the high point of their lives. As they were responsible before they left, they would be as responsible after they returned.[8] In 1927 and 1932 administrative changes were made in the procedures dealing with pilgrims, including issuance of special passes and the publication of a bilingual handbook containing the new regulations. Despite Hurgronje's assurances, Dutch officials remained concerned about the pilgrimage, and in 1927 limits on the total number of people allowed to participate were set, just for that reason. Also, there had long been concern about illnesses associated with the pilgrimage and these worries persisted into the twentieth century. In a medical study of the problem in the 1920s it was noted that several infectious diseases—malaria and smallpox among them—produced a death rate that was about 17 percent higher on the return trip than it was on the trip to Makkah; it was a dangerous undertaking. Finally, throughout this era travel to and from Makkah was handled by Dutch-owned shipping lines, purposefully to recapture some of the funds expended by the pilgrims.[9]

At the beginning of the era, circa 1900, the average number of pilgrims from the archipelago was 7,300. This expanded rapidly to 52,412 in 1927, but fell back to lower levels in the worldwide depression of the 1930s, with only 6,500 going in 1940, the last year of participation before the World War II.[10] Significantly, there was considerable debate on the economic consequences of the pilgrimage in the 1930s among Indonesian political factions. Muslim associations held that there was an intrinsic value to the rite, which was worth the expense because of the heightening of religious awareness and civic responsibility that it entailed, even extending to the nationalist movement. Nonreligious nationalists, such as Soetomo (d. 1938), argued that the loss of foreign-exchange earnings the pilgrimage entailed harmed both the economy of the Indies and the particular household economies of the people undertaking the pilgrimage. They maintained that the money could have been better expended in other ways, particularly on education.

Aside from the pilgrimage, there were Dutch agencies concerned with the administration of Islam, notably religious councils and the Office of Internal Affairs. Regarding the first, such councils were established in each regency and consisted of a religious judge as chair and five to seven other members who had charge of cases involving marriage, inheritance, religious endowments, and other strictly religious matters. The chief legal references were *The Gift* (known as *Tuhfah*) by Ibn Hajar al-Haytami (d. 1567) and the *End of Neediness* (known as *Nihayah*) by al-Ramli (d. 1596), which came to be regarded as authoritative even though other jurisprudential texts by al-Nawawi and al-Shafi'i (d. 820) were popular as behavioral guides among pious Muslims throughout the region. In 1922, as a result of a major Dutch rethinking, cases of inheritance were taken away from the Islamic courts and given to the regular land courts. The reasoning was that Islamic religious law had not supplanted customary law in the matter of marriage, and that the land courts were therefore the more appropriate place to deal with matters of custom.

The Office of Internal Affairs was created in 1899, with C. Snouck Hurgronje (served 1989–1906) as its director. The office undertook studies designed to reveal the needs of various Muslim populations under Dutch control and give advice on upgrading the general welfare of those populations. Not surprisingly, it became highly attentive to the rise of the nationalist and communist movements in the first quarter of the century, which led Indonesians involved in the these movements to view the office as a security arm of the government. For example, the office reported on the Gedangan affair in 1904 and the Tanjung Oost disturbances in 1916, where participants in "disorderly" protests were exhorted to use "holy war" *(sabililah)* against the Dutch. When the office reported on these events, the Indonesian nationalists regarded it as a tool of the government. Obviously such reports were of value to the government, but the advice of the office was seldom viewed as useable, since policy makers were convinced that a strong, unequivocal response to nationalist and communist activities would preserve security and the general welfare. The office was viewed as too temporizing.

In 1893 the Dutch administration decided to divide education into two types of schools. The one designed for the general public was very basic, intended for a people who were to be engaged in agriculture or craft activities, while the one designed for the gentry had a richer curriculum, which included natural history, geography, and history. In both systems the instruction was in Malay or a local language. Within the first twenty-five years of the new century the curriculum in schools for the gentry's children was lengthened from five to seven years and a junior high school was added. Senior high schools on the European model were later established at Jakarta, Semarang, and Surabaya. A medical school and the six civil-service academies begun in the nineteenth century continued to function. Pedagogical institutes prepared educators for teaching in the village school system. In 1907 the Peoples' Schools, with a three-year course on basic writing, arithmetic, and practical knowledge, were inaugurated as an advancement on village education for agriculturalists. They were supported by the villages themselves, although some government subsidies were available to needy villages. Despite the financial burden on the local population, this system grew rapidly, so that in 1930 there were 9,600 schools of this type. Moreover, the number of Indonesians in the Dutch-style education system was 84,609 students, and at the university level there were 392 indigenous students.[11] Education was popular.

Indonesian reaction was strong concerning this educational system, as is evident from the numbers of children who went to private schools, including those attending religious schools and those enrolled in mission schools. The most rapid rise, however, was shown among the Muslims, who expanded the number of "Qur'an schools," mentioned earlier, where pupils learned to read and write Arabic and received basic instruction in Islam. There was also the classic Muslim boarding school, where classes were conducted in Arabic and a local language that explored standard religious texts. The number of schools continued to grow and other types of schools came into existence alongside them. Islamic organizations of this era, such as the *Muhammadiyah,* the Orthodox Scholars association–NO (Nahdatul Oelama), and the Movement for Islamic Education–Perti (Persatuan Tarbijah Islam), founded schools that mixed Western subject matter and Islamic lessons in forms that took the names "schools" and *madrasah.* No good statistics exist for all of Indonesia in this era, but in 1933 in west Sumatra there were about 1,213 Muslim schools serving 69,938 pupils, over twice the number of

Dutch schools operating there. By 1942 on Java, there were 1,831 Muslim schools with a total of 139,415 students, representing a number nearly the same as that of government schools, below that of the Dutch numbers but still significant.[12]

Obviously many people sent their children to Muslim schools because they wanted them to learn religious principles, but the issue apparently extended beyond that. There simply were not enough places in the government-sponsored schools for everyone who wanted to attend, and most places were reserved for children of the gentry. Moreover, the schools that were open—that is, the village schools—were not up to the level desired by the parents and were not accessible in most cases, since a large portion of these students lived in urban areas. The *Thawalib* schools in western Sumatra and the *Muhammadiyah* schools in Java were especially cognizant of these shortcomings and tailored their schools to provide the broadened Western-style educations desired in middle-class Indonesia. Dutch officials regarded the number of private schools as excessive, consequently the "Teachers' Ordinance" was passed in 1925. That law placed government regulations on private schools, including those with religious sponsorship, which in turn was greeted with protests from Muslim political groups of the time as a blatant attempt to deny (Muslim) children entry into the better jobs of society. While the issue abated somewhat during the remainder of the era, the Dutch remained obdurate about control, and the Muslims kept on creating schools.

An open declaration of anti-Dutch feeling came with the rise of political movements about 1912 and continued on through the remainder of the era. It started with the manifestos of the Islamic Association (Sarekat Islam) from 1912 to 1926 and continued with the calls of "Indonesia for the Indonesians" made by Soekarno and his nationalist colleagues in the Indonesian nationalist parties in the 1920s. It was further enunciated in the legislative proposals made by the Indonesian political confederation Gapi (Gabungan Politik Indonesia) in the 1930s. All made unambiguous statements that the indigenous peoples of the archipelago found the Dutch system and its policies intrusive and wrong, and called for them to turn the government over to the local peoples themselves.

Dutch efforts to suppress such expressions of dissent were strong, as they always had been, with arrests of those who were found to be fomenting action against the Dutch administration or were even suspected of contemplating such action. Reaching a crescendo of antigovernment animosity in the mid-1920s, this anti-Dutch attitude ebbed to a seething resentment in the 1930s. In 1941 the situation was regarded as a crisis for the Dutch administration, which prompted Queen Wilhelmina (r. 1890–1948) of the Netherlands, then with her government-in-exile in Great Britain (because the Netherlands itself had fallen to German invasion), to promise reforms within an "international Dutch community" after the world war ended, presumably meaning that the East Indies would remain under Dutch control even at that time. With nearly all the nationalist leaders in prison or exile in remote parts of the archipelago, there was almost no public sympathy for any statements of a defeated regime's promised good intentions at some unknown future date. Consequently there was almost no Indonesian resistance to the coming of the Japanese in early 1942.

Several different relationships emerged between the Dutch and the various peoples of the Indonesian archipelago. The case of the Minangs of west Sumatra is outlined here to illustrate how a local Islamic political entity, heavily affected by custom, underwent a crisis that involved both an Islamic and a European assault on its values and political integrity.

Minangkabau in West Sumatra

At the beginning of the nineteenth century the Minang political system was matrilineal and decentralized, with meaningful government mostly at the local level. It was truly representative of the community model of societal organization outlined in the last chapter and could be considered that model's archetype. This local system featured a council of elders and a headman that decided customary law cases, usually matters of inheritance. In this customary law system Islam was included as a factor, sometimes becoming an intrinsic part of the custom, or as an alternative to generally accepted custom by some small groups of believers.

The political system also included governance at the level of the province, which operated according to custom but had a particular set of institutions of its own. At the highest level there was the west Sumatra ethnic nation itself, which had three rulers with each assigned a set of functions. One of the three was designated the central ruler, holding a slightly more senior place over his colleagues, the ruler of custom and the ruler of worship. Each of these three rulers, however, had his own buildings, staff, and councils in the several capital cities they occupied throughout the era. The Minang royalty operated at the top of this decentralized system and were expected to have their own sources of income and, pointedly, did not have any direct taxing powers on the population. Mostly funds for their support came from a small excise tax levied on ships entering the ports of the area. The political and financial weaknesses of the rulers denied the "national" level the funds necessary to administer matters that it might normally be expected to regulate, such as the trade in agricultural products or commerce throughout the entire country. In particular, there were difficulties with pervasive banditry, the regulation of the markets, and the creation of roads, trade centers, and other facilities to serve general trade.

Islam was represented in the formal political system at both the local and the national levels. At the local level persons were chosen to serve as guardians of Islamic ceremony, recorders, assisters in life-cycle events, and guardians of custom itself; these persons were specialists and peripheral to the system, dealing with very mundane matters. We know little about the "ruler for worship" at the national center other than that he had a sizeable organization of specialists presumably concentrating on ceremony and recording important events at that level of operation. There was an unfavorable reaction to this political system in some quarters, especially those engaged in mercantile activity. Their criticism related directly to unsafe marketplaces, poor roads, and pervasive banditry. Importantly, it was Muslim leaders from the large, private religious centers that sought to bring order to this chaos through efforts to introduce Islamic commercial law. While there were various official and private efforts to curb brigandage on the trade routes, the major effort at instituting societal reforms to address the entire problem of trade came only with the Paderi movement at the opening of the nineteenth century.

The Paderi movement was an adaptation of Wahhabi ideology from Arabia, which called for close attention to the basic rules and teachings of Islam and ridding religious practice of tendencies they regarded as "non-Islamic," such as saint worship and mysticism. In west Sumatra the Paderis began by seeking converts in target villages and, at the same time, moved against villages that allowed their members to rob merchants moving goods between the upland markets and the two coasts. The Paderis insisted on adherence to the Muslim commercial code, which provided guidelines for free trade, ethics in the marketplace, and the right of merchants to move their goods across territory free of interference. The Paderi were also moralists, regarding market towns as lax in good Islamic behavior. In particular, they loathed gambling, cock fighting, and opium use, which were common in most major market towns.

The value system of the Paderis was societal in scope as well as economic, and consequently the entire matrilineal system espoused by customary law also came under attack. While they dominated a wide number of villages at the height of their power in the 1830s and 1840s, in most cases their reforms were not long-lasting. Apparently Paderis were themselves deeply imbued with the values of the established Minang system and were not ready to do harm to their own female family members by destroying the matrilineal order of society. But they were more successful in persuading the population to devote greater attention to religious practice and thereby increased prayer and Islamic observances. While their efforts to change the local governmental structure were only partially accepted, the Paderis unhinged the political system by deposing the Minang ruler in 1821 and installing their own leader as ruler in his place.

The Paderi success in establishing itself as controller of considerable territory, and its attempts to bring other areas under its jurisdiction, produced a strong reaction from people outside the Paderi zone of influence. The deposed general ruler, representing the views of large numbers of the local chiefs, approached Dutch authorities, asking them to intervene in the war and remove the Paderi presence. In the war between 1821 and 1838 the Dutch ultimately won a bitter campaign, but only after a series of military expeditions into the Paderi-held territory. Fighting as guerrillas, the Paderis garnered support from the local population for a considerable period of time by claiming that the war was a campaign against "disbelievers" *(kafir)*. In truth, it became evident in the latter half of the campaign that the Dutch were seizing political control that would not be relinquished at the conclusion of hostilities. Even the reinstated general ruler of the Minangs, who had been in favor of Dutch intervention in the first place, found Dutch attempts to control the region too invasive; he was removed by the Dutch in 1833, never to be replaced.

Imam Bonjol (d. 1864), the last major leader of the Paderis, used the anti-disbeliever theme quite effectively in the final wave of resistance to Dutch operations; indeed, the legend he created through that resistance ultimately led to his "canonization" as an early "nationalist" leader by the Indonesian Republic in 1945. At the conclusion of the war the militant Paderi ideology dissipated as Minang society made some compromises in order to keep its basic structure. Accordingly, better habits of worship appeared and there was a greater identification of both men and women with Islam, even if most of traditional Minang life continued as it had existed earlier, especially with regard to matrilineal inheritance. In one sense, the Paderis had been successful in changing attitudes about Islam, but only at the price of allowing the Dutch to gain political control over the entire west Sumatran region.

Other Territories under Dutch Control

On Java two "native" states were allowed to exist under the control of Javanese rulers. Two "senior" monarchs ruled at Yogyakarta and Surakarta respectively, each with a junior prince. While European education and lifestyle became increasing popular at these courts, rulers retained important contact with traditional Javanese culture and promoted the arts common to the area prior to the arrival of the Europeans. While a few rulers were pious Muslims, most were inclined toward Javanese values with only nominal allegiance to Islam. Consequently, court custom and intellectual life showed a penchant for Javanese symbolism, Javanese ethical and cultural concepts, and placing Islam in a Javanese cultural context. In each of the two Javanese states an office for religious officials was located in the capital city, usually next to the chief mosque. The office of religious affairs oversaw the placement of mosque officials throughout the realm, gave guidance on matters of religious importance, often through the use of jurisprudential opinions *(fatwa)*, and assumed the preservation and upkeep of holy places, including the tombs of the earlier rulers of each state. The religious functionaries in those institutions were recruited from within the administrative class, and within that group, from descendants of officials who had held those positions earlier. Outside of this "official" Islam there were a large number of independent clerics operating throughout society, most being connected with private religious schools that acted as centers of influence in rural areas. They taught the local population the rudiments of Islam and often acted as religious intercessors for the nearby nominal Muslim population.

Regarding Aceh, the Dutch signed an agreement with the English in 1871 verifying Dutch rights throughout Sumatra in order to preclude British assumption of control there. To strengthen their claims of authority the Dutch then sent two expeditions to Aceh; the second one successfully occupied the capital at Kuta Raja in 1873. The sultan and his court fled to the interior and called on all elements of the society to "expel" the foreigner, with both the traditional chiefs and the independent Islamic clerics joining in that resistance. This war lasted nearly forty years, until approximately 1912, during which time the Dutch were alternately beleaguered in the chief port or forced to carry out expeditions into the interior. Muslim clerics were very prominent in the Acehnese military operations against Dutch units, serving as militia and, on occasion, as military leaders. Dutch control over the territory was finalized by decisive campaigns in 1903, when the sultan surrendered. During the pacification the traditional Acehnese political system continued to function, even though the sultanate was located in Pidië, a city in the interior. Regional chiefs who came under Dutch military control usually chose to cooperate with the Dutch, without, however, abandoning their allegiance to the Acehnese ruler in principle.

The British Colonial System

The British leased the island of Penang from Kedah in 1769 to establish a way station between India and China for its ships engaged in trade between those two regions of Asia. When "temporary control" of Java and other Dutch Company territories occurred in the Napoleonic Wars, there was a faction, with Thomas Stamford Raffles its most pronounced proponent, that wanted to expand British influence throughout the Southeast Asian region. Accordingly attempts were made to secure trade arrangements with independent rulers on Sumatra, on the Malay Peninsula, on northern Borneo, and in the Sulu area. This sense of British mission, eventually known as the "Forward Movement," was not generally supported by the British administrators in India, who only wanted safe sea lanes and some intermediate ports in Southeast Asia to enhance its prosperous trade with China. However, both sides were pleased when Raffles signed a lease with the Malay ruler of Singapore Island in 1819 and built a port there. Singapore and Penang, along with two later additions, Melaka and Province Wellesley, were known as the Straits Settlements.

The prosperity of the British operations at Penang and Singapore attracted the attention of the rulers of the Malay states, who began copying some of the British institutions. They also welcomed British commercial operations—in agriculture, jungle gathering, and using imported Chinese labor. In the 1870s there was enough British investment in the states that there were calls by British businessmen and officials for British control of the region; subsequently intervention took place. British advisers were assigned throughout the area, with four states—Selangor, Pahang, Perak, and component parts of Negri Sembilan—brought together in the Federated Malay States. Johore was not included, and the northern states of Perlis, Kedah, Trengganu, and Kelantan remained as Siamese vassals until 1909, when they too were transferred to the authority of Great Britain. These latter four states, with Johore, were known as the "unfederated" states.

In the northern Borneo area in 1846, a private kingdom headed by James Brooke (r. 1848–1868) was established in Sarawak, and in 1877 the British Borneo Company was established in the Sabah region, both having treaty ties to the British and tapping into private British capital in the Straits Settlements. In 1888 a British protectorate was established over Sarawak, North Borneo, and the Malay state of Brunei.

Governance in the Straits Settlements and Labuan Island off Brunei was based on a Royal Charter of Justice of 1826 that called for a British system of public and private law "based on common law, equity, and local and imperial legislation." This applied to everyone living in the Straits Settlements, but decisions in petty civil matters were delegated to the local "captains" of the Malays, Chinese, and Indians respectively, who were to use good judgment and the customs of their communities. In the Malay community some "Islamic" principles were used for adjudication when Muslims were involved in marriage, divorce, and inheritance disputes. As well, these "captains" were required to keep registers of marriages, births, deaths, and the arrivals and departures of members of their communities. The district police also came under the supervision of the captains. In 1880, under pressure from the Muslim community, an ordinance was passed permitting the British governor to appoint a religious judge, actually selected by the Muslims of an area, who was given jurisdiction over cases of marriage and divorce among Muslims. Later legislation defined the legal authority more fully. The Mohammadan Marriage Ordinance gave power to religious judges to register marriages and divorces and to set the rules for resolving marriage disputes. In the early part of the twentieth century, an appeals process was instituted and an Islamic legalist *(mufti)* was attached to each registrar to give jurisprudential advice on appeals involving Islamic principles.

Religious endowments were governed by the Mohammadan and Hindu Religious and Charitable Endowments Act of 1905, which allowed the governor to appoint persons to oversee endowments that, in the governor's opinion, needed government supervision. British subjects formed the boards for such oversight, which created some mild resentment in the religious communities affected, even though all parties regarded such boards as a necessity. It was the composition of the boards that was at issue, of course, as they contained no local members, only expatriate British.

The pilgrimage was of special concern, as Singapore was the primary departure point for Muslims in Southeast Asia undertaking that rite. In the nineteenth century the number of pilgrims was in the hundreds; in the twentieth century, the low thousands. In 1900 nearly 14,000 pilgrims departed from Singapore, most of them in British ships, but the number rose and fell throughout the era, with some 11,374 departing from Singapore in 1939.[13] Many prospective pilgrims from the Dutch areas used Singapore, since strictures and limitations were placed on the pilgrimage at Dutch ports. Private pilgrim agents were established in Singapore to facilitate the traffic, making considerable profit by arranging passages and providing accommodations in Singapore and Arabia. Some of these agents were honest, while others lacked integrity. Especially disturbing were the work contracts made for transient pilgrims from the Indonesian territories, who were assigned work on plantations in the nearby Malayan states. They were often mistreated and overworked for very low pay.

The British were usually concerned with the health conditions of the pilgrimage because the ships frequently carried contagious diseases from port to port. Late in the nineteenth century there were several international conferences to address this problem, and in 1894 an international "sanitary convention" was signed to which, inter alia, the Ottomans and the British were signatories. In Singapore this led to the promulgation of the "Indian Pilgrims Regulations and Passenger Ships Ordinance of 1897," which set out regulations on shipping schedules for the timely delivery of pilgrims and laid down regulations concerning inspection and hygienic arrangements. In 1905 the "Pilgrim Passenger Brokers Ordinance" was enacted to licence pilgrim brokers and assure that they followed regulations for pilgrims regarding proper documentation and medical tests. As well, every Muslim had to have a valid British pilgrim's pass, register with the pilgrim officer at the British consulate in Jeddah upon arrival of the ship, and deposit the return portion of his ticket at that office. The pilgrim officer, usually a Muslim Malay from Singapore, accounted for all the pilgrims and arranged for the personal belongings of pilgrims who died to be sent on to their kin. These acts and ordinances were updated several times during the era.

Early British education policy regarding Malays was undefined, piece-meal, and adaptive to conditions, especially when the jurisdiction applied only to the Straits Settlements. At Singapore the first schools taught general subject matter in the morning, while the afternoons were reserved for Qur'an learning, which most Malay parents regarded as essential. In Province Wellesley, the Qur'an schools were promoted as Malay language schools with general education and Qur'an learning. In general, British administrators were skeptical about such schools, regarding them as lacking proper levels of mathematics, science, and English-language training.

Later in the nineteenth century, particularly when the Federated States were formed, the policy was more defined, for it was decided that Malay officials should receive European education with English as the language of instruction because they would constitute a new governing elite. The remainder of the Malay population was to have a basic education suitable for agriculturalists. There was no provision for training people to fill administrative posts in the new civil service and private-sector firms. With the posting of a permanent education officer in 1903 this policy was changed to allow more children entry to the system, but education policy always aimed to serve upper-class Malay children. Particularly in the era between 1916 and 1931, Malay education was upgraded with the founding of the Sultan Idris Training College–SITC to prepare teachers for the general Malay schools, and the Malay College at Kuala Kangsar was structured to train the children of the elite. By 1941 the number of pupils in various schools totaled 316,000, mostly in elementary education, but some craft and technical schools had been instituted as well.[14]

The Muslim response to education took several directions. First the Islamic religious schools using Arabic and Malay as languages of instruction continued to operate and the numbers of students and graduates increased during this period. The largest gains were in the "unfederated" states of Perlis, Kedah, Kelantan, and Trengganu. The "Tok Kenali" schools of Kelantan in the 1930s, which attracted students from throughout the Malay world, including Indochina, were a special addition to this effort. The system's founder, Syakh Tok Kenali (d. 1933) introduced general subject matter into the curriculum in addition to religious subjects, and he employed styles of teaching not ordinarily used in the Islamic intermediate schools. In 1935 there were fifty-eight government schools in Kelantan with 4,863 pupils, while students in the Tok Kenali schools were only slightly below that figure.[15] In addition, a new Muslim secondary school (madrasah) was introduced by the modernist Muslims, where Islamic sciences and general subject matter existed alongside one another, and nearly all subjects were taught in Malay. At the senior levels of this new system, such as the Madrasat Al-Hamidiah, founded in 1906 near Alor Setar, religious scholars were found who had some knowledge of general subject matter such as elementary science, mathematics, and Malay literature. In Johore around 1895, both an education department and an Islamic affairs department were established, which broadened education considerably while imposing standards for common operation and curriculum supervision. At Muar an institute for pedagogy was founded where Islamic sciences, general knowledge, and teaching methodology were taught as a means of providing teachers for the entire system.

Nationalist sentiment was slow in forming in the British Zone, with the first organizations devoted to attaining independence appearing only in 1945 and 1946. Prior to that, in the late 1930s, Malay groups were founded that called for a united Malay political front. The Kesatuan Melayu Muda–KMM (Young Malay Union), the Malayan Democratic Union–MDU, the United Malay National Organisation–UMNO, and the Malayan Indian Congress–MIC all came into existence during that time period, and the Malayan Chinese Association–MCA a few years later. These associations did call for an eventual end to British colonialism, but mostly the groups applied pressure politics to narrower goals concerned with the advancement of the particular ethnic group with which the association identified itself.

The Federated Malay States

One group of states has been chosen to illustrate how Malay-Muslims were organized politically and how they fared in the British colonial system. This particular grouping, the Federated States, consisted of Pahang, Selangor, Perak, and the components of Negri Sembilan. Using the typology for Islamic states outlined in the chapter these states fit well into the vassal model. Each state was headed by a ruler bearing a royal title, usually "sultan" or "maharaja," and also the older Malay title of "paramount ruler" *(Ieang Yang Pertuan),* who had high respect in his state and was accorded honor through a sophisticated court ritual. The ruler's position was hereditary but usually confused by the contending claims of other members of the royal family. A group of state officers assisted the ruler in administering the state, with personnel usually drawn from the extended royal family. Principal among whom were the chief minister, the defense and police minister, the treasurer, the heir apparent, the keeper of the royal household, and often, the harbormaster. The ruler's symbolic control extended throughout the state, but his real control was limited to the area that he himself ruled directly and where his economic resources were concentrated.

Within each state, outside the direct control of the ruler, there were areas similar in size known as a districts, each of which was under the control of a district chief, who occupied a hereditary position. Each of these subordinate rulers was assisted by a group of retainers, some free and some slaves, who undertook matters of administration, including that of providing law courts and a system of justice. Prior to British control these district officials lived off the economic resources of their own areas of control and were often wealthier than the state rulers, sometimes competing with them for political influence. In this highly decentralized system the ruler and the district chief traditionally engaged in petty warfare to gain control over territory and enhance their own reputations, but the warfare contributed to general unrest. District chiefs usually ignored the commands and advice of rulers and only reluctantly acceded to the ceremonies of homage required of them during the reign of a state ruler. With the arrival of the British the state ruler was made paramount, challenges to his rule were reduced appreciably, and in no case was there a resort to warfare to resolve such issues.

There was also a subdistrict, centered about a mosque and a large enough number of families to constitute a quorum for Friday prayers. This unit usually consisted of several villages, with a headman and his retinue living in one of the hamlets. He gave direction to the local society and economy of the subdistrict, especially assuring that the appropriate stages of the agricultural cycle started on time and observed accepted custom. He also provided order through a constable, named the people who were to take part in corvee and defense levies, and looked after the welfare of the village in general.

One set of religious specialists was located at the village level under the jurisdiction of the subdistrict chief. They were comprised of the personnel responsible for the mosque and consisted of the prayer leader, the sermon reciter, and the prayer caller. There were no officials at higher levels of government dealing with Islamic matters until late in the century, although on important occasions in the Muslim calendar the rulers at the major population centers did use private Islamic scholars or learned community leaders to give public addresses and prayers.

When these four states came under British control as a result of the Pangkor Engagement in 1874, which the rulers of all four states endorsed, British officials were assigned to each state government. The British resident met regularly with the state ruler and a council of state to discuss state policy; the advice of the British resident was nearly mandatory and, in most cases, adopted as official policy. As a first order of business state revenues were improved, largely by extraction of raw materials, such as tin where it was available, and moving to large-scale agricultural endeavors, particularly rubber and palm-oil plantations. The net effect of this policy was to give considerable wealth to the Malay ruling class and Chinese investors from Singapore, but it marginalized the common Malays, who had before engaged in jungle gathering. They were removed from their homesteads when their land was included in agricultural plantations and forbidden to use the jungles, as they traditionally had, without paying fees. Since Malays lacked capital, education, and technical know-how, they did not usually profit from the economic expansion in the way the Chinese did, which set the stage for resentment and later racial difficulties.

All four states created hierarchies of religious officials, who were given state salaries and made responsible for state religious ceremonies. Mostly such officials were recruited from the traditional Muslim schools operating in the four-state region. Significantly, the new cadre of officials produced law codes incorporating Islamic principles for use in the courts and for religious interpreters of jurisprudence. Religious courts continued to function as they had before the arrival of the British, when they had jurisdiction over all cases concerning Islam, but particularly marriage and divorce. District leaders also had courts of their own; general matters of public welfare and law were at the residency level, where European court personnel were sometimes involved. Judges for the religious courts were appointed by the ruler in council and could be removed by him in the same manner. Between 1901 and 1915 an attempt was made by the British to centralize all courts including those dealing with religious matters, but in 1915 the power to hear appeals from religious courts was returned to the control of the state ruler, who was free to hear the appeals himself or to form a special body to hear those cases, which occurred in most cases.

Other Territories under British Control

As stated above, Kelantan, Trengganu, Kedah, and Perlis were ceded by Thailand to the British in 1909 and, along with Johore, were known as the "unfederated states," in which a British resident advised the state ruler on all matters except religion and custom. There were religious courts, always with control over marriage, divorce, and inheritance, and sometimes with jurisdiction over matters of morals and ethics. Punishments varied but, unlike in the Federated States where fines were light, more serious punishments sometimes were imposed. For example, in Kedah, flogging and dismemberment, while seldom applied, were inflicted at times. Despite periodic attempts by the British to narrow the jurisdiction of religious courts in the unfederated states, those courts retained a great deal more power and vigor than those in the Federated States.

In Sarawak a British adventurer, James Brooke, signed an agreement with the sultan of Brunei in which he was given control with the title of "Raja." Using the Malay elite already in place, he established rule over the inland peoples and generally "tamed" the countryside, even stopping the traffic in slaves. He was succeeded by two descendants, who ruled until the Japanese invasion in 1942. Great Britain established a protectorate over Sarawak in 1888. There were three chief administrators, all of them Malay, with one given responsibility for the Islamic matters. In the early twentieth century this official was assigned the title of "Lord Religious Leader" and was designated the official head of the Islamic religion in the state, while a second official, the "Lord Judge," was the chief authority on Malay custom and Islamic law. Mosque officials fell under the jurisdiction of the "Lord Religious Leader," where there were three officials for each mosque: again, the prayer leader, the sermon reciter, and the prayer caller. At the main mosque in Kuching these specialists were given the honorific "sir" before their names, were usually of aristocratic birth, and received a government salary. The Lord Judge headed a religious court system that dealt with matters of Malay custom and Islamic law. The Muslim community was apparently satisfied with the control of two officials over religious matters until the rise of the modernist movement in the 1920s, when modernist Muslim advocates charged that the system—dominated as it was by traditionalist-minded officials—did not seek to advance the cause of Muslims as much as was possible, although they were not really very specific as to the meaning of that criticism.

The sultanate of Brunei entered the nineteenth century in a weakened political and economic condition, and it steadily lost territory, population, and influence throughout the century. The 1906 treaty between Great Britain and the sultan of Brunei retained the protectorate but allowed Great Britain to assign a "resident" to Brunei to give advice on all matters of state except that concerning Islam. The sultan agreed in advance to follow that advice. It was specifically mentioned that an attempt would be made to bring state matters into the same general framework as that already existing in the Malay states, with the implication that Brunei's future was to be tied closely to developments there.

Two pieces of legislation were enacted in the early part of the period that determined the Islamic infrastructure of the Brunean state. They were the "Mohammadan Laws Enactment of 1912" and the "Mohammadan Marriage and Divorce Registration Enactment of 1913," which reflected similar legislation enacted in the federated Malay states during the same period. That legislation laid the framework for the Islamic court system in which religious judges and legalists operated, drawn from the learned Muslim population. Mosque officials existed throughout the countryside, with the standard offices being prayer leader, sermon reciter, and prayer caller; the mosque at Brunei city was designated the state mosque and its officials awarded the special title of "honorable" to set them off from functionaries of other regions.

The Siamese Region

The strongest indigenous Southeast Asian state during the nineteenth century was the Thai kingdom of Siam, the successor to Ayuthia, whose rulers stressed centralization and integration of territory already under Siamese control, along with a feeling of nationalism among the people in that territory. It fit the hierarchy model of government and societal organization outlined in Chapter 2. The political system constructed by King Mongkut (r. 1851–1868) and King Chulalongkorn (r. 1868–1910) provided a general pattern of Siamese officialdom over like-sized provinces, owing responsibility to a larger unit called a region, which was in turn responsible to the royal government in Bangkok. Officials at the local level were regarded as employees of the national government who were expected to know the Thai language and the etiquette of the Siamese court and government. The mores and values existent in Bangkok, many of them based on Theravada Buddhist practice and the remainder on Thai ethnic culture, were deemed the standard for all parts of the kingdom. In the Malay south, political consolidation consisted of bringing some of the areas into the kingdom itself and building a series of vassal states for the remainder. The major arenas for this effort were at Patani, Kedah, and Perak. While this policy had some success, British inroads on the Malay Peninsula checked Siam's efforts, and in 1826 the British-Siamese Treaty recognized Perlis, Kedah, Kelantan, and Trengganu as under Siamese suzerainty, while states to the south were regarded as falling in the British zone of protection.

The state of Patani was placed under the control of the Siamese governor of Songhkla in 1791, and shortly after the start of the nineteenth century it was divided into seven parts. The Malay Muslim ruler, Dato Pengkalan (ruled 1791–1808), was removed, sent into exile, and not replaced. Further attempts to centralize were made in 1901–1902 by King Chulalongkorn, and in 1932 when Siam became a constitutional monarchy.

Siamese policy during this entire era was aimed at forcing a change in attitude and custom among the Malay-Muslim population. King Chulalongkorn regarded them as totally foreign in all matters and readily used the derogatory term "alien" (khaek) in referring to them. He also came to the conclusion that their "foreign" ways could not be allowed to continue and insisted that Muslims adopt Siamese culture, particularly in language and dress, as indications of their membership in his nation. Malay-Muslim reaction to such Siamese attitudes was hostile, and throughout the era there were low-level insurgencies—the most serious was at Ban Nam Sai in 1922 —that were put down by Siamese security forces.

Throughout this era there were no Siamese officials or institutions that assisted the Islamic community with the administration of Muslim matters. However, there was an accommodation made in the late Chulalongkorn era when Siamese civil judges were assigned cases regarding marriage and inheritance that previously had been handled by local Muslim religious judges. The new arrangement allowed a Siamese judge to assign one Muslim religious judge from a pool at his disposal to hear a case involving religious law and then to either verify or change the decision made by that official. Further accommodations were made in 1923 when King Rama VI (r. 1910–1925) issued a proclamation stating that the practice of Islam was permitted and that any laws conflicting with it should be removed, which had some effect in lowering administrative harassment of the population and allowed courts to consider Muslim cases on the basis of decisions of Muslim judges. However, with the end of the strong monarchy and the institution of the Constitution of 1935, nationalism became important again, and new laws were enacted in 1940 that had an adverse impact on the Malay region in the years immediately afterwards.

The vassal states of Perak, Kedah, Kelantan, and Trengganu retained limited autonomy throughout the period of Siamese overlordship. The rulers regularly sent the traditional triennial tribute as a sign of their vassalage, but they maintained their own government structure, which was similar to that of the Malay principalities in the British zone. However, when Siamese administrative techniques were introduced in the vassal states, there was greater control by the ruler over subordinate officials because another layer of government was installed. There was a strong reaction to Siamese overlordship in Kedah in the 1840s when an attempt was made to bring that state into the central administrative system of Siam. However, the Siamese were dissuaded from that venture after religious scholars declared a holy war (perang sabil) and popular Malay militias moved north, destroying Buddhist shrines. Otherwise opposition to the Siamese was not strong, largely because these states were on the periphery of the Siamese kingdom and were generally left alone. The most notable local Muslim ruler of the age was Ahmad Tajuddin I (r. 1802–1821, 1841–1854) of Kedah, who challenged Siamese authority, insisting on a vassal relationship when the Thai government wanted central control of the area.

Throughout these vassal states a mosque organization existed at the local level, which was larger than in the Malay states to the south. Significantly, the most prominent Islamic schools were located in Kelantan and Trengganu, and their trainees filled many of the local positions of government and the Muslim communities within those states. Also, in each state there were officials at the sultan's court charged with administrating Islamic matters. In Kelantan, for example, a jurist at the royal court compiled a complete listing of the mosques and prayer houses throughout the state, enabling the royal court to assert a nominal jurisdiction over these institutions and the personnel that served in them. At Trengganu there was an official called the chief Islamic scholar (shaykh al-Islam) who was an adviser to the sultan on Islamic matters and served on the state council, and another official undertook the role of chief jurist (mufti). In this respect the development of state institutions dealing with Islam were slightly more apparent than at the courts of Malay states under British control.

In the Siamese vassal states only a few schools operated with Westernized curricula and Malay instruction; they were all in Kedah at Changkon in 1892, at Kulim in 1896, and Alor Setar in 1897. But, throughout the century the Qur'an schools described earlier were in existence and provided a rudimentary Muslim education for a considerable number of males. There were intermediate Islamic schools that offered learning at a higher level of Islamic education; the most renowned were located at Duyung and Paloh in Trengganu, and at Kota Bharu in Kelantan. At Kota Bharu those schools were located near the central mosque and consisted of small huts of bamboo and *attap* where religious teachers taught students from throughout the region. They ranged in size from several persons up to several hundred. They were often boarding schools where students assisted in the occupation of the teacher, frequently agriculture or trading, and they studied traditional Islamic sciences. In general the trend was very much like that in the federated Malay states, with a slightly greater role played by Islamic specialists in the vassal states.

The French Colonial System

In the late nineteenth century the Indochina region came under French colonial control and consisted of Cochinchina (southern Vietnam), Annam (central Vietnam), Tonkin (northern Vietnam), Cambodia (Khmer), and Laos. The French system varied across Indochina according to the area, but it was a dual system, with French officers serving alongside indigenous administrators and giving them "advice." The French decided that, since the customs of the two Muslim groups in Indochina—the Malays and the Chams—were different from those of the local Annamites and Khmers where they resided, they should be classed as special population groups, in some cases with their own governors and local headmen.

In Cambodia the French resident there adopted policies that had the effect of stripping the Cambodian monarch of administrative and fiscal authority but left undisturbed his control over the local court system, the village education system, and religious institutions, especially the Buddhist sangha but including the Muslims as well. The Muslim response to the state-sponsored schools was poor. In 1941 it was reported that only seventy Muslims were in the state-sponsored system and all of them at the lowest level. Muslims clearly preferred traditional Muslim education.[16] The exact number of Muslim schools was not given by ethnologists of the period, but there was mention in their findings that there were many "low-level" religious schools, similar to the intermediate Muslim schools of the Malayan states, and that there were several more advanced schools, often run by religious scholars from Kelantan or Patani. In great part, however, those Muslims students seeking to become religious scholars themselves went to study in Kelantan, Patani, Singapore, and Makkah.

The Spanish Colonial System

At the beginning of the nineteenth century, the Spanish claimed jurisdiction over the southern islands of the Philippine chain, although they occupied only strong points at Cagayan de Oro on the north coast of Mindanao and at Zamboanga on the western side of that island. Otherwise, the Spanish simply reacted to slave raids in the Visayan Islands carried out by groups from the Muslim territories, usually from well-known slave centers on Jolo, at Illana Bay, at Pollok, and several other ports on Mindanao. In the second half of the nineteenth century, the Spanish became fearful that other countries might take over the Muslim territories for their own colonial interests, so they coerced treaties with local rulers, carried out campaigns against resisting rulers, and occupied key population points and overland routes. The military campaigns were long-lasting and had to be repeated several times. However, by the 1890s the entire region was generally under Spanish control, although the collection of taxes was difficult and military action continued against small groups engaged in sudden raids. Although earlier Spanish efforts included Christianization, at this time they only placed missionary-priests in the region without insistence on conversion. With the withdrawal of Spanish troops in the Spanish-American War of 1898 de facto political control reverted to local rulers.

The Tausug of the Sulu Archipelago

The Tausug state in the nineteenth century affords us another opportunity to observe the workings of an Islamic sultanate up close. During the first seventy years of the nineteenth century, the Sulu sultanate controlled this region—politically, militarily, and economically—under the control of the Tausug elite, which brought together the other peoples of the region, including those on the coastal areas of north Borneo, parts of the southeastern coastal areas of Mindanao, and the southern reaches of the island of Pahlawan. The structure of the sultanate was less hierarchal and more representative of public interests than that of its neighbor Brunei; accordingly, it fit the vassal model described in Chapter 2 and was similar to that of the Malay sultanates on the Malay Peninsula. The officers of state included the chief minister, the chamberlain, the fort master, the harbormaster, a state treasurer, a minister for internal security, a guardian of customary law, and a naval minister. The sultan and the sultanate were financially supported through profits from crown lands, by the profits of trading arrangements made in partnership with private entrepreneurs, through the booty of military expeditions, and from a portion of fines and fees levied throughout the sultanate. In particular, the excise taxes from trade with China were sufficient to make the ruler independent enough from feudal dues to allow him to build an imperium.

The political system was organized by districts, with a governor *(panglima)* in charge of each who became the military commander during times of war. Usually district officers were not from the aristocracy and could be from the subject peoples in the sultanate, such as a Samal or a Bajau, and sometimes were even former slaves. Commanders were assisted by subdistrict officers. Local chiefs *(dato)* exercised almost absolute control over the people in their localities, which might only be a small canton or, in other cases, large areas with many villages and a scattered population. This control was mitigated in some situations by the use of councils, usually consisting of important people, elders, and some religious officials. At all levels there were personal retainers who assisted state officers, many of them free, some slave. Rulers at all levels acted in their own stead, usually not as consensus makers of the population they ruled, confirming the judgment that they were part of the vassal pattern and distinctly not related to the community model.

In religious matters the ruler appointed a chief judge, usually a foreign Muslim with considerable learning in Islamic sciences, who resided at the capital. He advised the sultan and others on matters involving Islamic requisites, even to the point of sometimes reviewing decisions of the state council for conformity with Islamic standards. The chief mosque also had one prayer leader, four sermon reciters, and four prayer callers, who were appointed by the sultan and received a state stipend. There were prayer leaders at all the mosques and prayer houses throughout the capital city, but it is uncertain whether they owed their position to the sultan and whether they received a state stipend. Finally, a number of Qur'an schools were maintained by the sultan, especially on the island of Sulu, and were paid for either from the proceeds of donated property or by a direct stipend of the sultan. He also supported traveling holy men who claimed descent from the Prophet.

The Tausug sultanate was built on an economic system that gathered goods from outlying areas and then sold them to interested parties in and outside its own area of control. Many jungle products were sold to the British in the east; some goods, such as birds' nests, were sold to Chinese traders; and slaves were sold throughout the region. Slavery was the lubrication that enabled the system to function, as the Tausug were short of labor and relied on slaves to open new agricultural lands, gather produce, and assist with shipping. Employing the slave raiders of Balangingi and Iranum in particular, the sultanate sponsored the capture of slaves in the Visayan islands, on Borneo, in the highlands of Mindanao, in Maluku and Sulawesi, and other places, for use throughout the Sulu zone. Slavery was highly important as a supplement to existing labor pools, and the social system was tolerant enough to allow for some social mobility, so some slaves were able to attain their freedom or even become part of a Tausug family. But, in large part, the Spanish action against the Muslim areas in the latter part of the nineteenth century was a direct reaction to slave taking in the Visayas, even if other causes existed as well. Considerable numbers of people were engaged in the slave business in one way or another and it was a source of investment and profit. Moreover, those with other economic interests used slaves extensively, and even individual households stood to gain with the addition of slaves to do the labor needed there. It was a popular institution that did not easily disappear.

With the drive of the Spanish to completely dominate the Muslim territories of Sulu and Mindanao in the latter part of the century, the sultanate was severely strained; some of its territory was taken over for direct rule by the Spanish, like the island of Jolo itself, and the sultanate lost much of its ability to affect events throughout the territories it supposedly controlled. Reaction of the Sulu population to the Spanish was strong. The presence of Spanish priests and missionaries, with their constant requests for conversion to Christianity, was particularly disliked. Alongside this, the institution of the head tax and the overweening nature of Spanish military occupation caused strong resentment. The most serious reaction took the form of terror attacks made against non-Muslims—sometimes Spanish, often the Chinese, and sometimes local Christian converts—by dedicated "suicide commandos" (*juramentado; orang jang perang sabil*) who ran amok and indiscriminately struck down all people in their path until killed themselves. Actually, those attacks were not very effective, though unsettling to all non-Muslims.

Other Territories under Spanish Control

The strongest state in Southeastern Mindanao between 1865 and 1885 was the Buayan sultanate, located inland on the Pulangi River. Throughout this period it continued taking captives from the mountain country and trafficked in slaves generally, defying Spain's prohibition on that practice. Power in the Buayan sultanate rested, not with sultan during this era, but rather with an important chieftain known as Datu Utto (r. 1861–1899), although at the end of his career he did in fact proclaim himself sultan. He created a federation of small states and established a capital at Bakat, whose location barred the entry of Spanish forces into the interior. He governed with the assistance of a council and a small administration, but his rule was built on personal following. Accordingly, he had a large retinue of adherents, mostly purchased slaves, who accompanied him, defended him, and carried out his orders. He received the strong support of Muslim teachers (*ʿalim*), and used suicide commandos, dedicated by those Muslim functionaries, against the Spanish, once using forty of them in a single campaign. Neighboring states feared him more than they did the Spanish and consequently made agreements with the Spanish to oppose him. Ultimately,

Spanish diplomacy was successful in wooing all of Dato Utto's allies away from him, so he was isolated and rendered ineffective as a political personality. At this time the Maguindanao sultanate was in decline and chose not to oppose the Spanish conquest of the area. The Maranao in the north-central region around Lake Lanao was militarily reduced in the 1890s, but resistance continued in the form of suicide commandos, ambuscades, and attacks on Spanish outposts.

The American Colonial System

The United States replaced the Spanish in the Philippine Islands in 1898 as a result of the Battle of Manila Bay, and its control was verified shortly thereafter in the Treaty of Paris. The Spanish assertion that the southern islands of the archipelago were part of the colonial possessions it was turning over to the Americans was accepted. The Bates Treaty of 1898 between the United States and the sultan of Sulu, Jamal Kiram I (r. 1894–1904), gave the former further legitimacy in the region, although it was not until after the Philippine-American War (1900–1906) that the United States sent in forces to assert an actual claim. There followed the establishment of army camps and administrative centers from which U.S. officials attempted to enforce their governance.

The American system was centered at the capital, Manila on the island of Luzon, which had also been the Spanish capital. In the Muslim territories of the south the "Moro Province" was established, with governors, military officers on active duty except for the last one, who was a civilian. This arrangement lasted until 1916 when the region was divided into "presidencies" along the lines of the Philippine administrative arrangements elsewhere in the archipelago. The welfare of the Muslims was also safeguarded by the Bureau of Non-Christian Tribes, later the Commission for Mindanao and Sulu, and was charged with preparing the Muslims and other minority peoples for entry into full participation in Philippine society and government. In general, however, limited protection of established customs, and very little preparation for "integration" into wider Philippine society, actually occurred.

There was considerable Muslim displeasure with the entire governmental system imposed on the Muslim population. Initially the population disliked American military and constabulary presence because it interfered with the long-held practice of intergroup feuding, in which neighboring groups bearing grudges attacked and counterattacked one another in low-level fighting, that was sometime mock battle and at other times in earnest. The Americans countered these conflicts with military expeditions, with disastrous results for the Muslims opposing them. These "uprisings" continued throughout the era, although they lessened considerably in intensity and number by the late 1920s, when the governorship of Frank Carpenter (term of office 1914–1920) brought most Muslim groups to acceptance of American rule. There was also considerable unhappiness over the decision of the United States to combine the Muslim territories into the Philippine Republic, as it handed control of the Muslim areas over to a government of Hispanicized Christians who had long been enemies of the Muslims.

No attempt was made to structure institutions that would assist the local Muslims to realize their religious obligations, although some nonofficial institutions did function. The headmen governed using local custom as a guide, and custom was inextricably entwined with Islamic injunctions and interpretations. Later, under the period of the Bureau of Non-Christian Tribes, some field agents of that unit called for the use of customary law courts *(agama)*, which were to handle Muslim marriage, divorce, and inheritance cases, but the idea was never officially permitted.

American officials sometimes spoke out about Muslim religious practices that they found "unhelpful" in their "civilizing mission." The pilgrimage was one of the practices that was regarded as having a pernicious influence on the inhabitants. Officials observed that "fanaticism"—namely, anti-American attitudes and hostile action against Americans—was often associated with Muslim clerics and those Muslims who had been on the pilgrimage.[17] While the Americans placed no limitations on the pilgrimage, and officially it was stated that Muslim acts of worship and ceremony were left to the Islamic community itself to support and undertake, administrative impediments to such travel were not removed to assist those undertaking the journey.

American-style schools were established in the Muslim territories beginning in 1903, but Muslims used them rarely. For example, in 1914 there were ninety-seven schools, with a total of 14,800 enrolled in public school and another 4,272 in private schools out of an estimated 126,000 children between the ages of seven and fourteen. The number of Muslims in those schools constituted less than 2,000 pupils. By 1939, however, the ratio was considerably better, as Muslim suspicions had lessened due in large part to the Muslim elite, which saw advantages in the American system, especially in gaining appointed positions.[18] There are no figures, however, for attendance at the Muslim religious schools; but the figure was certainly higher than for the public schools throughout the period. The languages of instruction in the local school system were Arabic, often Malay, and local languages, all written in Arabic script.

Japanese Domination (1939–1945)

Japanese domination of Southeast Asia began in 1939 and ended in 1945, a period of time that changed the political landscape markedly. This short historical epoch arose out of Japanese nationalism, which, following a particular interpretation of imperial practice, strove to bring all of East and

Southeast Asia under Japanese control and to subjugate the economic and political resources existent there to the advancement of Japan. In 1940–1941, Japan moved into the fringe areas of Southeast Asia, insisting on military occupation of Indochina so that it could establish bases there. In December 1941, military, naval, and air attacks were directed simultaneously at the Malay Peninsula, Java, and the Philippines, which generally eliminated the British, American, and Dutch forces and brought all of Southeast Asia under Japanese control by May 1942. The Japanese drove into the Southwest Pacific area as far as the Solomon Islands, where the Allied counterattack beginning in late 1942 eventually reached the Philippines in 1944. When Japan surrendered in 1945, the remainder of Southeast Asia was still under its military jurisdiction, but was passed back to previous colonial control.

Japanese control in Southeast Asia was a combination of military (or naval) presence and special arrangements made with the indigenous elites of the regions it occupied. Military government was instituted in most places, with one commander per region, who had an administration consisting of bureaus manned by Japanese personnel in the fields of general affairs, internal affairs, justice, police, finance, traffic, propaganda, and religion. These replaced the colonial administrations, but integrated many of the local personnel from the colonial systems into the new Japanese organization. Except in Indochina, former European administrators were interned and replaced by local administrators who took directions from Japanese officers. Japanese military government varied in its relationship with local officials. In the eastern Indonesian archipelago, where the Japanese navy was in charge, Japanese officials kept indigenous participation in administration under close scrutiny and quashed all attempts of the local peoples to seek any kind of control over their own affairs. On the other hand, where army control predominated, as in the Philippines and on Java, efforts were made to encourage local political participation and the development of some nationalist identity, even if it was carefully controlled and directed.

The Japanese were engaged in a war of tremendous consequence, and indeed, Japan's very survival in the form that it existed depended on success in that endeavor. It is not surprising, then, that Japanese attitudes were highly nationalistic and reflected the overriding consideration of winning that war, with all other goals subordinate to ultimate military victory. At the same time, behind that immediate priority lay the long-range purpose of an international order for East Asia, guaranteed by Japan, which featured a series of Asian states, controlled by local peoples, with an interconnected economy that would fuel the industry of Japan and allow it to become a world power. This theme was generally given the name "Greater East Asia Co-Prosperity Sphere," and, while certainly important to propaganda, it was viewed as coming to fruition only after the Pacific War had been success-fully completed.

In the meantime, the primary policy was to redirect all the economies of the Southeast Asian territories wartime needs, with goods crucial to the war effort given priority and the entire population mobilized to that end. Rubber, oil, and metals were particularly necessary. The new conditions resulted in a striking loss of production, ultimately reduced to about one-fourth of what prewar production figures had been throughout the region. Food production lagged badly so that general hunger was common, and textiles were in very short supply. The war effort also demanded the forma-tion of labor battalions to serve throughout the Japanese-controlled region, often under extremely bad conditions, and some women were taken to serve in Japanese military brothels. The result was that Japan did obtain the supplies it needed to carry out the war, but the relentless collection poli-cies, along with harsh treatment of civilians, created extremely low morale among most peoples of Southeast Asia.

The Japanese attempted to win the Muslim leaders to their cause and use them to control the population. They allowed religious officials in the Malay states to retain their high status as members of the religious councils that had received legitimacy during the British period, even though their work was undercut by the Japanese military administration to some degree. The Japanese also tried, unsuccessfully, to nourish good relations with the religious officials at royal courts. Further, on two occasions they sponsored conferences of Muslim leaders and notables. The 1942 meeting in Singa-pore brought together the Muslim leadership from Sumatra and Malaya to enlist their support and receive advice on how some sources of irritation to Muslims might be changed for the benefit of both Muslims and Japanese. The meeting in 1944 at Kuala Kangsar discussed details of Muslim worship and devotion, while the Muslim audience also had to listen to speeches about Japanese war aims. In Aceh new Muslim laws was instituted that cov-ered marriage, divorce, inheritance, pious endowments, and welfare (bayt al-mal) issues. The staffing of the new courts was turned over to the Persa-tuan Ulama Seluruh Aceh–Pusa (All-Aceh Union of Religious Teachers), a religious scholars' organization that was highly disposed toward Japanese authority.

On Java, the Japanese installed an office of religious affairs, which took over some of the personnel, records, and duties of the Office for Internal Affairs from the Dutch period. It was initially headed by a Japanese officer, who had his Japanese staff members dress in the white robes that pilgrims often wore, pray in mosques, and generally act like Muslims. The office was later reorganized to give local personnel important positions, with Hoessin Djajadiningrat (served 1943–1945), a noted Sundanese scholar, as office director. On the other hand, the Japanese did not employ this strategy in

the Philippines or the eastern Indonesian territories because Muslim officials there were regarded as intractable and opposed to Japanese aims. In
the eastern Indonesian Islands, the Islamic policy consisted of attaching a
group of Japanese scholars to state administrations to foster better ties with
key Muslims, but they were not very successful in that endeavor.

There was support for the Japanese among some Muslim groups, who
willingly acted as guides upon the Japanese arrival and assisted them
throughout their sojourn in Southeast Asia. In Singapore and the Malay
Peninsula region, the Young Malay Union–KMM greeted the Japanese when
they arrived, offering to be their guides, and formed two home-guard units
at Japanese request. In 1945, KMM mobilized Malay support for inclusion
in "Greater Indonesia," which the Japanese were interested in promoting,
but the project was stillborn. In Aceh, Pusa assisted the Japanese in their
landing in March 1942 in the face of Dutch resistance. Not influential at
first, Pusa became prominent midway in the period and occupied many of
the seats on advisory councils in Aceh. On Java, the Japanese replaced the
Muslim unity association, the Majelis Islam A'la Indonesia–Miai (Higher
Islamic Council of Indonesia), formed a short while before the arrival of
the Japanese, with the Majelis Shuro Muslimin Indonesia–Masjoemi (Consultative Council of Indonesian Muslims) in 1943, which took on the role of
mobilizing the Muslim community to assist Japanese war efforts. Masjoemi
raised several units of home guards and held cadre-training sessions that
included indoctrination in Japanese war aims. This sort of cooperative
response was lacking in the southern Philippines and in eastern Indonesia.

In many places there was considerable reaction to Japanese presence
and policies, especially in the last two years of the occupation. First, Muslim leaders disliked imperial ceremonies, particularly the bowing toward
Tokyo at public ceremonies, which seemed too much like the prostration
toward Makkah in standard Islamic prayer. Second, Japanese used mosques
freely, for commemoration ceremonies for fallen Japanese soldiers, as storage areas, and as bathing places. Furthermore, the Japanese usually insisted
on prior censorship of the Friday sermon, or forbade it altogether, as happened in parts of Sumatra for a time. People in home-guard and administrative positions were discouraged from fasting during Ramadan.

There were isolated uprisings against the Japanese, as in Tasikmalaya
and Ceribon in 1944, because rice deliveries to those cities were severely
curtailed. There was rioting in Blitar in 1945 because of poor treatment of
volunteer recruits receiving military training there. At Amuntai in South
Kalimantan there was an attempt to drive the Japanese out and establish an
Islamic state; it failed. Throughout 1944 the Dayak people of West Kalimantan, including many Muslims, killed individual Japanese in ambuscades,
indicating weaknesses in the Japanese security system.

The most serious resistance to the Japanese, however, took place in the southern Philippines. There the Muslim population was divided in its response to the Japanese. Some of the elite, particularly those families with considerable land, felt obliged to cooperate, while other parts of the population resented the Japanese presence and either tacitly or openly supported the anti-Japanese guerrillas. Retaliation against local populations for guerrilla actions led to a revival of the suicide commando *(juramentado),* who attacked small groups of Japanese and died in the fighting. Also, there were guerrilla units dominated by Muslim fighters. The most prominent was that formed by Salipada Pendatun (active 1944), who led a joint Christian-Muslim force, known as the Maranao Militia, that operated in the central Mindanao region. The southern Philippines theater was more roundly anti-Japanese than other areas of Southeast Asia.

Finally, the impact of the Japanese period on the history of Southeast Asia was profound and had both short-term and long-range effects. First, it interrupted European and American colonial control of the region, which was never to reestablish itself with the strength it had had earlier. Second, it unleashed incipient nationalist movements, at first only as a means of controlling the territories with their new leaders but that led to the eventual emergence of new nation-states. Third, it severely harmed the economies that had been crafted by the colonial powers and made reconstruction of them so difficult that they never reemerged with their previous efficiency and power, thereby leaving the way clear for the eventual development of new national economies in the second half of the twentieth century. Fourth, the total-war mobilization caused severe hardships throughout the region that had a profound impact on all the populations that survived. Islam underwent no great changes during the war and its followers suffered as much as any other group, even though at times they were given "special treatment" in some places. Muslims and Muslim institutions survived, but significantly emerged from the period with about the same strength vis-à-vis other actors as it had possessed going into the Japanese period.

The Muslim Community

Religious Elements
Islamic Specialists
There continued to be five Muslim specialist groups in the Muslim Zone throughout this era: government officers concerned specifically with Islamic matters, functionaries dealing with the operation of mosques, private scholars undertaking the dissemination and furtherance of Islamic knowledge, leaders of "Islamic" movements, and intellectuals. Alongside these specialists, several groups of adherents were visible for their supporting roles, although they were not themselves in positions of authority or masters of religious knowledge. Here one can define those who had under-

taken the pilgrimage, disciples of mystic saints, those who were students or followers of particular teachers, and those who were activists following an Islamic leader. They informally composed a cadre for the Muslim community.

Muslim advisers, most of them scholars (ʿalim) at the royal courts, underwent significant change in this era. In the Malay states the advisers were elevated in importance because religion was deemed an important part of each ruler's responsibilities not subject to the scrutiny of British advisers, and more attention was devoted to Islamic education; hence, more Muslim specialists were needed. The opposite occurred in the American zone, where the eclipse of the existing sultanates meant that religious advisers, along with regular officials, were swept away, while those outside the royal courts were deprived of the high moral support and modest financial assistance they had received earlier. In the Netherlands Indies general erosion of the position of the court scholars occurred because the centralizing efforts by the Dutch ended many royal courts and diminished the influence of those remaining. Religious advisers were losers as a result. Much the same was true for judges (qadi); many lost their positions or had their jurisdictions altered as a result of changes in laws or assignments of cases to particular courts. Overall, there was less room for Islamic law in the colonial world, whether it was applying the principles of Syafiʾi jurisprudence (fiqh) or attempting to attain some approximation of sacred law (shariʾah).

On the other hand, the legal reforms of the Dutch in areas under their direct control, especially Java and Madura, produced "religious councils" at the district level of administration, which placed the council members (mufti) in paid positions, with authority to interpret religious law for the courts and local administrators. That was undoubtedly a gain for the specialists involved. A similar trend was apparent among the Chams and Malays in Indochina, where state-sponsored Muslim religious officials were installed at the district level to serve some of the religious needs of the population. Two examples serve to illustrate these advisers. Sayyid Uthman al-ʿAlawi (d. 1914) was employed at the height of his career by the Dutch administration as "honorary adviser for Muslim matters," wherein he explained intricate matters of Muslim jurisprudence to Dutch officials. Abdul Razak bin Hassanudin (d. 1939) was a religious judge, then minister of religion, and finally a member of the council of state of Brunei.

Mosque specialists were standard across the Muslim Zone, with the prayer caller, prayer leader, and sermon reciter usual in most locations, performing fairly common duties and responsibilities. In some mosques, however, there was also a reciter of religious texts, who performed at feasts and private residences when asked to do so. These officials had no fixed salary, but received presents at each rite and ceremony performed. The Javanese system was more elaborate, however. At Gresik in the nineteenth century, for example, the regional governor was assisted by eight district prayer leaders *(penghulu)*, who oversaw lesser mosque officials, conducted prayer, registered marriages and divorces, and looked after the graves of holy men in the district. The prayer leaders probably had control over endowments and the tax revenues devoted to the care of the shrines. There were also 63 sermon reciters *(khatib)*, who assisted the prayer leaders in services and carried out most of the administrative duties of the mosques, including general upkeep. There were 70 custodians for the mosques and 466 "small group prayer leaders" *(modin)* who prayed with worshipers at the mosque, signaled the holy days with the beat of the giant drum on the verandah of the mosque, and washed and wound corpses. This group of officials was supported by government salaries in a few cases, but mostly by a voluntary tax on grain harvest and taxes on livestock, precious metals, and trade activities.[19] There was also the curious practice of any father who had twenty-five children "giving" the last child to the religious officials of the local mosque, who then allowed the child to be redeemed for a modest contribution.

Private religious scholars *(ʿalim)* remained important during this epoch and the schools where they taught increased appreciably in number. At Muslim boarding schools in central and eastern Java, religious scholars who taught there enjoyed great prestige among their students, former students, and the population near the school. They were independent of civil authority and often critical of life in the courts of the rulers and urban life. They usually, but not always, identified with the local population in the neighborhood of the schools, serving as a source of religious advice. Emblematic of such scholars was an important group in Kelantan noted for their piety, adherence to Sunni theological teaching standards, and association with established mystical orders. Nearly all studied in Makkah at some point in their careers and adapted Arabic textbooks to the needs of their Malay students in Kelantan. The most noted was Abdul Samad b. M. Saleh (Tuan Tebal; d. 1891). Not only did Tuan Tebal teach, he published a religious magazine and offered advice to those from the surrounding region who sought it.

In the cities religious scholars fulfilled the roles of teaching at mosques, in free-standing schools, or as advisers for the general population; some even specialized in propagation or "revivalist" activities. In the early twentieth century, in particular, these religious scholars took a pronounced role in founding organizations that were intended to serve the Muslim community. They remained very much the influential class they had become in centuries past, but whereas their predecessors had been mystics, the new scholars were given over to religious law and societal activism. An example of this type of religious leader was Abdul Halim Hasan (d. 1969), who taught and worked in and near Medan on Sumatra in the latter part of the era. He was a teacher of religion, a writer, and a producer of a commentary/translation of the Qur'an.

Mystics *(sufi)* were popular in the nineteenth century, but faded in importance after the turn of the twentieth. From the middle of the nineteenth century to its end, there was an appreciable rise in the activity of the Naqsyabandiya brotherhood, while other orders began to fade. Two of its suborders, the Khalidiyah and the Mazhariyyah, targeted local elites where they operated, while a third suborder, the Qadiriyah wa Naqsybanidiyah, used already established organizational cells, continuing to do ongoing work in the general population. The three component suborders differed mostly on methods of inducing the mystical trance, the central feature of mysticism. In Indochina, for example, in the nineteenth century there were a series of mystic teachers from Kelantan who were active among the Muslim population in Cambodia and Vietnam. Immigrant Kelantanese scholars taught the Islamic sciences in schools and many practiced mysticism, in some cases becoming well enough known to be regarded as "blessed." But in the early twentieth century, Islamic modernism laid stress on the fundamentals of religious action and eschewed mysticism as being "passive" and out of step with the times. Since there were ample opportunities for new religious expression and a new world filled with Western entertainment, the pool of people interested in mystical experience declined appreciably.

In the category of "other specialists," a number of activists in "antiauthoritarian" movements were prominent during the nineteenth century. The first case occurred early in the era and centered around Pangeran Diponegoro (d. 1855), a secondary prince of the Yogyakarta palace. He rose in rebellion against the ruler and his Dutch allies because he held that the protocol and customs of the court, reflecting Hindu and Buddhist rituals, were contrary to Islam. He charged that the courtiers were so ignorant of religion that they were scarcely Muslims. He disliked, in particular, their use of Dutch styles in clothing, education, and general living. Leadership and military support for his rebellion came from individual Muslim teachers in the nearby private boarding schools, where he was regarded as a personification of the Islamic messiah *(mahdi)*. The local agricultural population, which believed they were overtaxed and otherwise abused by royal authority, allowed Diponegoro and his supporters refuge and passage through their territory and occasionally fought with his forces. They regarded him as the personification of the Javanese messiah *(ratu adil)*. His revolt, which he and his followers labeled a "holy war," lasting from 1825 to 1828, was ultimately put down by Javanese, Makassarese, and Dutch troops after an intense and expensive military campaign.

A second example of the "antiauthoritarian" leader was Matt Saleh (d. 1901) in north Borneo. His rebellion, 1895 to 1905, was aimed against the established political authority, although general conditions of social life may have been the real cause. He insinuated that he was the long-awaited Muslim messiah, and he gave his followers Islamic symbols—flags, standards, and parasols—as a means of identification with Islam and as holy relics capable of generating power to aid them in their endeavors. (As in the last chapter, intellectuals will be discussed in the sections on ideology and literature.)

Education and Intellectual Centers

In the nineteenth century, the number of Islamic schools on Java grew from 1,853 Islamic boarding schools with 16,556 students to 14,929 schools with 222,663 students by the end of the century; of course, there were many more in other parts of the Muslim Zone of Southeast Asia.[20] The schools varied in size. With minor exceptions, all these schools had a common outlook on religious matters: they followed Ashʿarite theological doctrine and creed, adhered to the Shafiʿi school in jurisprudence, and belonged to the al-Junayd (d. 910) pattern of mystical belief and practice—all elements that constituted Sunni orthodoxy at the time. Teachers at these schools taught several of the Islamic sciences, usually the structure and orthography of the Arabic language *(balagh* or *sharaf)*, Qurʾanic commentary *(tafsir)*, sources of Islamic law *(usul al-fiqh)*, sources of Islamic religion *(usul al-din)*, Islamic philosophy *(filasauf)*, mysticism *(tasawwuf)*, and Islamic history *(tarich)*. These standard "sciences" were essentially the same as in the previous period, although the availability of texts and the learning of the instructors were considerably improved. Much of the study was done in Arabic, but some subjects, and particularly the commentary on various texts, were in Malay or, sometimes, a local language such as Javanese.

Education was pursued through the elucidation of old texts, usually reading them in a "circle" and having them explained by the scholar himself or, if the exercise was repeated, by one of the older students to the younger ones. As in the former period, there were no formal programs of education and a student stayed as long as he wished and/or could afford, with the more advanced students moving on to some other scholar with different texts and subject matter.[21] Apparently during the nineteenth century the number of new scholars available for staffing these schools grew appreciably, almost all of them coming from within the Muslim Zone itself, even though many had had to go to Makkah to complete their educations.

Two systems were used to teach Arabic, which C. Hurgronje referred to as the "local" and the "Makkan" systems.[22] In the local system, an Arabic text was placed before the student and the scholar explained the meaning and intent of the text, which the student then wrote in Malay as an exposition of the Arabic text, later returning to learn by heart both the original text and the commentary. In the Makkan system, the student was taught the elements of Arabic grammar, followed by more advanced elements, and then the relationship between Arabic and Malay, culminating eventually in the mastery and translation of texts. Hurgronje found no great difference in their understanding of Arabic texts in students using either of the two systems, but assessed that those who studied grammar in the Makkan system were able to read Arabic regularly, while those pursuing the local system could not. Numerous Arabic texts were used to teach Arabic grammar, usually starting with the *Alphabetical Essence (Alfiyya)* of Ibn Malik al-Taʾi (d. 1274), the *Proper Measure (Kafiya)* by Ibn al-Hajib (d. 1249), and the *Introduction (Muqaddima, or al-Ajurrumiyya)* by Ibn Ajurrumiyya (d. 1323), all of which were generally used along with the commentaries of one or more later scholars. Islamic education of the era was an extension of Middle Eastern education adapted to the language conditions of the region, but kept doctrine, texts, and teaching methods intact.

During the early twentieth century, the realm of the private entrepreneur-scholar who operated boarding schools alongside other economic enterprises underwent considerable change and for schools to survive adjustment was necessary. Midway in the era, around 1925, several organizations of teachers appeared, the *Nahdatoel Oelama*–NO association in Indonesia being the most notable, which brought together religious teachers for common action. These networks were concerned to preserve the basic system of education, with its stress on the standard texts of Islam and teaching through the "learning circle." At the same time there was some individual experimentation with different teaching methods and the inclusion of some new subject material that lay outside the normal curriculum, such as mathematics.

Challenging this entire traditional system were new schools founded by one group of scholars educated at the boarding schools and at Makkah. They broke with their teachers to establish new schools with a different emphasis, using newly written texts, usually in the vernacular, changing some teaching techniques—for example, the graded classroom—and bringing in "secular" subjects of the time. Some of the early schools were in west Sumatra and the Singapore area, but later there was a strong development on Java. Some of these new institutions were boarding schools still concentrating on the fostering of a new type of religious scholar, but this purpose was usually set aside for the development of the *madrasah,* a school that offered a dual curriculum of general subjects and Islamic sciences, at graded levels, with a certificate at the conclusion. Graduates of these new schools were not intended to become teachers themselves, but to participate in society in general.

An important intellectual center at Patani produced Islamic literature for use in the Muslim Zone. The writers there concentrated exclusively on the translation, commentary, and exposition of texts of Arab religious masters. Actually, it would be more correct to say that religious scholars from Patani migrated to the Middle East, to Makkah and Cairo, primarily for religious study; and, once they had become established there, their writings found their way back to the Southeast Asian region through students who studied with them at Makkah. The most noted writer was Daud bin Abdullah al-Fatani (d. after 1843), who wrote nearly thirty books on Islamic sciences, including law, mysticism, Traditions of the Prophet, and jurisprudence. His important works were the *Students' Desire (Bughyat al-ullab)*, a guide to proper religious observance based on al-Nawawi's well-known *Students' Guide (Minhaj al-talibin)*, and a guide for proper procedure regarding all aspects of daily life. Ahmad bin Muhammad al-Fatani (d. 1906), somewhat less prominent than Daud, issued a book on the creed of Islam, and a set of jurisprudential opinions in which he gave answers to intricate religious questions sent to him by Southeast Asian Muslims. These two writers wrote in a mixture of Arabic and Malay, using as a base text the work of some noted Arabic scholar, with a Malay commentary detailing the meaning of the text and the keys to its translation. Often the commentary was a simple paraphrase of the Arabic text, but at other times substantial explanations were included that elucidated the subject under discussion in the Arabic portion.

There were several important scholars who, individually, were important contributors to Islamic thought. Nawawi al-Bantani (d. 1897), originally from north Java, like some of his colleagues from Patani, spent most of his career in Makkah and did almost all his writing in Arabic. He gained some fame in Southeast Asia and the wider Islamic world for his works on Qur'anic commentary, the life of the Prophet, jurisprudence, and mysticism. On the other hand, Ahmad Ripangi (d. 1875) stayed in Southeast Asia. He wrote over twenty treatises on theology and jurisprudence, all of which were used widely without any sort of formal publication.

In general, the scholars of the region continued to contribute to the religious literature needed by the Muslim community of the zone, but it had to depend heavily on Arabic-language works, first in the operation of the schools and second as the source material for the writing of new textbooks and study materials. In fact, there was little innovation and a slavish use of Arabic source materials, with little beyond paraphrasing in the way of rewriting. Still, the passage of these materials into Malay and other languages of the region was not inconsiderable and constituted a contribution to the education of the community.

Islamic Thought and Ideology

NINETEENTH-CENTURY EXAMPLES. In the nineteenth century the most prominent use of Islamic ideology occurred with the Paderi movement in west Sumatra, discussed earlier in this chapter. The Paderis followed the teachings of Muhammad Ibn Abd al Wahhab (d. 1791), a scholar-activist located near Riyadh, Arabia, which aimed at clarifying the teachings of Islam to "give God all honor and worship." The teachings asserted that only prayer directed to God was legitimate, and that, accordingly, saint worship was religiously wrong. Further, the principles of religious law could only be acquired from the Qur'an, the true Traditions of the Prophet, through consensus of the scholars, and from the insights of the first several generations of Muslims. Once in Southeast Asian society, the Paderis attempted to instill an Islamic outlook and ethic in a society that they regarded as woefully lacking in Islamic identification and perspective. They insisted that white clothes, symbolizing purity, be worn, that women cover their faces, and men were encouraged to wear beards. Gold ornamentation and silk clothing were viewed as unsuitable because the Prophet had regarded them as signs of vanity. Many practices common to the Southeast Asia of the time were labeled as "indulgent" and as directly or indirectly forbidden by the Prophet; these included the use of tobacco, cock fighting, gambling, opium, betel chewing, and alcohol. The Paderis also held that the Islamic commercial code should be observed and that commercial courts should be established in different parts of the west Sumatra interior.

The leading thinker of the movement, Tuanku Nan Rinceh (d. 1832), maintained that the use of "striving," or "holy war" (*jihad*), was an appropriate way to disseminate the Paderi revivalist message. This involved, in order of use: "striving with the heart," "striving with the tongue and hands," and "striving with warfare." "Striving with the heart" meant an individual effort to perfect oneself, especially by clearing away bad thoughts and resisting untoward behavior, so that the true Muslim spirit would emerge. "Striving with the tongue and hands" involved dedication to fashioning a society of believers whose members collectively would understand the real message of Islam and avoid behavior prohibited by Islamic teachings. "Striving through warfare" meant using force to compel others to accept the conditions of a correct society and the rulings of Islamic law. The best ways of achieving the goals of a true Islamic society were to use the first two methods, and indeed, "striving through warfare" should only be used after the others had been tried repeatedly. But ultimately the use of force could be used to extend the realm of the believers in God and to disseminate and enforce the holy laws of religion.[23]

In another case, that of Aceh, the invasion of the Dutch was countered by Acehnese resistance in the form of guerrilla warfare and Islam was used as a rallying cry. Midway in the war some pamphlets were issued justifying resistance to the Dutch and the use of "holy war" (*perang sabil*) that had already been proclaimed by religious officials there. A tract by Teungku Kuta Karang (active 1890) used arguments similar to those of the Wahhabis by calling for a grand sacrifice in which all the people would be mobilized and all the wealth of the country amassed to finance the war against the Dutch at a level that would assure victory. The tract argued that the holy war was the highest obligation a Muslim could fulfill, taking precedence over all other obligations because the very existence of Islam was at stake. Moreover, the reward for participation—namely, martyrdom—was likewise higher than other religious rewards, so the Acehnese should undertake the task very seriously and hold back nothing. He stated that the threat to Islam in Aceh was not imagined but real, and that one only had to observe the fate of Islam in the colonial cities of Southeast Asia—that is, at Batavia, Penang, and Singapore—to understand that Islam was under attack to its very core.[24]

Other indications of Muslim thought did not have the same degree of urgency about them, nor were they so passionately argued. The clearest example occurred at Riau, where several writers lamented the passing of traditional society and a voiced their distaste for the rise of the commercial and urban lifestyles introduced by the Dutch and British. The leading scholar, Raja Ali Haji (d. 1869), made a case for the revitalization of traditional society in which the rulers of the state—the Malay sultan and the Bugis regent —would put aside pride for the good of the kingdom, so that an honorable society steeped in Islamic values could emerge and award the population with "justice and prosperity."[25] This vision of an ideal society from the past was portrayed as a sharp contrast to the westernized city of Singapore that was emerging nearby and was attractive to many people in the Riau state. There was considerable support for that position in many parts of society, and particularly among the local elite.

MODERNIST ISLAM. In the twentieth century, Muslim intellectual thinking focused on the development of modernist Islam. This was an ideology developed in the Middle East by a number of thinkers, primarily Muhammad ʿAbduh (d. 1905) and Muhammad Rashid Rida (d. 1935), and spread throughout most of the Muslim world in the last years of the nineteenth century and during the first half of the twentieth. In the Southeast Asian Muslim Zone it had its greatest and most long-lasting impact on the Dutch-controlled region, while in the British-controlled, French-controlled, and Thai regions it had a strong initial impact, with diminishing effect thereafter. It had a weak impact on Sarawak, and almost no influence on the other northern Borneo states or the southern Philippine Islands.

The first modernist message arrived in Southeast Asia in the early years of the twentieth century. It was carried by young Minang Muslim scholars who came in contact with the ideology during their study in Makkah, and they attempted to follow those teachings when they returned to Southeast Asia. In Singapore and the neighboring Johore area, Tahir Jalal al-Din al-Azhari (d. 1957), Sayid Shaykh al-Hadi (d. 1934), and their compatriots spread a message urging Malays to adapt to the changing times by accepting new knowledge and modern methods of learning, and by assigning rational thought an important place in their reasoning. Their message also struck hard at continuing use of animistic practices among the faithful that they believed hindered the acceptance of both standard Islamic teachings and modernization. In 1906 they founded the newspaper *The Leader (Al-Imam)*, which served as a sounding board for the modernist message to other religious scholars and to the interested public.

In west Sumatra a similar movement was led by Haji Rasul (d. 1944), who called for the Friday sermon to be delivered in local languages because few indigenous worshipers understood them in Arabic. He also urged drastic revision of mystical practice so that it no longer competed with regular worship activities or challenged the central role of religious law. Haji Rasul took part in publishing a magazine called *The Light (Al-Moenir)*, which gained an important audience among religious officials in the region. The third major figure of this first wave was Agus Salim (d. 1954), also from west Sumatra, who had been educated in the Dutch educational system. His arguments centered primarily on the exploitation of Southeast Asians from the colonial system, and he promoted the intellectual interests of young Muslims in Dutch schools.

A second modernist message arrived on Java around 1912. Achmad Dachlan (d. 1923) at Yogyakarta stressed Islamic activism by establishing new schools that combined Western-style teaching methods and subject matter with standard Muslim subjects. Later, he opened clinics and hospitals using new medical practices from the West. The organization that Dachlan founded, the Moehammadijah, captured the attention of middle-class Muslims and gained strength rapidly, reaching a membership of twenty-four thousand in 1930, with over four thousand pupils in fifty schools that the movement established. It was an urban-centered movement and concentrated on the social needs of Muslims living in cities, such as polyclinics, libraries, mosque building, and "information sessions" *(tabligh)*.[26] In the same time frame Achmad Surkati (d. 1943), a Sudanese Arab resident in Jakarta, worked within the Arab community to reform education there, also introducing general subject matter, and revised ways of presenting classical Muslim teaching subjects.

A third wave of modernist reform occurred in the mid-1920s at Bandung when Ahmad Hassan (d. 1958), established a printing press and gave guidance to a group of ideologues called the Islamic Union–Persis (Persatoean Islam), covered earlier. Over the next fifteen years this group examined all the issues of modernism in its magazine *The Islamic Defender (Pembela Islam)*. Hassan urged a rethinking of Muslim jurisprudence—which he regarded as hidebound and filled with unwarranted conclusions—by concentrating on the scriptures of Islam, the Qur'an and the "firm" Traditions. Of all reformers he was the most strident and uncompromising, even labeling his opponents with pejorative epithets and calling into question their very belief in Islam.

A fourth wave of modernist activity occurred in the 1930s in Perak and Sarawak, apparently inspired by *The Leader* in Singapore earlier. Abdu Bakir Bakir (active 1935) established a school at Perak in 1935 named the Reformist Academy–Miagus (Maahad El-Enya Assyarif Gunung Semanggul), with teachers trained in Makkah, Egypt, and India. Members of Miagus wrote in the leading vernacular press of the time and later became active in the Young Malay Union–KMM. In Kuching, Sarawak, the modernist movement came via the Pen Pal Association, through which upper-class Malays corresponded with Muslim modernists from the Penang region. Letters to the editor of the *Sarawak Gazette,* and later in the modernist magazine *Sarawak Dawn (Fajar Sarawak),* focused on the need to overcome attitudes of fatalism and, at the same time, prepare poor Malays to meet the changing economic conditions that were beginning to affect them. The letters also called for improving the status of women and reallocating spending away from elaborate feasts and gifts in celebration of life-cycle events, which the writers regarded as wasteful.

There was considerable reaction to the first three waves of modernist Muslim activity, especially on the part of other religious scholars who believed that the standard teachings of Islam did not need much "updating." In response, the opposition argued that the subject matter being taught in Muslim schools was suitable and that reform was not needed in religious practice. These "traditionalist Muslims," as they came to be known, reacted to the modernist message that was presented to them in hostile, ideological terms and applied their own derogatory religious labels to the modernists. At the height of the dispute in the 1920s, the two sides were so polarized that they labeled one another "heretics" *(murtadd)* and often denied burial to a deceased member of the opposite side in a cemetery that fell under their jurisdiction or control. The primary organization that emerged on the side of the traditionalists was the Nahdatoel Oelama–NO, in league with smaller organizations of the same outlook found outside of Java and Madura.

NATIONALISM. In the Muslim Zone nationalism first developed on Java and in west Sumatra. As mentioned above, in 1911 the Sarekat Islam came into existence and became the leading advocate for nationalism in the Dutch East Indies. The movement was supposedly religious in outlook, but it was actually a mass political organization without regard for religion, ethnicity, or ideology, which brought Muslim activists, secularists, and communists together to work against Dutch authority. The Sarekat Islam remained a legal movement for over a decade, due to the careful political balancing acts of its principal leaders, Umar Cokroaminoto (d. 1934), Abdul Muis (d. 1959), and later Agus Salim. By 1915 a split had developed in the organization between militants, who wanted confrontation with Dutch authorities in order to press for nationalist demands, and the moderates, who wanted to use measures short of direct confrontation. The association was badly fractionalized in 1926 when the militants called for strikes in the public sector. Dutch authorities responded by arresting most of the leaders of the strikes and placed such restrictions on the Sarekat Islam as to make it politically ineffective; subsequently, its membership evaporated.

A second "Muslim" endeavor occurred late in the 1930s with the creation of the Higher Islamic Council of Indonesia–MIAI, a confederation consisting of the leading social and religious associations of the time that allowed some participation with other nationalist organizations outside the Muslim-oriented group. Overall, the Muslim wing in nationalism was important early on but faded in importance as the era proceeded.

The second trend in nationalism was given definition in the 1920s by the Indonesian National Party–PNI (Partai Nasional Indonesia). PNI leaders called for a new independent nation-state, referred to as "Indonesia," to be formed from the territories of the Dutch East Indies. The "nationalist" call was intended to supersede the "smaller" nationalisms of Java, Sumatra, Sulawesi, and other places, and it was pointedly nonreligious so that members of all religions could be included in the effort. The primary leader, Soekarno (d. 1970), attempted to fashion a new ideology not hitherto recognized. In particular, he believed that it was paramount to revivify the merging of diverse factions he found in archipelagic society—notably, an Islamic identity, a socialist or communist inclination, and a nationalist commitment. He maintained that these three diverse trends needed unity and direction, which he hoped to be able to provide through exerting his own charismatic personality.[27] Another nationalist leader, Muhammad Yamin (d. 1964), provided the historical foundation for the new nationalism by evoking the classical Javanese empire of Majapahit as the prototype for the new Indonesian nation.

The PNI leadership was arrested by the Dutch in the 1920s and its leaders sent either to prison camps or into exile in the outer islands. However, the remaining nationalist leadership joined with other parties in the late 1930s in a union called the Indonesian Political Federation–Gapi, mentioned earlier, to push its nationalist program, particularly in regard to the debates in the Peoples' Chamber concerning autonomy/independence. There has been a split among later Indonesian Muslim intellectuals as to whether the PNI trend, and Sukarno in particular, represented Muslim political action in a secular guise, or whether nationalism truly stood outside the Islamic movement.

In contrast, in the zone of British influence two trends were of special interest to nationalist development: one that centered on Malay interests and the other that took a strong interest in Islamic matters. Not surprisingly, the two were sometimes intertwined. The first significant organizations in this dual configuration were the Singapore Muslim Association and the Malaya–Singapore Union in the early years of the twentieth century, which became rivals in seeking membership on a government council as representatives of the Malays. The Singapore Muslim Association was elitist, its leadership drawn from the Arab and Javanese communities, while the Malay–Singapore Union was middle-class, with Malay leadership. The union won the competition and came to be recognized as the voice of Malay community consciousness in Singapore.

In the late 1930s the Young Malay Union–KMM appeared, which, while espousing Malay nationalism, was leftist in orientation, with an agenda that opposed British colonialism, all forms of capitalism, and chastised the Malay rulers for "selling out" Malay interests. That organization and many other minor organizations from throughout the Malay States and the Straits Settlements came together twice in the late 1930s to discuss common Malay problems. The National Congress of Malay Associations met in 1939 and 1940 to discuss the perennial question of leadership among Malays, Arabs, and Javanese, with all three groups vying for that role. The Malays eventually gained control of the agenda, giving them the leadership. The congresses also discussed the issues of Malay difficulties in entering the civil service and lack of educational opportunities for Malays but did not, significantly, call for independence. In the mid-1940s, as World War II ended, there was a sharp rise in political organization among Malays in response to Chinese communist organization and British plans for creating a multinational state.

Nationalism did exist in Siam and the Philippines, but it was confined mostly to the people identified with the social elite in the capital city and promoted the dominant ethnic group in each country. So in Siam it favored Thais and Thai culture, and in the Philippines it favored the Luzon-centered elite and the population with a culture bearing strong Spanish and Christian values. In both countries Muslim elites did not belong to the national elite, so the nationalism developed in the capital cities there did not much affect them, except in a negative way. However, there were anti-authoritarian revolts in the Muslim territories that displayed some nascent nationalistic tendencies and called for an end to outsider control of Muslim areas.

In the Philippines there were significant revolts led by Datu Ali Bayao (d. 1905) in 1904 in Magindanao, by Panglima Hassan (d. 1904) and his followers in Sulu between 1903 and 1905, by Jikiri (d. 1909) in the wider Sulu Archipelago in 1907, and by Datu Alameda Macog (active 1916) in Lanao. The leaders were all members of local elites, often part of royal families, and they were supported by religious officials, who encouraged the revolts as action against disbelievers. In the last phase of the Panglima Hassan revolt, a holy war *(perang sabil)* was declared, giving it special religious meaning. In addition, two large battles at Bud Dajo and Bud Bagsak, in 1906 and 1912 respectively, were large-scale revolts without clear leadership, but had the support of the religious leaders and teachers.

In Thailand the situation was much the same. In 1922 civil unrest occurred in the Patani region mobilized by Haji Sulung bin Abdul Kadir (d. 1952), the former raja of Patani, assisted by a large number of returned pilgrims and a sizeable number of agriculturalists. These popular uprisings lacked doctrinal perceptions or clear statements of political intent, but were expressive of an overall popular sentiment calling for local control of their political destiny. They lacked the ideological underpinnings necessary to identify movements as nationalist, but bore enough of a resemblance that they can be labeled as early nationalist movements.

The Pillars of Islam

The nineteenth century was marked by a greater appreciation for the standard procedures and observances of worship than had existed in the eighteenth century. Foreign-born Muslims, mystics, and scholars were still the pacesetters, but there was no longer such a wide gap between their behavior and that of much of the indigenous Muslim community. While some Southeast Asian Muslims took their obligations seriously, other indigenous groups were much more casual about religious worship and identification. Such a bifurcation was clear on Java, Sumbawa, and in the Khmer area. Among pious Javanese Muslims there was recognition that recitation of the "confession" was important. In regular Muslim practice this was accomplished through the reciting of standard prayer, hearing it in the call to prayer, and including it in the marriage contract. In the Khmer region, nonbelievers who wished to marry a Muslim were required by custom to convert. They did so with the words "I accept," but pointedly did not recite the "confession" itself, calling into question whether an actual conversion had really occurred.[28]

On the Malay Archipelago many people considered themselves devout Muslims but prayed only occasionally and seldom visited a mosque. On Java "committed" Muslims prayed five times a day and males attended the communal worship on Fridays, but nominal Muslims did not concern themselves with these obligations. In addition, the standard evening prayers during Ramadan were observed and many people recited short utterances common in Islam, such as the "remembrance" *(zikir),* the "confession of faith" *(shahadah),* and, using a rosary *(tasbih),* the repetition of the ninety-nine "names" *(asmaul husna)* of God. Observers remarked that many people did not know the proper procedure for prayer and, when forced to participate in worship, were at a loss as to how to proceed. Consequently, some committed Muslims asked for laws to force males to attend prayers, but almost always officials were against compulsion. Universally the Friday sermon was given in Arabic and usually taken from a set of writings passed from teacher to pupil among sermon givers. Such sermons consisted of quotations from the Qur'an and from well-known Muslim writers of previous centuries, but without much care for the original sermon, so that errors, incompleteness, and inappropriate additions made many of them unintelligible, even to those who understood Arabic.

On Java the fasting month was observed by some of the population with a wide variety of attitudes about it. Nominal Muslims often did not fast at all; this constituted a significant sector of the population. The pious fasted for all or part of the month, many performed evening prayers, and some paid the rice tax near the end of the month. A large number of Muslims prayed in the evenings on the last days of the month as being an especially propitious time to do so because the Qur'an was revealed then. Besides the obligatory fast during the month of Ramadan on Java, some pious Muslims also observed voluntary fasting during the first week of the month of Syawal, the ninth day of Zulhijah in conjunction with the pilgrimage, the ninth and tenth of Muharam, the "white days"—that is, the thirteenth, fourteenth, and fifteenth of each month, because the moon was white at that time—as well as Monday and Thursday of each week.[29] Fasting for the pious was a continuous obligation, but the numbers of those who observed all those fasting days seem to have been very small.

Throughout the Muslim Zone the rice tax was paid out from each household on the twenty- seventh day of Ramadan and divided among the local mosque personnel. At all places it was a voluntary contribution and a set amount, not a tithe on crop yield. There was general recognition that the poor should be assisted by pious contributions, but this particular tax was not regarded as the vehicle for such contributions. That began to change somewhat with the rise of the modernist movement, and the mosques established by its followers continued in that direction in the next era.

Many sources report that the pilgrimage was popular, both with civil servants of the Malay states who received special stipends and time off to travel and with many others who saved their money over long periods to undertake it. Returnees were regarded as "learned" in Islam and could be expected to find employment in mosques and religious schools, and to be considered in public discussions as people worth listening to. Nationalists in Indonesia in the early 1930s criticized the pilgrimage as detracting from nationalist goals and suggested that those who were imprisoned at the Digul prison camp for opposing the Dutch authorities should have higher status than the pilgrim. This assertion set off a storm of debate among different factions, but it did not dampen commitment for the pilgrimage, or for nationalism.

Qur'an learning among children was common throughout the zone, and recitation was taught so that standard styles that traced their beginning to Makkah at the time of the Prophet Muhammad were common. Recitation of particular sections were believed to be capable of driving away an evil spirit, especially among the insane. Further, the Qur'an was cited at certain life-cycle events, such as after the birth of a child, at a circumcision ceremony, or as a form of entertainment for guests at a wedding.

Religious Practice

During the nineteenth century Southeast Asian Muslim students studying at Makkah frequently joined mystical groups for worship sessions and to learn the science behind the practice. Some of these pilgrim-students became proficient enough that a mystic master would name them as his agents in their home areas, where they were expected to form new groups and continue the spread of the mystical order. Shaykh Isma'il Minangkabawi (d. 1865), a member of the Khalidiyah order, was representative of such agents. Located at Singapore, he first attached himself to Temenggung Ibrahim (ruled 1841–1861), the Malay ruler of Johore, then to the Bugis royal family on nearby Penyengat Island. Later he journeyed northward as far as Kedah, establishing similar groups in Malay areas. In another case, the activist Shaykh Jalal al-Din (active 1860) operated in west Sumatra around Cangking, where a sizeable portion of the highland's population became members of the Khalidiyah order, nearly one-eighth according to a Dutch official. Because of their emphasis on standard Islamic practices, these activists were precursors of the modernist Muslim groups that followed a half-century later.[30]

During the early twentieth century there was a rise in the amount of revivalist *(dakwah)* activity taking place throughout the Muslim Zone, in large part an outgrowth of the many Islamic organizations that came into existence. Among revivalists there was a common belief that Islamic worship should be undertaken regularly and individual religious behavior should be more apparent in the lives of believers. While most organizations devoted some of their effort to such intensification of observances, it was Persis that organized itself specifically toward upgrading the religious behavior of the general Muslim community. Its techniques focused on four major activities. First, the members organized "information" *(tabligh)* sessions, which were open to the general public and highly publicized in the press and at local mosques. At those meetings speakers from the association outlined proper behavior in regard to the major obligations of Islam, such as prayer, fasting, or the pilgrimage. A second effort of Persis was placed on public debate, where a personality from the association would challenge the representative of some other viewpoint, so that the "proper" interpretation of Islamic teachings would be made clear to the audience. Again, great emphasis was placed on publicity, and the "results" of the debate would be distributed through pamphlets, handbills, and press articles in order to generate awareness of the issue in the Muslim community. Third, the association held short intensive courses, again focusing on the primary obligations of religion, which were held at a series of evening meetings or on a weekend. Fourth, regular magazines were published that carried inspirational articles, interpretations of contemporary affairs and the need for greater Muslim involvement in them, with many admonitions for readers on how to live good Muslim lives. Detractors called Persis members fanatical, but most modernist Muslim organizations found these efforts laudable and gave them a great deal of support.[31]

Local Customs and Islam
Shamans, Saints, and Amulets

In the Malay states the position of the shaman *(bomoh, dukun)* was central to the community life of the countryside. He gave the instructions for most of the daily routines of life, particularly planting and harvesting, the life-cycle events of birth, marriage, and death ceremonies, and the prevention of disease and health care in general. The shaman was almost always male, learned his craft from his father, and accepted small gifts for his services. Few shamans were rich men, but they made a modest living and commanded a great deal of quiet awe on the part of the villagers around them because of their knowledge of how the spirit world worked and their access to hidden powers that could be used by them on their clientele's behalf.

The most challenging work for a shaman was dealing with the ill. He was not a surgeon, so most of his task was to diagnose illness. Curing was done by drawing out the spirit that had caused the illness, often with massage, but sometimes by way of a trance in which incense, holy water, and power gained from it could be applied to the infecting spirit. The imagery used by the shaman in his incantations drew on the cosmogony of the Islamic world—jinn and demons—of the Hindu world—Kala, the god of death—and mythical references, such as ʿUmar Ummaya, the hero of an Arabic romance. If the occasion was an illness, the effort was usually directed toward luring the offending spirit causing it to move onto a model ship or mosque so that it could be removed, after which holy water was sprinkled and incense used for fumigation.[32]

For the shaman, the rice field was a continual arena of action to handle the spirits that dwelt there. First he would clear the rice field of general spirits, so that planting could be done without harm from them. Then he nurtured the spirits of the new rice so the crop would be good and there would be no untoward occurrences that would upset the spirits of the new rice crop. When harvest was ready, the shaman spent several evenings collecting the "souls" of the rice, then selected seven stalks that he first bound together to represent the rice's spirit. After prayers from the mosque official and a general harvest meal, the shaman fumigated the selected stalks and sprinkled rice paste on them; with a tiny blade he cut the ears. This "soul" of the rice was then received into the home of the agriculturalist as a baby and treated like one for a week's time, when it was stored for use in the seed beds for the next rice planting. In the first two days after taking the soul of the rice, a small basket of rice was gathered, dried, and winnowed, after which children performed a dance on it, followed by its grinding in a pestle—the names of Allah and the Prophet were intoned. It was then made ready for eating at a village-wide harvest festival including games, recitations of popular poems, and other entertainment. The rice tax was paid to the mosque and a fee given to the shaman. So, although the shaman was animist in character, he used enough references to Islam that many believed him to be in tune with the religion.

Shrines were an important feature of most villages in the Muslim Zone, but it was unclear whether they were really part of Islam or outside of it. In the case of Malay villages, such a shrine might honor a tomb, an unusual tree, or a stone marker, which were regarded as having a spirituality about them that demanded respect and veneration. Some places harbored sites regarded as the graves of a "founding father" of a village or a pious personality, where votary offerings were brought in order to gain some desired outcome for the person making the offering. The grave of Dato Machap (d. unknown) on the Malay Peninsula was used for swearing serious oaths; indeed, an oath made there was regarded as more binding than simply swearing by the Qur'an. Such sites, including those of former rulers, were used by people who left small gifts of white and yellow cloth tied to nearby trees as offerings. Village shrines and the saints' tombs often blended in with one another, and devotees might be pious Muslims, nominal Muslims, or even non-Muslims.

In the early twentieth century Muslim saint cults remained important. As we have seen, on Java the graves of the "nine saints" were popular. There were cults at each grave and attendants to assist visitors and to keep the site in good order. The princess Kartini (d. 1904) observed in her diary that some of the tombs of former rulers were regarded as important and that one specific tomb was reputed to assist barren women, who would visit it to offer gifts of flowers and incense wafers.[33]

Amulets were in great use during this era and justified on the basis that Muhammad himself was said to have countenanced their wearing against the "evil eye," for snakebites, and against some diseases, although the Prophet himself preferred to rely on prayer. The popular amulet was the six-sided star of the Prophet Sulayman, which could be used to counter madness and demon possession. Verses of the Qur'an written on paper hung on a person were believed to protect against convulsions or earaches. The magic square written on a leaf and buried in a rice field would protect the field from pests and varmints. Writing a Qurʾanic verse on a piece of paper, rinsing it with water, and drinking the water would assist the doer with concentration and the ability to perform well whatever activity was at hand. The injunctions of the Arabian cosmology were given attention; for example, the use of the phrase "In the name of God, the Merciful, the Compassionate," when recited repeatedly, had magical effects in gaining desired ends, and when written repeatedly could make the "barren fruitful and attract fish to the net."[34] In the same way, philters made from the ashes of a burnt black cat, the blood of various animals, and other unusual ingredients could be smeared onto the flesh to assist in gaining desired ends. In general, the population of the Southeast Asian Muslim Zone existed in a world dominated by spirits, and placating them was essential to survival. If one could control them, it was possible to prosper. This belief was not directly sanctioned by Islam, but neither was it popularly regarded as opposed to Islam.

Life-Cycle Events

The customs surrounding birth, circumcision, marriage, and death all reveal that Islam was involved in the life-cycle events of the peoples of the Muslim Zone. As in matters of healing and agriculture, the operative element was usually the custom of the region, and Islam entered in to different degrees depending on the particular life-cycle event. In general, Islam was nominally involved in marriage but dominant in burial practice.

Regarding marriage, in Aceh an expectant mother engaged a midwife in the seventh month and a religious specialist could be asked to attend to deliver prayers. At birth, after the umbilical cord was cut, the father usually recited the call to prayer in the right ear of a boy, followed by the "exhortation" (kamat) in the left ear; in the case of a girl, only the exhortation was said. These whispered messages informed the child it was a Muslim. The area around the birth site was strewn with raw rice, amulets were hung on the walls, and certain fruits and thistles were placed there with the purpose of warding off evil spirits. On the seventh day after birth, there was a tonsure ceremony with a large festival for both families and other guests. Some particularly poor but pious people were often invited so that part of the meal could be given to them as alms, considered a meritorious act on the part of the family. On the forty-fourth day after birth, the mother ended her confinement, during which time she had been confined to a bed over an oven to keep her very warm. On this occasion the mother was bathed with various liquids; the midwife performed a ceremony to drive away evil spirits, frequently invoking God's name; and a festive meal was held. Afterwards the baby was taken to the tomb of a Muslim saint, its head bathed, and an offering of flowers, incense, and cloth was made as a means of invoking the blessing of the saint.

Again in Aceh, genital cutting was performed on girls before the age of awareness, but the event was regarded as a private ceremony involving only the women of the family. A bowl of yellow glutinous rice was sent to a religious functionary as a gift, with the request to utter a prayer on behalf of the giver. No detailed description was given of the procedure, but the midwife was often the "surgeon," making a small incision on the tip of the clitoris. Boys were circumcised at the age of eight or nine. This occasion was a festive one, with the boy dressed in finery and often mounted on a horse as he arrived at the place where the procedure was to be performed. Beforehand he usually visited the tomb of a Muslim saint, where his head was washed at the foot of the tomb and a festive meal was served. After returning from the saint's tomb, he was washed again, and then the foreskin was cut away by a Muslim functionary while a prayer was recited as a means of stanching the blood.

Marriage in Aceh was conducted according to custom and direct Islamic involvement was limited to a few items. The marriage contract was completed several days before the wedding, when the men of the two families, acting on behalf of the bride and groom respectively, went to the mosque and met with a religious specialist to certify the terms of the marriage and its related financial arrangements. After that certification a short sermon was given and the opening chapter of the Qurʾan was recited to give the union a blessing. Several witnesses were present for verification. Otherwise the very involved betrothal negotiations, the preparations of the bride and groom, the meeting of the bridal pair at a feast, and the entertainment connected with the entire affair had little Islamic content except for the occasional reference to God or the Prophet, which more often than not was merely common speech idiom, not recognized as Islamic religious expression.

Again in Aceh, when death was near and the dying person was aware of it, he might ask forgiveness of those around him. The standard reply was that it was God who forgave, but sometimes those so addressed indicated that they did indeed grant their forgiveness. Sometimes everyone present recited the confession of faith. When the person had died, a ritual washing took place, usually done by a religious specialist in the case of men, and a woman funerary specialist in the case of women. After the body was carefully wrapped, it was transported to the cemetery where regular prayer was performed, usually by the religious specialist alone, or with the entire assembly of guests if the guests were well versed in performing prayer. The shrouded body was then laid on its side in a grave with the face toward Makkah and buried. Afterwards the religious functionary recited the "prompting" *(talkin)* to the deceased about meeting the angels Nakir and Munkar, who would test his knowledge of religion and determine if he was a pious and believing person. The "admonition" provided the answers to the questions the angels were expected to ask. Then the "remembrance" *(zikir)* was pronounced one hundred times, declaring that "there is no god but God," the funeral prayer was recited, and refreshments were given to all those attending. Later, at the home of the deceased, a rice meal was served to relatives and the general public.

For a number of days after death the family might employ a religious specialist to recite portions of the Qur'an for the merit of the dead. On the third, fifth, and seventh days after death the nearby public was often invited to a meal served with yellow glutinous rice. Before eating there often was a recitation of a portion of the Qur'an, followed by a prayer always said at the conclusion of such a recitation. On the later remembrance days, that is, the tenth, thirtieth, fortieth, hundredeth days and yearly anniversary of the death, a ceremony was held at the home of the deceased for close relatives, a number of poor people, and a few other invitees.[35] At this ceremony readings from the Qur'an were offered by religious specialists with closing prayers. On the forty-fourth day, women of the family visited the grave site to pour water on it, leave flowers, and eat plantain at the grave site. There might be a Qur'an recitation, if any among the women were able to give it, and in some cases women specialists were hired for that purpose.

Obviously the social world of the era was regulated by custom in which Islamic incantations and prayers were assigned a sanctifying role. Throughout their lives Muslim peoples in the zone lived in a world of spirits, in which only correct behavior verified by custom and accompanying Islamic injunctions and pronouncements made it possible to survive and to die safely. It was not so much that Islam verified these local customs as that Muslims used Islam as an additional assurance in the performance of these customary acts.

Muslim Celebrations

The holidays noted in the nineteenth century were fully described by observers of the time. The following celebrations were performed in Aceh during the latter part of the nineteenth century and provide a solid example of how important these holidays were to the societies of the wider Muslim Zone.[36]

The tenth day of Muharam was intended among Sunni Muslims to be a supplementary day of fasting and was considered "meritorious" but not "required." Hence it passed almost unnoticed in many Sunni communities of Aceh. In the small Shi'ite communities and among many Indian Muslims, the day celebrated the death of Imam Husayn (d. 680), one of the chief figures of early Shi'ism. Among these groups there were bonfires, repetitions of the "remembrance," and reenactments of the massacre of the martyr Husayn, along with much emotional wailing and self-mortification with sharp instruments. Sunnis observed this rite as a curious spectacle, but did not participate or feel particularly connected with it.

The last Wednesday of Safar was a day of ablution in which believers bathed in the sea, a river, or some bathing site, using water that had been consecrated by touch with certain verses of the Qur'an. Some of the water might be drunk as a means of amplifying the blessing. In some places there were voluntary worship services, but these were not countenanced by some religious authorities as having justification in religious sources. Beforehand religious specialists prepared slips of paper with the seven verses from the Qur'an in which God addressed humans with the word "peace," and these were cast into the sea, river, or well where the rite was taking place.

In Rabiulawwal the birthday of the prophet Muhammad was celebrated with a recitation from long poems prepared by al-Bukhari (d. 870) or by Ja'far al-Barzanji (b. 1765). Trained specialists took turns reading, using a variety of styles that were regarded as fashionable. Some people knotted black thread during the reading to use as amulets, since the reading was believed to radiate a blessing. At the conclusion of the reading a long prayer was given. Afterwards there was a feast to which the entire community contributed and all men, women, and children attended. Such celebrations rotated among villages or city quarters during the month so that people could participate in more than one. On the anniversary date itself a large feast was held at the tomb of a popular saint, Teungku Anjung (d. unknown), where several carabao were slaughtered for the festivities.

The night of the fifteenth day of Syakban was believed to be the time when God set the fortunes of mortals for the coming year. According to popular legend, there was a celestial tree of life the leaves of which represented all humans, and on the fifteenth of Syakban the tree was shaken and the leaves that fell represented those people who would die during the coming year. Obviously such an occurrence agitated the general population. Accordingly, in the evening the men gathered in the mosques and the women in private homes to pray, after which a special meal was held in each place. The prayers were designed for the occasion, and often the "gloria" (tasbih) was recited as well.

Fasting was observed during the entire month of Ramadan. According to Islamic law, no food, liquid, or other substance was to be ingested during daylight hours, although there were frequent departures from fasting by users of drugs, smokers, and those unable to bear the strain of going without food all day. However, the practice was very popular and there was heavy participation in the first several days, even though many participants were not otherwise regular worshipers or very knowledgeable about religious practice. Special prayers were recited in the mosque during the evening along with recitation of the Qur'an. The special prayers were well attended but often only listened to, as few people knew the actual prayers, which were lengthy. Afterwards a selection from the Qur'an was recited, with alternating recitations spoken by professional readers and devoted believers. In some places the "remembrance" *(zikir)* was substituted for the Qur'an recitation, in which the word "God" was repeated over and over, louder and louder, and faster and faster, while participants swayed back and forth, causing some to reach a state of ecstasy. Near the end of the month the date when the first section of that scripture was given to Muhammad was celebrated by lighted lanterns in homes, and children shot off fireworks.

The first of Syawal was the great feast day marking the closure of the fast of Ramadan. Men took a ritual bath in the morning and then attended a special prayer service at a mosque, although attendance was always poor in Aceh. Women assembled elsewhere under well-known female devotees. Men paid the capitation tax for those for whom they were responsible to a religious functionary, supposedly the intermediary who would use it for religious purposes. New clothes were donned by everyone who could afford them, all family members duly congratulated one another, and special respect was shown to elders.

During the pilgrimage on the tenth of Zulhijah, pilgrims at Makkah offered their sacrifices at Mina as part of the required ritual. In Aceh, in honor of this occasion, beasts were sacrificed, usually by a religious specialist, who distributed the meat among the members of the village. Lengthy prayers and a sermon were given in the mosque early in the day and that evening fireworks and popular entertainment were staged. In general, the calendar was rich with Islamic festivities and there was considerable participation by the general public.

Cultural Development
Urban Design and Architecture
The downfall of the principal rulers and passage of political and economic power to occupying Europeans forestalled any significant development of architecture as had been so apparent in the preceding era. There was some new building of palaces, particularly in the Malay Peninsular states. Many schools were built as well, although these structures were usually functional and what decoration was added had to come from the teacher-owners, who operated on rather thin financial margins. Consequently there were practical limits on architecture in this particular area.

At the end of the nineteenth century the palace at Kota Bahru in Trengganu was described as comfortable but not pretentious.

> The Sultan's palace, which with its dependencies, surrounds on three sides
> a court of sand, is closed on the fourth by a wooden palisade with one great
> central gate flanked by smaller gates on either side. A second and similar set

of gates forms a further enclosure, about a hundred yards nearer the river. From the outer portals to the river stretches a long straight road, and, on occasions of great ceremony, the visitors whom the Sultan delights to honour will find this road lined, on both sides throughout its entire length, by spearmen, while the principal chiefs and a great posse of retainers escort the guests from the landing-stage to the hall of audience, where the Sultan receives them. Beyond the palace, the town, the houses, and gardens of rajas and chiefs, the country is highly cultivated as far as the eye can reach.[37]

A further development in construction was apparent in general descriptions of the layout and architecture of Muslim schools in the second quarter of the twentieth century. Muslim schools throughout the Muslim Zone were often built in the vicinity of a mosque, or else the mosque was an intrinsic part of the life of the school, with its premises being used for regular prayers and at other times for certain lessons undertaken as part of the curricula of the school. There were a variety of architectural styles, depending on the wealth of the school owners and their willingness to spend funds on more than the essentials. At Sabak Bernam on the Malayan Peninsula, the Madrasah Muhammadiyah building stood on a footed foundation with two stories, topped with a slanted tin roof. Parts of the exterior walls were wooden, but ample space was left open to the outside air. It had a decorative facade made of wooden slats cut into two scalloped archways. Students stayed in small buildings mounted on poles, with no windows and simple thatched roofs.[38]

During the nineteenth century a new wave of foreign influence affected mosque construction, mostly from the central Islamic world. Several of the mosques that reflected this change were actually built by Dutch architects as public projects, such as those at Medan and Aceh. The Sultan Deli Mosque at Medan emulated Ottoman architecture with a massive center dome and four side domes in a square around the center, along with arabesque windows and doors and four matching minarets. The Raya Mosque at Kutaraja used a combination of Mughul and Andalusian styles, incorporating onion-shaped domes, arabesque arches, and ornate facades. Mosque building on the Malay Peninsula employed the Mughal style, although on a much smaller scale than at Kutaraja Aceh. The design of a mosque on Penyengat Island in the Riau Archipelago also reflected influences from elsewhere in the Islamic world. It was erected on a raised section of land with a graceful flight of thirteen steps leading to the structure itself. The mosque proper measured 19.8 x 18 meters and was supported by four pillars constructed from a mixture of sand, gravel, and cement. The roof featured thirteen cupolas, some four-sided, some six-sided, and others eight-sided. It was surrounded by four minarets, each with its own steep staircase winding around the outside of the minarets. A widely told story related that egg whites were mixed with lime to strengthen the cement used in the construction of the cupolas, minarets, and other strategic parts of the structure.[39]

In the early twentieth century new mosques featured building styles that were in keeping with earlier architecture. They frequently had rectangular floor plans and were laid out on a flat, stone base that avoided any use of poles and elevation of the floor as some prayer houses did. They had pointed roofs with two to four levels decreasing in size to the top one—that is, the mastika style described earlier. They faced toward the west or northwest so that the prayer niche could be located appropriately in front. They frequently had an open or closed veranda on one or two sides and were surrounded by a wall with one or more gates in it. Significantly, in some places the dome had made an appearance, as at Tasikmalaya, Surabaya, and Sukabumi. Arabesque arches were common in some places, as at Tuban, but semicircular arches were in common use in most places. In west Sumatra at this time, the dome was in use and minarets were also apparent at some mosques. In the Malayan area, mosques often used the Moorish building style favored by the British authorities at that time, which consisted of large onion domes over the central area, with minarets rising on the four corners of the mosque with domes over them and spires over the domes. There were colonnades at the entrances with arches and heavy decoration, making them very ornate. On the other hand, in Jolo, southern Philippines, the main mosque was a hacienda-style house with a boxlike structure over part of the roof, with a small, pitched roof slanting down from it toward the front of the building; it was undeveloped in structure and ornamentation. In general, there was variation in the style of mosques in this era; however, the main tendency was toward adoption of styles from the central Islamic world, though they were often mixed with local building styles prevalent earlier.

Language and Literature

During the nineteenth century the literary scene showed the same sort of diversification as the eighteenth century, but some of the locales where literature was produced were different. There was a subtle shift in the type of writing as the printing press made its mark in this century by making more publications and wider distribution possible. However, the older style of copying by scribes continued to disseminate many of the works on Islam, especially at religious centers away from the commercial cities of Singapore and Batavia. Accompanying urbanization, a new kind of literature emerged, the beginnings of a shift in the type of writing that was to burgeon in the early twentieth century.

At Singapore, one kind of Malay writing emerged that had a considerable effect on the wider Malay region. The leading literary figure was Abdullah Abdul Kadir Munshi (d. 1854), who was considered the first "modern" author to write in Malay, though he used Arabic script. His books about his own life, both his autobiography and accounts of his travels on the Malay Peninsula, were regarded as Malay masterpieces for their use of language and became standard readings in the Malay schools of Singapore for many years to come. Also, Abdullah made a new translation of *The Story of the Two Jackals (Hikayat Khalila Wa Dimnah)* a well-known book of Indian tales reworked for a Malay-Muslim audience, and he produced a new edition of the *Malay Annals* that was used as a standard reference throughout much of Southeast Asia.

At Riau in the mid-nineteenth century, a renaissance in classical Malay writing took place. There, members of the royal court were versed in poetry writing and in the production of manuscripts on various subjects, including religion. The most prominent scholar from the royal family was Raja Ali Haji, mentioned earlier, who wrote *The Precious Gift (Tuhfat al-Nafis)* a chronicle of the Bugis entry into the Malay areas and their absorption into the Johore state as important officials and vassals. Alongside the Riau royal family, a number of important religious writers from elsewhere were assembled from the Middle East, South Asia, and elsewhere in Southeast Asia—probably as mentors for the royal family—but many of these did writing of their own on various religious subjects.

Throughout the Malay world of the nineteenth century, accounts of the fifteenth and sixteenth centuries were popular, including new versions of *The Malay Annals, The Story of Iskandar Muda,* and *The Gardens of the King,* and folktales about the local heroes Hang Tuah and Hoja Memum. Also there was a wealth of proverbs, and the ever-popular poetic *pantun,* described in Chapter 2. At some places older Muslim literature was used, such as the famous *Thousand and One Nights,* and even the tales in the Hindu epic Ramayana were popular. In Aceh there were abundant translations of Arabic sources and a reworking of classical literature from the Arabic in Acehnese and Malay writings. Other works drawing on Arabic sources without attribution and written anonymously included Islamic lore about the Prophet, heaven, hell, creation, and true belief.

By the 1920s the reading audience had matured significantly over that of the turn of the century, and new themes and genres were necessary to fulfill expanded intellectual appetites. Consequently, a spate of short stories was published in Malay-language journals in the Straits Settlements, most of them dealing with the disjunction between Western, Middle Eastern, and Asian values and ways of life. The themes of "forced" marriage and the difficulties of adjustment to urban life were common. Stories often dealt with Muslims, but the content or problems connected with religion were seldom issues of any moment. One prominent Muslim intellectual, Syed Shaykh al-Hadi, took part in this literary development, apparently because it allowed him to make a living while he carried on his intellectual writing in ideological magazines. He was well known for detective stories—starting with *The Tale of Rokambul,* which ran serially in *Friendship (Saudara)* magazine—emphasizing the struggle between good and bad. A leading Muslim intellectual, Za'ba (d. 1974), was preeminent for his studies on the development of the Malay language in its modern usage, one of a small number of such critics in the Malay-Indonesian world of the time.

In the Netherlands Indies, the primary outlet for new literary works appeared later in the era, such as *The New Poet (Pudjangga Baru)* magazine, operating between 1933 and 1942, which promoted prose, poetry, essays, and even a novel and a radio play. The movement promoted by the *New Poet* group greatly enhanced the new national language and acted as a forum for a long-running debate over the desirability of accepting Western values and styles as opposed to promoting a modernized version of Asiatic values and styles. Armijn Pané (d. 1970), Muhammad Yamin, and Amir Hamzah (d. 1946) were the leading writers of prose and poetry of the era, while Takdir Alisjahbana (b. 1908) was the conceptualizer and promoter of the language.

One important writer, Abdul Muis—largely because of his political career—did use religion as an important theme in his works. One of those works, *A Wrong Upbringing,* focused on the problems of a Western-educated youth who lost his cultural moorings because, in the view of the author, he turned his back on standard Islamic education when he had the opportunity to study in schools with a Dutch curriculum. Outside this circle of Westernized literati there were still a few writers educated in the traditional Muslim way but still writing in the new style that was evolving. Of these Hamka was the most important, who drew heavily on his reading while a student in Egypt and particularly that of the Egyptian writer al-Manfaluti (d. 1924). In *The Protection of the Ka'abah (Dibawah Lingdungan Kabah)* he used some religious references as a setting, although it was not essentially a religious story, a fact his Muslim critics were quick to indicate when they proclaimed it "frivolous."

There was further development of the Javanese language, especially at the royal courts of Surakarta and Yogyakarta. As we saw in the last chapter, belles lettres became prominent at Surakarta, particularly in the person of Jadisapura I. His offspring were to continue the tradition, making it a family specialty, with his son Jadisapura II (d. after 1825) and his great-grandson Raden Ngabei Ranggawarsita (d. 1873) providing the high points of that line of succession. All three were concerned to perpetuate old Javanese values and tradition, not only at court where the influence was strongest, but in Javanese society in general. Belief in Islam was regarded as an important feature of that Javanese identification, but Vishnuite values of conduct and deportment were the most important feature. Such mixing of Javanese cultural values with Islam was regarded as "genteel" and culturally acceptable in a way that would not be true without the Old Javanese tradition.

In the last part of the nineteenth century and the first half of the twentieth, Javanese writers concentrated on retelling stories popular in the past. This genre included *Lives of the Nine Javanese Saints (Suluk Wali Sanga)* and many stories about the martyred Siti Jenar, the saint who was put to death as a punishment for his esoteric religious beliefs who, predictably, then became a martyr for the constancy of his faith. *Lives of the Nine Javanese Saints* became a leading source for Muslim writers in the latter half of the twentieth century as a reference to the early Javanese tradition of Islam, even though the stories were literary creations rather than factual history.

In some quarters of the literate Javanese population a subtle anti-Islamism continued to express itself, revolving largely around the belief that Islam had weakened Old Javanese tradition, morality, and perspective. That attitude was kept alive by some of the gentry and members of the royal courts on Java, in large part as a reaction to the literature of the time that glorified the spread of Islam among the Javanese. One work reflecting this viewpoint, *The Story of Dermagandul,* written in classical style, appeared during this time period and upset committed Muslim sensitivities. It stated that the Islamic propagator saints of Javanese history had been interlopers whose actions merely undermined an old, illustrious, and valuable culture. The work strongly attacked the famous Sunan Bonang, charging that he had been particularly underhanded in his treatment of the Javanese rulers of the Majapahit kingdom, which had been the great carrier of Javanese culture. Muslim organizations of the time, including the Muhammadiyah, protested the appearance of the manuscript, apparently without much effect.[40]

Language development also occurred in southern Sulawesi where the Bugis language, written in a unique script, developed its own poetry, sagas, court chronicles, and religious literature. In particular, Islamic writings of four general types paralleled the growth of Islamic literature in the Malay world and on Java. The first group was concerned with stories of the prophet Muhammad, his companions, and the early personages of Islam, along with religious tracts on various matters of dogma and sermons to be recited in the mosques. A second group of writings were translations from Malay that dealt with the prophets of Islam, such as Ibrahim, Musa, and Salman, as well as the immediate family of Muhammad, such as Fatimah and ʿAli, the Prophet's daughter and son-in-law respectively. A third group consisted of descriptions of mystical practices and the admonitions of learned mystics on proper belief and attitude. The fourth part contained prayers, religious formulas, and various incantations. In addition there were also translations from Malay of standard entertainment literature with Muslim themes, such as *The Story of Bakhtiar.* This Islamic literature was not much different in form and content from that found earlier and contemporaneously in the Malay and Javanese areas, so it seems the tradition simply spread into a new language, probably with a minimum of adaptation.

In the Dutch-controlled areas of Southeast Asia, Dutch was the language of the elite and was used throughout the administrative services. There was a small amount of Islamic literature written in Dutch by Muslims who used that language regularly, particularly by those who had attended Dutch schools. The Young Muslims' League–JIB (Jong Islamieten Bond), at Batavia published an intellectual magazine *The Light (Het Licht)*, which contained the writings of its members and interested outsiders, mostly in Dutch. The mentor of the organization, Haji Agus Salim, also wrote a series of works about God, religion, and the requirement in Islam for the separation and differentiation of the sexes. One of the later leaders of JIB, Moehammad Natsir (d. 1993), published a series of booklets with similar themes.

Finally, the Arabic language suffered considerable loss of influence during this period, even if its status was not particularly eroded. The rise of an entire new literature in Malay/Indonesian began to replace the books that had formerly been the mainstay of the cultural and religious systems. Still, local scholars who mastered Arabic were able to go to the sources of the religion and were highly regarded for their knowledge of that language. Religious scholars still had to know Arabic and, on average, the mastery of Arabic during this era was at a much higher level than previously, as Islamic schools began to pay more attention to understanding the language and perfecting reading and writing along with mastery of standard texts.

Music and Dance

A nineteenth-century painting from Java indicates that royal processions and parades continued to be held and that musical instruments were a vital accompaniment to those events. During the nineteenth century a genre of singing developed in the Malay Archipelago region that adopted the name *hadrah*, apparently in reference to the supposed origin of the musical form brought there by Hadrami Arabs. Initially the genre was spiritual in purpose, concentrating on praise of God and the Prophet, similarly to the classical odes *(qasidah)* found in the central Islamic world. This genre rapidly transformed into a form of entertainment useful at weddings and other life-cycle celebrations, where praise was given to the individual or to the marriage couple being honored. This form of music was accompanied by dancing, using local traditional steps, and later developed some plot lines so that it began to resemble theater. Traditional Malay dress was the general attire of the performers.

In the Malay areas encompassing the territory from Trengganu in the south to Patani in the north—namely, that area under Siamese control—a form of classical Malay dance remained popular; for a time it was performed in Riau and Deli as well. The form drew heavily on animistic mythology and Hindu-Javanese deities common to the area in earlier times. Its continuing use long after the arrival of Islam, was justified by the claim that the dance patterns had originated with the first man, Adam, implying that it was thus allowable under Islamic doctrine because it was connected with an early prophet. In essence, however, like many other traditional dances of the zone, these were not connected with Islam in any real way; still, in actuality, committed Muslims before the arrival of reform movements did not find the dances offensive to Islam either. The modernists, of course, did regard such dances as heavily laden with animism; as such, they were questionable activities for Muslims.

Courtly dancing continued to be used even in the twentieth century. At the Sultan of Sulu's reception for the American commissioners in 1901, court dancers gave several performances. The first group consisted of petite women dancers who were carried into the performance area and placed on white mats. "They wore long yellow silk skirts, white waist bands, silver belts and suspender-like bands of silver ribbon crossed over their breasts."[41] The dancers wore elaborate headdresses over hair pulled together in a knot at the back, held there by horn combs, from which hung spangles of red and blue silk that moved about as the dance proceeded. The dance consisted mostly of swaying to and fro, while the hands and arms moved in intricate patterns, and faces maintained a stony composure. This style was in marked contrast to the dancing of the non-Muslim women from the mountains. They wore heavy brass rings on their ankles and a large number of brace-lets on their forearms; their feet were mostly stationary, but their bodies moved in a lithe, snakelike writhing. There was nothing particularly Islamic about the dances, but they were performed in the court of a Muslim ruler and must have reflected what he regarded as acceptable.

Finally, throughout the region there was common use of the "Birthday of the Prophet" (mawlid) recitation, the performance of the "piercing" (dabus) ceremony among mystical groups, and praises sung to God and the Prophet. All of these have been outlined in Chapter 2, but they continued to be used in this era because they were part of the standard repertoire of the various performing troupes and were well understand and enjoyed by wide numbers of people in the population.

Conclusion

Politically, this era was a cataclysm for many royal families widely through-out the Muslim Zone of Southeast Asia. Large numbers of them were swept away by colonial administrations that perceived them as unneeded, unco-operative, or standing in the way of colonial policy. Rulers were removed and never replaced in the Dutch, Thai, and American zones. Also, in many places royal rulers who remained were placed under surveillance and had their political powers tightly regulated, as in the case of the Javanese rulers in central Java. Only in the case of the rulers of peninsular Malaya was there any elevation to a new level of status, but even there their authority was carefully directed to achieve colonial perceptions of what was good for those states. In the last period, that is, the first half of the twentieth century, new elites began to appear that sought to control indigenous society, both Muslim and secular. Those who sought to be spokespersons for the indigenous population were placed under surveillance, limited in their activities, and in some areas imprisoned or isolated. Committed Muslims were found in all three leadership categories—royal, local, and new elite—and experienced the colonial occupation in the same way that their less pious or non-Muslim fellows did.

Politically, the forms of government underwent change that was not to the benefit of Muslim leaders. At the highest level of society increasing foreign control of government organization and power established the goals of colonial systems as top priority. Southeast Asian forms of rule were rejected as unviable, and the Dutch, French, Americans, and British all placed new administrations over the political operations that had existed earlier, so that the new systems reflected their own methods of rule and styles of governing. Moreover, change was initiated at all levels of administration, as the British example in building the federated states on the Malayan Peninsula revealed; but the Americans in the southern Philippines and the Dutch in the same time period did the same. By the end of the era these political systems no longer had the appearance of being indigenous in form or content.

Economically, the peoples of the Muslim Zone were losers and Muslim enterprises were among those hard hit by the changing economic conditions that occurred during this era. Muslims had been the leading traders in the preceding era, and their local efforts in forest- and sea-gathering occupations and their entrepreneurial efforts along the coasts and waterways were crucial economic processes of the time. In the new colonially controlled economies that emerged, new products, new methods of capital funding, and new methods of gathering and processing goods for the international market were introduced that pushed the local workers and traders into ever more disadvantageous conditions. In several areas, such as the Malay states, Chinese workers and traders were introduced as a cheap source of labor and as providing a more efficient form of business than local peoples could provide, so that the latter were shut out of prosperous enterprises and marginalized. Even where Muslims showed innovation, as in the cloth industry of central Java in the early twentieth century, the market proved too limited to support the numbers of Muslim businesses that entered it. The system was geared to an international market controlled by foreign interests.

The indigenous societies were also affected socially, although it took a long time to transpire. Islamic penetrations of local customs in the preceding era continued to be accepted and even strengthened during this time, so that very common patterns of life-cycle events had a universal Islamic element. The acceptance of these Islamic interpretations of life-cycle events gave the Muslim Zone a cohesion that was always lacking in the political realm. In point of fact, Islam penetrated the societies of Southeast Asia through their observance of certain of its social institutions more than its political or religious ones. The analysis above shows a continual strengthening of these institutions throughout the time frame until the mid-nineteenth century, although they began to undergo some changes in the early twentieth century as urbanization began to affect social organization.

Socially, Muslims were transformed along with the rest of society as the new technical civilization of the West penetrated Southeast Asia in the late nineteenth and early twentieth centuries. Indigenous groups in administration in all parts of the region profited the most from the new educational systems that were introduced. Committed Muslim communities often went their own ways with improvements to their religious educational systems or the introduction of hybrid systems that combined traditional Islamic and Western education. The changes split the societies in some respects, and the results were most apparent in the differences between the northern Malay states and those in the south, in the American area of the Philippines, and in the Javanese and west Sumatra areas. Two streams of education emerged, with graduates often finding themselves at odds with one another and with different outlooks on the desirability of future political and social arrangements of the societies and governments of the region. In this dramatic development Muslims seem to have been the losers.

Religiously, this was a period of growth and maturation that changed the nature of religion in Southeast Asia from a generally nominal adherence to Islam to a more thorough commitment to that religion by the closing years of the era. A continual transferal of Islamic lessons and literature from the Middle East, almost all of it from Arabic-language sources, occurred during the period. Along with the influence of the schools and teachers in Makkah, the lessons of Islam were transported back to Southeast Asia so that the general religious outlook moved through a Hindu-Buddhist era, over to a heavily mystical stage, and from there to a time of general reform stressing jurisprudence. This development belied the presence and high influence of intrusive foreign powers because the efforts were continuous and vital, setting the stage for further maturation after the intruders left.

Culturally, this was a period of broad expansion in Muslim thought and literature, with a considerable array of thinking and writing in several principal areas of the Muslim Zone. Language often used the Arabic syllabary, even though European and Thai authorities sought to replace it with other scripts and over the long run were successful in making the transition. Local literatures were strengthened with an infusion of tales, stories, and literary devices used in the Middle East, and these became an important part of the local traditions. In all cases, the literatures found room for considerable development of Islamic literature devoted to explanation of the Islamic sciences in understandable idiom. This genre underwent startling development in this time span, beginning with mere translation and commentary from Arabic and moving to the production of entire books in the vernacular by the end of the era. In general, Muslim thought and practice matured considerably during this time period as a result of the new literature that evolved.

In sum, then, the Muslims of the Muslim Zone survived the colonial period in a weakened political position, but strengthened their hold on Southeast Asian societies and increased their orthodoxy and commitment to Islam. By the end of the era, Muslims were a vital part of the societies of the Muslim Zone but by no means the prime determiners of the new world that would emerge as the colonial forces receded.

Key Readings

Benda, Harry J. 1958. *The Crescent and the Rising Sun*. A description of developments in the Indonesian Muslim community during the last decades of Dutch colonialism and the Japanese occupation.

Gullick, J. M. 1990. *Malay Society in the Nineteenth Century*. An overview of the political, social, and religious life of the Malays during the early days of British colonial expansion in Southeast Asia.

Kobkua Suwannathat-Pian. 1988. *Thai–Malay Relations*. A study of the Thai monarchy's efforts to extend the nature of its control over the Malay states of the Malay Archipelago.

Kumar, Ann. 1997b. *Java and Modern Europe*. A description of the political, social, and cultural developments on Java in the eighteenth and nineteenth centuries and the reaction of various societal groups to Dutch intrusion.

Majul, Cesar Adib. 1999. *Muslims in the Philippines*. A common history of the various Muslim peoples of the Philippines stressing the role of Muslim commonality.

Matheson, Virginia, and Barbara Watson Andaya. 1982 and 1985. *The Precious Gift*. The chronicle of the last century of the Johore kingdom, with a nostalgic look at the passing of traditional society.

Matheson, Virginia, and M. B. Hooker. 1988. "Jawi Literature in Patani." An investigation of Islamic textbooks prominent in Southeast Asia emanating from the Patani writers of the late nineteenth and early twentieth centuries.

Noer, Deliar. 1982. *The Modernist Muslim Movement in Indonesia 1900–1942*.

An account of the political and social movements organized by Muslims in the last period of Dutch rule in Indonesia.

Reid, Anthony. 1980 and 1993. *Southeast Asia in the Age of Commerce.* An anthropological account of the peoples of Southeast Asia in the period marked by the entry of Europeans into Southeast Asia.

Reid, Anthony, and Lance Castles, eds. 1975. *Pre-Colonial State Systems in Southeast Asia.* Articles on the political structure of states in the eighteenth and nineteenth centuries throughout maritime Southeast Asia.

Roff, William R. 1967. *The Origins of Malay Nationalism.* An account of the rise of Muslim modernism in the Singapore and peninsular Malay states during the first half of the twentieth century.

Warren, James Francis. 1981. *The Sulu Zone 1768–1898.* An analysis of the economic structure of the Sulu state and its dependence on slavery.

Wilkinson, R. J. 1925. "Life and Customs." An anthropological description of the living conditions and customs of the Malay peoples of the Malay Archipelago at the turn of the twentieth century.

Yegar, Moshe. *Islam and Islamic Institutions in British Malaya 1874–1941.* 1979. A careful description of Muslim institutions of the Straits Settlements during the British period.

4 Nation-States and Civil Values (1945-2000)

> Islamic resurgents want a new social order.... Countless seminars
> and forums have called for the establishment of an Islamic edu-
> cation system, an Islamic economy, an Islamic political order,
> an Islamic legal framework. Most of all [they] want an Islamic
> State.... The passion behind it, fortified by the enthusiastic
> support of a growing number of young adherents, is an unmis-
> takable sign of our times.

General Context

The Greater Asian Setting

The three regions of Asia endured, but with different political configura-
tions and changed economic importance due to the shifts in international
power relationships. Petroleum was king during this era, and the presence
of large amounts of it in certain parts of the Middle East and Southeast Asia
gave added importance to those regions. The Cold War between "East" and
"West" produced pressures on the new nations of the Asian region, and they
divided between the two camps. The new nations that arose had to define
themselves both to their own peoples and to others.

The Middle East entered this period with a large number of independent states and others were added during the era. Significantly, the region
continued to have an impact on the Southeast Asian Muslim Zone. First, two
different political systems were used in the Middle East that seem to have
been parallel in development to those of Indonesia. The political system
established in the 1960s by Abdul Gamal Nasser (ruled 1952–1970), which
featured strong executive rule with other political forces forced into weak
opposition roles, was also used by Indonesia in the Sukarno era. In a similar way, military rule in Syria, Iraq, Egypt, and Sudan may have constituted
some examples for Indonesia in the early Suharto years. Second, the operation of the Muslim proto-states of the Arabian Peninsula and the Persian
Gulf region may have been a model for the Brunean state. There were parallel developments in the Middle East and Southeast Asia, but out-and-out
imitation in either direction probably was not done, as individual events
produced their own localized reactions.

Developments that occurred in the Middle East did affect Southeast

Asian nations. There were changes in the pilgrimage whereby newly independent Southeast Asian countries negotiated directly with the Saudis for pilgrim allotments. The founding of the Organization of Islam Conference by Saudi Arabia with worldwide membership gave the Middle East status with Southeast Asian Muslims. Indeed, an early secretary-general came from Malaysia. Equally important, however, was the intrusive role that several Muslim countries were willing to play internationally—notably Libya, Saudi Arabia, and Iran—in influencing events that enhanced Muslim fraternity or communal cohesion. These nations used money from petroleum development for aid programs throughout the Muslim Zone of Southeast Asia, and they were particularly involved in the politics of the southern Philippines and southern Thailand, where Muslim minorities were disgruntled with the majority, non-Muslim rule. Through direct and indirect contact with the elites of the Muslim minorities and with the governments of the Philippines and Thailand these three Middle Eastern governments negotiated for political settlements that would protect the interests of the Muslim minorities. All told, there was an increase of contact and interaction between the two regions.

South Asia was further divided as a result of the colonial withdrawal; four nations appeared where the British had previously ruled. In the late 1950s and early 1960s, two of those states—India and Sri Lanka—sought to create a new bloc of nations capable of exerting international pressure on international bodies, particularly the United Nations. Indonesia, in the person of President Sukarno (governed 1945–1966), was so taken with the project that he hosted the Afro-Asian Conference in Bandung in 1954, although the inspiration clearly came from Indian prime minister Jahawaral Nehru (governed 1947–1964). Later contact was light, but some Muslim influence was apparent through Pakistan, where the writings of the Sayyid Abu A'la Mawdudi (d. 1979), a leading fundamentalist ideologue of the era, became recognized for his statements about the centrality of Islam in human life. As well, there was the continuing exportation of Ahmadiyah Islam, with its controversial claim of possessing a "renovator" or "prophet," which caused difficulty among committed Muslims in many places, including Southeast Asia.

China underwent similar change as the other two regions, but of a different character altogether. The Chinese were ideologically committed to communist ideology, which they attempted to spread through the Southeast Asian region, unsettling the peoples who lived there. During the 1950s and early 1960s communist insurgencies were promoted in Malaya/Singapore and the Philippines, and in the mid-1960s Chinese communists colluded unsuccessfully with the Indonesian Communist Party to institute a government that would be either communist or "near-communist." But despite this ideological interference, the image of China as a struggling nation attempting to modernize itself without much outside help offered an inspiration to Southeast Asians that earned it considerable respect and admiration.

Several other countries of North Asia—South Korea, Taiwan, and Japan—were crucial to the economic reconstruction programs undertaken in this time frame, which drew worldwide acclaim. Obviously such programs served as an important catalyst to the governments of Southeast Asia, and many of their characteristics were imitated, particularly their paternalistic governments, economic policies, and efforts to harness religion as a legitimizer of modernization and development. Malaysia, in particular, afforded these countries great respect when it inaugurated its slogan "Look East." Indonesia also attempted to apply the principle of religious certification to its development policies, apparently in imitation of East Asian success.

The Southeast Asian Setting

The beginning of the era was engaged in decolonization, starting with the Indonesian and Burmese declarations of independence in 1945 and concluding with Brunei's celebration of its independence in 1980. However, in the period from 1945 to 1958 most of the states in Southeast Asia were recognized as independent even though former colonial powers still exercised considerable influence throughout the 1960s. The new nations that arose were amalgams of territories held by previous colonial powers, with some shaping by national elites that arose at various centers—for example, Jakarta, Hanoi, Kuala Lumpur, and Rangoon—to decide which territories would be included in the new nations; if they erred, it was on the side of inclusion. These new nations spent much of the time until 1980 handling problems of national political integration and meeting some very severe setbacks along the way. The largest disruption was the Vietnam War, which had the practical effect of bringing about the unification of Vietnam, but geopolitically placed the nations of Laos, Cambodia, and Vietnam in the "communist world" and the nations of Thailand, Malaysia, Indonesia, and Singapore in the "free world" camp. As a result, political consolidation occurred under two vastly different ideological systems, with centralized forms of authority being established in the communist states and limited representative systems rising in the noncommunist grouping. In the latter, authoritarian forms of government emerged to dominate in all cases, although in the Philippines that authoritarianism was later rejected. By the end of the era, political consolidation had progressed far enough that observers were discussing the formation of civil values in many of the states of the region.

The latter half of the era was dominated by the economic cooperation of the southern states in the Association of Southeast Asian States (ASEAN) and by the economic expansion of the region under the direction of international development banks (i.e., the International Monetary Fund, the

World Bank, and the Asian Development Bank). Elites in these states were paternalistic and at times repressive, regarding their own well-being as inextricably tied to development of flourishing national economies. While all states except Brunei opted for representative government in the beginning, most had difficulty sustaining this choice, moving toward authoritarian forms and almost always limiting political participation. The role of Muslims within these societies varied according to their places in the power structures, but usually they were politically disadvantaged in most of the countries of the region.

People and Their Activities

Indonesia

Demographers identified sixteen major languages with about a hundred dialects in the Republic of Indonesia alone. About 57 percent of the population lived on Java, making the Javanese-Madurese groups the largest racial grouping of all. Other groups with appreciable numbers were the non-Muslim Balinese, Bataks, Dayaks, Papuans, and Chinese, and the Muslim Malays, Minangs, Acehnese, and Makasarese-Bugis. Of the total population 87.21 percent were Muslim, 9.71 percent were Christian, 1.83 percent were Buddhist, 1.03 percent were Hindu, and 0.31 were other believers.[1] Association with particular religions and degree of involvement with religion varied among ethnic groupings. Islam was strong among the Acehnese, the Malays, and the Minangs on Sumatra, among the Sundanese and Madurese on and near Java, and among the Makassarese and Sumbawans in the east. Islam also had pockets of strength among the Javanese on Java and the peoples of Maluku. Hinduism dominated Bali and had many followers in East Java. Buddhism was strong in parts of Java and north Sumatra, while Christianity was strong in sections of north Sumatra, in north-central Java, and on Sulawesi.

Anthropological studies revealed further divisions. In the 1950s Clifford Geertz described Javanese culture as grounded in three major groupings: the "gentry" *(prijaji),* the "committed Muslim" *(santri),* and the "Javanists" *(abangan).* The gentry served as a kind of a cultural corps, applying the concepts of custom and traditional values and giving general direction to society. Some of this class were devout Muslims, but most regarded their own cultural views, infused with Vishnuite values, as the guiding factors in their lives. The committed Muslims pursued trade and business and built a communal structure based on classical Islamic civilization, applying it to local conditions. The Javanists assumed the agricultural and labor activities of society. They looked to the official class for cultural advice and to the committed Muslims for spiritual help, while continuing to hold animistic values as central to their own well-being.[2] Despite severe scholarly criticism of the categorization, until late in the era this conceptualization was regarded as useful as a cultural measure and was applied widely by scholars and the media, not only to the Javanese, but often to other nearby peoples in Southeast Asia.

Malaysia

Malaysia was a multiethnic state with four major groupings: Malay, Chinese, Indian, and indigenous Bornean. Divisions in society reflected the viewpoints of the ethnic communities, and ethnicity often determined religion. Malays were nearly always Muslim, only small numbers of the Chinese had converted to Islam, and the Indians had a percentage—about one-third—that identified with Islam. Chinese were Buddhists and Taoists, and Indians were largely Hindu. Considerable change in demographics occurred in the era. For example, 1979 figures were 5,975,000 Malays, 3,850,000 Chinese, and 1,144,000 Indians, with Malays constituting more than 60 percent of the population in the northern states. Malays formed a general majority in the central state of Pahang, while non-Malays outnumbered Malays in the western and Bornean states. By 1991 there were totals of 8,918,000 Malays,

TABLE 1. Muslim Percentages of Total Population in Southeast Asian Nations

Country	Year / Total Population / %Muslim			Year / Total Population / %Muslim		
Indonesia	1965	120,000,000	90	1995	231,000,000	87
Malaysia	1969	10,200,000	50	2000	23,000,000	>50
Brunei Darussalam	1984	200,000	70	1991	260,482	67
Singapore	1969	2,000,000	17	2000	4,500,000	17
Thailand	1969	33,000,000	3	2000	62,000,000	4.1
Philippines	1975	42,200,000	3.75	2000	76,506,000	4.9
Cambodia	1969	6,600,000	1	2000	13,000,000	5
Vietnam	1969	(So.) 33,000,000	1	2000	81,000,000	>1

Sources: Kurian 1990; Singapore, 1989, 28; Che Man 1990, 19, 36.

5,215,000 Chinese, 1,429,900 Indians, and 2,765,100 other (mostly indigenous races) for a grand total of 18,379,700 people. Malays constituted over
70 percent in the northern states, and over 50 percent in Johore, Melaka,
and Negri Sembilan. Non-Malays outnumbered Malays in the states of the
west and in the Bornean states. But, while the figures show majorities, in
general Muslims were spread across the entire country and played an
important, usually dominating, role in political activity in all parts of the
country.[3]

Attitudes toward racial identity were important. In areas where Malays
were the majority, as in the northern states, there was strong sentiment for
tying religion and politics together and seeking an Islamic state. In some
areas of the country where large non-Muslim ethnic groups were present,
Malay attitudes were inclined toward racial accommodation, even though
Malays still sought a strong government relationship with Islam. However,
among Muslims of different ethnic groups there were some tensions. In
general, the Indian group tried to use association with Islam as a means of
becoming identified with the Malays, but this was hindered by tight restrictions on membership in the Malay community because of the government's
affirmative-action program for that group. A number of Chinese converts
to Islam in the 1970s faced the same barriers, where religious identity alone
was not sufficient to make one a native Malay or to allow assimilation into
that community.

Brunei Darus Salam

The Brunean state, operating with an Islamic ruler and a large majority of
its population as Malay Muslims, sought a high identity of state, society, and
population with Islamic and with Malay custom. The two points of identity,
religion and ethnicity, were regarded as supporting one another and as a
suitable basis for building a twentieth-century state. Ethnic minorities were
given some rights to worship freely and to follow their own customs, but
they were expected to recognize Malay custom and rights as paramount in
the functioning of the state and society. Although prevailing political realities were sometimes questioned during the era, the state reliance on custom and Islam were never at issue.

Singapore

Singapore society in many respects was a continuation of racial relations
found in Malaysia, with the Chinese, Malays, and Indians constituting the
three main ethnic groups. The Chinese made up about 75 percent of the
population, the Malays 15 percent, and the Indians about 6.5 percent, giving the Chinese the opportunity to shape the political and cultural landscape. None of these ethnic groups was a united entity in itself, with the

major groupings consisting of several subcategories marked by further social division. The 1980 census set the Muslim population at 292,174 Malays, 27,823 Indians, and 1,222,000 Chinese. There were also a small number, in the hundreds, of people from the Middle East, some of them Arabs from the very important Hadrami community, although intermarriage placed many of them in the Malay grouping.[4]

Thailand

The 1980 census figures in Thailand indicated that there were 1,714,689 Muslims in the entire country, with the largest concentration in the southern region where 1,371,784 were located, followed by the central region in and around Bangkok, with 329,611. There were 2,712 Muslims in the northeast and 10,582 in the north. The statistics also made urban–rural comparisons, showing that only 84,583 Muslims were found in urban areas, while 1,287,201 were in rural regions. Groups living outside the south spoke the Thai language almost exclusively, while those in the southern provinces spoke both Malay and Thai, with the use of Thai growing steadily throughout the era. In Satun Province more Thai was spoken than in the other three southern provinces. Malays formed the largest grouping of Muslims, but there were small groups of Chams, Indians, and Chinese who were also Muslim. In the 1960s and later in Bangkok, a Shi'ah community of about 2,000 members was clustered about four mosques who were descended mostly from earlier migrations of Persian traders to the region. Thai was the language of social intercourse in this community, and though Arab lessons were given for the study of religious sources, there was an attempt to translate leading books on Islam into Thai.[5]

The Philippines

The 2000 figures for the Philippines show nearly all Muslims located in the southern region of Mindanao and Sulu except for slightly less than sixty thousand in the metropolitan Manila area. Scholars identified thirteen separate ethnic groupings who were Muslim, with the Magindanao, Iranum, Tausug, Maranao, and Samal constituting 90 percent of the total.[6]

Cambodia

In Cambodia the Cham population, which was predominately Muslim, was located near the banks of the Mekong, through Kampong Cham and Phnom Penh to the Vietnamese border. In 1975 there were nearly 250,000 Muslim Chams, about 3 percent of the total population, with an annual pilgrimage representation of eighty and with a smattering of scholars educated at Islamic educational institutions, including Al-Azhar University in Egypt.[7]

Vietnam

The ten thousand Muslims in Vietnam at the era's end consisted mostly of Cham, largely in the countryside, with a grouping of Indonesians, Malays, Pakistanis, Yemenis, and Algerians, mostly in Ho Chi Minh City. The Muslim Cham referred to themselves as "southern Cham" to distinguish themselves from the Cham who were Hindu and lived in the central highlands, who referred to themselves as "pure Cham." In general, the Muslim community of Vietnam was isolated from the larger Southeast Asian Islamic community and exhibited some particular characteristics of practice and belief.[8]

The Political Situation

In this time frame, eight nation-states emerged in the Muslim Zone. The retreat of colonial powers from Southeast Asia allowed both the combining and the division of previous territorial units, yet the countries that emerged bore strong identification with the territories assembled by the colonial powers during their ascendency. Hence, Indonesia corresponded generally to the Netherlands East Indies; Malaysia, Singapore, and Brunei emerged from the British-controlled area; Vietnam and Cambodia were once French holdings; and the Philippines emerged from the Philippine Islands controlled by the Americans. The remaining country, Thailand, of course did not come under any foreign control and constituted territory roughly the same as Siam had before World War II.

An outstanding feature of these states falling completely or partly in the Muslim Zone was their ethnicity, which included a large number of competing groups. This multicultural characteristic was a primary divider of societies and, when these divisions ran on ethnic lines, religious identification was very frequently a factor in ethnic makeup. Subsequent discussion will show the extent of such subgroup identification.

In all eight countries of Southeast Asia attempts were made to establish civil values, usually based on concepts of nationalism, religion or religious toleration, ethnicity or intercommunal tolerance, selective histories, common language(s), and support of some common political system or ideology. In the three countries where Muslims formed the majority—Indonesia, Malaysia, and Brunei—and in Singapore, where Islam was a minority, relatively successful civil cultures were constructed that were accepted by the Muslim populations, and in fact Islam was effectively recognized as an ingredient in those civil values. In two countries where Muslims were in the minority—Thailand and the Philippines—civil values were established that did not give much consideration to the Muslim populations as part of the national community, and hence Muslims had difficulty identifying with

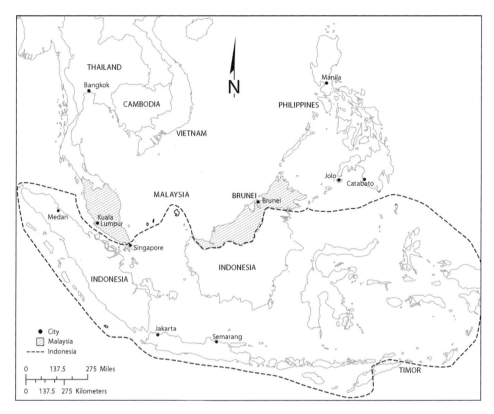

6. Nations of Southeast Asia

those nation-states. In the case of two other countries where Muslims were minorities—that is, Cambodia and Vietnam—incomplete or unsuccessful civil cultures were constructed by elite groups that were not accepted by the entire population and were also suspect among the Muslim populations.

Further, in all the countries of the region governments established administrative agencies that were intended to handle religious matters within their territorial boundaries. Often they were called "Ministry of Religion," but not always. In countries where Muslims were a minority, the ministries were usually preoccupied with a more dominant religion, often Buddhism; consequently Islamic affairs were given light attention. Moreover, because religious matters were not so easily defined in isolation, many areas, particularly law and education, were handled in other government departments. The ensuing discussion attempts to describe the effect of government policy regardless of the ministry involved.

Also, alongside Muslim identification or lack of identification with nation-states within the region, the participation of Muslims in their political systems was equally important. When elections were held, Muslims were able to vote in the national elections of every state in the Muslim Zone and were able to become members of whatever councils, parliaments, or offices that were contested by election. But more was at issue than merely voting and sitting as representatives, as we shall see. The openness of any political system to including Muslims in administrative positions at various levels, becoming teachers in the school and university systems, and eventually persons of influence and decision-makers was important as well.

Muslim Majority States

Indonesia
The Return of Dutch Colonialism

When the Dutch attempted to reassert authority over the former East Indies after World War II there was Indonesian resistance. On August 17, 1945, the Republic of Indonesia proclaimed independence and sent paramilitary units to occupy as much territory as possible given the constraints of manpower. It was successful in establishing political control over some areas of Java and in several outlying areas, such as Aceh. Muslim paramilitary units trained during the Japanese period, the Army of God (Hizbullah) and the Martyrs of God (Sabillah), formed part of that armed force. Realizing that the earlier colonial system could not be reimposed, the Dutch adopted a new strategy in which a series of states consisting of regions within the archipelago were created with Dutch leadership. That ploy was successful for nearly three years, but by late 1949 the Dutch were forced by international pressure to pass sovereignty over to a United States of Indonesia, which consisted of the Republic of Indonesia and the Dutch-created states. The following year most of the Dutch-created states disbanded and relinquished political control of their territories to the republic, putting an end to Dutch colonial presence in the Southeast Asian region, except for the area of West New Guinea. That territory was passed to Indonesia in a later agreement in 1962.

During this short period of four and a half years between the declaration of independence and passage of sovereignty, several developments occurred that affected the Indonesian Muslim community. In the first instance, a ministry of religion was established in 1945 in the republican area of control and its early work dealt mostly with recording marriages, with local registrars being located at the prominent mosques in key cities and towns. In 1948 the ministry took on its wider mission of handling a religious court system, supervising Muslim education, setting standards for general worship, and assisting in the repair and building of houses of worship. Given the unsettled conditions of the revolution, this wider mission was implemented only in part—little was done with the pilgrimage, for example—and it was not until the next era that the general work of the ministry became a reality.

In a second development Indonesian associations and organizations revived, many with specific Muslim purposes. The Muhammadiyah and the Nahdatul Ulama–NU associations continued as they had in the late colonial and Japanese periods, and they were joined by numerous others, which organized women, students, labor, intellectuals, and other groups in Muslim society. The most important Muslim organization of the time was the Indonesian Muslims' Consultative Council, Masjumi, an umbrella political union modeled after the Muslim federation organized during the Japanese period. Party membership was general among Muslims and attempts were made to create unified Muslim political goals, but common aims were elusive. Party representatives took part in all governments throughout the period, but the factions included in the coalitions were different for each new government. Masjumi leaders did not put forward an "Islamic" agenda, contending that cooperation with non-Islamic parties was essential and that such issues as the role of religious principles in a state could be decided after independence was fully achieved.

There was reaction to the creation of a nonreligious state on the part of some Muslim groups. The most significant response occurred in West Java, where a secondary Muslim leader by the name of Kartosuwirjo (d. 1966) had control of Muslim paramilitary forces. In 1948 Kartosuwirjo established himself as "Islamic leader" *(imam)* of an Islamic government. In the area he controlled, largely inaccessible to the Indonesian and Dutch armies because of the rugged terrain, he collected taxes from the villages, established military courts using a form of Islamic justice, and began the establishment of Islamic institutions. In 1949 he declared his state, called the "House of Islam" (Darul Islam), to be operative throughout the entire country, even though it garnered only limited loyalty in several isolated regions. Republican leaders saw his actions as clearly those of a renegade, but Masjumi leaders attempted to negotiate and persuade him to join the republic. National Party leaders, on the other hand, wanted him treated as an outlaw, and this view prevailed.

Independent Indonesia

Indonesia's political system changed dramatically when the Dutch transferred sovereignty in 1950. During the first era (1945–1958), known as the Liberal Democracy era, Indonesia had a nominal president and a strong legislature operating a cabinet system. There was frequent change of prime ministers during this period and little political stability as a result. By the end of the period in 1957, widespread elite and popular feeling was that liberal democracy had been a failure and had not resolved major problems confronting the nation. The second era (1958–1966), referred to as the period of Guided Democracy, featured an authoritarian president, with politics based on a balance between the army generals and the communist party. President Sukarno played the two power factions against one another and enticed them to compete with one another to advance his agenda, which aimed at eliminating the Dutch ownership and influence in the economic life of the nation. He largely accomplished that goal, but the cost was high in economic terms. The period ended when the balance among factions was upset and the country was in economic ruins. In the third period (1966–2000), known as the New Order era, a paternalistic government was established under President Suharto (served 1966–1998), which eliminated most political opposition and made massive efforts to modernize the economy. As a result of a government based on generous agricultural subsidies, large-scale modernization loans from abroad, and massive education schemes, the country experienced a thirty-year period of economic growth. At the end of the period, when public confidence had been lost and an economic crisis occurred, President Suharto was forced from office. That system was then replaced with a reconstituted system of liberal democracy.

Civil values were consciously installed in the constitution of 1945, consisting of five principles, called *Pancasila,* which formed the basis for the political culture throughout the period. The five principles—that is, "belief in God the Only One," "nationalism," "democracy," "humanitarianism," and "social justice"—were generally accepted as the underlying themes of nationhood by most elements of the population, but at first were not accorded top priority among many groups because of religious, ethnic, and regional differences. Many committed Muslims regarded *Pancasila* as a simple national motto and wanted Islamic standards to be the basis of state operation and the creation of civil values. A crisis of identity occurred in the 1950s when national values were at issue in an election campaign, in the constituent assembly, and in armed resistance in the provinces. The matter was settled unilaterally by President Sukarno and the Indonesian military, who put down the rebellions, decreed *Pancasila* as official, and ended the public debate about the nature of Indonesian nationhood. Under the New Order government *Pancasila* became standard national doctrine in schools, in government-employee training, and in government propaganda materials aimed at the general public. By the 1990s the government was strong enough that it was able to insist that all social organizations regard *Pancasila* as the basic philosophical underpinning of their organizations, insisting that any conflicting ideology or religious outlook had to be cast aside or made amenable. Muslim associations did this with great reluctance.

Muslim response to the founding of the Indonesian state was positive, and there was always a strong identification with it on the part of most Muslims throughout the era. Indonesian Muslims were involved in the establishment of the nation, composed the greater part of the administration of the government, and were leaders in many sectors of society. There were, however, a few notable exceptions to this identification. In the early part of the period, particularly when the Indonesian republic was establishing itself, several insurrections based themselves on Islam. One, Kartosuwirjo's Islamic state, described earlier, was ideological, with the expressed aim of establishing an "Islamic state" with "Islamic law." The movement did control a small population, which it tried to rule with a version of Islamic law, but was too peripheral to the thinking of the time to gain much popularity, as large numbers of Muslims identified closely with the Republic of Indonesia. Three other Islamic movements based on regional aspirations were located in Aceh, southern Kalimantan, and central Sulawesi. For a time they made common cause with Kartosuwirjo, but there was never coordinated policy or action, and even religious teachings were different among the groups. In West Java the leadership was modernist, while in the other regions it was traditionalist in outlook. All four insurgencies were ended in the 1960s through government counterinsurgency measures, amnesty arrangements, and negotiations initiated by the army. Kartosuwirjo's movement, in particular, left a legacy with later governments—to wit, that the republic was under a threat from the religious right and that security forces had to stay alert to prevent their reemergence. Periodically governments made arrests of small groups of Muslim militants they regarded as posing a threat to the republic, after which they reiterated the constant danger of militant Islamic movements.

The reaction of Muslims to civil values was mostly positive. Muslims generally supported *Pancasila* as a political statement concerning the Indonesian state and its operation. However, many Muslim activists found the creed inadequate or inappropriate for the functioning of wider Indonesian society, where they believed Islamic values had greater possibilities and support among Muslims. The first principle, "belief in God the Only One," received most of the attention and was the subject of much discussion among Muslim groups. The tenet concerning God came to mean that the state recognized three specific religious traditions—Islam, Christianity, Hinduism-Buddhism—and that a state agency, the Ministry of Religious Affairs, was charged with handling administrative matters concerning those communities. Christians, Hindus and Buddhists, and nominal Muslims accepted the state interpretation of the principle easily, and often enthusiastically, since it was viewed as protecting them from the zealotry of some Muslim groups who wished to impose their versions of Islamic values. In general, these groups saw the *Pancasila* as a safeguard for them.

Many committed Muslim groups had difficulty with the *Pancasila* as any sort of a replacement for religious values, and throughout the era there were discussions about the proper place of Islamic laws and values in any state dominated by Muslims. Some groups, such as the Islamic Union–Persis in the 1950s, Carriers of Revivalism (Media Dakwah) in the 1980s, and the Army of Martyrs (Lasykar Jihad) in the late 1990s, asserted that Islamic values had necessarily to be accepted more fully by the state. These groups held that the entire nation must obey the dictates of Islamic law as laid out by the appropriate Islamic documents on the matter—either the Qur'an and Traditions of the Prophet, or Islamic jurisprudence, depending on the group making the assertion. Other groups, especially the leading associations, Muhammadiyah and Nahdatul Ulama–NU, while maintaining that Islamic values had to become the guiding principles of nationhood for Indonesia, were not in a hurry to make that happen. They professed that the form of such values needed attention and adaptation to the Indonesian environment, and were ambivalent about the application of such values to the non-Muslim sections of the population. Muslim activists near the end of the era often expressed their frustration with the statement that "Islam in Indonesia [where the vast majority of people were Muslims] functioned like a minority," meaning that Islamic values were not sufficiently incorporated into state principles, state policy, or state behavior.

Muslim reaction to the various regime changes was varied and, indeed, these changes had varying impacts on different Muslim groups. In the first period, the era of Liberal Democracy, there was unrestricted political activity marked by competition among a wide spectrum of parties, including four Muslim parties. Either Masjumi or NU was included in all the governments of the period, indicating the political importance of the Muslim vote in national politics. As discussed in the last section, Masjumi was the unity Muslim party founded in 1946 and a major political actor on the national scene until its demise in 1958. As the major representative of an important portion of the Indonesian population, Majumi was accorded considerable political status in the legislatures and cabinets of the time. Two prime ministers—Mohammad Natsir and Sukiman Wirjosandjojo (served 1951–1952) —and a number of cabinet ministers all came from Masjumi.

During this period, however, Masjumi's unity was fractured when groups within the party withdrew to seek their own political opportunities. The Indonesian Islamic Alliance Party–PSII (Partai Sarekat Islam Indonesia) established itself as an independent party in 1947, and the NU did the same in 1952. The loss of the NU deeply affected Masjumi, since the NU took with it most of the private religious scholars who constituted the backbone of the Muslim community in rural Indonesia. The result was that the NU became a key political actor in forming cabinet coalitions and replaced Masjumi as the partner-of-choice of the nationalists, who found it much more amenable than Masjumi as a political partner. The split in the Muslim political forces at this time reflected some substantial differences on doctrine and religious practice, but actually the failure really rested on elite jealousies, and there was not enough political patronage to satisfy all factions. After the 1955 election, Muslim parties commanded about 43 percent of the vote and about 30 percent of the seats in parliament, but suspicion and enmity among Muslim groups prevented them from cooperating with one another to form a coalition cabinet with an "Islamic" base to it.

In the second period, that of Guided Democracy, power moved to the presidency, the armed forces, and leftist political movements capable of mobilizing popular rallies in support of their goals. Political parties steadily lost strength. Among Muslim parties, Masjumi went out of existence because of its association with a rebellion attempting to replace the Sukarno government, while the NU and two other Muslim parties continued to exist, gained cabinet posts, and had access to government leaders. In general, however, these parties were considered peripheral and were awarded only subordinate posts in government bodies, which limited their participation. In general, social organizations declined during this era, and Muslim associations reflected this trend by losing large numbers of their members. Leading modernists were arrested as potential enemies of the state late in the era, and several who led key organizations were politically discredited through harassment campaigns conducted by the communist party.

As the Guided Democracy period came to a close in 1965 and 1966, Muslim personalities and organizations reasserted themselves and became active in trying to define a new political order, playing a secondary role in the emergence of a new government. On a negative note, Muslim intercommunal tension between "committed" Muslims and "nominal" Muslims occurred in East Java. Thousands of non-Muslims accused of being communists were killed in night raids, with Muslim youth organizations involved in the killing with the tacit approval of the local army units. Overall, this was not a good period for political Islam.

In the third period, that of the New Order, power resided in the military and in the presidency, with important groups of technocrats and businessmen allied closely with government leaders. At the beginning of this period several political parties existed; two Muslim parties, the NU and the Indonesian Muslim Party–Parmusi (Partai Muslimin Indonesia) were the most prominent. Periodic elections were held, but the undisciplined behavior of several parties in parliament appeared to the government as contributing to a loss of national direction. Accordingly, it decided to downgrade the role of political parties and create a flexible parliament that would support, largely without question, the policies of the government. Consequently political parties were required to combine, so that only the government-sponsored party and two other amalgamated contenders remained.

All individual Muslim parties were required to merge into the Development Party–PPP (Partai Persatuan Pembangunan) and lost much of their previous dynamism. Alongside this shrinking of political party life, a campaign was undertaken to remove all religious symbols as political identifiers, so that, for example, the PPP could not use the image of the holy structure (Ka'aba) at Makkah as its symbol. Neither could the mosque be used for political activity, and the Friday sermon had restrictions placed on the political viewpoints and preferences that could be expressed from the pulpit. Government statements insisted that worship should be important to the believer and a source of spiritual strength, but that faith was not an influential factor in politics. The government made little secret of its policy of "taming" Islam and removing it as a source of political mobilization.

Within the population that identified itself as Muslim there was a belief that Muslim political activism never accomplished what it was intended to, namely, to make Islam the cornerstone of the Indonesian state and enable Indonesian Muslims to be regulated by Islamic law. Throughout the era Muslims complained that they were not accorded a proper role in political life. In particular they held that they were systematically excluded from policy-making bodies and from political activities that would allow them to build the Islamic outlook they regarded as necessary. This is how things stood at the point when the events of 1998–1999 removed the New Order from power. After that, Muslims organized parties again and contended for power, even placing one of their own politicians into the presidential palace and having another chosen as speaker of the parliament.

The Ministry of Religious Affairs developed further in this era. Although it was responsible for all the major religious communities in the country, Muslim and non-Muslim, most of its efforts went to serve the Islamic community. It established courts to handle cases concerning Muslims regarding marriage, divorce, reconciliation, inheritance, and religious endowments, but these courts were made advisory to national law courts, which actually tried the cases. The ministry fairly early brought all private religious schools under its jurisdiction, then established its own school system incorporating all these private schools. The ministry then made further arrangements with the Ministry of Education and Culture for the eventual integration of these schools into a national system of education, with that integration still taking place at the end of the era. The ministry also established an extensive pilgrimage service, which set quotas for pilgrims each year, established a system for selecting them, provided them with appropriate instructions for undertaking the rite, transported them, fed them, arranged guides for them, and took care of their travel documents. Also, the ministry established local units that coordinated holy days among local prayer congregations, approved local mosque organization, certified persons servings as Friday sermon givers and, when the government had regulations regarding it, enforced restrictions placed on the subject matter of the Friday sermons. Further, working with local religious organizations, mosques, and worship groups, the ministry coordinated major religious holidays and the services connected with them. It also gave its certification to the publication of key religious texts, such as the Qur'an and its commentaries. Muslims generally approved of the work of the Ministry of Religion and regarded it as suitable that a government agency should perform such functions for the Muslim community.

Government policy regarding education aimed at creating a national system that would eventually lead to a common curriculum and educational standards for both national and private schools. The national system of education built on the schools established earlier by the Dutch. That system emphasized general subject matter and employed teachers who were graduates of secular teaching colleges. In 1950, there were 5 million pupils in elementary education, which increased to 80,000 schools, with an enrollment slightly over 15 million in 1976 and to 29 million in 1996. At the secondary level the gains were equally impressive, with 8,265 schools in 1976 serving slightly more than 2 million pupils at the junior secondary level, and 3,141 senior secondary schools with a total enrollment of 933,000 pupils. In 1996 at the junior secondary schools, there were 8.7 million students, and at the senior level 5.4 million students. Universities grew as well during this era, and in 1996 there were slightly over 3 million students attending them, with another 15,000 in graduate degree programs.[9] Muslims constituted the overwhelming majority of students and teachers in this system.

At the beginning of the era it was decided that, since there were not enough public schools to train all the children, private schools, largely the domain of religious associations in the Muslim and Christian communities, should continue to offer classes. From the early 1950s on working committees were established to try to bridge the differences between the many educational tracks. Some private Muslim schools were incorporated into the government system and received subsidies for their participation, agreeing to curricula that hypothetically gave Muslim pupils and students equivalent educations to their counterparts in public schools. Transfer points were made in the two systems, although the students from religious schools seldom found it advantageous to transfer, because their knowledge of general subjects was not at the same level as that of students already in the public schools. Diplomas were given equivalency as well, although government employers and institutes of higher education showed a clear preference for graduates from the public schools. Correspondingly, religious school graduates were relegated to schools specializing in Muslim higher education and to work in the low-paying Ministry of Religion. Parents of Muslim middle-class families often sent their children to public schools in the morning and to afternoon religious classes, assuring them of "balanced" educations.

Finally, there was an issue of Islamic identification that led to conflict in the Javanese countryside and in the Muslim community. It involved religious sects in central Java that drew heavily on values and practices reflecting Hindu and Buddhist rites that had preceded Islam. The sects numbered slightly less than two hundred, with membership in them ranging from less than fifty to several thousand. Most were local, some were regional, and a few achieved international importance. They varied in style; many adopted a mystical format, others were concerned with theosophy, a few espoused moral and ethical teachings, and some were devoted to magic and occultism. Committed Muslim organizations considered the members of the Javanist sects to be Muslims who were unacquainted with the proper teachings of Islam, especially those engaged in mysticism, where the goals and practices of regular Islamic mysticism bore a similarity with those of the sects. However, the members of the sects noted a pronounced difference between themselves and committed Muslims, preferring their own practices to those of Sunni Islam. To establish their own religious activities as separate and unique, the sects joined together early in the era to proclaim their own identity through a formal association and to work with the government about their status.

Largely through their lobbying efforts, in 1973 the sects were declared to be "cultural" groups rather than religious ones, and were placed under the jurisdiction of the Ministry of the Interior. This move afforded them protection against heavy pressure exerted by Muslim revivalist groups and the Ministry of Religion. For the purposes of this study, it can be concluded that the Javanist sects were at best a fringe group of Islam, but certainly not a functioning part of the Muslim community of Java, despite the general acknowledgment of their status as "statistical Muslims."

Malaysia
The Return of British Colonialism

When British authority was reimposed in 1945, the Straits Settlements were not reconstituted, but rather Singapore was given separate, Crown-colony status, while Melaka, Penang, Province Wellesley, the Federated States, and the "unfederated" states, including those returned from Thailand, constituted a new colony outside of Singapore. The new political arrangement created a federal government over all these territories, following the model of the Federated States used prior to the Japanese period. In northern Borneo the territories of Sarawak and North Borneo were both made Crown colonies, and the protectorate was reinstated in Brunei.

On the Malayan Peninsula the new federation installed by the British diminished the jurisdiction and sovereignty of the individual state authorities, particularly the ruling sultans. Consequently those rulers and their followers were particularly concerned about the new arrangements. The first attempt to form the federation, then called the "Malay Union," was stillborn when the state rulers reneged on their original consent, partly because of loss of royal prerogatives and partly in response to massive public protest against recognition of the Chinese and Indians as political participants on a par with the Malays. Eventually the Malay rulers agreed a second time to unity, but only after assurances were given that their place in the system was secure. The Malay public was pacified as well, since the new political arrangement recognized the Malays as the original inhabitants of the Malay states and gave them a special political role in the new governing system.

The Malay Union dispute was a catalyst for the formation of political groups and parties among the Malays, with the United Malays National Organization–UMNO and the Malay National Party–MNP splitting the Malay activists in the 1946–1947 period. UMNO, under Dato Onn bin Jaᶜa-far (d. 1962?) represented continuity by seeking to secure the place of the Malay sultans in the new political system and to work with the British in organizing the new state. UMNO also sought a balance between protecting Malay rights and seeking cooperation with the Chinese. The MNP, under Burhanuddin al-Helmy (active 1945) favored radical change designed to protect Malay rights. Al-Helmy wanted political union with Indonesia and called for removing British influence as soon as possible through revolution, if it could be supported by the Malays.

Of the two groups the MNP was initially more successful in mobilizing Muslim groups, particularly those who had connections with religious schools or close ties to religious teachers. In fact, this group of committed Muslims founded several other organizations that worked in concert with the MNP. The All-Malaya High Islamic Council–MATA, aimed at general improvements in Islamic religious life, such as heightening Islamic belief, welfare, and education, but its chief political goal was to create a new body of elected Islamic scholars to operate Islamic affairs departments then under the authority of the individual state rulers. The All-Malaya Malay Economic Bureau–Perpermas aimed at upgrading agricultural and economic enterprise among Malay-Muslims. The Muslim Party (Hizbul Muslimin) was interested in independence for the Malays, construction of an Islamic society, and realization of a Muslim state.

These Muslim organizations first gathered support from the countryside, but were banned by the government and many of their leaders arrested in 1948 with the declaration of the "Emergency," which was intended to halt a communist insurrection. Obviously the government used the occasion to remove its noncommunist political opponents as well. The effect of this punitive action against these militant religious associations was to drive many of their members into UMNO, which then held the Malay political arena relatively free of competition for a time. In 1951, however, the elements that had formed those Muslim organizations reemerged to found the

Pan Malayan Islamic Party–PAS or PMIP, which, over time, was to emerge as a rival to UMNO.

British attention during this period was monopolized by the communist insurgency from 1948 to 1960. The anti-insurgency policies of the British included resettlement of some Chinese villages; security sweeps; tight control over food, ammunition, and other supplies that could be used by guerrillas; and incessant propaganda to check support for the guerrillas. The second British government policy in this era aimed at passing political authority over to local political leaders; this was deemed to create a coalition of political parties committed to racial pluralism, and an elite that was strongly anticommunist and capable of winning support through elections. Political parties formed during that era generally reflected ethnic orientation, but a breakthrough was made by the Malayan Chinese Association–MCA and UMNO when they formed an electoral front that won elections for municipal offices in 1951, which in turn cleared the way for the creation of an independent state.

Independent Malaysia

In 1957 an independent Federation of Malaya was recognized by Great Britain consisting of the British holdings on the Peninsula, but without Singapore. In 1962 an independent Malaysia was formed, consisting of the Federation of Malaya and three British Crown colonies—Sabah, Sarawak, and Singapore. Singapore left Malaysia in 1965 because of a dispute over the political aspirations of Singaporean leaders, which Malay leaders in Kuala Lumpur found unacceptable. Malaysia adopted the Westminister parliamentary model, with a rotating monarchy and actual political power wielded by a prime minister beholden to a regularly elected parliament. Regime change was very slow throughout the era.

In the early years Tunku Abdul Rahman (governed 1957–1969) held the prime minister's post, supported by a political coalition of Malay, Chinese, and Indian politicians. The coalition changed somewhat during the succeeding years, but managed to keep a series of Malay political leaders in power for the remainder of the century. Tun Abdul Razak (governed 1969–1976) was replaced by Hussein Onn (governed 1976–1981), who, in turn, was replaced by Datuk Seri Dr. Mahathir Mohamed (governed 1981–2003).

The civil values of Malaysia were officially addressed in 1970 with the Pillars of State *(Rukunegara)* declaration, which established the principles to be "belief in God," "loyalty to King and country," "constitutionality," " the rule of law," and "good behavior and morality." These principles were explained in terms that stressed freedom to practice religions, customs, and cultures consistent with national unity, and it called for a fair distribution of economic wealth for all groups in Malaysian society. Several agreements made by the Malaysian political leaders concerning pluralism further defined civil values in relationship to specific communities, but the Pillars of State was always acknowledged to be the final authority on the matter.

The principle of communal cooperation, in which Malay rights were regarded as superior to those of the other communities, was originally enunciated in a campaign manifesto in the 1955 election and won political power for the coalition of parties signing the manifesto. The principle was an important element in political affairs after that time. Other communities, that is, the Chinese and the Indians, were regarded as having rights of citizenship and opportunity, but in somewhat less equal terms than the Malays. Economic opportunity in particular, where the immigrant communities had greater skills and resources, was viewed as an equalizer. This principle came under serious attack several times during the era, especially from younger Chinese who did not regard themselves as "immigrants," but it remained a cardinal principle of national character to the end of the era. In 1991 these civil values were given amplification by Prime Minister Mahathir in a speech wherein he stated that rebuilding the social and economic structure had placed all the communities on an even footing and that it was time to move into a new era. In his Vision 2020, he stressed three elements: greater communal cooperation, deemphasis of racial differences, elimination of all forms of extremism, and achievement of economic excellence. Few believed, however, that this statement changed the relationship of the various communities in any appreciable way or that Malay political dominance was to be discontinued.

Special Malay political rights included allowing the Malay sultans to retain governing authority in their respective states and to choose the paramount ruler of Malaysia from among their number. Malay ascendency also expressed itself in leadership at the federal level, where Malays occupied both the prime minister and deputy prime minister posts throughout the era. The special position of the Malays was further advanced in the New Economic Plan of 1971 when policy was implemented to upgrade Malay economic status in society. This economic provision came under attack several times, particularly from the Chinese community, which regarded the control of universities by Malays and of certain state investments on behalf of the Malays as undue favoritism.

In terms of Islamic identification, documents outlining civil values stressed the Qur'anic admonition that Muslims were the stewards of the earth, assigned that role by God. Consequently, it was a Muslim obligation to build a prosperous economic system so that some of the produce of economic activity could be used to fulfill God's commandments about aiding the poor, orphans, and others who suffered. Consequently, economics was a matter of high importance in the operation of the Malaysian state and directly related to the emergence of the reinvigorated Muslim society within it.

The third principle of civil values was the federated nature of Malaysia, which made state governments the primary governing agents in the nation with the authority to formulate policies and regulations that affected the welfare of their own populations. This institutional arrangement allowed the ethnically different populations of the Bornean states, Sarawak, and Sabah, to operate according to their own traditions in a federation that was otherwise dominated by the Malay and Chinese communities. The final point in civil culture was to Islamicize the political system and society as much as the constitution would allow. In fact, the constitution was fairly liberal on that point, clearly stating that government financial support for the Muslim infrastructure (i.e., mosques, pilgrimage office) and its operation was allowed. That clause was used to justify a number of institutions, some not envisioned at the time of the adoption of the constitution, such as the Pilgrims Management and Fund Board, an Islamic insurance company, and an Islamic bank.

Muslim reaction to civil values also varied on the same lines as it did on state identification and support of particular regimes. The Muslims in general, being mostly Malays, all supported the continuing special status of Malays, with Islamic opposition parties wanting legislation that would significantly increase Malay rights and prerogatives. PMIP members called for policies designed to give Malays greater preference and assistance in the social areas, in education, and in support of Islamic institutions. Few Muslims called for reform of the state sultanate system or the system of rotating the paramount ruler's position among state sultans. A considerable difference existed in the desire to assign Islamic values a greater role in the operation and structure of the national government, even to the detriment of the non-Muslim communities. In the last two decades of the century there was a growing, and politically loud, Malay-Muslim demand for the institution of Islamic values across society, with no exceptions made for non-Muslims. Understandably, such attitudes provoked hostility in the Chinese and Indian communities. But Malay-Muslim groups calling for the one-sided changes were seemingly oblivious to the feelings of other ethnic groups and unduly preoccupied with their own religious-political agenda.

In the Malaysian constitution Islam was designated as the official religion of the country, and all of the state constitutions, except those of Penang, Melaka, and Sarawak, acknowledged Islam as the official religion of the country. In the federal constitution, administration of Islamic affairs was assigned to the sultans of the various states, while in those states that did not have a sultan—Penang, Melaka, Sarawak, Sabah, and the federal territory—the paramount ruler was assigned that function for those territories. Shortly after independence, the Administration of Muslim Law Enactment was ratified by all state governments. This legislation recognized the state sultan (where there was one) or the paramount ruler as the head of the

Islamic religion and created a "council of religion" with powers to determine what the principles of Islam were and to advise the head of state on religious matters. The legislation also established religious courts, presided over by a religious judge, and a religious court appeals committee. The enactment defined specific regulations for ruling on family matters, religious offenses, and witnessing. As in the colonial period, religious courts were ranked as subservient to regular civil courts.

In the 1980s new legislation was passed in all the states redefining marriage law so as to strengthen the standard provisions protecting women. It also recognized religious courts as separate from the civil court system and allowed issues other than marriage—specifically inheritance, worship, and morals—to be handled by the religious courts. Alongside the operation of religious courts were also a series of religious offices in each district headed by a religious judge, responsible to a department of religious affairs located in the capital of the state, or in Kuala Lumpur for those states without a sultan. The district office was charged with the administration of mosques, coordination of common religious observances, and fostering "revivalism" of religious behavior. The office also registered marriages and divorces, authorized the division of property according to the law of inheritance, served as sponsor for women marrying who had no male family member to undertake that role, and mediated family disputes.

There was criticism within the Malay-Muslim elite about the organization of Islamic administration, some political activists advocating a national office of religion to better coordinate religious administration throughout the country. Opposition of the sultans and their supporters to such a proposal prevented that centralization from being seriously considered. A different response arose from the various "revivalist" movements and some Malay political parties, particularly the PMIP, that urged that a full range of religious regulations be placed on Muslims. In particular, those suggestions called for application of the "harsh penalties" *(hudud)* involving death and dismemberment for certain crimes. Some proponents of these penalties wanted them applied, not only to Muslims, but also to non-Muslims, which had the effect of badly frightening members of other ethnic communities. But, even when the proponents of such views gained political power in individual states—as PMIP did in Kelantan and Trengganu—they did not attempt to pass legislation to make such regulations applicable.

Two reasons were cited for this reluctance to take action on a matter the party endorsed as a principle. First, proponents believed that society had to be prepared in order for such measures to be fair and effective; obviously Malaysian society was not at that stage, especially the non-Muslim community. Second was the fact that the federal constitution would need amending to allow such regulations to go into effect since freedom of religion guarantees and other restrictions hindered the application of such penalties. The ruling elite of UMNO never supported the harsh penalties, apparently out of respect for its non-Muslim political allies, but probably also in part because UMNO itself advocated a cautious approach to Islamization.

The first two five-year plans (1955–1960, 1960–1965) were intended to rectify the wide economic disparities among ethnic communities. The thrust of the program was toward improvement of the living standard of those people living in rural areas, mostly Malays. Pioneer settlement on lands newly opened from cleared jungle areas allowed a considerable number of Malays to upgrade their economic positions, and the conversion of Chinese-owned rice mills to Malay cooperatives afforded them further economic gain. The New Economic Policy (NEP) in 1971 was designed to increase the number of "modern" jobs for Malays and upgrade their economic status. The goal was to raise Malay ownership from 3 percent to 30 percent in twenty years and to increase Malay presence in government jobs. Substantial goals of the NEP were achieved, although not entirely. For example, Malay ownership of economic assets reached slightly less than 20 percent in 1985, but the economy had expanded significantly by that time so that the amount of Malay holdings clearly exceeded the original targets in gross monetary figures.[10]

Education was affected by Islamic considerations. In the closing period of British rule it was planned to create a national education system with Malay as the language of instruction. To that end the large number of private, religious, and communal schools were absorbed into the new system, but the use of one national language was never enforced. English and Malay were made the two languages of instruction for the public schools, although at the primary level vernacular languages could be used if courses in English and Malay were part of the curriculum. At the secondary and university levels in the public system, only English and Malay could be used and standard government proficiency exams were in those languages. However, vernacular schools and universities were allowed to operate at nongovernment expense, and the government agreed to allow such private education to exist in the face of considerable opposition by Malay activists.

The university system grew throughout the area and consisted of several institutions, notably at Penang, Banggi, and Kuala Lumpur, each with a particular educational specialty. The numbers of Malay students in those universities was considerably higher than those of the immigrant communities, but educational specialists complained that there was an unusually high number of graduates in the humanities and religious studies rather than in economics, the sciences, and various technologies that the nation needed badly. After the creation of the Federation of Malaya, regulations imposed in the schools that later became part of the national system (including nearly all the missionary-sponsored schools from the pre-independence era) put an end to any non-Muslim religious instruction and did not allow instructors from those schools to teach religious subjects in supplemental classes. At the same time, classes on Islamic history, values, and practices were incorporated into schools as part of the normal curriculum, although they were intended only for Muslim students.

Alongside the national education system private Islamic education continued to function, but attempts were made to bring the standards of those schools into conformity with those of the national system. In the late 1960s and early 1970s, the students in those schools began sitting for the required national exams at various levels. Based on the results, most states with extensive Islamic school systems—Trengganu, Kedah, and Kelantan—made changes in the curriculum and administration in order to better meet national standards. Significant reorganization was necessary in Sabah and Sarawak, where test scores were much lower than on the Malay Peninsula. Secondary education institutes were identified in several places—the Islamic College of Malaysia, the Islamic College at Klang, and the Sultan Zainal Abidin Islamic College.

Brunei
The Return of British Colonialism

The British protectorate was reestablished in 1945, but in 1959 a new treaty established home rule for Brunei. It recognized that executive power rested with the sultan, assisted by an appointed executive council and a legislative council composed of appointed and indirectly elected members. In 1967 the sultan, Omar Ali Saifuddin III (r. 1950–1967), resigned but served as regent for his son until near to his own death in 1974, actually exercising all the powers of sultan during that time.

Much of the Brunean elite favored rule by the regent and protection by Great Britain as the best means of guaranteeing the continued independence of Brunei in the face of dynamic neighbors and republican ideology. The elite feared that those outside influences, especially in neighboring Sarawak and North Borneo, would contaminate Brunei and might even force a merger with them, which they believed would be to Brunei's disadvantage. The continuing rule of a traditional ruler with strong, even authoritative, powers was regarded as a hedge against such unwanted change. On the other hand, some sectors of the Brunei public were equally aware of the populist trends elsewhere in the region and favored their adoption in Brunei. This identification with republicanism was apparent in the groundswell of support in 1960 when elections for local government councils were held. The spokesman for the populist viewpoint, the Brunei People's Party–PRB (Partai Rakjat Brunei), won nearly all the contested seats. The party favored, in particular, union of Brunei with Sarawak and Sabah, with the Brunean sultan as titular ruler over the new expanded state. When the sultan rejected such a role, party leaders engineered a coup d'état in Brunei and proclaimed a "state of north Kalimantan." However, British forces defeated the small army that had been raised and the leaders of the uprising either fled or were arrested. Considerable sentiment for the PRB's goals continued in the general population, but with the crackdown on party activity in Brunei there was less opportunity for the expression of such viewpoints.

In the mid-1950s a series of Islamic institutions were established by the Brunei government. The Islamic Religious Council of Brunei was created in 1954 to handle matters of custom, Islamic religious affairs, and religious welfare concerns. In 1955 an act formally established religious courts for family law, and in 1956 religious taxes *(zakat, fitrah)* were introduced for Muslims, with the proceeds being used for charitable purposes. The 1956 legislation recognized the office of "legalist" *(mufti)*, which was common in the states on the Malay Peninsula, who had the responsibility of researching Muslim jurisprudence to arrive at precedents to be used in specific court cases or matters of government policy. Finally, in the constitution of 1959 Islam was made the state religion, but non-Muslims were recognized as having freedom of worship. The creation of these institutions had the support of religious teachers and of the teachers' association of the public school system, the two organizations regarded as spokespersons for the general population.

The chief policy initiative of the ruler during this period related to the 1963 creation of Malaysia, discussed earlier. There was an expectation that Brunei would become a state within Malaysia and that Great Britain would support that union. However, the sultan decided not to join, because the condition for Brunei's entry was the surrender of oil revenues to the Malaysian federal government after a period of ten years. Financially, this was considered too great a sacrifice, as Brunei at the time was the leading producer of oil of any Southeast Asian nation. There was the additional annoyance that the sultan's position on the list of rulers would be last and that therefore his chance of becoming the "paramount ruler" of Malaysia would necessitate a long wait. This unfavorable view of Malaysia on the part of the ruler was shared by both the elite and the general population, which saw Malaysia as constituting "outside rule." A United Nations' investigative committee polled popular opinion in Brunei and found it heavily against such an association, preferring political association with the other north Borneo states.[11]

Independent Brunei

In 1984 Brunei was recognized as independent by Great Britain. Its constitution gave executive power to a hereditary sultan. There was only one ruler between 1984 and the end of the era in 2000, Sultan Sir Hassanal

Bolkiah (1967–). During that time span the system remained politically paternalistic, with well-to-do families and a newly educated class staffing the senior positions of government and the bureaucracy. The government continued to rest on the authority of the sultan, who ruled with the aid of an appointed executive council. Political parties were allowed to exist, but this was contingent on registry with the government. In 1992 local government was revamped and the principle of appointment to local offices and councils by the sultan's officers was reaffirmed, but initial choices for candidates were voted on by the people at the village and county levels. In addition to their local duties, these officials became members of "consultative councils for local government officials" in various districts of the country, which received directives from higher officials and passed on their recommendations to higher authority in return. Selected school administrators and mosque officials were also members of the consultative councils. This arrangement was viewed by the elite as fulfilling Islamic injunctions that rulers should consult with their subjects; pointedly contemporary conceptions of democratic representation were avoided as inappropriate.

According to government statements issued at several points since 1984, the basis for civil culture was the Islamic sultanate itself and the necessity for all peoples in the state to acknowledge its authority and identify with it. This policy was given the name "Brunei, Islam, Malay"–BIM. In accordance with the views of the sultan, the Malay language in Arabic script was the official language, Islam was the state religion, and Malay custom was operative in society. Furthermore, learning in the sultanate was based on the "Islamization of knowledge" approach in which Islamic principles were incorporated in the learning of all disciplines. In 1991 a report issued by the government reported on the progress of the state's effort to make the principles of BIM civil culture operative in society. The report stated that ethnic groups were overcoming their separation from one another to forge a common identity, that government policies in all areas were having a positive affect on the population, and that, as a result of those gains, a common way of life was emerging in Brunei.

In 1992 BIM was introduced as a mandatory subject in the education system. In this school version, Islam was featured as the guiding principle of the nation and constituted a "shield" for Bruneans, while the other two principles of "Malayness" and the sultanate acted as instruments to fulfill the commands of God. Muslim students were required to complete courses on the history and cultural attainments of Islam, and on the practice and behavior of Muslims in properly fulfilling the demands of their religion. Non-Muslim students were required to take a course on "appreciation of Islam" and Islam as a guide for daily life since these principles constituted public morality. They were not required to take the courses on practice and behavior, because, as non-Muslims, they were not required to pray or perform other Islamic rites as part of their religious or civic duties.[12]

Muslim response to the sultanate continued to be mixed as it had been in the preceding period, with considerable support for the ruling dynasty. However, there was concern on the part of some about the lack of limits on the power of the sultan and the failure of the government to specify a clear and suitable role for the population in political matters. On the other hand, the adoption of BIM as the basis for civil values was generally understood and accepted, apparently even among non-Muslims. The concept of fostering greater religious knowledge and respect in society was supported. Even if the Muslim community itself sometimes fell short of those values, it was regarded as an ideal to be attained.

Much like sultans in the Malaysian states, the sultan of Brunei was constitutionally the official head of religion and, by custom, charged with administering Muslim institutions. He had the added responsibility of applying Islamic law based on the Syafi'i school of Muslim jurisprudence. Most of the formal institutions of Islam were found in the Ministry of Religion. Some were overseen by the chief religious judge, who was responsible for enforcing laws concerning marriage—namely, registration, handling contentious separations, and divorce proceedings. The ministry also regulated mosques throughout the country, arranged the proper appointment of officials, supervised worship, and provided for the regular delivery of Islamic sermons. Communal activities, such as the collection and distribution of the "poor tax" and the administration of alms, were undertaken. The ministry also had a section that conducted "propaganda and Islamic revivalism programs" aimed at upgrading the faith and practice of Islam and inculcating an understanding of Muslim duties and morals among the citizenry. In addition, the ministry issued religious pronouncements on important matters of religion when needed, such as "the dangers of secularism," the raising and selling of pigs, and the place of the Bahai religion in Brunei. In addition to the work of the ministry, several other institutions were established, such as the Brunei Islamic Trust Fund–TAIB and the Charitable Foundation.

These institutions were widely accepted by the Brunei population and were not the subjects of protest by local consultative councils, probably indicating positive support for their work and the manner in which they functioned. The ability of the Islamic Trust to draw nearly Brunei $100 million in deposits from the public in its initial period of operation indicated strong support for a bank employing "Islamic principles" of economics and investment. Religious scholars were participants in the work of Islam and supported the institutions strongly, even to the extent of approving the sultan's stress on making Islamic institutions a means of gaining support for the monarchy.

Muslim Minority States

Singapore

From 1945 to 1963 Singapore was a crown colony of Great Britain with an appointed governor assisted by an executive council and an elected legislative council. In 1963 the British transferred control of Singapore to Malaysia with the permission of the Singapore Legislative Council, and in 1965 Singapore separated from Malaysia to become an independent nation-state. Its territory was small, limited to the island of Singapore and a few offshore islets. The government was modeled on the Westminister parliamentary system, but the ruling party, the Peoples Action Party–PAP, effectively eliminated serious political opposition early in the era and ruled unchallenged thereafter. Elections were regular and apparently fair, with prescribed campaign periods scrupulously observed. Since political challenge from inside or outside the party was very weak, PAP leadership was stable and regime change slow, reflecting generational shifts more than ideological or political controversy.

The development of a pronounced civil culture was an aim of the PAP government throughout the period. It called for a "democratic, prosperous, and just" society, and a number of policy initiatives supported that ideal, which were constantly iterated in speeches of the primary leaders, in the public relations materials of the government, and in the policy documents of the regime. Central to the civil conception was the goal of creating a harmonious interracial and interreligious society. To this end, the primary languages of each of the constituent communities—Mandarin Chinese, Tamil, and Malay—along with English, were recognized as official languages, with conscientious efforts to make everyone in the city-state at least bilingual. Religious freedom was guaranteed in the constitution and such freedom prevailed throughout the period.

A second theme of the civil culture was the creation of a "prosperous society," which reflected the mainstay of PAP ideology that economic betterment was a legitimate goal of national life. Economically, the government promoted Singapore as the leading entrepôt port of the Southeast Asian region and consolidated it as the financial center of Southeast Asia. Education through the university level was established in order to provide the trained human power necessary to achieve its economic goals, and all citizens were expected to work diligently to improve their skills and marketable knowledge. Further, the PAP government attempted to provide social benefits for all sections of the population, particularly by upgrading housing and creating an economy that provided the highest standard of living in Southeast Asia.

In 1989 civil values became a major point of public discussion when the

PAP leadership opened a public debate on national ideology, claiming that an effort was necessary to give definitive character and spirit to the Singapore population. The debate revealed widespread fears about the effects of Western culture on Asian society and there was general consensus about the need to adopt positive Asian values to act as a shield against that intrusive culture. Four key values were isolated for this national ideology: "placing society above self," "upholding the family as the basic building block of society," "resolving major issues through consensus instead of contention," and "stressing racial and religious tolerance and harmony." These themes were regarded as correctly Confucianist in tone and intent, which was suitable for a country in which Chinese were a overwhelming majority.

Muslims of the three major ethnic communities supported the PAP governments, with the Malay-Muslim politicians a part of the ruling coalition, and the Indian and Chinese Muslims supportive of politicians from their own ethnic communities who were participating in the government. The first president was a Muslim from the Malay community, and throughout the era, several cabinet members were Muslims as well, although not in positions of primary importance. In large part, government policies designed to advance the members of the Malay and Indian communities economically probably convinced the Muslim population to support the PAP governments politically. Muslims entered educational institutions, the workforce, and participated in public affairs with positive attitudes toward the state and government and, despite some frictions caused by majority–minority status problems, generally regarded themselves as belonging to the Singapore nation.

State institutions were created to assist in the administration of Islamic religious affairs soon after independence. The Islamic Council of Singapore–MUIS (Majlis Ugama Islam Singapura) was originally an advisory group to the president but later was given administrative duties. In particular, it operated a mosque-building program, organized pilgrimage affairs, oversaw the use of the mosques, including holy day celebrations, and administered religious endowments. One of MUIS's offices, the Registry of Muslim Marriages, reviewed applications of Muslims for marriage and ascertained that the petitioners were of legal age—that is, sixteen years or over —and provided premarital counseling sessions. An Islamic affairs court handled cases of divorce among Muslims and other cases involving marriage disputes. The court retained several Muslim social caseworkers to assist couples to come to agreement about the terms and conditions of divorce.[13]

In policy deliberations the government of Singapore decided that the apartment house would be the standard dwelling for all income groups, and that the government would promote ownership by the people residing in them. People with adequate financial resources were encouraged to buy their apartments, and those who did not have that funding rented from the government with the option to buy at any time. Because families were assigned by economic ability, not by race, there was some mixing of ethnic groups, which broke down barriers and encouraged people to have social interactions with people from other ethnic groups and religions.

Initially Malays resisted the new housing schemes because the people living in the hamlets of the island liked village life. Culturally, Malays did not like the impersonal life of large apartment housing in which they were always a minority surrounded by Chinese residents, but they apparently adapted to the change. Middle-class Malays, particularly trained technocrats, adjusted to the city landscape and had few complaints about isolation. Importantly, they founded Malay neighborhood associations to encourage normal Muslim religious activity, particularly by promoting Qur'an recitation activities and the observance of religious holidays. They also formed networks to convey information, such as news about funerals in their neighborhood. Related to the housing program was the mosque-building program, which the state undertook to assure that the new housing patterns would have a sufficient number of places of worship for Muslims in the various sections of the city.

In regard to education, the Singapore government's aim was to produce a population of English-speaking, well-educated, and well-trained workers. Consequently it invested considerable effort and resources in its schools, deciding to separate out students heading for the secondary track by sending those with potential academic abilities into the university entry stream and directing those who demonstrated less of those abilities into technical programs. Abilities were measured by standardized testing. By the 1980s there were concerns about the comparative lack of success of Malays in this system. In the 1983 competition, nearly 60 percent of the Malay students were sent to technical education, vis-à-vis the norm of 40 percent for all. Government and PAP leaders regarded the problem as a failure of the Malay community and urged—actually demanded—that the community itself do something about it.[14]

The Malay Youth Literary Association and the Torch Movement (Gerakan Obor) were prominent in directing the discussions and public fora that constituted the communal soul-searching of this issue. Discussions focused in part on some of the structural obstacles Malay students faced to succeeding in public schools, particularly scheduling difficulties, which worked to their disadvantage. Also, stereotyping by Chinese teachers verified the well-known "self-fulfilling prophecy" whereby Malay students did poorly because they were expected to do so. But cultural traits were identified as lying at the heart of the problem. Malays tended to be educated in Malay rather than English, which was less valuable in economic and educational terms. Malay parents were often poorly educated and lacked knowledge about how to assist their children's educational progress. Malay culture deemphasized economic and social competitiveness in favor of family and communal harmony. Furthermore, there was discussion about the role played by Islam in the issue, with those who were critical of Malay performance asserting that the Malays of Singapore used a variation of Islam that was "old-fashioned" —marked by passivity because of fatalism, "a penchant for magio-animistic explanations" of the universe, and a fondness for "enjoying life" instead of striving and attempting to improve conditions. Despite some protests about such stereotyping, this view of an outdated form of Islam prevailed. In many respects the communal soul-searching was a harsh lesson in modern reality.

The government response was to create a new social welfare organization called the Educational Council for Muslim Children–Mendaki which was community oriented and intended to address education primarily and social welfare in a broad sense. The thrust of the new organization was to help Malays set aside the prevailing character of Muslims and to establish new values more in keeping with the times. At the Mendaki congress in May 1982, an overall plan and seven detailed programs were outlined, starting with preschool nutrition and preparation, proceeding through the educational process, and ending with securing employment in "skilled jobs and creative work."

The programs of the agency centered on the family, and through "speeches, media coverage, booklets, marriage-guidance courses, sermons in the mosque, and community level meetings" they sought to disseminate ideas about developing the "new Islam." Along with encouraging them to do homework for school and study at higher levels of proficiency than earlier, Mendaki literature also called upon parents to remind children that "Islam values education," called for adoption of student prayer, and for parents to give their children Islamic greetings and blessings when they went to or returned from school, so that a "loving, concerned, and religious atmosphere" would pervade the home. A new effort was made to target newlyweds to give them early training about their duties as parents and to help them guide their children through the system with improved attitudes about Islam and education.[15] This theme of making Islam compatible with the values of the modern East Asian state was clearly evident in the Singapore situation, but actually it was a trend throughout most of the nations with sizeable Muslim populations in the latter part of the twentieth century, even if the issues were not so openly discussed.

Throughout the era there was criticism by PAP officials about the low scores on standardized tests earned by students in the private Muslim educational institutions. Periodic attempts were made to upgrade the six religious schools that existed in Singapore, serving about four thousand students. The criticism was that students who attended those schools lagged behind other students in the general school system, and consequently they were not likely to go on to institutions of higher education in the numbers that could ordinarily be expected. When such statistics were first revealed in the 1970s, prominent personalities in the Malay-Muslim community claimed that the figures were irrelevant, because students attending those religious schools were interested in learning about Islamic fields of study—which they did very well—and paid limited attention to the general curriculum that was taught alongside religious subject matter. Singapore government leaders, however, held that it was incumbent on Malay youth to attain good educations as defined by the government, lest the Malay-Muslim community fall further behind that of the Chinese. Efforts were made to improve the test scores of these students, without great success, but such concentration of course detracted from Islamic subjects, which had been the purpose of the schools in the first place.

Finally, there were part-time schools operating outside the educational system that taught rudimentary Arabic lessons, religious behavior, and ceremonial conduct, and gave introductory work in some of the Islamic sciences. These were not publicly criticized by the government or PAP leadership because they were defined as part of general religious instruction belonging exclusively to the Muslim community and clearly outside of the school system. As such they were not subject to government standards.

The reactions of Muslims to the educational policies of the Singapore government were mixed. Higher economic groups were supportive of the Mendaki programs, while other sectors of the Malay population, though participating, were less enthusiastic. More political in its response, however, was the challenge in 1990 by the Association of Muslim Professionals–AMP, which found the Mendaki plan not achieving its goals, especially in meeting educational standards, and blamed the Malay politicians in PAP for the shortcoming. The charge was that those politicians had constituencies beyond the Malay community and could not concentrate on Malay needs. The PAP leadership suggested that the AMP try its hand at operating Mendaki and stated that the government would supply the same level of funding. The AMC accepted the challenge and achieved about the same level of results as had emerged under the earlier plan.[16]

In general, the Muslims of Singapore occupied a unique position throughout the area, being a minority in the Singapore state and nation but part of a Malay/Indonesian majority when the neighboring areas were considered. The nearby presence of large groups of other Malays undoubtedly had an impact on the attitudes of Chinese leaders of Singapore, but it appears that those leaders were concerned in any case about making the Singapore society more dynamic and the Muslims simply could not be left behind in that effort.

Thailand

In 1946 Siam joined the United Nations with the name of Thailand and by that act was newly recognized as an independent nation-state. Thailand functioned as a titular monarchy, with a parliamentary system investing power in a strong prime minister and cabinet. The army officer corps and senior civil servants were strong political actors working in concert with politicians dependent on the support of those two dominant groups. Military leaders prevailed early in the period, while civilian leadership was pronounced at the end of the era.

The political culture of Thailand during this period owed its beginnings to King Chulalongkorn in the early twentieth century, who proclaimed "school, monkhood and the bureaucracy" as the identifying elements of the nation.[17] Later, Phibul Songkram (governed 1947–1957) removed the king from actual power, but kept him as a symbol of the Thai nation and a point of identification for the state. Premier Phibul also asserted that the historical tradition of Buddhism and its values of "merit, deference, loyalty, and dependence" were essential to Thai notions of nationhood; this assertion tied the majority Buddhist population closely to the state. Phibul promoted a vibrant nationalism through the use of the flag, an anthem, a common Thai language, and the identification of a territory with clear boundaries known as Thailand. In 1989, most of these values were renewed in a security act that defined offenses against the nation, religion, and monarchy; offenses against the democratic system under a constitutional monarchy; and offenses against the country's culture and tradition.

Muslim identification with the Thai nation-state was weak at the beginning of the era, tenuous through much of the period, and somewhat strengthened at the end of the time span. At the beginning of the era in the late 1940s, there was considerable resentment of Thai efforts to overturn the traditions of the Malay peoples of the south and make them culturally Thai, especially by demanding that they change their clothing, learn the Thai language, and act in accordance with general Thai codes of cultural conduct. In response, a local Malay-Muslim leader named Haji Sulong put forward a petition calling for a reversal of the cultural policy, the restoration of Malay identity, and the institution of local administration operated by the Malays themselves. At the same time, a secessionist movement, allied with groups in Singapore and the Federation of Malaya, called for the four Thai provinces with majority Malay populations to be united with the Federation of Malaya. Demonstrations, riots, some guerrilla warfare, and armed confrontations took place throughout the southern Thailand region. Sulong was arrested on the charge of treason and ultimately convicted of slander against the government.

The Sulong uprising was the high-water mark for general Malay nationalism, which garnered support in Malaya, Singapore, and southern Thailand and aroused sympathy in the international press, in several United Nations' bodies, and among members of the Arab League. However, the sympathy for political separation from Thailand went for naught when Great Britain decided not to seek control over those four provinces and publicly reassured the Thai government that it recognized Thai jurisdiction over them. The UK-Thai accommodation did not end Malay irredentism from Malaya, nor did it end the efforts of several Malay "liberation groups" operating along the border, but it did remove the issue from the headlines and set the official policies that would be followed thereafter.

After the Sulong uprising, Thai officials reviewed their policies toward the Malay-Muslim population and sought new solutions. As a result, Friday was restored as part of the weekend, Islamic family law was reinstated, traditional Malay clothing was again allowed, and general freedom of worship was affirmed. The schools also dropped Buddhist ethics as a subject from Malay-Muslim schools while adding Islamic history and study of the Malay language. The new policies also asserted that Thai administrators assigned to the area would have better knowledge of Malay culture, and there was a commitment to recruit local advisers to help Thai officials learn about Malay culture and local ways of doing things. At the same time that accommodations were being made, all recommendations or calls for independence or autonomy were flatly rejected as inimical to the integrity of the Thai political system. The government buttressed its position by taking closer action with the British in patrolling the frontier against communists and other dissidents.

The government policy of assimilation continued throughout the era. Muslims were assigned the label of "Thai-Islam," apparently to replace the pejorative term "alien" *(khaek)* previously used by non-Muslim Thai in reference to Muslims. At the same time, the word "Muslim" was not used, on the theory that it promoted identity with groups outside of the country whereas "Thai-Islam" indicated national as well as religious identity. There were attempts to economically upgrade the southern area where most of the Muslims lived, both to improve the low living standards prevailing there and to convince the Muslim population that the Thai government was concerned about its welfare. A mosque-building program was launched with considerable financial support from the government. Some effort was made to enlarge the number of government functionaries from among the Muslim population itself, but this only occurred at the lowest levels, while intermediate- and high-level positions continued to be drawn from ethnic Thais.

In keeping with the centralized state, Muslim affairs remained under the control of an administration in Bangkok, which handled general matters of Muslim education, the pilgrimage, and coordination of communal worship activities. The king became the patron of Muslims, which allowed him to make inquiries about controversial issues, to suggest legislation, and generally to be interested in Muslim welfare. This policy of "attraction" had a positive impact on many Malay-Muslims. The number of them conversing in Thai increased in all southern provinces during the era, but particularly in Satun Province; much the same seemed true about identification as citizens of Thailand. Significantly, the number of Malay-Muslims seeking elected office in the southern provinces increased and greater numbers of them were successful in becoming parliamentary delegates. Near the end of the era, there were enough Muslim elected officials that it was deemed feasible to form a political bloc in the legislature to act as a voice for the southern population and work for public policies that would favor the people of that region.

State institutions were established at the beginning of the era for addressing Islamic religious matters throughout the country. The major holidays and events of the Muslim calendar were recognized officially so that they could be celebrated by Muslims throughout the country. There was a hierarchy of religious officials with government-assigned responsibilities at the national, regional, and local levels. Muslims in the northern and central parts of the country apparently accepted these institutions without difficulty and regarded them as important mechanisms for assisting Muslims. The record in the south was more problematical, with little identification by the Muslim community early in the era but growing acceptance as time passed.

Starting in the mid-1940s, small units of Malay-Muslims in Thailand and some groups from the northeast states of Malaysia engaged in sporadic warfare against Thai security forces in the southern provinces. They consisted of the National Liberation Front of Patani–NLFP (Barisan Nasional Pembebasan Patani), the Liberation Front of the Republic of Patani–LFRP (Barisan Revolusion Nasional), and the Patani United Liberation Front–PULO (Pertubohan Persatuan Pembebasan Patani), with PULO showing the most staying power. A number of groups espousing Islamic fundamentalism and operating from Kelantan participated as well, notably the Martyrs of God (Sabilillah), the Patani Islamic Movement–GIP (Gerakan Islam Patani), and the "Black December" organization. These "liberation groups" were never united and, even within their own groupings were extremely loose-knit, giving considerable freedom to each unit, which probably accounted for the difficulty of police units on the border to contain them. Their activities consisted mostly of "hit-and-run" raids, although for a period of time in the 1970s one group was able to claim a small area in an isolated region along the border as free of Thai security forces. Direct support for the liberation groups was limited, although people directly affected by their raids paid "taxes" to be identified as friends and avoid being raided.

Malay-Muslims elsewhere in the south were tolerant of the violence used by the dissident groups, whether or not they agreed with their aims.[18]

Thai policy directions in the Malay-Muslim area were most apparent in education. In the 1960s the government moved to include the general schools in its national system by giving aid and accreditation to schools that would include the use of the Thai language and certain subjects found in regular public schools. Over four hundred of the religious schools accepted these conditions in return for financial support. However, this action was important only for elementary education, while the numbers of secondary schools remained small, perhaps because good command of Thai language skills was necessary for completion, which did not generally exist in the Malay population. This in turn depressed numbers of students suited to go on to teacher-training schools or national universities. An effort to raise the number of university graduates in the southern provinces was encouraged with the establishment in 1967 of the Prince of Songkhla University, with its main campus located at Songkhla and its school of education at Patani.

Response among Malay-Muslims toward educational change was generally passive or noncooperative early in the period, with eventual grudging acceptance, and some degree of cooperation later in the era. In the beginning there was a desire that Malay education and Islamic training be emphasized, which allowed general schools to thrive. Moreover, advanced learning was not much valued, so primary school education was generally considered sufficient by large sections of the Malay population. However, when the technological revolution swept the world, it became apparent to Malay-Muslims that they needed to have access to the tools of that revolution. The immediate answer rested with the Thai school system that reflected the new educational system prominent in Asia during the latter half of the twentieth century. Consequently, greater numbers of students began attending schools for longer periods and more went to the Thai public schools. In a trend similar to those found elsewhere in Southeast Asia, the tendency to offer religious education alongside secular learning became a common pattern. Thai schools met in the morning and the general schools in the afternoon, with many students attending both. Also, with the availability of higher education in the region, more students were preparing themselves for entry to those institutions. In the 1990s a new trend developed of expanding the religious schools operated by the mosques so that students could attend them and receive suitable Islamic educations at the same time that they were undergoing their required schooling mandated by Thai law.

As for the Muslims existing in the central part of the country, they used Thai as everyday speech and were integrated into the economic life of the central Thai nation. Their religious lives centered around the 150 mosques that existed in and around Bangkok, and their religious materials, including their Qur'an commentaries, were written in Thai. In general the Muslim position in central Thailand was viewed in a positive light by Thai authorities and the general Thai population. Among the Cham population in Bangkok and toward the east employment was still heavily dependent on service in the military and navy, while those who remained civilian were often limited to low-paying agriculture jobs, which presented a particular challenge to the development policies of the government.

The Philippines

In 1945 the Philippines were returned to American control, and in July 1946 the nation became independent. The Muslim areas on Pahlawan, Mindanao, and the Sulu Archipelago were included as provinces. The Philippine governmental system was based on the American model of a strong president formulating policies for internal welfare and foreign affairs, with an independent legislature making laws and raising taxes for support of the government's programs. In the first era between 1948 and 1963, presidents from the landed gentry ran the nation, with one, Ramon Magsaysay (governed 1954–1957), rated highly as a problem solver, while the country suffered from growing lawlessness and uneven economic development. In the second era between 1953 and 1986, there was only one president, Ferdinand Marcos (governed 1965–1984), who manipulated the electoral system to stay in power, with the military supporting him. In the last period, 1983–2000, presidents were popularly chosen—the first a woman fulfilling her martyred husband's aspirations, the second a general in mufti attempting to usher in political stability, and the third a popular actor who did not complete his term because of corruption charges.

Creation, manipulation, or use of civil values was not a major aim of the Philippine elite, but several key values were intrinsic to the system. First, there was a strong sense of nationalist identity arising from the historic effort to rid the country of foreign control, and pride in finally accomplishing that feat. This was reflected in widespread use of the flag, the deep reverence for the writings of the nationalist hero Jose Rizal (d. 1872), and acceptance of the Philippine state as encompassing popular political aspirations. Second, there was a respect for democracy and human rights as enshrined in the constitutions. Third, there was considerable identification with the Catholic Church and a belief that its programs were closely associated with the good of Philippine society. The *Pasyan,* the epic poem of Christ's life, was a strong influence: it was commonly recited in the family or performed in public passion plays, and its values permeated social and political life. Fourth was the strength of family ties, which controlled much of Filipino social relationships, and its transference into political life in the form of patron–client relationships.

Patron–client relationships in politics demonstrated themselves in the formation of "political clans," in which certain families, along with their

allies and retainers, controlled political power in a region and used government patronage (i.e., appointments, contracts, and special beneifts) to
reward their clients. The chief patron received the most lucrative post—
often that of senator, congressman, or governor—while other supporters
and subpatrons were given correspondingly lesser positions of prestige and
importance. Political parties consisted of alliances of chief patrons throughout the country seeking mutual assistance.

There was an inherent regionalism, whereby people from particular
regions of the country identified with one another. Even in urban settings
where rural families had migrated regional languages and customs prevailed. Lastly, because the Philippines still was a rural country, the goal of
land reform was important, particularly early in the era when there was a
very strong desire by the large agriculturalist class to own land for sub-
sistence.

Initially, Muslim acceptance of the Philippine nation-state was mixed,
with some of the population willing to accept inclusion while others
opposed it. Several prominent families on Mindanao became part of the
Philippine elite through their control of the elected positions in their home
districts, including the powerful post of national senator. The Alonto, Piang,
and Madale families represented this trend. These groups, somewhat reluctantly, accepted the nation-state of the Philippines and saw Muslim territory as part of it, making the best of their situation. However, a strong identification with the nation-state of the Philippines never emerged among
the population; rather, primary identification remained with ethnic groups
within the southern region. As we saw in the last chapter, many people from
the south advocated Muslim autonomy, free of northern Filipino control;
others advocated outright independence. This feeling was manifest in the
early days of the republic in a revolt led by a Sulu Muslim leader named
Kamlun (active 1954), followed a decade later by several other movements
calling for political independence.

Muslims questioned Philippine civic values and identified only with
regionalism and patron–client relationships. Muslims could relate strongly
to regionalism as their own societal system was ethnically diverse and historically divided politically and socially. Local control was important and
welcomed. Patron–client relationships were as strong in the south as they
were elsewhere, and so the political system and, indeed, much of the rest
of society, was controlled through that system of social interdependence.
These two factors probably kept the Muslims in the Philippines during the
early years after independence, substituting their own conceptions of a
Muslim political heritage and Islamic values for the two Filipino values of
patriotism and Catholicism.

It was only when the "independence" movements appeared in the
1970s, largely in response to Christian paramilitary incursions and military

heavy-handedness, that the Muslim population saw their situation as better served by Islamic values than by the Philippine nation-state. Again, with the return of elected regimes in Manila at the end of the era, Muslim populations were willing to set aside hopes for independence in return for autonomy over the territory they occupied in the southern Philippines. In general, then, Muslims were very selective about their identification with civil values of the Philippine nation-state.

At first, in 1945, there were few government agencies to support Muslim matters. Religious *(agama)* courts were allowed to have a legal role after a quasi-legal existence under the Americans. These courts allowed Muslims to come before a local Muslim magistrate who would render verdicts according to local custom, including some Islamic precepts, on matters of family concern, such as marriage, divorce, and inheritance. The institutions were regarded by Philippine national authorities as temporary, as it was planned to phase out such courts in time.

In 1954 the Commission of National Integration–CNI was created in response to the investigations of a congressional committee examining the integration of Muslim populations into the Philippine political system. They found education and economic underdevelopment to be the key hindrances to such integration. The commission recommended increasing public education at all levels and providing scholarships for Muslims to institutions of higher education in the Philippines and abroad. Further, the commission was charged to improve agriculture, provide electrification, and generally strengthen community life among Muslims in general.

Midway in the era the Philippine government began to create more infrastructure for the Muslim community. In 1977 President Marcos issued a presidential decree that comprised a code of Muslim personal statutes for the Philippines. This law, and its successor a few years later, established a series of Islamic courts in Muslim areas to deal with matters of marriage and divorce among Muslims. It effectively replaced the earlier courts, which were regarded as ineffective because of the low caliber of judges and the application of customs rather than statutory law. The presidential decree also established standard Muslim holidays and recognized ancestral rights to certain land in the south that was contested by Philippine settlers from outside the Muslim area. President Marcos also created an office on Muslim affairs, which had responsibility for a large number of matters, including the pilgrimage, religious endowments, and Muslim schools. The office also was given the task of coordinating with foreign Muslim governments on matters of religion. This last action was meant to facilitate the Saudi and Libyan governments' attempts to give assistance to the Philippine Muslims for mosque construction and with small development projects.

Throughout the era there were also policies and state actions that worked against the Muslim population. In the late 1940s resettlement projects originally begun in the 1930s were reinitiated, in large part because of the communist threat in the poor, densely populated districts in the central Philippines. It was felt that migration to Mindanao would help to improve economic conditions for the new settlers and alleviate population pressures in the areas they left. The drive to the south was complicated by the tendency of pioneers to clear land without establishing ownership yet claiming it as their own. Since local Muslim populations occupied land on the basis of customary communal ownership, which did not deal with titles or other legal documentation, much land was claimed by the settlers without much legal recourse. Initially, Philippine officials in charge of the land registration sided with those who had filed the claims, but in a change of federal policy the validity of historical claims by Muslims was recognized in a presidential decree in 1973 and legislative acts in the 1980s and 1990s, all of which declared certain lands held by Muslim groups as inalienable. Still, the settlement of large numbers of Christians on Mindanao changed the ethnic composition of the area, often giving Christians the majority in some provinces previously controlled by Muslims.

Muslim independence movements appeared in the 1960s, when a strong sense of frustration existed among many Muslims caused by land grabbing and poor economic prospects. The catalyst for the founding of such movements was the Jabideh massacre in which a group of Muslim trainees for a clandestine operation on Sabah were executed by their Catholic Filipino trainers, which created a firestorm of protest among Muslims. This was followed by the actions of Christian Filipino gangs on Mindanao and Sulu who terrorized the local Muslim populations to assist attempts by the Christian Filipino population in the area to gain political control. As a result, President Marcos' declaration of martial law and subsequent efforts to disarm Muslim groups in the south met with great resistance, particularly among Muslims, who saw a plot to annihilate them. Initially, three independence movements arose. First was the Moro Independence Movement–MIM, formed by an old-line Muslim politician, which disbanded quickly when its leadership decided not to pursue the issue. The Moro National Liberation Front–MNLF then gathered the young people from the disbanded MIM who wanted to create opposition to the gangs that had terrorized the Muslim population. Gaining arms and military training from neighboring Sabah and from several Middle East countries, especially Libya, the movement had the sympathy of large sectors of the Muslim population of the southern Philippines. Later, the Moro Islamic Liberation Front–MILF challenged the MNLF for leadership of the independence movement with its ideology that reflected fundamentalist Muslim principles.

The strategy of the Philippine government under Marcos was to use the Philippine military to defeat rebel forces in the field while keeping the local Muslim population under close scrutiny. The military did have some success in holding the urban areas, but was not successful in bringing the guerrilla forces of the independence movements to bay. Still, tight control over the settled populations did dampen enthusiasm for the rebel organizations, although army presence was disliked by the local population. Eventually the Marcos regime decided to address long-term Muslim complaints and issued several decrees, outlined above. The regime also began negotiations with Saudi Arabia and Libya, which offered to act as negotiators for the Muslim population to bring an end to the Muslim uprising. In 1989 an accord between the government and the MNLF established the Autonomous Region for Muslim Mindanao–ARMM, which was to be created from territory in the south that chose, through a series of provincial plebiscites, to constitute that territory.

The response of the Muslim population toward the policies of the government regarding the independence movements was mixed. By and large there was strong identification with the movements, and the promotion of Muslim unity as a basis for any new state had considerable appeal. Throughout the crisis the independence movements, both MNLF and MILF, enjoyed widespread support among the Muslim population. Still, there were divisions, with many people opting for continued inclusion in the Philippine political system, others wanting independence, and still others calling for a settlement that would give Muslim peoples control over their own local affairs. Strikingly, the old Muslim political leadership clearly sided with the Philippine system whereby they had access to public office and administrative positions. Although younger family members initially started the independence movements, they soon recanted and gave support to the Philippine government as well. Consequently a new Muslim leadership arose, consisting largely of those who had fought with the rebels, were not from the prominent families, and had studied abroad, sometimes in the Middle East. Importantly, religious scholars became more prominent in their own right and began to have more influence in societal matters than their predecessors had earlier, but they still did not achieve political authority.

At the end of the era, after a decade of self-rule, it was generally agreed that the administration of the autonomous region had been "poor" by general standards of political expectation, and that Muslim administration drawn from the independence movement was marked by inefficiency, lack of ability to solve problems, and corruption. These were the very problems that had haunted earlier provincial administrators and been part of the reason that Muslims had been unhappy with Philippine government rule.

Cambodia and Vietnam

The French attempted to reinstitute their colonial administration in Indochina using a federal structure to incorporate the local states, but political desire for independence led to such disruption that the system never functioned well. The Paris Peace Accords of 1954 recognized several independent states, even though the French presence continued until 1963.

Independent Cambodia

In the 1954 accords, the French recognized an independent kingdom of Cambodia under French protection. Like most of the Indochina area of which it was a part, Cambodia experienced a tumultuous period in which several ideologies came into sharp conflict several times during the era. In the early period until 1970 Prince Norodom Sihanouk (r. 1954–1970) ruled as a monarch and there was popular voting for the legislature. Cham and Malay populations generally supported the Liberal Party, a relatively small one composed of traditional leaders and the administrator-gentry class. They also accepted the Cambodian state, as evidenced by Prince Sihanouk's regular visits to Muslim areas and his gesture of goodwill toward them by meeting them at their mosques. Sihanouk went into exile in 1970, but his successor, General Lon Nol (governed 1970–1975), was able to gain the support of the Cham and Malay populations as well. Many of them traditionally served in the armed forces, and their presence in that force during this period was particularly apparent.

In 1975, however, the Lon Nol government was replaced by the Khmer Rouge communist movement, which renamed the country Kampuchea and purged the population of those it regarded as having identified with the West or had other outlooks inimical to the radical communism it advocated. Muslims were designated as one group judged as exhibiting unacceptable values and behavior, and they were severely persecuted for it. Muslim women were forced to cut their hair. Prayer and religious devotion were banned, and those found practicing Islamic rites were arrested and, in some cases, executed. Apparently with the aim of eliminating the leadership of the Muslim community, an estimated thousand returned pilgrims were imprisoned in prison camps and badly treated, only thirty surviving the ordeal. In addition, the destruction of Muslim scholars, teachers, and officials was high, and it was estimated that over two hundred thousand Muslims may have been put to death. To survive, many Cham adopted Khmer clothing and lifestyles, hiding their ethnic identity and religion, and not even switching back when the Khmer Rouge government was replaced. A number of them fled abroad, especially to Thailand and Malaysia.[19]

Mutual antagonism between Kampuchea and Vietnam led the Vietnamese to invade in 1979, and the Kampuchean government was replaced by a communist leadership that was linked closely to that of communist Vietnam. The Muslim population was no longer brutally treated, but was designated a special nationality group to be closely watched and regulated, while new efforts were introduced to integrate them into the society that the new communist government was attempting to install across the nation. Muslims apparently regarded their situation as dire, and significant numbers continued to flee abroad.

An initiative of the Association of Southeast Asian Nations in the early 1990s led to the formation of a unity government in 1993 under the nominal leadership of Norodom Sihanouk. Restrictions on the Muslim population were lifted, they were given the label "Khmer Islamites," and a Muslim administration was set up to give identity to the Muslim community. It was headed by the Chief of Islam (Sheikh ul Islam) with its headquarters at Cherui Chengvah near Phnom Penh. That official led the important celebrations connected with the holidays of the Muslim calendar, dealt with the small Muslim law courts that existed for family matters, and received international visitors to the Muslim community. Religious schools were reestablished after having been closed during the Khmer Rouge era, and some religious scholars from Kelantan contributed to that religious education. The return of political parties allowed the Muslims to organize politically, and they divided fairly evenly among the three leading political parties, with one Cham personality being elected to the National Assembly.

Early in the era, Malaysia attempted to act as an Islamic "lifeline" to the Muslims of Cambodia by including them in the annual Qur'an recitation competition, allowing students to enter Malaysian religious schools, and assisting Cambodian Muslims with pilgrimage arrangements. After the end of communist rule, several Muslim nations, Saudi Arabia and Brunei prominent among them, gave aid to the Muslim community of Cambodia, aiming particularly at creating an Islamic infrastructure, mostly by building mosques and schools. Some schools were influenced by Wahhabite teachings from Saudi Arabia as a result of this assistance, but schools in Kelantan appears to have remained a primary source of religious teaching.

Independent Vietnam

In 1954, two independent nation-states were recognized by the French as existing in Vietnam until arrangements could be made for unification. Twenty-one years later, in 1975, North and South Vietnam were united into a single nation-state called Vietnam through military action by the northern Vietnamese state. A communist government ruled in the united Vietnam with a centralized economy, so that state planning, state-owned industry, and agricultural collectives intruded heavily on the lives of the general population.

The Cham Muslim relationship with the historical Vietnam state were often troubled, and this remained true in this era. During the brief period prior to the advent of communism to the southern part of Vietnam, when a U.S.-supported state existed, the Muslims of the country, both Cham and Malay, were strongly anticommunist, but apparently retained some distance from the South Vietnamese regime at Saigon. They were exempt from conscription into the army and were generally left alone by the communist forces then attacking the supporters of the government in Saigon. After the unification of North and South Vietnam in 1975, efforts were made to bring all elements of the population into ideological conformity with the communist principles outlined above. The Muslims were labeled as a group in need of special handling. Some of their numbers were sent to indoctrination centers, while the entire Cham and Malay population were designated as a national minority, which meant that they were a target group for efforts aimed at overcoming their ethnic and ideological differences from the mainstream population. As a result of this negative attention, some Cham began to acculturate themselves by taking Vietnamese names, clothing themselves like Vietnamese, and using the Vietnamese language, while dropping Cham, Malay, and Arabic identifying characteristics. Late in the era a Malaysian delegation visited several Muslim communities in Vietnam, especially those near Saigon and Hanoi, and reported that Muslims in those places regularly used mosques and observed the normal celebrations of the Muslim calendar, which indicated that freedom of worship was allowed. The delegation did not report on the general social conditions of that population or their attitudes toward communist rule.

The Muslim Community

Religious Elements
Islamic Specialists
The new nation-states increased the number of government officials dealing with Islam, while mosque personnel changed as a wave of populism swept through the region. In addition, the role of independent Muslim scholars altered markedly while mystics remained relatively unimportant, continuing the decline noticeable in the previous era. Finally, there was an explosion in the number of "other" Muslim leaders due to the creation of new specialities in education and "revivalism," as more activists and leaders arose in response to changed conditions. This era revealed nothing less than a complete revolution in the kind of leaders necessary to meet Muslim needs in a period of development in Southeast Asia.

All nations of the Muslim Zone, whether containing Muslim minorities or majorities, designated special personnel to handle certain Muslim matters. The number and range of activities differed according to country, with Malaysia using the most and Vietnam the least. The range of specialists required by the Islamic Council (MUIS) in Singapore is particularly instructive. It included specialists to handle marriage registration, family court matters, education and propagation, pious endowments, food certification, mosque building and administration, pilgrimage preparation, and coordination for worship activities.[20] In Indonesia the situation was only slightly different. A quasi-governmental agency, the Council of Religious Scholars, illustrates the expansion of Islamic specialists needed to operate a new service organization of government. The council considered contentious matters of morals, ethics, and religious ritual and made recommendations to the government and the public on how those issues might be addressed in light of Islamic teachings. This called for the use of persons trained in Islamic jurisprudence and familiar with the process of extracting Islamic principles for use in contemporary cases, which demanded considerable experience as well as basic knowledge. As the council had subcouncils operating in every province, several hundred such specialists were required.

In Thailand the situation was much the same as in Singapore and Indonesia. A sizeable administration of Muslim specialists was appointed by the Thai government to operate offices dealing with Muslim matters at three different levels of administration. At the national level there was a central committee for Islamic affairs headed by an official called the Chief Islamic Community Leader (Chularatchamontri, or Shaikhul-Islam), who was appointed by the king from among prominent Muslim scholars of the kingdom. This national committee was responsible for overseeing the administration of Islamic religious life among Muslims throughout the country. Its responsibilities included the regulation of mosques, translating religious materials into the Thai language, supervising the national Qur'an recitation competition, conducting training sessions for religious officials, and representing Thailand at international meetings of Muslims abroad. In provinces with substantial Muslim populations, elected committees for Islamic affairs were established to coordinate between the national committee on one side and local government and mosque leaders on the other. These committees met annually in a general conference held in Bangkok to interact with several ministries in the fields of education, social policy, and economic development. The standard Muslim scholar (*ʿalim*) who had commonly staffed such agencies was still needed, but in addition other clerical, legal, and administrative professionals were required by the greater specialization of tasks to be performed. This organization involved hundreds of people.

In the mosque there was also a multiplication of functions and new specialities sprung up there as well. During this time span the mosque became much more than a place for formal devotions, although that remained its primary purpose. Learning centers, libraries, youth groups, and various social welfare projects were attached to mosques, so that administrators (*nazir*) appeared in many places and assumed responsibility for the new range of services and functions. Importantly, there was a sense of popular participation throughout the Muslim Zone about how mosques should be operated, so local councils were created in most places that gave direction for worship activities and other mosque affairs. The three central figures of prayer leader, prayer caller, and sermon reciter were still important, but prayer leadership often rotated among senior worshipers, outside speakers regularly gave Friday sermons, and the use of loudspeakers and recorded prayer calls diminished the need for a professional caller on every occasion. Worshipers themselves were included in these functions as a general rule, often relegating the formal holders of those titles to an instructional and coordinating role.

Mosque committees were given responsibility for fund-raising in order to meet expenses for the mosque and for the payrolls of specialists that worked there. Such committees also raised funds for building and renovations, with governments sometimes providing assistance in new construction and upgrading. The rice tax that had been used for mosque support earlier was removed in most places, and the "poor tax" collected by the mosque from its members was now given over to support of the indigent, changing the mosque from a receiver of alms to a facilitator of social welfare on the behalf of the wider Muslim community. Personnel capable of executing these new financial functions became important additions to the mosque organization.

Religious scholars and specialists associated with mosques still relied on traditional sources of income: assistance at corpse-washing ceremonies, circumcisions, marriage-contract preparation, and teaching introductory Qur'anic Arabic to children. In general, however, there was less work for these traditional specialists. The healing art was lost as people turned increasingly to practitioners in the medical profession, the movement toward urbanization rendered the harvest rituals obsolete, and state-operated schools severely curtailed education in the mosque. In general these positions, which formerly had commanded considerable respect, did not continue to carry the same status or potential for community service. Overall, there was a general lowering of prestige for the traditional specialists located at the mosque but a rise in that of people who fulfilled the new administrative and financial functions.

The prestige of private scholars (ʿalim) remained high but underwent some change in the course of the era. Traditional scholars who taught at private schools did remain influential and important, although their numbers began to dwindle somewhat. Throughout the region these scholars served as a backbone for the local Muslim community and dealt with religious, ethical, and societal issues that concerned their respective populations. Hence, in the Philippines, calls for political autonomy and independence had the support of most Islamic scholars, and in Indonesia the government's policies of economic development received the blessings and encouragement of scholars.

At the same time, the rise of national education systems placed pressure on religious teachers to "upgrade" their own curricula, both directly from state officials and indirectly from students who chose to attend, or not, based on choice. Though significant adaptations took place, the religious educational systems languished during the era and there was general inability on the part of religious scholars to promote their profession as dynamic to young men who had once been attracted to the field. On the other hand, the number of teachers trained in departments of pedagogy increased appreciably as the number of specialized Muslim schools and other institutions combined Islamic subject matter with general educational materials. The importance of the shift was evident in Indonesia, where two ministers of religion at the end of the era were former chancellors of Muslim universities, whereas the earlier tendency had been to choose important religious scholars to fill that post, who did not have connections with "higher education." But further, a new group of religious scholars arose throughout the region who had basic Islamic education in their backgrounds but chose national or international universities to learn about Islam. Consequently, these graduates brought a new perspective to the study of Islam that was markedly different from those of traditional scholars, and they dominated the agenda in the final fifteen years of this era, particularly in Indonesia. Brunei, northern Malaysia, and Cambodia, however, were much less affected by the change, and in those countries traditional scholars retained prestige and influence.

The "other" Muslim leaders category blossomed during this era. Reflecting a trend that had begun in the nationalist era, Muslim associations produced a new generation of Islamic leaders who could mobilize sectors of their communities for some particular Islamic goals. The numerous revivalist organizations in Malaysia, the large Muslim community associations in Indonesia, and the Islamic service societies of Singapore were representative of this type of organization. Leaders of these groups were important spokespeople for Muslims and, because they represented important national groups with political, social, and economic interests, they became influential. While a few were important in wider society, such as Amien Rais (b. 1944), leader of the Indonesian Muhammadiyah movement in the 1990s, most were not prominent outside of their own local and regional milieus but were highly influential and respected within them. There were several hundred of these organizations throughout the region, of all sizes, influence, and direction, so the leaders and elites represented very diverse outlooks, while developing similar skills and outlooks in providing leadership for those organizations.

A large number of Muslim political leaders emerged, ranging from those who led legitimate political parties contending for power in competitive political systems to leaders of insurgencies against established national governments. For the most part these Muslim political leaders had been educated in government schools rather than Islamic institutions, with some notable exceptions. This group of Muslim personalities, from a wide variety of backgrounds, garnered respect and great influence. Three people illustrated this leadership. In Malaysia, Anwar Ibrahim, from a middle-class background, started as a revivalist organizer, headed the "reform wing" of the ruling political party, and served as deputy prime minister (1997–1998). In Indonesia, Abdurrahman Wahid, the scion of an influential family of religious scholar-administrators, acted as general chairman (1984–1999) of the Nahdatul Ulama organization and later assumed a prominent role as outspoken advocate of Muslim political interests. At the end of the era he was elected president of Indonesia. In the Philippines, Nur Misuari rose from an obscure background to lead the Moro National Liberation Front–MNLF in an insurgency against the Philippine government. Afterwards he became governor (1996–) of the Autonomous Region for Muslims.

Islamic Associations

Some of the Muslim movements that had religious, educational, and social welfare agendas took on quasi-political roles at times. In Indonesia, the Muhammadiyah, the Nahdatul Ulama–NU movement, the Muslim Educational League–Perti, and the All-Aceh Union of Religious Teachers–Pusa each served a sector of the Muslim community as a major mobilizing center for Muslims engaged in politics, social change, educational reform, and religious activism. There were other Islamic associations in specific areas of societal work, such as intellectual activity, education, and labor. The principal organization involved in intellectual activity was the Muslim Students League–HMI (Himpunan Mahasiswa Islam), which was the motivating force behind the Islamic "reconstructionist" intellectual movement of the 1970s and 1980s. There was also the Islamic Intellectuals Association of Indonesia–ICMI (Ikatan Cendiakawan Muslim Indonesia) in the 1990s, which was intended to revitalize Muslim thinking regarding Indonesian economic development policies of the era but never quite realized its goals. Finally, a set of nongovernmental organizations (NGOs) late in the era undertook to organize committed Muslims in human rights, education, and other fields considered important to the development of civil culture. In general a rich tapestry of organizations reflected the widespread interests of the Indonesian Muslim community.

In Malaysia there were a number of strictly religious organizations, including the Muhammadiyah, which was modeled on the Muhammadiyah of Indonesia, but they were small in number, limited in activities, and influential only in certain places; national organization was not the norm. "Revivalist" organizations were much more prominent, as they captured the interest of the general Muslim population, at least in the western part of the country. They constituted a societal force that had influence on politics, at times even challenging the government. The two most prominent of these revivalist movements were the Muslim Youth League of Malaysia–ABIM (Angkatan Belia Islam Malaysia) and Arqam (Darul Arqam). ABIM drew largely from young middle-class students (numbering forty thousand at its height) and served as a "critic" of Malay society, the Islamic community, and government policy. Arqam drew on a similar membership and had nearly sixty thousand members at its height. In 1994 the government, concerned about its growing militancy and impact on politics, moved against Arqam because its founder asserted that he would be reborn as the Islamic messiah *(mahdi)*, a teaching regarded as at odds with orthodox Sunni Islam.[21] While tolerant of the revivalist organizations for the most part, the Malaysian government did attempt to limit their influence by sponsoring its own organizations, apparently to control the tone and direction of the leadership of revivalist action. Its two groups were the Islamic Welfare and Missionary Association–PERKIM (Pertubuhan Kebajikan Islam Malaysia) and the National Muslim Student's Association of Malaysia–PKPIM (Persatuan Kebangsaan Pelajar–Pelajar Islam Malaysia).

In Brunei, social associations were sparse, but many of the same trends occurred as in Malaysia. The Brunei government founded its own revivalist movements, and it criticized the Arqam movement in 1991, even before Malaysia did, as espousing doctrines and using approaches to Islamic revivalism that were seen as upsetting some Muslims. Significantly, the Brunei government, always suspicious of nongovernmental organizations that had a popular following, attempted to make revivalism a function of the Ministry of Religion, where the zealotry of activated Muslims could be channeled into politically safe activities.

In Singapore there were "voluntary associations" organized by the Malay-Muslims. Some, such as the Muslim Missionary Society of Singapore and Muslim Converts' Association of Singapore–CMCAS sought to convert Indian and Chinese residents to Islam. Other organizations reflected popular concern throughout Singapore for "modern-day" problems connected with development. The Young Womens' Muslim Association–PPIS (Persatuan Pemudi Islam Singapura) concentrated on issues of family law, especially women's rights in marriage, divorce, and separation. As part of its mission, PPIS established a day-care center and a single-parent family service. The Adult Religious Students' Association–Perdaus (Pergerakan Dakwah Singapura) drew its membership from Malay intellectuals and administrators, concentrating on modern education. It operated an Islamic middle school, but insisted that its students attend public schools and study modern subject matter not available in Islamic schools. In general, associations in Singapore reflected the larger society in which Muslims lived, which was interested in overcoming community problems that needed solutions to assist Singapore in its drive to become a leading nation in the region.

Three general types of Islamic association existed in southern Thailand: revivalist groups, mystical cells, and fundamentalist organizations. The fundamentalist organizations were described above in the section on political matters. The revivalist movements were strong throughout southern Thailand, even as they were to the south in the peninsular Malaysian states, some having the same association names. There were also numerous Islamic mystical cells, with the most prominent identifying themselves by the titles "Green Robe," "Red Robe," and "Sheik ʿUsman" orders, all of which were connected with other mystical orders operating throughout Southeast Asia mostly in the Naqsyabandryah order. Because Thai authorities were concerned about security and believed that "secret" organizations were especially suspect, many of the mystical orders were raided at times, and a few of the cells were disbanded on the grounds that they might be connected with insurgent movements.

In the Philippines there were a few organizations directed toward the entire Muslim community of the Philippines. These included the Muslim Association of the Philippines, which for a time in the 1960s played the role of spokesgroup for Muslim interests in the Philippine nation-state even though it was little known outside of Manila. Other organizations filled a similar role later, such as the Muslim Lawyers' League, the Muslim Youth National Council, and the Muslim Students' Association of the Philippines. At another level, several associations advocated regional grouping of Muslims, such as the Sulu Muslim League and the Sulu Islamic Congress. Usually they were sponsored by one prominent family or another for their own purposes. On the other hand, the Tableegh and the Shahab were leading revivalist movements that did cross ethnic lines to some degree, carrying out their activities across the southern Philippines wherever Muslims were located.

In general, there were a considerable number of organizations and associations operating throughout the era to accomplish the general goals of Muslims in all countries of the region. Significantly, only a few were organized across national boundaries, and none were prominent throughout the entire Muslim Zone. Some were highly respected, while others were barely tolerated by the wider Muslim community; but their existence indicated that the Muslims of the zone were active in pursuit of their goals and capable of mobilizing to advance their cause. In truth, they were highly reflective of the wider societies of Southeast Asia, which regarded associations as a legitimate and effective means of achieving success in societal ventures.

Islamic Thought and Ideology

In Indonesia, intellectual currents were important in the era. At the beginning of the time frame several themes permeated intellectual thinking, which could best be described as variations of the modernist and fundamentalist messages known elsewhere in the Islamic world. The modernist thinkers, epitomized by the political activist Mohammad Natsir, mentioned earlier, made a case for Indonesia developing itself as a Muslim society through Islamic awareness and transformation. The immediate goal for Indonesian Muslims according to Natsir was to cement the relationship between Islam and the new Indonesian state by a statement in the constitution that Indonesia was an Islamic state or that Islam was the state religion. Such a statement would serve to motivate all Indonesians to follow productive paths of national development and assure that Islamic principles would be used in the operation of the state and in determining state direction. The fundamentalist message, expressed by M. Isa Anshary (d. 1967), a disciple of Ahmad Hassan, discussed in the previous era, called for a total transformation of the Indonesian state to Islamic law, the institution of Islamic rulers, and the adoption of Islamic policy, whereby even non-Muslims would be expected to live in accordance with Islamic regulations. Anshary did not want to build toward an Islamic identity, as he believed that already existed among many Indonesian Muslims, but rather to create a state infrastructure in which Islamic principles would immediately be the crucial determinants of state policy and action. These two intellectual constructs were widely discussed in the first decade of Indonesia's independence, and then presented before the constituent assembly in 1957.

Both Islamic views were opposed by the secular vision of President Sukarno, himself a Javanist with nominal views regarding Islam. He held that the *Pancasila* (five principles) was admirably suited to be the state philosophy, as its principles encompassed the major patterns of political aspirations found in the various peoples of Indonesia. Sukarno and some later government ideologues argued that *Pancasila* actually constituted a form of Muslim government because it had been created in the midst of a debate over the proper role of Islam in the state early in the republic. This debate was a leading public issue until the fall of liberal democracy in 1958, when the Sukarnoist state materialized and put an end to any consideration of Natsir's, Anshary's, or anyone else's conception of an Islamic state. *Pancasila* became the unchallenged state philosophy and remained supreme throughout the remainder of the era.

With formation of the New Order state in Indonesia in the late 1960s, a new line of Islamic political and social thought emerged. It called for "renewal," defined as a transformation of the Islamic message to allow Indonesian Muslims to support modern political and economic development and the creation of a modern social state in Indonesia. The new thinking was launched by the Muslims' Students League–HMI with Nurcholish Madjid (d. 2005), in particular, giving early direction. The intent of the new approach was to transform the Islamic community from a conservative intellectual tradition to a "progressive mind-set." Promotion of intellectual freedom, pursuit of the idea of progress, and cultivation of open attitudes were regarded as necessary to begin the process. The heart of the matter, however, was "secularization," defined to mean separating the truly transcendental in religion from those matters that should properly be regarded as temporal. Madjid argued that Muslims had made too much transcendental which God had not really meant to be that way, and that most aspects of human life were intended to be left to the human intellect to decide. He maintained that new social and political constructs were possible without violating any Islamic tenets.[22]

Later, Madjid and several of his colleagues, most notably Dawam Rahardjo (b. 1942) and Kuntowijoyo (b. 1943), provided further rationales for Muslim support of government action to modernize Indonesia, justifying that support with arguments drawn from Islamic scripture, history, and cultural essence. The approach, however, was not universally accepted by other Indonesian Muslim intellectuals, who found the reformers' use of social scientific methodology questionable and the lack of attention to matters of worship and piety wrongheaded. By the end of the era many of the intellectual constructs of the "reconstructionists" were still being debated, but the issue of compatibility between Islam and economic development was widely accepted.

Muslim intellectual thinking in Malaysia was less concerned with the political world than in Indonesia. Sayyid Naguib al-Attas (b. 1931) was a proponent of an intellectual approach called "Islamization of knowledge." In this approach it was incumbent upon Muslims to learn and use knowledge only in ways that enhanced the principles of Islam and to avoid those applications that were detrimental to it or supported some rival.[23] Accordingly, science could not be separated from ethics, and principles of management had to have a moral base. In fact, all fields could only be properly studied when placed in the context of their relationship with the guiding principles of Islam. Al-Attas was reacting, of course, to the general Western approach to learning in which various fields were dealt with separately without an overarching moral and ethical framework. Obviously he regarded the Western view as totally wrong. Islamization of knowledge gained considerable followings in Malaysia and neighboring Brunei.

The second trend in Islamic thinking in Malaysia was put forward by

Chandra Muzaffar (b. 1947), primarily in his elaboration of the term "unity of God" *(tawhid)* as it applied to contemporary Malaysia. He maintained that when applying the concept to politics the best features of governance known to humans should be used, including democratic rights, elected legislatures, well-reasoned laws, and fair judiciaries. Instituting vague "Islamic laws" or "Islamic states" would miss the mark, in his view, unless proper attention was devoted to a perception of "justness" in the social and political workings of a society. He was reacting strongly against the rise of neo-fundamentalism in Malaysia, which, to his mind, placed too much emphasis on Islamic identity and piety without regard for long-founded principles of law and government that Muslims as well as the West had developed. In practice Chandra Muzaffar was a social and political commentator whose analyses of Malaysian public policy were usually careful, thoughtful, and responsible, but were often viewed by government leaders and revivalist activists as unduly critical.[24]

In the Philippines the major intellectual issue was the future of the Muslims of the region and whether they should be independent or part of the Philippine nation. One Muslim writer, Saleh Jubair (active 1990), affiliated with an insurrectionist movement, promoted the concept that Muslim peoples in the southern Philippine Islands constituted a distinct group with a common religion and history that made them a nation. The idea had already been proposed by others, but his study traced the history of the Muslim peoples of the Philippines, emphasizing points of commonality, shared experience, and like traditions. Jubair chose the long three-century warfare with Spain and the American occupation of the first half of the twentieth century as the crucial periods in which the traditions and commonalities that made the Muslim population a nation developed.[25] He concluded that this identity was justification for having a separate state and government.

An approach favoring continued association of the south with the Philippine nation was apparent in the views of Michael Mastura (active 1996). He laid stress on building Islamic institutions—an Islamic legal system and religious courts, and a modernized Muslim school system, in particular—that would provide the foundation for further development of a healthy Muslim entity. He argued that a number of key state documents guaranteed the Muslims a place in the Philippine nation that would respect Muslim identity and aspirations. He saw the Muslims as having autonomy in political, social, and religious matters—which was what eventually happened, although Mastura would have liked a better result.[26]

In general, during this particular era, Muslim intellectual thought in Southeast Asia was concerned with the role of Islam in the nation-state and with the need for it to express itself effectively in the governing process. As a rule, the thinking that emerged focused on modern requirements for governance and the manner in which Islam might be included in the mix. It asserted that Islamic values and essence would prove advantageous to the body politic, as well as satisfying the Muslim concern that Islam should necessarily include the political dimension of life.

Education and Intellectual Centers

General trends in education have been covered in the political discussion as part of state policy and do not need further elaboration here. However, some comment about the content of specifically Islamic education is appropriate in order to understand how the treatment of the Islamic sciences changed, or did not change, in comparison to earlier eras. Several writers have addressed this issue. One study listed and categorized over nine hundred pieces of material containing subject matter taught in the Muslim boarding schools throughout the Muslim Zone. About 50 percent were concerned with jurisprudence, doctrine, or Arabic grammar, which traditionally have formed the core of the Muslim educational system. About 55 percent of the works were written in Arabic, 22 percent in Malay-Indonesian, 15 percent in Javanese, and the remainder divided among Sundanese, Madurese, Achenese, and Buginese. Actually, great similarities existed between this list and those outlined in previous chapters, indicating that there was continuity in the lessons taught in the traditional religious schools of the Muslim Zone. At the same time, some texts from earlier were viewed as outmoded, often being replaced with a "commentary" or updating of the earlier text by another scholar, so that the essence of the message was carried forward in a slightly different format.[27]

Another study of Islamic education emphasized the teaching aspects of religious schools in the Malaysian world. The author noted that there was still great emphasis placed on the "learning circle" as the general teaching technique and that most of the classical sciences were taught. Study of the Arabic language was the mainstay of the curriculum and was viewed as the key to the rest of the educational process. Outside of those basic requirements, however, stress on subject areas appear to have shifted somewhat from concentration on law over to study of the Qurʾan, especially involving commentaries and memorization of the text itself. Study of the Qurʾan as a "useful" tool in assisting Muslims to live and work in Malaysian society was sufficient justification.[28]

One study addressed the changing nature of Islamic education in Indonesia. It was noted that the Islamic boarding schools produced good results, particularly by developing moral young men and women, but that the schools themselves had been instructed by the government to contribute in a greater degree to the "development" of the nation. Accordingly, it was decided to add more general subject matter to their offerings, mostly in agricultural science, handicrafts, technical subjects, and science. This would allow the students to participate in a type of vocational education at the same time as they completed their religious education. The study provided insight into how Islamic schools, generally considered productive by a major part of the committed Muslim population, were required to adapt to changing conditions in the name of "progress."[29]

A study on learning in the Sulu Archipelago discussed differing perceptions of the subject matter that needed to be mastered. One group insisted on the importance of classical Muslim learning, while the other group opted for technological subjects and general knowledge found in the national school system. It was concluded that the two approaches produced different religious and societal perceptions. In general, study of classical Islamic texts provided limited learning but developed an outlook that made the rural, somewhat isolated world comfortable to the learners. Those who studied in the public schools were made aware of the wider world—Muslim and international. Muslims throughout the region were confronted with this educational dilemma, and as a result the classical style of learning was under considerable attack from parents, governments, students, and even teachers.[30]

Beyond formal education attempts were made throughout the era to increase the amount of literature available in local languages for the study of Islam and the edification of Muslims. One important trend in the 1960s, 1970s, and 1980s stressed Qur'anic commentaries and translations of the Traditions of the Prophet. Commentaries were essentially translations of Arabic versions of the Qur'an into Malay/Indonesian or another local language, with some notes of explanation. Indonesia was the center of this development, but most areas of the Muslim Zone produced their own commentaries as well. Four of the first five Indonesian translations appeared in the mid-1960s and were made by A. Hassan, T. M. Hasbi Ash Shedieqy (d. 1975), Dr. Hamka, and a group led by A. Halim Hasan. The *Qur'an and Its Translation,* published slightly later by the Ministry of Religion, had a lengthy introduction that propounded the modernist message regarding the history and development of Islam; and *Qur'an and Its Commentary* expanded that message into nine volumes. All of these commentaries, with the exception of the last, proved to be very popular, receiving many reprintings in Indonesia, and were available throughout much of the Muslim Zone of Southeast Asia until the end of the era.

As it was universally agreed that the Qur'an existed only in Arabic, any attempt to even approximate it in other languages was a sensitive issue, so the Indonesian Ministry of Religion set up a review process for all such commentaries and rejected several contributions that failed to meet its standards. The most notable case was that of H. B. Jassein (b. 1917), a literary critic who was not a trained Qur²anic specialist, who used Yusuf ʿAli's rendering of the Qur²an into English—highly regarded for its literary quality in translation—as a model. He even produced rhymed Indonesian verses to resemble the Arabic text. His version was withdrawn from bookstores until a team of Arabic specialists could strengthen the Indonesian text and rid it of discrepancies in the translation. Ultimately it received approval, but of course the text lost much of its Indonesian literary appeal in the revisions.

While more commentaries by Indonesians did appear later in the era, the pace slowed considerably, and the trend moved toward translation of commentaries by Arab intellectuals into Indonesian, with those by M. al-Shaltut (d. 1964) and A. al-Maraghi (d. 1945) probably most popular among Muslim pietists. At the end of the era the Indonesian intellectual M. Dawam Rahardjo published a highly acclaimed *Encyclopedia of the Qur²an,* which was billed as a sociological commentary on the *Qur²anic* message, corresponding with the Indonesian drive toward political and economic development. Accompanying these commentaries was a relatively large literature of materials regarding the recitation and memorization of the Qur²an.

Outside of Indonesia, the writing of commentaries also occurred. *The Guide of the Merciful (Tafsir Pimpinan Ar-Rahman)* was published by religious scholars in the Office of Islamic Affairs in Kuala Lumpur, and also enjoyed general success in Aceh, Singapore, the Malay States, Brunei, and southern Thailand. It had the advantage of appearing in both Malay scripts, that is, Arabic and Roman. At Singapore, the *Commentary of the Qur²an* was prepared in the 1970s by Ahmad Sonhaji Mohammad (b. 1922), first as a series of radio addresses, and then in refined written form. At Brunei, the Ministry of Religion published the *Commentary of the House of Peace (Tafsir Darus-Salam),* which was specifically intended for Brunei Muslims and pointedly not distributed to outsiders or shipped abroad to other areas in the Muslim Zone. There were also several full commentaries in Sundanese, one in Javanese, and two in Thai, one of the last being issued by a group of Thai Muslims in Bangkok who had attended Al-Azhar University in Cairo.

Finally, there were collections of Friday sermons, some books on Muslim jurisprudence, various primers, and specialized literature on prayer, religious duties, and the role of women. As in the other categories, Indonesia witnessed the greatest production of such works, with the other areas of the Muslim Zone issuing fewer publications, with the lowest production evident in the Philippines, southern Thailand, and the Indochina states.

The Pillars of Islam

Newspaper coverage at Medan in northern Sumatra from 1984 to 1986 provides us with an example of the appearance and importance of the fundamental obligations of Islam in the public life of that city. It was a model that could have been compiled for many other urban areas of the Muslim Zone.

The confession of faith was recited continually as a part of Muslim ritual, so it would not be a point of interest to the media in that context. However, reporters did refer to its use in conversion to Islam, when it occurred in a news story. Most press coverage of these events noted that the "confession of faith" (syahadat) was repeated twice as an act of identification with Islam. Usually reports mentioned individuals or a family, but occasionally more were converted, as in May 1985 when 297 Karo Batak people embraced Islam in a common ceremony.[31]

Aside from informal prayer settings, such as in personal homes and places of business, formal prayer locations were numerous, with 309 mosques, 523 prayer sites, and 43 prayer houses within Medan. The formal prayer sites were used for all five of the standard prayers during the day, the number of participants increasing with each prayer throughout the day, primarily men, but women were likely to attend the "sunset" and "evening" prayers.[32] In some sites women heavily outnumbered men at the evening prayers, but this was the only prayer time when this occurred. Alongside regular prayer there were other actions that were regarded as devotional in nature, such as Qur'an recitation or memorization sessions, and super-rogatory prayers, often between the usual prayer times or late at night.

At the Friday noon prayer, a sermon was given by a visiting speaker, approved beforehand by the local office of the Ministry of Religion, who was aware of topics regarded as off-limits, notably political matters. These speakers were seldom trained religious scholars but often university graduates who received a fee for their services. The sermons were usually about good behavior and proper intention in leading pious Muslim lives. During Ramadan evenings, special prayers, interspersed with lessons, inspirational talks, readings, and recitations, were held that drew large crowds, especially in the first few evenings of the month, but the size dwindled after the first week. Also, on the two major festivals of Islam, 'Id-al-fitr and 'Id al-adha, some larger mosques were used for special prayers and a sermon, while major open areas in the city, such as the great square in the city center, were marked off for large public prayer sessions involving thousands of people.

The media said very little about fasting during Ramadan, but implied that it was being done and that it was a challenge that Muslims confronted for their faith and, interestingly, for their nation. Some of the coverage centered on the "breaking of the fast" each day, when one or another of the various civilian and military officials would hold prayers, a meal, and provide a speaker or a Qur'an recitation with religious specialists and other guests.

A great deal of attention was given to economic conditions: the rise of prices during Ramadan (they rose 5 percent over pre-Ramadan prices in 1986), the availability of foodstuffs and special Ramadan delicacies, and the price of clothing given as gifts at the end of the month. As well, there was reporting on the other important days of the Muslim calendar that fell into this time frame—Muhammad's night journey *(Isra')* and ascension *(Mi'raj)*, and the revelation of the Qur'an—where the prayers and addresses commemorating those events took place in mosques and other important buildings. There was also coverage of the train, flight, and bus schedules and the cost of transportation in general, because so many people were under way at the end of the month trying to "go home" for the Lebaran holidays immediately after the end of the fast.

On the final days of Ramadan the contribution for the poor *(zakah al-fitr)* was collected from Muslims and distributed to the needy. The local office of the Ministry of Religion acted as coordinator, with mosques and associations serving as collectors and distributors of the funds that were garnered from those voluntarily contributing. The figure to be raised from each individual in 1986, for example, was 3 kg of rice or Rupiahs 1,050.* Written notices of this amount appeared in the local media and on the bulletin boards of most mosques around the city. Amounts collected were relatively small, given a city of about 1.2 million people. Several groups of mosques reported giving funds to people in their own city quarter known to be poor, while the other groups donated their funds to religious schools and local social welfare institutions, particularly orphanages.

The pilgrimage was important to Medan as the site of one of the departure points for Muslims going to the holy land. In 1986, 5,500 aspirants from Aceh, Minangkabau, eastern Sumatra, and north Sumatra came through that center and were flown to Saudi Arabia by Garuda Airlines. At the Medan center on the way to Arabia all aspirants were given a final health check, issued pilgrimage passes, received final familiarization with travel arrangements, and then began the religious prayer and contemplation necessary to prepare themselves spiritually. The trip was regarded as strenuous, given the great amount of walking required to circumambulate the Ka'abah shrine between points and the large distances that had to be covered in a crowd of nearly 2 million people. The newspaper kept a running record of the number of people who died on the pilgrimage, which was over two hundred Indonesians in 1986. They were listed as "martyrs" *(syahid)* by the media, in conformity with general Islamic belief about the merit of dying on such a quest.[33] In general, newspaper reporting revealed

---

*US$1.05 exchange, approximately US$10.00 local buying power.

a society that was Islamic in spirit, with many people engaging in the required practices of the religion. The portrait did not indicate either obsessive devotion or lack of concern, but rather a religion operating as a normal part of human activity.

Religious Practice

The spread of "revivalism" *(dakwah)* throughout the Muslim Zone in the 1960s, 1970s, and 1980s was as meaningful as the spread of the modernist ideology in the last era, but had a more pronounced influence because it was a popular movement rather than being confined to the religious elite. Revivalism consisted of two elements: the inspirational message and the techniques used to capture the attention of a target audience. The message can be ably illustrated by an example from Indonesia, and the techniques can be observed in an example from Malaysia.

Syahminan Zaini (b. 1933), a teaching staff member at a State Institute for Islamic Studies–IAIN, wrote a series of booklets that presented the upgrading of Islamic belief and practice in terms similar to popular self-help manuals such as those popularized in Europe and North America. Indeed, the author lauded some of these foreign writers for inspiring their readers to improve their own lives through self-help methods. Zaini often addressed three themes in his writings and speeches: "God," "humankind," and "the world." His remarks on humankind stated that people have to contend with conflicting attitudes that exist within them: the "pure" and the "true" on one side and "passion" and "deceit" on the other. Humans were commanded by God to emphasize the first and tame the latter. In particular, the author laid stress on the importance of shunning the "easy" way in life that leads to sloth and indulgence—and here the West received the author's condemnation as representing the epitome of such living. People who showed proper reverence for God and put aside their own corrupting impulses were truly those who followed the "way" of God. Zaini's remarks, of course, were intended to convince and even overwhelm the reader with the sense that only by living a life totally devoted to Islam would it be possible to meet God's expectations.[34]

In Malaysia revivalist organizations used a variety of techniques to achieve their goals. In the first instance, members of an association worked in teams of two or more to open an area to their influence by talking to people on a university campus or going door-to-door in a neighborhood asking the males to attend prayers and lectures in a nearby mosque. People undertaking such activity were given the title of "preacher" *(mubaligh)* or "propagator" *(da'i)*. Once a group was assembled, the message of the revivalists was presented at the meetings: emphasizing Muslim identity, wearing appropriate clothing, and carefully fulfilling the ordinary requirements of religion. A second technique was to bring speakers to an area, often members of a revivalist association, or persons selected from a list of other speakers known to be sympathetic. People attending such sessions would be asked to return to attend worship sessions and symposia where the issues raised by the speaker could be discussed in greater detail.

A third technique was to organize retreats where readings from the Qur'an, discussion, and worship constituted the formal agenda, while integration into a community was the real objective. At such retreats participants prepared their meals together, ate as a group, worshiped alongside one another, and slept dormitory style. A fourth technique was to sponsor schools, particularly at the secondary level, to assist those students who had not passed their national proficiency exams to prepare for the next round of testing or to undertake revivalist enterprise as a career alternative. Emphasis in such schools was placed on fulfilling the obligations of Islam and making religion the central purpose of one's life. Finally, some economic and social welfare efforts, such as starting cooperatives, clinics, or small shops, were undertaken by members of the association to perform service for the Muslim community and to attract attention so that other people would consider joining the movement. In general, all activities were aimed at attracting new members to the revivalist association or at intensifying the Islamic identity of its members. Supporters of these associations praised the dedication of the participants and the gentleness of their approach, while detractors charged that the message was unduly narrow and that a great deal of social and peer pressure was placed on people to participate.[35] Similar sentiments about revivalism were common throughout the Muslim Zone.

Mysticism was acceptable in many places in Southeast Asia, but it was carefully watched by all governments and by most of the leaders of Muslim communities lest it stray from acceptable forms countenanced by Sunni Islam. In many traditional Islamic schools throughout the region, mystical practice was part of the religious experience, and students were often introduced to it there, but as an adjunct to their studies, not as a principal activity. Further, in some mosques there were groups of worshipers who used mystical experience as supplemental, designed to heighten regular worship. In general, while mysticism (tasawwuf) was regarded as a legitimate subject of inquiry and practice, there were fewer committed practitioners (sufi) than there had been in previous eras.

Small mystical "cults" also sprang up that broke with standard Sunni orthodoxy, often challenging the authority of the governments as well. Such sects were judged by religious scholars as lying outside of Islam and were frequently banned by governments as a threat to security. The number of such suspect organizations was not unusually high, but at least one such cult was banned every year in one or another country of the zone. Some of their leaders attained brief notoriety as a result of their activities.

In general the number of "legitimate" mystic leaders was relatively small, and they did not generate the kind of public attention that they once had.

Customs and Islam
Shamans, Saints, and Amulets

At the beginning of the era, modern health and medical practice were making inroads into the traditional healing practices of the shamans in east Java, and the general population grew skeptical about the efficacy of their powers. Still, sections of the population held that some shamans were effective, but most were middle-aged or old, with young people seldom going into that line of work. In the latter half of the era, the shaman was still strongly connected with rural life and no village organization was really complete without one. But there were questions in the minds of committed Muslims as to whether he was an Islamic figure, with the general conclusion that trafficking in hidden knowledge unconnected with Islam made him highly suspect.

Generally speaking at this time, shamans and the general population did not believe that most sickness was caused by spirits or "possession," but rather by "bad blood" due to stress, poor diet, and inappropriate behavior. Some diseases were believed to have been caused by other (unscrupulous) shamans applying sorcery or that some people were truly possessed by demons. Cases of demon possession would be marked by violent stomach sickness, vomiting of blood, and raging fevers, or the appearance of nails, glass, and other foreign objects in the bowel movements of a person. These cases could only be handled by a shaman able to harness "power" to overcome the strength of the superhuman adversary. There were lesser instances of sorcery, such as commanding people to be in a specific place at a certain time or making a person fall in love with the shaman's client. In practice, cases of bad luck were apt to convince some people that their enemies had placed a curse on them, and they might consult a shaman to have that curse removed. All in all, there were ample reasons why shamans remained useful, even though the general usage of them fell off dramatically throughout the era as modern health practitioners and facilities became available.

Visitation to holy tombs, such as those of the nine propagators of Java, the Islamic rulers, and prominent Sufi practitioners, remained popular on Java. Every Thursday night thousands of pilgrims visited the royal graves at Imogiri where Sultan Agung was buried. Most Sundays saw thousands of people visiting the tombs of the former rulers of Banten and the grave sites of the former Demak rulers. Holy tombs usually came under the control of a royal overseer, a mosque official, or some other administrator, who set the conditions of visitation, including the time of the visit, what sorts of behavior would be allowed at the shrine, and appropriate apparel. For example, at most holy places pilgrims were admonished to recite *Surat Ya Sin* from the Qur'an and not to substitute some other formula. At the rulers' shrine at Surakarta, kneeling and obeisance of the pilgrim were required as if he were at the ruler's court, and at Kota Gede court clothing was obligatory when visiting the shrines of the rulers there.

Supposedly, the pilgrim who made a visitation to a shrine was rewarded with blessing, which removed sin and added heavenly merit, allowed the pilgrim to live happily and have good fortune, and, perhaps, allow for some good thing to happen that the pilgrim desired. The pilgrim might, in fact, ask for a special favor when he visited the tomb. Visitations were most common among pious Muslims with a traditionalist orientation, since modernists usually ridiculed the value of such ritual, but many Javans lightly associated with Islam found it useful to visit these sites, as well as to maintain their own village shrines, which had no particular relationship with Islam.

Amulets, always popular, constituted an entire line of business and were of various kinds. The most common type were those written in Arabic, such as Qur'anic verses, that were encased and worn somewhere on the body. They were intended to prevent sickness and guard against sorcery. In this regard they differed little from those observed in earlier eras.

Life-Cycle Events

The complexity of life-cycle events in the Muslim Zone endured and, as in the past, Islam pertained in different measures across the societies of the region. The case of the Tausug in the Sulu Archipelago is instructive because it describes how a society, long associated with Islam, dealt with the problems of adjusting religion to ordinary living. Ideally, the first words a child should hear after birth were those of the call to prayer, with the first part recited into the right ear and the second half into the left. It was considered best if a religious specialist could be employed and waiting nearby at the birth scene to perform this act, but more often it was the midwife or the hospital nurse who did the recitation.

On the seventh day after birth, a ritual was performed in which the baby's hair was cut, a name given, weight taken, and a goat sacrificed on its behalf. At this ritual, in addition to members of the immediate family, there would be invited guests and from three to fifteen religious specialists, depending on the status and wealth of the family. The goat was sacrificed first, with the meat going to the preparation of a meal held later in the day and the remainder given to the religious specialist doing the slaughtering. This sacrifice was regarded as necessary in case the child died young, because the dead child would otherwise not know how to find its parents in paradise, whereas if the ceremony was performed, the spirit of the sacrificed goat could identify the parents and remind the child of its obligations toward them. Later in the day the religious personages seated themselves around a large prayer mat on which there was a lit incense burner and a container of artificial flowers made from woven coconut fronds, in symbolic acknowledgment of the prophet Muhammad's mission. After sections of the Qur'an were recited by these religious personages, a group of adolescent sponsors presented the infant to the religious group, who acknowledged the child as a member of the Muslim community. In some places a weighing of the baby took place at this point in the ceremony. The child's weight was measured in terms of rice to an equal amount, which afterwards was given to the attending religious personages as the poor tax—the child's first fulfillment of that religious obligation. The hair of the infant was then cut, the locks placed in a coconut shell, and the shell resealed and hung in a tree near the infant's home to bring good fortune. A meal followed, although this was regarded as a simple act of hospitality and pointedly not considered as having any special religious significance.

Earlier in Tausug history, circumcision was regarded as a significant rite of passage and consisted of an elaborate celebration involving the community of which the boy was a member. In this era the circumcision was performed in the office of a Muslim physician, where it was a routine medical procedure, not a religious rite. A private prayer for the family might be held afterwards. Taking the place of circumcision as a rite of passage was the first prayer said in the mosque for a boy, who was given elaborate instructions about procedure, especially ablutions beforehand, but also about the proper movements of standing, kneeling, and prostration required in the performance of formal worship. Female cutting was done when a girl was between six and seven years of age. It was usually performed by a midwife or folk healer and consisted of cutting away the tissue connecting the clitoris to its hood. Male members of the household were not privy to or even knowledgeable about the rite, it being regarded as a female matter. Its believed purpose was to assure cleanliness rather than having any religious significance. Particular care was taken to make the procedure as painless as possible, lest there be trauma connected to it that might have long-term negative affects on the girl's personality.[36]

Religion was peripheral to betrothal and marriage. In the former, after lengthy negotiations had taken place between the two families and a dowry due the bride agreed upon, there was a final negotiating session attended by a mosque official or a religious scholar as impartial observer, to review all the arrangements made up to that point and certify that both parties agreed to them. The marriage ceremony was very similar to the first official meeting of the groom and bride at their betrothal, except that a larger number of religious specialists were present, rings were exchanged, and a sermon was delivered in Arabic by one of the specialists. The wedding celebration usually included the extended families on both sides and often large numbers of other people, especially community leaders. At another point in time, there might be a civil ceremony, a practice dating to the American period, which imitated a Christian wedding in the West. The cost of the civil ceremony and its accompanying festivities was usually a part of the bride's share.

At death a body was prepared for burial through a series of purification steps laid out in the Sunni books of jurisprudence. First was a thorough washing of the body. The body orifices were cleaned and plugged with cotton, after which the body was dressed in a loosely fitting white shroud. On the evening before burial, prayers were said for the deceased, and young women expert in Qur'an recitation performed in order to increase the amount of religious merit accruing to the deceased. A final prayer and a reading from the Qur'an was given over the body at the home of the deceased, after which the body was carried to the cemetery on a bamboo stretcher and buried on a shelf in the ground with the face toward Makkah. The religious specialist then read a short exhortation in the form of a prayer over the grave informing the deceased that he was indeed dead and must accept his new status; it was believed that those who did not receive this reading would be confused and might wander the earth as spirits. Water was then poured on the grave, whose purpose, according to some informants, was to cool those souls already in hell. Prayers were said for the deceased for several nights after the burial and especially at a seventh-day ceremony, which included a large feast for the extended family. Further, the deceased was remembered at a day in the month of Zulhijah dedicated to the observance of ancestors. In general, Islam was an important component in all of these life-cycle events and sanctified the most crucial affairs in the lives of believers.

Muslim Celebrations

An important anthropological study on North Java reported that a number of holy days, such as ʿId al-fitr and ʿId al-adha, were observed by all Muslims and were celebrated with a great deal of enjoyment in Cirebon and other north-coast cities. Each celebration combined special elements such as invocations, prayers, and the preparation of special food.

Suroan, the first day of the Islamic and Javanese lunar calendars, marked the anniversary of the flight of Muhammad from Makkah to Madinah. Many other important events happened then as well, including the birth of the prophet ʿIsa and the martyred death of the grandson of Muhammad. Consequently, ʿAsyura was celebrated with a ritual meal consisting of a rice porridge with coconut milk and various vegetables, fish, and eggs offered to guests. The meal was regarded as alms, because it was shared with others and hence, constituted an act of worship. Some committed Muslims felt that instead of the meal it was more appropriate to celebrate by fasting, offering voluntary prayer, and giving alms to the poor.

Sapar, the second month, was regarded as unlucky. The most precarious moment of the month was thought to be Rebo Wekasan, the last Wednesday of the month. To mark the occasion many people went to the Drajat River to bathe, where they recited the "remembrance" *(dhikr)* or the "confession of faith" *(shahadah)*. On the next evening, after night prayers, youngsters who were learning the Qurʾan went from house to house in their neighborhoods to ask for small change, which they used to buy snacks later on. This practice may have originated in commemoration of Shaykh Lemah Abang, namely, Sitti Jenar in the sixteenth century, who was executed for heresy. After his widely mourned death, his followers had been allowed to move among villagers and pray for the general prosperity of the population and were given small amounts of money as recompense.

Mauludan, the birthday of the prophet Muhammad on the twelfth of Rabiulawwal, had considerable importance. There was a public festival in Cirebon focusing on the heirlooms of the palace. Each piece was displayed, including large porcelain plates with the Confession of Faith written on them in enormous Arabic letters, believed to have been prepared by Sunan Gunung Jati, one of the proclaimed nine propagators of Islam on Java and a founding father of the city. A special rice, cooked with turmeric and spices, was served to the assembled crowd, whose members competed with one another to obtain portions of the rice, as it was believed to be blessed.

There were also lesser celebrations sponsored by individuals or groups at which the story of Muhammad's birth was recited. Usually, either the commemoration poem *(mawlid)* of al-Barzandji or of al-Daʿiy (d. unknown) was used for recitation and response. The audience was frequently separated by gender, with each group having its own reciters, both male and female. The main reciter introduced new material, and the other participants formed a chorus that responded with a refrain after each section. At the verses describing the imminent birth of the Prophet, the entire assembly stood up and recited twenty-two verses in chorus, after which everyone sat down again for the remainder of the performance. When the recitation was complete, a prayer was said, refreshments were served, and the guests departed.

Rajab or Israʾ-Miʾraj commemorated the ascension of the prophet Muhammad and his return. It was celebrated with a short exhortatory sermon, in which the events of the journey from Makkah to Jerusalem were described and how the ascension and return occurred, as well as something about the nature of the conversation that transpired between God and the Prophet on that occasion. The sermon ended with an appeal to Muslims to live pious lives in accordance with the teachings of Islam.

Ruwahan or Nisfu Syakban reified the widespread belief that on midnight of the fifteenth of Syakban the tree of life was shaken at the will of God and certain leaves, with the names of people written on them, fell from it, indicating who was to die during the coming year. Devout Muslims fasted on that day and read *Surat Ya Sin* of the Qur'an three times after the evening prayer. Some people were known to go to the grave of Sunan Gunung Jati to recite a religious formula and then visit the graves of several other prominent people, such as the founder of the village in which the worshiper lived.

Syawalan, which was on the tenth day of Syawal, marked the occasion of the end of the lesser fast, which was a voluntary but meritorious act on the part of pious believers. In Cirebon it became an opportunity to visit the tomb of the Sunan Gunung Jati and the graves of other rulers of Cirebon buried nearby. A procession was held in which the two living sultans of Cirebon led the way to the tombs and later gave a feast at the cemetery for the guardians of the shrines. In the city near the palace, large crowds of people, numbering as high as 150,000, often gathered to see the two sultans and the procession.[37]

Such celebrations correspond with the descriptions from Medan about the observance of the pillars of Islam, where large portions of the population were involved with religion throughout the year. On one level, there was piety and a concern on the part of many individuals that the ceremonies be properly observed for their religious value. On another, more public level, they were societal occasions which were celebrated by the public and an Islamic atmosphere was made manifest. Nor was the degree of celebration necessarily unique, for such celebrations would be common in many other regions of the Muslim Zone.

Cultural Development
Urban Design and Architecture

During the era the capital cities of Indonesia, Malaysia, and Brunei underwent considerable change as a result of national projects designed to express the cultural aspirations of the governing elites. The same impulse was present in the countries where Muslims were in the minority, but because the majorities there were from other cultures, Islamic or Muslim themes were not in evidence, even in provincial cities dominated by Muslims. Indonesia had the longest period of independence and probably developed the most complex architecture and public design. Under the first president, Sukarno, the nation was poor and preoccupied with political restructuring, so that urban design and architecture commanded only a small part of the government's attention. However, what was planned and built did have considerable significance. The national monument, in the shape of a candle, was constructed to give symbolic representation to the new country and to the revolution fought to attain independence. Later, a sports complex consisting of a stadium and an arena was constructed for the hosting of the Asian Games in 1962, a bypass highway from the port to the interior of Java resolved some heavy-transport problems, and a multistoried hotel of international standards was constructed to handle the growing tourist trade. A national mosque was planned, and at the very end of the regime a complex of buildings intended to house the international organization that Sukarno proclaimed as ready to replace the United Nations, so that the West could no longer dominate the international system so thoroughly. Sukarno was replaced before either of these last plans came to fruition; the mosque was ultimately built, but the international complex was scrapped. In general, except for the mosque, architecture did not reflect any Islamic themes during this era. This outlook reflected the attitude of an elite that was only nominally Muslim and was intrigued with modernization, namely, Westernization.

Under President Suharto economic conditions improved considerably and more technical competence was harnessed by the government for an extensive public-works program. That program was both practical and expansive of Indonesian culture. The national mosque was completed, the "Beautiful Gardens of Mini-Indonesia" (Taman Indonesia Mini Indah), an entertainment park featuring the cultures of Indonesia, was built; the Sukarno-Hatta airport was opened to expand international and domestic operations; a series of tollways and ring highways were built to handle the growing size of the capital; multistoried building complexes on Kuning and Soedirman Avenues in Jakarta were constructed; and a mosque-building program was initiated. Finally, in the New Order period the suburb of Pondok Indah was constructed in south Jakarta with upper-income homes and shopping centers reminiscent of Western cities, but the houses were shrouded by fences and gardens and bore architectural designs consistent with houses from Javanese tradition. Again, Islam was not a theme in this physical development, except for the national mosque.

In Kuala Lumpur beginning in the 1980s, but more apparent in the 1990s, several projects were designed to display "the biggest and the best." Accordingly, a 421-meter telecommunications tower, the Maybank Towers, the National Science Centre, and the 88-floor Petronas Tower were constructed. A national mosque was built, and in each state capital there was a state mosque; they represented a variety of styles. Along with the public construction projects, a new kind of condominium structure was designed that incorporated features from the classical Malay hamlet, which was a modernized and stylized representation of a traditional living style. As in the case of Jakarta, a new upper-middle-class suburb for the capital was built at Petaling Jaya. Some effort was made to blend Islam with Malay culture in this venture, certainly by choosing mosques as an architectural vehicle and also in using Islamic themes for the adornment of certain buildings.

In Bandar Seri Begawan, a similar intensification of public construction took place after independence in 1984, with the new palace as the centerpiece of that activity. The palace, named the Istana Nurul Iman, was located on a slight plateau next to the city, which gave it the appearance of being higher than it actually was. Other important structures in the capital included the Foreign Ministry building and the Brunei Arts and Handicrafts Training Centre, which were landmarks for the city. Slightly upriver, a new city was constructed over water to provide housing for about twenty thousand people to match Kampung Ayer, an older city built over water located in the heart of the capital. Hence a modernized version of the traditional living style was re-created in a familiar setting. A similar attitude regarding Islamic expression in architecture prevailed in Brunei as it did in Malaysia.

A significant trend emerged in the building and beautification of mosques and prayer houses throughout the entire Muslim Zone. In Indonesia the Independence Mosque, laid out in the 1960s, was completed in the 1970s and served as a site for national observances of key moments in the Muslim calendar, as well as being used as a favorite Friday communal prayer site. It had a capacity of twenty thousand people. In other major cities of Indonesia central mosques were also constructed. Like the Independence Mosque, these large mosques were attractively constructed and served as important centers for community activities in the city or province they served. They usually drew on modern Arabic building styles, employing columns and subtle arabesque windows and openings for architectural effect but eschewing the more ornate Moorish architecture popular at the end of the previous era. Furthermore, there were private mosques built on endowed land financed by fund-raising drives among local populations; mosques built as part of schools, whether boarding schools or universities; and those constructed as part of an Islamic association's drive to deepen the religious life of its own members. In general, mosques in Indonesia became important sites for the Islamic community during the period, especially in the 1970s and 1980s when revivalism was high. They served as special places for instruction, centers for Islamic vigils, sites for libraries and reading rooms, and in a few cases locations for special services such as legal aid, health dispensaries, and child care. In general, mosques were a very apparent manifestation of the strength of Islam in Indonesia during the era.

In the New Order period, President Suharto founded the Pancasila Muslim Charity Foundation to raise money for building new mosques and prayer houses throughout the country, particularly in locales that had no such prayer facilities. The foundation furnished standardized and partially prefabricated buildings modeled on the profile of the great mosque at Demak, which featured a three-tiered, square-hipped roof. On the roof a lightning conductor had a pentagonal frame—to symbolize the state motto of *Pancasila*—within which the Arabic lettering of "Allah" was inscribed.

The large number of mosques—of all sizes—that were pervasive in both urban and rural areas indicated a society with an Islamic identification, even if other structures did not have an apparent "Islamic" theme.

In Malaysia a trend on the same order occurred, the culminating architectural high point being achieved in the official mosque at Shah Alam, the capital of the state of Selangor, and the National Mosque of the Federal District. Here the architecture continued to stress the Moorish form popularized by the British in the public buildings of Kuala Lumpur built in the early part of the twentieth century. In southern Thailand and the southern Philippines fewer mosques were built, but in important cities some did appear during the period. In Thailand some building was done at government expense, while in the Philippines several of the larger mosques were gifts of Middle Eastern countries using aid money to upgrade Islamic infrastructure in areas regarded as poor and undeveloped. A similar trend took place in Cambodia after the end of the Khmer Rouge period, when Middle Eastern countries assisted in rebuilding an Islamic infrastructure. In Brunei a great mosque was built at Gadong; it too used the very ornate Moorish architecture found in Malaysia. In the same year the government of Brunei created a department to oversee mosque construction and upgrading, so that all Muslims would have adequate learning and resource centers alongside formal prayer space. Bandar Seri Begawan, the capital, also completed the elaborate Asri Hasanul Bolkiah Mosque in the 1990s as a counterpart to the "national" mosques of neighboring countries.

In Singapore the drive from 1960 to 1990 to reconstruct the city for apartment living resulted in the destruction of many places of worship. Chinese temples were most affected, although a large number of mosques were destroyed as well. It was public policy to rebuild all places of worship but relocate them in areas where people could use them. To finance the rebuilding, the Mosque Building Fund was created in 1975. According to this scheme all Muslims were charged fifty cents a month at first, later one Singapore dollar, and still later a dollar and a half, to create a fund to finance the building of new mosques. By 1981, over S$7 million had been collected and six new mosques had been constructed, and in 1989 a second stage of building was undertaken that provided another nine mosques. These mosques came in various styles, with some simple variations of the Moorish architecture used in Malaysia, while others drew on newer styles from the Middle East. They were built to serve as community centers as well as for general worship.

Language and Literature

Variants of Malay-Indonesian became the national language in all three states with Muslim majorities, and in Singapore it was accorded official language status as well. In Thailand and Cambodia it was used by many people. The major development of the language occurred in Indonesia and Malaysia, where literary movements led the way and government agencies supported the work of publishing dictionaries and manuals for the study of the language in schools. Malay-Indonesian was the major language of the Muslim Zone and the lingua franca for about three-fourths of its area.

In Malaysia the Malay literary movement after World War II, especially the "50 Generation," sponsored a series of language and literature conferences in the early and mid-1950s. The conferences advocated the continued use of both Roman and Arabic scripts and urged that Malay be made the national language of the Federation of Malaya. Those efforts were successful, with the Malay-controlled government choosing to follow the recommendations of the conferences. In addition, a government-sponsored intellectual outlet, called the "House of Language and Printing," was founded to sponsor the production of Malay-language publications. (Actually it was a continuation of the British-founded literary outlet discussed in the previous chapter.) In Indonesia the decision to use Malay-Indonesian as a national language had been decided earlier in the 1920s, and the 1945 constitution certified the national status of the language. In Brunei as well, the use of the language was never in question before independence and was merely certified as the official language at independence.

The development of a common Malay-Indonesian language was given special impetus during this era, especially when a joint Indonesian-Malaysian committee made recommendations for the simplification of the language and rationalization of common standards to be applied in the two countries. In this reform, the Roman script was given preference and spellings were made uniform. In the case of Indonesian, this meant that some vowels and diphthongs drawn from Dutch practice were dropped for those used by the Malays, who drew theirs from English. The stress on the development of Malay-Indonesian in a Roman script had a strong impact on language development, as it opened the way to greater facility in learning English, which uses the Roman script as well. Brunei, on the other hand, which followed Malaysia in many matters of language and government, did not go along with the changes, but the sultan repeatedly noted the importance of Arabic script as providing identification with Islam through the use of Arabic letters. He stated that, in time, all Islamic courses in Brunei schools would be taught using the Arabic script. Street signs continued to use that script as well. There were other attempts to save Malay written in the Arabic script, such as a joint committee of officials from all the areas of Southeast Asia that continued to use it to keep that version of the language from falling into extinction, arguing that it was an important part of the history of the region.

Substantial schools of literature existed in Malaysia, Indonesia, and the Philippines during this era, and Muslims participated in the literary work.

That literature concerned itself with fiction, essays, and literary criticism. But these literatures were not much concerned with Islam; rather they focused on non-Muslim traditions, as in the case of the Javanese, and dealt with themes explored in Western literature—that is, the power of nature, the growth of national identity, and the moral dilemmas facing humankind in general. Muslim writers participated in this literature, but they were what some writers termed "deconfessionalized Muslims"—secularized persons—who regarded their own religious tradition as incidental to their literary exercises.[38] At the beginning of the era, three prominent personalities stood out: Za'aba in Malaysia, Muhammad Yamin in Indonesia (Java), and Takdir Alisjabana in Indonesia (Minangkabau). They were all discussed in the context of the last era, but deserve mention here as well. Za'aba was concerned with the growth of a Malayan literary movement; Muhammad Yamin dealt with historical antecedents of the modern Indonesian state; and Takdir Alisjabana was prominent in his examination of the modern Malay/Indonesian language. Of the three, Za'aba might be considered "in" the Islamic community; Alisjabana was on the edge, and Yamin probably stood outside of it.

In Malaya in the 1950s, the 50 Generation used poetry and the novel as the primary media of expression, with the competitions at the Council for Languages and Libraries being the catalyst for their development. A. Samad Said (b. 1935) and Ibrahim Omar (b. 1936) were the prominent writers of the sizeable literary movement. Those writing verse no longer used the *pantun* and *syair* forms that had dominated up until the 1940s, adopting instead the *sajak* form, which used free verse. Mostly, such poetry emphasized the sad condition of humankind and the distant hope of attaining human love; references to Islamic themes were seldom apparent. Many were especially popular as novelists, with two special treatments of Islam apparent. Ahmad Lutfi's (d. 1966) novels in the immediate post–World War II period concentrated on the abuses perpetrated by traditionalist religious scholars, especially charging that their multiple marriages and divorces used women capriciously and left them destitute and without honorable prospects. The author was roundly condemned by religious scholars, who took offense at being singled out in this manner, but he refused to drop the theme, even in the face of heavy criticism. Later, in the 1960s, Ahmad Shahnon's (b. 1933) novels depicted the values of a rural religiosity, hinting that it could be transferred to urban life. His characters were conservative and deeply pious, which set them at odds with Malay society in general, as it was undergoing rapid change due to the national drive toward economic development. For the most part, Malay authors identified being Muslim with being Malay, so they could bypass the subject of Islam without great offense while developing themes that dealt with the other issues, such as the Malay position in the new Malaysian state.

Later, short-story writing emerged that did have a strong Islamic element in it. Especially in the late 1970s and the 1980s, efforts were made to create a literature that would correspond with the "revivalist" movement then in full force in Malaysian society. The movement received the name "Islamic Culture" from an article of the same title by Shahnon Ahmad, in which he attempted to inspire other writers to take up the Islamic cause. One effort gave rise to an "Islamic poetry night" in the capital, where inspirational readings were held. Another activity produced a magazine called *Inspiration (Dakwah)* that published Islamic-oriented writings. In addition, beginning in 1975, the federal prime minister's office sponsored a competition for the best Islamic short stories, with over two hundred manuscripts being submitted in 1982. Largely written by amatuer writers, these stories were mostly about Muslims who "sinned" in some way but how they, or others near them, took that fall from grace as inspiration to lead godly lives themselves. In essence, such themes were consistent with the revivalist calls for a heightened Muslim awareness.

In Singapore, Malay arts and letters flourished as well, fed by intellectual developments in the wider Malay world and the status of Malay as one of the official languages of the Singaporean state. Singapore Malays wrote poetry, novels, essays, and drama for an annual arts awards competition. Significantly, religious life was not an important theme in these writings, although the acceptance of Islamic identity was apparent and formed a backdrop against which the plots evolved. Critical assessments of the contributions, however, indicated that the quality of writing of the participants was below that of writers in Indonesia and Malaysia and, moreover, that the viewpoints expressed were reflective of racial separateness in a non-Muslim state, a finding that troubled Singapore's Chinese authorities, who had expected a more open, multicultural attitude to reveal itself.

Malay literature in Brunei took a different turn than it did in Malaysia or Singapore. There were several dramatic works written for radio and television, and poetry appeared in newspapers and magazines. The dramas all had Islamic themes, often set in the historical context of classical Islam, while the poetry evoked Islamic imagery and/or ideals of morals and ethics. In this respect it reflected Islamic values that were quite traditional and rural, largely unaffected by the urban influences of Malaysia and Singapore. In southern Thailand some political literature was written in Malay to justify the Malay-Muslim separatist cause, but a literary movement associated with the Malay-Muslim community did not develop. There was very little writing of this sort among the Muslims of Cambodia and Vietnam.

The Indonesian variant of Malay-Indonesian was the primary vehicle of government communication and literary development, with the continuous publication of several important literary forms throughout the era. The early literature was dominated again by the Minangkabau writers, with

Chairul Anwar's (b. 1922) poetry setting the tone for a new Indonesia with its highly passionate portrayal of life and strong calls for full expression by writers. The group revolving around Anwar became known as the "45 Generation." A statement in its journal, *Arena (Gelanggang)*, proclaimed the movement's identification to be humanist but realist, and the legatee of culture from across the world, not simply from the Indonesian area. Two of its writers, Mochtar Lubis (b. 1922) and Pramudya Ananta Tor (b. 1925), achieved international reputations, particularly the latter, who was viewed as a martyr for the cause of leftist political aspirations after his imprisonment for involvement with the abortive power seizure by the Communist Party and its allies in 1965.

Almost none of these national Indonesian writers identified themselves as Muslim, and only occasionally were Muslim themes used in their literary works. A. A. Navis (b. 1924) published some material that dealt with Muslim life and its problems, but he was careful not to question the rules of Islam, merely noting the untoward results of not following religious dictates. Djamil Suherman (active 1965) and Muhammad Diponegoro (active 1965) also produced writing that reflected similar outlooks toward Islam and the Muslim community. The use of Muslim themes might have been greater had it not been for the anticipated negative reaction on the part of committed Muslims, who almost always regarded modern literature as morally wrong and as popularizing subjects that were offensive. The most notable example was the reception accorded A. K. Mihardja's (active 1949) novel *Atheist*, which related the story of a young man confronted with modern urban life who could not reconcile it with his religious upbringing, as a consequence of which he denied all religion, repenting only on his deathbed. Muslim critics termed the work an unjust criticism of religious training. In a later case, the poet Danarto (active 1985) published a lyric poem called "Adam's Insight" *(Adam Ma'rifat)*, which was a strong statement about the need for understanding creation through a mystical approach and the necessity of attaining a "pure heart." This was viewed as "heterodox,"—namely, "sinful"—by some committed Muslims because it did not follow generally accepted teachings in Islam. In general, committed Muslims were strongly critical of the literary movement in Indonesia, regarding it as un-Islamic and dealing with themes frequently offensive to them.

Beginning in the 1960s, Western learning in religious matters became important to a number of scholars at Indonesian national universities and the state institutes of Islamic studies. In large part this learning was based on the social-scientific methodology that dominated the study of comparative religion at the time. A number of scholars returning from study abroad began to apply that acquired knowledge to Indonesia's own problems of religious and national renewal. The precursor to this group was Deliar Noer (b. 1926), whose career endured from the 1960s to the end of the century, and whose works centered on Indonesian Muslim political development. Abdul Mukti ʿAli gave a crucial set of speeches and seminar sessions highlighting his belief that religion and modernity were not only compatible, but a historic necessity. The third writer, Harun Nasution (d. 2000), was controversial for his assertion that rationalism was a major movement in Islamic history, as epitomized in the discredited "Freethinkers" *(mutazili)* of the ninth century. He claimed that they had cleared the way intellectually for the rise of classical Muslim civilization, and he wanted this trend to reassert itself in Indonesian Islam. His writing created such a firestorm of reaction that the government ultimately called an end to written debate on the subject.

Following these three writers, another generation of intellectuals was concerned about the importance of economic modernization in the country. Over a thirty-year period, they wrote a number of crucial articles and books attempting to convince the Indonesian middle class to support the government's efforts in that regard. Nurcholish Madjid, covered earlier, was the leading writer among this group.

Javanese continued to be the primary language for over 25 million people in Indonesia and consequently remained important, even though the official attitude of the government was that it was a regional language so accorded it limited support. The period was particularly rich in the production of Javanese literary materials using contemporary Javanese life, Indonesian nationalism, and Western plot lines recast for local audiences as common themes. Significantly, studies listed no writers with a particularly Islamic outlook that could be regarded as prominent. Anthropological studies indicated that Islam had a peculiar development on Java, and that the language developed its own concepts and terminology to deal with that religion. These studies described the rituals, language, and concepts appearing in Javanese, showing that the language found suitable terms to express the broad range of Islamic teachings. In addition, Javanese received an abundance of new Islamic terms from Arabic as standard Sunni practices became more widespread in Javanese society and its rituals and doctrine created a need for appropriate terms in Javanese for easy identification and acceptance.

In the Philippines English was used extensively as a language for writing about Islam by Filipino-Muslim authors, particularly those writing from Manila, where some of the educated Muslims lived and worked. In the 1960s the Muslim Association of the Philippines published a group of tracts in English written by Pakistani writers—Syed Zafar-ul-Hasan (active 1965), Hassan Suhrawardy (active 1965), Muhammad Abdul Aleem Siddiqui (active 1965), and Muhammad Fazl-ur-Rahman Ansari (active 1965)—intended to defend Islam against general attacks from outside and to promote a feeling of pride among the Muslim population of the Philippines. For a time a magazine titled *Philippine Muslim Bulletin* was published that gave attention to common Muslim identification as opposed to narrower regional and ethnic ones. Mamitua Saber (active 1979), a trained sociologist and university administrator, wrote important descriptions of Maranao society. Cesar Adib Majul, at the University of Manila, explored the entry of Islam into Southeast Asia early in his career and later concentrated on the historical development of the Muslims of the Philippines. Samuel Tan, Abdullah Madale (b. 1937), and Carmen Abubakar (active 1991) also wrote scholarly works on Islam in the Philippines using English as their medium of communication.

Singapore was a second locale where English was used by Muslim writers. In the 1960s the Malaysian Sociological Research Institute published three high-quality studies on Muslim law, the arrival of Islam in Southeast Asia, and modern practice of mysticism among the Malays. Later in the era, the Institute of Southeast Asian Studies (ISEAS), made one of its foci the study, elaboration, and publication of studies about Islam throughout Southeast Asia. Revolving around the editorial work of Ahmad Ariff (active 1991) and Sharon Siddique (active 1995), a series of important anthologies and studies were published in the 1980s and 1990s that substantially expanded the scholarly understanding and perception of Islam in the Muslim Zone. These works brought together Muslim writers from the zone who wrote analytically about their own societies, so that comparative studies emerged on particular subject matter. The third locale for the use of English as a cultural medium was Malaysia, where several Muslims published in the language. The two most eminent writers were Sayyid M. Naguib al-Attas and Chandra Muzaffar, who have been covered elsewhere in this study.

Arabic continued to be used as a religious language, although the rise of English as an international means of communication in trade, technology, and education did have an adverse impact on its usage. In addition, the rise in the use of a new Islamic literature written in the vernacular had a dampening effect, even though the message previously contained in Arabic was much the same in the local languages and, indeed, was often merely translated from it. But the popularity of many titles in Arabic remained high, particularly older studies of the Qur'an, Traditions, and jurisprudence *(fiqh)* by al-Sayuti, al-Nawawi, al-Baydawi, and Ibn Hajar al-ʿAsqalani. Later writers, such as M. Rashid Rida, al-Maraghi, and Sayyid Qutb, also sold well. Book handlers in various parts of the Muslim Zone were in agreement that Arabic titles were not best-sellers, but that sales were steady and worthwhile.

Basic Arabic continued to be learned as a means of reading scripture, particularly the Qur'an, and reciting prayer. Neither of these fundamental Islamic concerns could be erased by use of the materials in the vernacular, since it was commonly recognized that those two activities could only be accomplished in Arabic. Also, many people attempted to memorize the Qur²an, a particularly meritorious action in the view of the Muslim community. The art of Qur²an recitation, which had long been popular in the entire region, underwent a growth of interest in the period, with the governments of Indonesia, Malaysia, and Brunei instituting official competitions. In addition, the religious schools throughout the Muslim Zone relied heavily on Arabic texts, as we have seen. The general use of Arabic as a scholarly language was important enough that several dictionaries and word lists of Arabic were developed to assist in learning and translating.

Finally, local languages were important for the publication of Islamic materials in a few instances. In the 1980s and 1990s some Islamic writings appeared in the Tausug, Maranao, and Magindanao languages. In particular, translations were made from Arabic and Iranian Muslim writers in those languages, many of them dealing with contemporary political issues facing Muslims in the Middle East and the plight of Islam throughout the world. New works by local Muslims, however, apparently were not written in those languages in any significant amounts.

Drama

Theatrical productions were well developed in Java, including several versions of the shadow play, folk productions, and modern plays, but most of these came from non-Islamic origins. Similar productions existed throughout the wider zone, even if not on the same scale as on Java. Large numbers of pious Muslims shunned such dramas as questionable or even harmful to their Islamic perspective. There were two developments, however, that were aimed at specifically Muslim audiences. Beginning in the 1960s, an important genre appeared known as media drama, initially geared to radio and television. While most of that drama was concerned with general subjects common to Indonesian society, there was a development of special drama for Islamic holy days, very much the same way that highly patriotic drama appeared on national holidays. Several Muslim writers were associated with the creation of such drama: Junan Helmy Nasution (active 1965) was a pioneer in the 1960s, and Kuntowijoyo was prominent later in the era. These efforts produced a number of plays about the early Muslim community in the days of the prophet Muhammad, but there was considerable opposition from traditionalist Muslims, even though the playwrights avoided characterization of the Prophet. Several of the dramas eventually became part of the regular media offerings for Muslim holidays. Similar television plays appeared on Malaysian television, arousing some of the same apprehensions on the part of Muslims opposed to this art form.

In a second development, an offshoot of theater productions dealing with general life in Indonesia, some stage companies catered to a constituency of committed Muslims. One particular play, entitled *Pious Family*, sponsored by the Women's Section of the Muhammadiyah movement, was representative of this genre. It centered on the decline in moral values occurring in a Muslim family because of the pressures of modern life, particularly among the youth. For the most part, however, this kind of theater was not aimed at the discussion of Islamic issues and themes.

Music and Dance

There were popular music developments in both Indonesia and Malaysia during the era. In Indonesia the popular music of the area, often distributed via cassettes, produced songs that were strongly critical of the government, the society such a government fostered, and the general social injustice that was a common complaint throughout the era. In particular, one type of music, called *dongdut,* was more antiestablishment than others. Its "superstar," Rhoma Irama (b. 1947), called for greater attention to Islam as a means of instituting social reform. The Islamic message fit well with the revivalist movement that was under way, and Rhoma himself identified with the Islamic political opposition for a time, asserting that it offered some hope against the authoritarianism of the Suharto regime. The mention of Islam as a cure-all for the ills of society was a lyrical fad that did catch the attention of a considerable number of people, but it carried no real Islamic message otherwise. Ironically, the music of *dongdut,* particularly in its later phases, prompted dancing exhibiting a form of sensuousness somewhat startling to Indonesian audiences, and anathema to committed Muslims.[39]

During the 1980s and 1990s, a singing genre *(nasyid)* emerged in Indonesia, especially among young women, that attempted to imitate Arabic singing popularized by the Egyptian singer Umm Kalthum (d. 1975) in the middle years of the twentieth century and immensely popular in the Middle East until the end of the century. The genre involved the use of a quavering voice reminiscent of the popular Egyptian singer, while drawing on themes of Islamic identity, morality, and communal commitment. Commonplace in many parts of Indonesia were troupes of singers who took part in "revivalist" activity and in formal competitions, even becoming an important part of the national Qur'an recitation celebrations. This type of singing stood in marked contrast to the popular style of the time period, when pop singing emphasized romantic love and nostalgia.

In Malaysia and Singapore throughout the era there was a popular music that reflected trends common in the West and East Asia, albeit in toned-down Malay and Chinese versions. The songs expressed themes of love and nostalgia without much social message, as in Indonesia. Among a few groups, such as rural agriculturalists, Indonesian performers were popular, but this was largely absent in the urban populations. Rather than being a vehicle for Islamic revivalism as the *dongdut* style suggested, pop culture

—both singing and dancing—were viewed by many Islamic groups as evidence of degenerate Westernism, and some of these groups demanded that such detrimental cultural influences be eliminated.

Visual Art

In Jakarta and several other Indonesian cities, and in Kuala Lumpur and Penang in Malaysia, painters were active. In Indonesia the subject matter centered on depiction of Javanese classic dancers; nature scenes, often with Indic-period architecture visible; and modern urban scenes. In Malaysia, where most painters were Chinese, the subject matter concentrated on nature, human impositions on nature, and folk scenes. In both countries several media were employed, color was bright and sometimes explosive, and different schools of painting were apparent, mostly following Western developments. There was little use of Islamic subject matter, except as incidental to the subject at hand.

At Yogyakarta some artists working with traditional batik techniques produced new forms based on Javanese historical styles. A few "Muslim" artists appeared in this colony, such as A. Pirous (active 1989). In one of his paintings, a section of the Qurʾan was depicted, white on gray, with a surrounding field of orange on which further Arabic writing appeared in the form of the traditional glosses found in a "yellow book," a study guide of an Islamic boarding school.[40] Here a religiously charged item was presented as art. Such expressions of Islamic identity, however, were quite limited, and those that did appear tended to be calligraphy.

Working in print on paper in Malaysia, Sharifah Zuriah al-Jefferi (b. ca. 1955) used Arabic inscription, employing it as a central motif in her paintings. Al-Jefferi used only a single letter or very short words, so that inscription dominated the entire piece. Her colors were displayed in line patterns of circles, ovals, and seemingly unplanned shapes, with forms seldom apparent. The color tones were chosen to fit the artist's mood for each piece; mostly, she saw an unjust world filled with human transgression. Like many other international Muslim painters of the period, her works evoked common Muslim themes, such as "Bosnia" and "Compassion." In general, the number of Islamic artists appearing in this era was quite limited, and they made no grand impression on the wider art scene in any of the countries of Southeast Asia.[41]

Conclusion

The Muslim Zone remained politically fragmented during this period, with Muslims included in the several nation-states of the region. Tellingly, there were no "pan-Islamic" or "pan-Muslim" movements for the zone, which aimed at uniting all groups into a common Islamic political entity. Within the nation-states, elites gained power who were not interested in advancing Islam as the primary identification, except possibly in Brunei, although the period of independence in that country was too short really to measure that identification. In Indonesia and Malaysia, the governments were controlled by elites who looked to cross-cultural and cross-racial solutions for the conduct of national affairs, while in the states where Muslims were in the minority the Muslim elites usually identified with non-Muslim national elites who had no interest in promoting Islam whatsoever. In two of those states, the Philippines and Thailand, the refusal of national elites to accept any part of the Muslim's local culture was deeply resented and led to insurgencies to gain concessions from the national governments. Significantly, only in the Philippines was the insurgency fought with "Muslim identity" as the central theme, which appeared to be the only common point of culture that the rebels had with one another, since they consisted of several ethnic groups.

Except in Malaysia, there was no Islamic agenda in the political realm, where Islamic issues and identity were major topics of political activity, and there it was gathering momentum at the end of the era. In Indonesia, such an agenda was controlled and suppressed by the elite, and it was only very late in the era that the issue of whether such a discussion could be held was apparent. That is not to say that the nation-states ignored Muslim political considerations, for they did not in any of the seven countries involved. Muslims were always included in political parties and pressure groups; Islamic issues were discussed and debated in public and parliamentary fora; and Muslims received attention politically, in most cases. Muslims certainly did not get everything they wanted in any of these countries, but they probably got as much as any other group. Despite this, very few committed Muslim groups were of the opinion that they had received as much as they deserved, and regarded themselves as having been held in check or forced to give in to other groups on key issues.

In the realm of religious practice, expressed in a wide sense, Muslims continued to worship freely. The one exception was in Cambodia during the Khmer Rouge period. Otherwise there were no restrictions on their religious duties or ceremonies in the main, although states sometimes did interfere with the Friday sermon and placed restrictions on the message that could be relayed in that way. Otherwise, the general practices were widely observed, mosques were built and maintained, Muslim revivalist teams were given access to most Muslim audiences, and often to non-Muslim ones, and there were no forced conversions from Islam except, again, for a brief period of time in Cambodia.

Life-cycle events connected with Islam changed to some degree as those events were altered in response to cultural adaptation, but the underlying Muslim role was preserved, as in the case of circumcision where the practice moved from the village specialist to the local doctor, but the affirmation of Muslim identity remained a part of the procedure. Yet Muslims regarded their institutions as under attack throughout the era and feared that "Western culture" or "nationalism," or some other force regarded as malign was poised to change, corrupt, and distort these Muslim obligations and points of identity. In general, Muslims were probably stronger at the end of this era than they had been at the beginning, yet there was a sense that great danger loomed. Further, it was here that one could see the unity of the Muslim Zone, where common standards of ceremony, behavior, belief, and institutions of religion remained very much the same regardless of national boundaries.

In the expression of culture, Islamic themes and identification lost considerable ground as the new nation-states developed cultural forms in architecture, arts, and literature that reflected global culture, and there was a further move away from identification with Arabic and other Islamic forms. The role of the West and the conceptions of nationalism promoted local artists to produce literature and aesthetic forms that were quite removed from those championed by historical and contemporary Islam. Brunei and Malaysia maintained greater contact than others, but still followed the same trend. All told, however, the emphasis on mosque, prayer house, and schools still gave enough justification for Muslim architecture to allow an Islamic character to continue in that art form. In literature, the old poetry, sagas, and Islamic writings began to wane in importance as the world of the twentieth century provided new and exciting alternatives. The only part of Islamic literature that increased was the production of religious literature explaining Islamic beliefs and practices. It appeared in greater volume than earlier. Significantly, Muslims did not complain very much about the general trend away from the Islamic heritage, and that reaction was a bit unusual because they were so vocal about the other areas of national life where they did feel threatened.

Overall, the latter half of the twentieth century was a time of political loss, religious continuity, and aesthetic curtailment, during which Muslims felt themselves to be under pressure and in danger. Significantly, the end of the era was artificial, and the era itself continued into the twenty-first century, with final judgments about all these matters yet to be decided in the future.

Key Readings

Boland, B. J. 1971. *The Struggle of Islam in Modern Indonesia*. A description of the development of Indonesian Islam in the first decades after Indonesian independence.

Bruinessen, Martin van. 1990a. "Kitab Kuning. Books in Arabic Script. . . ."

The results of extensive research into the textbooks used in Islamic training schools throughout the Muslim Zone.

Chandra Muzaffar. 1987. *Islamic Resurgence in Malaysia.* An analysis of the rise of Islamic revivalist movements in Malaysia, with stress on case studies.

Cheah Boon Kheng. 2002. *Malaysia: The Making of a Nation.* An outline of the key policies followed by Malaysia's prime ministers throughout the entire era.

Dhofier, Zamakhsyari. 1982. *Tradisi Pesantren.* An analysis of traditional Islamic education on Java, explaining the network of teachers and students that gave great stability to an otherwise unregulated educational system.

Federspiel, Howard. 1999. "Muslim Intellectuals in Southeast Asia." An explanation of the types of intellectuals operating in Southeast Asia and samples of their contributions.

Malay/Muslim Professionals of Singapore. 1990. *Forging a Vision.* The planning documents of a nongovernmental organization taking on the upgrading of the Islamic community in Singapore at the behest of the Singapore government.

Riddell, Peter. 2001. *Islam and the Malay-Indonesian World.* An account of the development of Islam in Southeast Asia as viewed primarily through the work of its teachers and intellectuals.

Saleh, Fauzon. 2001. *Modern Trends in Islamic Theological Discourse in Twentieth Century Indonesia.* A comprehensive study of Indonesian Muslim intellectual currents in the twentieth century.

Stahr, Volker S. 1997. *Südostasien und der Islam.* A political description of the Muslim Zone in the 1990s from the interviews and findings of an acute observer of the Southeast Asian scene.

5 Themes of Southeast Asian Islam

> It should be remembered that Muslims have always regarded the principles of their religion as a frame of reference within which their individual, social and political life should be attuned. . . . Islam includes the spiritual as well as the physical, the worldly as well as the other-worldly, and the present life as well as the life hereafter.

Common Muslim Institutions

Nine historical institutions relating to the Muslim Zone of Southeast Asia have been selected for further consideration at this point. These institutions were chosen because they are most representative of a wider range of institutions that existed historically in the Muslim Zone.

Political Institutions

The Sultanate

This first level of the political system was a blend of three different political systems covered extensively earlier in this book. Consequently, the sultanate was not a common institution, but varied according to whether the original system had grown out of a vassal, hierarchy, or community model. But many commonalities arose, and it will be considered here as having a common identity, even if that view is idealistic. The institution first had pre-Islamic forms, but it shed much of its overt Indic characteristics relatively early in the era, except on Java where a Vishnuite form and style persisted. At the same time it took on a name and characteristic that tied the institution closely to Islam. The term "sultan" was assigned, albeit alongside other local and Indic titles, initially as an indicator of the association of the ruler with Islam and later as an inherited title of respect and veneration. The epithet of "the shadow of God on earth," a concept found in India and Persia, tied the Muslim perception of God to the ruler and endowed him with the standard duties and obligations of Muslim rulers, even though the monarchs themselves probably were not aware of that certification.

The strength of the sultanate resided in the council, state officers, and administrative units that were the adjuncts to the position. The personnel for those auxiliary positions provided duties and prerogatives for an extensive elite that acted as a curb on excessive power exerted by the ruler and also served, through the competition of the nobles, as a balancing of interests. In some places, apanages tied the elite to land, albeit in a feudal fashion and, in turn, connected the interests of local populations to the court. The weakness of the sultanate lay in the troublesome succession problem, since no arrangements proved capable of assuring a logical successor who could be installed with a minimum of difficulty in the transition. Rather, the opposite was true. As a result of multiple marriages, adoptions, and competitive family members, problems were common and often upset the court and the countryside as the pretenders sought to gain power and put down the claims of others.

In the classical period the sultanate evolved at Melaka and on the north coast of Java and then was used across the zone as Islam became a major identifier of a ruler's weltanschauung. Being a Muslim ruler, it was axiomatic that a sultan welcomed trade, particularly with foreign Muslims, but with others as well, that he subscribed to standards of legal procedure in broad areas of life, and that he worked for the diffusion of his faith into new regions. The sultanate was a very successful organizer and mobilizer of principalities and kingdoms within the region, and it provided for an international order to exist and operate within maritime Southeast Asia. In the middle era the sultanate experienced erosion, primarily loss of power and status, and many rulers were removed altogether from the political scene. Under the Dutch Company, and later the Dutch administration, some were demoted to the status of territorial rulers, some were converted by the Dutch into titular and symbolic officers, some were given small principalities to govern on strictly internal matters, and many were removed entirely. In the American and Thai areas of control, they lost their power and disappeared as the intruding powers replaced much of the existing political system with their own governing institutions. In the British areas, the sultans and sultanates survived, although their powers were greatly curtailed to conform to British ideas of their proper role in a remodeled political system, although the status of the sultans was somewhat elevated in the new system that emerged.

At the beginning of the final era, the sultanate was not a political unit of any strength, except perhaps in Brunei, and sultans had little standing, except for a few individuals. In the modern era, the sultanate survived as a ruling institution only in Malaysia and Brunei. In Malaysia sultanates were transformed into a series of state governments, clearly without sovereignty and autonomous only within the bounds prescribed by a constitutional document. Even within the state he ruled, the Malaysian sultan was compelled to share power with elected legislatures. Further, the system of electing one sultan from the group to serve as a head of state for Malaysia for a set period of time also reflected the limited nature of the institution, giving it a symbolic role in the political system of the country. Only in Brunei did the classical sultanate emerge with its powers intact, and was suspect by many in the population as a system resistant to representative institutions. The reigning rulers of the modern period in Brunei were to retain power in the person of the sultan, while rebuilding an elite of educated and influential people to assure exclusion of any political forces that would threaten the historical powers of the sultan. Those rulers regarded the sultanate as a viable form of government for the modern age. This position stood in marked contrast to sentiments held throughout the rest of the zone, where the classical sultanate was regarded as totally outmoded, out of touch with representative perceptions of governing, or even the power-gathering institutions of more autocratic elites. Except for in Brunei, it was regarded as an institution that could be used as a symbol, and only Malaysia was willing to use it in that way.

The obvious question is whether the new "rulers" of the Southeast Asian Muslim states who appeared in the second half of the twentieth century drew any of their authority or symbolism from the earlier position of sultan. The answer is no, as these positions—the prime minister's position in Malaysia and the president in Indonesia—were taken from more modern models in use elsewhere in the world, without much reference to Southeast Asian tradition. Those rulers followed modes of behavior common to many other rulers elsewhere in terms of how law, administration, and policy were derived and carried out. Attempts to use Islamic symbolism have been limited—in Malaysia because the state sultans and the king have strong claims on that symbolism, while in Indonesia the two dominating presidents tried to set limits on the role of Islam in the nation. Strikingly, in both Indonesia and Malaysia there is a general belief that the ruler should be a Muslim, but there seems to be no strong view of the ruler as a continuation of the sultanate; most Muslims regard contemporary forms of political office to be adequate to the times.

Judges and the Law

In the classical era Islamic rulers usually appointed justice officials, giving them Arabic titles such as "religious judge" (*qadi*) and "chief judge" (*qadi al-qudah*), as the situations at both Melaka and Aceh attest. In that formative age, rulers sometimes acted as judges, at least in major cases, so that judges were probably little more than their surrogates, filling in when the ruler was away or occupied with other matters. Over time they became established in their positions and took on the legal functions of their political systems. The first judges appear to have been well-trained religious scholars, often from abroad, but they had limited ability to apply any sort of standard Islamic justice because rulers tended to favor local custom, the fiats and decisions of earlier rulers, and their own inclinations to decide cases. There was some codified law at various places, established by ambitious rulers to give order and direction to the legal system; seldom was it reflective of the dictates of Islamic law except in some general matters, particularly trade, family affairs, and pious endowments.

In the middle era judges became specialized, some dealing with general matters of public and criminal law, and others concerned with personal and family law; one title *(hakim)* seems to have gone with the former, while the traditional title *(qadi)* was retained for the latter type of judge, perhaps because he involved himself much more in law as drawn from the standard books of Muslim jurisprudence. Law became more complicated and differentiated during this era, with instructions, decisions, and decrees of colonial governments becoming part of the overall legal system, affecting everyone to some degree, but groups in directly ruled territories the most. In indigenous law there was a bifurcation between custom and precedent important in public and criminal law, while Muslim jurisprudence *(fiqh)* was common in dealing with family matters and certain areas related to religious institutions of Islam, such as the pious endowment. The perception that the sacred law of God *(syariʾah)* was being applied by the state was widely held because of its application in family matters, even though that probably was not entirely true.

In the modern era, all governments of the various nation-states that arose in the Southeast Asian region adopted legal systems that relied on legislatures and/or executive bodies to formulate law and legal systems suitable to the politics of the time. For the most part, many sectors of law—such as commercial law, criminal law, public law, and several other fields—were handled through law codes adopted and adapted from abroad, often European countries, while family law and pious endowments generally continued to follow Muslim jurisprudence. The training of national judges was based on secular education with specialization in legal studies, which meant they had limited understanding of Muslim jurisprudence or God's sacred law. Near the end of the era, however, groups arose, especially in Malaysia but much muted elsewhere, that advocated that the state should apply greater portions of the sacred law—in other words, "Islamic" law should be more extensively adopted and used at the expense of other national law. The overall trend, however, shows there was a diminishing role for religious judges throughout the era, religious law having been used extensively at the very beginning of the first era and then shrinking to a small area of jurisdiction until comparatively recently, when there have been some attempts to resurrect its importance, though with only small increases in actual usage by the end of the era.

Customary Institutions

Shamanism

The healer/magician was a universal figure in most societies before the advent of modern medicine, when rudimentary medical usage, herbology, massage, and psychological manipulation were the methods used to treat sickness and maladies. In the history of the Muslim Zone shamans were ubiquitous; because they were deemed indispensable to ordinary living among all classes, they constituted the health-care practitioners of their eras. They sprang from societies that relied heavily on animism, seeing the life force in surrounding nature, which could be tapped by the shaman for healing and sorcery. Regarding "power" as residing in religious objects and language, the shamans converged with Islam in a fragmentary way, even as they had been merged with Buddhism and Hinduism in their time. Accordingly, some shamans attempted to incorporate Islamic knowledge, symbols, and prayers as part of their practice and repertoire. However, it was a specialized extraction without regard for the core meaning of the religion itself and concentrated on the use of religious terms and expressions in an attempt to draw power from their use, just as the animist tried to derive power from other animate objects. Consequently, there was always tension between religious teachers and shamans, intensified by the competition that existed between shamans and mosque officials for officiating at rites of passage, particularly births, but to a lesser extent those conducted during circumcision, marriage, and death ceremonies. Even in the practice of healing, mosque functionaries used prayer as important to curing some ailments, and the "blessing" of a saint was regarded as the ultimate device for healing, which competed directly with the shaman. Still, in people's minds there must have been a blending of the practitioners who really controlled Islam, and many probably did not differentiate among them very much.

The high era of the shaman occurred at the end of the nineteenth century when they were clearly the dominant figures in rural life, viewed as mediators with the spirit world in a society given to animism; but thereafter they went into eclipse. With the advent of modern medical knowledge and techniques offering effective cures, along with education that stressed a rational world, the usefulness of the shaman declined as new kinds of health-care practitioners came on the scene. Within Islam, the modernist Muslim began to "purify" religion and shun those practices connected with animism in particular, and shamans became a target of their preaching. These changes eroded the use of the shaman and led to a widespread changeover to more modern medical practice. As a result, a historical figure that was not Muslim at all but had sometimes been associated with Islam, was replaced by a more modern institution that also lay largely outside of Islam.

Life-Cycle Events

Birth, puberty, marriage, death, and other markers in human life were celebrated by societies within the Muslim Zone with rites or observances that mixed Islamic tenets with local practices. Islam entered into these observances in different degrees: for instance, some rites, such as those connected with circumcision and death, were almost totally defined by Islam; while others, such as childbirth, tonsure, and marriage, almost entirely followed local custom. Ear boring, teeth filing, and female genital cutting were hardly affected by Islam at all. Islamic functionaries were involved with male circumcision and burial, with Islamic prayers, incantations, exhortations, and procedures constituting an important part of the observances. In the second category of childbirth, tonsure, and marriage, religious functionaries might be involved at particular moments, and Islamic prayers and exhortations uttered at crucial moments, but Islam's role was limited. In the final set of rites—ear boring, teeth filing, and female genital cutting—Muslim functionaries were not used, and only occasionally were Islamic exhortations or prayers uttered.

While the relationships of Islam with local customs were worked out in the early period, by the middle period the amalgam of the two was set so that the sum total was regarded as properly Islamic, or at least sanctioned by Islam. Few judgments were made about those practices by religious reformers of the time, although there were minor attempts to eliminate some animistic or Hindu practices the reformers found particularly offensive. However, in the modern era, the life-cycle events underwent change as the societies of the region left their rural settings and urban life became the primary form of living. Those events of course continued, but they had to be expressed in a new context. For example, the practitioner who performed circumcision was changed to a doctor in many cases, weddings were set in new social contexts, and teeth filing and ear boring were cast aside. Still, the role of Islam endured in many of these events, such as final rites. In fact, this is the first of the institutions of Islam we have examined that has retained some strength and continuity in the contemporary age.

Religious Institutions

The Cleric (ʿalim)

The Muslim cleric, or teaching functionary, predated the arrival of Islam in Southeast Asia and was an immediate import into the zone when Islam arrived. The cleric was already established in the central Islamic world as a "student" of religion and the primary personage involved with the well-being of the community of believers at the local level. He taught the youth, mostly boys, the basics and essentials of religious lessons, but also fulfilled an important role as advice giver to rulers, individual believers, and groups of believers. As we saw in earlier chapters, these clerics were often local leaders, identifying with the communities they served. Sometimes they were mystics, but usually the mystics recognized as saints were not clerics. Some clerics were propagators of religion, most were religious teachers, some were attached to mosques, some were attendant at the courts of rulers, and some were simply adventurers wandering from place to place.

In the classical era, clerics were influential in the spread of Islam and the early political administration of the zone. They appeared in the chronicles as propagators, often converting rulers. They married the daughters of rulers, in several cases succeeding to the throne, and in other prominent cases serving as advisers. They were viewed by outside observers as influential in the policy decisions of the rulers' courts. As well, they were vital to the early practice of Islam and apparently served as teachers of both children and adults. In the middle era, their role in politics was greatly diminished, although still important on occasion, and their role as propagators lapsed with the end of widespread proselytization. Likewise, their role in the mosque decreased as less-learned men assumed the positions there. Mostly they were associated with schools, where they taught religious sciences, making them an integral part of the major institution for providing literacy and education in these Muslim societies. In the modern period, clerics have been marginalized in teaching with the rise of national school systems and a shift in education to general and scientific subject matter, along with the diminishing value of religious education in the employment and careers of peoples. At the same time, new opportunities have arisen in connection with the mosque, as that institution has been upgraded to take on professional religious leaders for a wide variety of functions, and as more opportunities have arisen in the revivalist field. These functionaries must increasingly compete, however, with new kinds of Muslim leaders—administrators operating religious associations, new scholars in universities and Islamic institutes, and journalists and government officials—as givers of advice to society in general. In sum, the cleric started in the first time frame as an important personage, suffered decline in the middle period, and faced severe challenges of redefinition in the final era.

The Propagator (da$i^{}$)

The propagator was a historical Muslim figure who attempted to proselytize non-Muslims into Islam and/or attempt to intensify the faith of those already in the Muslim community. Consequently, propagation was an imported institution that arrived with the advent of Islam and was regenerated in the Southeast Asian environment. Historically, such propagators have been enthusiastic proponents of Islam, energized by another propagator, by a trip to Makkah, or by belonging to some association, such as a mystic movement. Sometimes they were clerics or mystic leaders, but often laymen.

In the classical period the propagators, particularly those who belonged to mystical orders, were the "foot soldiers" of the religion, moving into non-Muslim areas to make conversions, sometimes before the royal court of the territory itself had converted, but very often in response to such conversion with the full support of the royal court. The "saintly" community of Giri was an important source of the propagators who moved into the Lesser Sunda island chain to spread Islam among a population brought under the control of Makassar rulers. In the middle era, this classical propagator continued to function in the frontier areas of Kalimantan and Sulawesi, but a new sort of propagator emerged with the reformers of Islam, as revealed through the movements of Paderis in west Sumatra and Diponegoro in central Java. In the early twentieth century propagators often belonged to modernist Muslim movements such as the Islamic Union–Persis, which, like the Paderis, were interested in removing animistic practices from Muslim society and furthering the cause of standard Islamic practice. In modern times the propagator became important in 1970–1990 as a wave of "revivalism" passed through the Islamic world in general and across the Muslim Zone in particular. While some efforts were made to proselytize non-Muslims, especially the Chinese and indigenous inland peoples, most of the efforts of the propagators went into revivalist activity among the believers. Particularly in Malaysia there were several associations devoted to this activity, and they stimulated strong identification with Islam that had important political overtones.

Propagation as a historical institution continually changed as conditions altered. Starting with the simple task of converting non-Muslims in frontier Islam, it evolved into an agent that consistently sought to strengthen and consolidate the Islamic community of the zone, and reinvented itself as an institution in each era.

The Mosque

Like the cleric, the mosque was an institution created in the central Islamic world and brought to Southeast Asia, at least in its conceptual form. The entire functioning of worship required a place for such practice, and mosques were established for that purpose at the very beginning of the religion. The physical forms they took in Southeast Asia, however, seem to have evolved from preexisting structures used for worship in earlier religions and, with adaptations, eventually developed a distinct architecture that differed from that in the central Islamic world. Practically, the mosque was always a center of communal activities for believers where prayer took place, particularly for men; but it was also the focal point around which other markets, villages, or educational institutions were erected. In Southeast Asia three primary functionaries were essential to the mosque: the prayer leader, the caller to prayer, and the sermon giver.

In the early period, the number of mosques was limited and the structures were fashioned on the model of earlier Balinese-style buildings used for worship there, although there also appear to have been Chinese influences, seen especially in the detail of multiple roofs in a pagoda style. The officials of the mosque were standardized during this period, and a voluntary rice tax was assigned in rural areas for the support of mosques, while rulers at various levels of authority supported their structure and upkeep in the cities. Mosques seem to have generally had limited use during the early era because disciplined forms of worship were apparently not common among the general population. In the middle era, the number of mosques grew as association with Islam became stronger among the general population; late in the era, the numbers of people using mosques increased appreciably. Especially late in that middle era, the mosque began to change its architectural form, taking on the Moorish style in some areas, particularly in the Malay states and southern Thailand, as an addition to the Southeast Asian style that had dominated earlier. In the modern era, the mosque underwent considerable architectural change, as large, showcase buildings were constructed by various governments, and international architects became available who drew on "Moorish forms" and "Arabesque styles," and created "neotraditional" Southeast Asian forms. Strong identification with Islam, promoted by the revivalist movement, prompted greater use of the mosque for worship by men, women, and children, so that prayer, basic religious learning, and social welfare activities became centered in them. The uses to which mosques were put reflected the needs of the mosque communities operating them, and they functioned at a level not apparent in earlier times.

In fact, it would appear that the mosque is an institution that has enjoyed greater usage and wider functions as time has passed. It has always been a symbol of Islamic presence, but its original role as a center of regular religious practice has expanded appreciably throughout the entire time frame.

Religious Schools and Literature

Schools predated Islam's arrival in Southeast Asia, of course, and were an important part of the Buddhist scene. With Islam's arrival, however, schools took on new names and subject matter, and changed their teaching mission, much of the change reflecting standards from the central Islamic world because the first teachers came from that region. It was the mosque that was the site of the first Islamic schools, where people received instruction on worship, general obligations of the religion, and what it meant to be associated with Islam. For advanced learning, formal schools with their own buildings came into existence. In the classical era, religious schools were sometimes located at royal courts for the education of children and adults there, but soon were established in outlying areas as private enterprises, sometimes combining trade or agriculture with study. Learning in the schools concentrated mostly on mastery of Arabic and the rudiments of the Qur²an, but with time enough students were found to focus more broadly on the Islamic sciences, including both jurisprudence and mysticism. In the middle period, the private schools became more important and evolved into self-contained social units that were often highly respected in the countryside they dominated. Students were widely drawn so that there was not a direct relationship between schools and local population, but local religious leaders were always consulted for their advice on crucial matters of faith and life in general. Late in the time frame, the schools continued their evolution when modernists founded new schools where teaching methods and curricula were changed to accord with new schools formed by governments, modeled on Western educational patterns. In the modern era, the schools lost considerable influence in the new nations formed then because their religious subject matter was deemed unsuitable for meeting the needs of a technologically oriented society. Many schools ceased to exist, others made changes, and still others were forced to adopt new patterns by governments so that they could be absorbed into national educational systems.

Importantly, religious schools constituted another institution that had a long, influential history but faded with the onset of the modern era because the environment changed so significantly. Late in the era, with the counteraction of the revivalist movement, those schools partly recovered, though reconstructed in their teaching methods and content.

Artistic Institutions
Literature
Literature in the Muslim Zone was partly homegrown, partly imported from the Islamic heartland, and partly from other external sources. In the early era, general literature showed a heavy influence from India and Persia, with materials relevant to religious obligations coming directly from the Arab world. Also, some materials from the Indic period of Javanese history remained, which was an important consideration for Muslims in north, east, and central Java. Muslim intellectuals began to use literature as a way of mobilizing support for their ideological positions and intellectual constructs, and for assistance in the task of teaching new generations of religious scholars the lessons of Islam. In the middle period, the Persian and Indic influences were modified to suit the Southeast Asian and Muslim context rather than purveying the original messages, which were often non-Islamic in intent, story line, and values. Javanese values remained important on Java—particularly in central Java—where there was a constant reinterpretation of old Javanese stories, texts, and themes with slightly modified story lines to make them acceptable to Muslim audiences, but not at the

expense of a strong continuing identification with pre-Muslim understanding of culture. Islamic literature on the study of Islam continued to come from the Arab world and was often reworked for use in the Southeast Asian context.

In the modern era, the basic literature was pushed into the background as new national literatures appeared and became prominent, usually reflecting Western themes and values, but also retaining a strong relationship to other non-Islamic values and conditions in Southeast Asian society—a sort of secular literature. Islamic literature on the study of Islam once again came from the central Islamic world, mostly Arab, but within a slightly wider context, so that some Persian and even Pakistani writings were included. Again, however, these works were revised by the local Southeast Asian scholars. However, other intellectuals in Southeast Asian societies began to create their own kinds of writing, most apparently in economics, government, and science, while in the field of Islamic study some thinkers emerged who used both Western methodologies and good knowledge of Islam to create a neomodernist school that relied on their own interpretations rather than those taken from the Middle East.

Overall, this review of eight institutions of Islam tells us that several have fallen into decay and are losing their influence, that several others continue to make a contribution, and that in a couple of cases it looks as though a restructuring might be under way that would lead to eventual revival.

Islam: Contributions and Accommodations

Indigenous Influences

Southeast Asian concepts and values had an important relationship with Islam. The political institutions all had an indigenous base and, with some exceptions for the sultanate, remained vital throughout the entire time frame of the study. The capsule descriptions above properly noted that these indigenous institutions all had Islamic functions attached to them that, in effect, served as vehicles for Islamic identification and values. Of these, the sultanate was the most symbolic and the royal courts the most functional, but none of the institutions really ever departed from being expressive of the general indigenous culture they served. The anthropological institutions were also autochthonous and provided a common cultural framework for the entire Muslim Zone, but validated many Islamic practices and customs to create a hybrid culture that incorporated Islamic values extremely well. Most of the religious institutions operated in reverse, with local influences having effect on customs, practices, and functionaries brought in by outside forces. Literature was expressive of local values in some genres, such as the poetry of the Malays, the creation cycles of the Bugis and Maranao, and the Panji tales of the Javanese, but for a long period it was dominated by foreign themes, styles, and even forms, although in the modern era indigenous themes and problems reasserted themselves. In sum, some institutions, particularly in governmental and societal organization, were furnished from within Southeast Asia and acted as a platform upon which some Islamic concepts and practices rested for utilization within the Muslim community.

Middle Eastern Influences

The study of institutions demonstrates that three influences came from the Middle East: Islamic religious values, Arabic language, and some literary forms. We have already seen that in the political and societal institutions Islam adapted to the locally created indigenous institutions. But imported concepts and practices accompanied Islam from the Middle East; there was also considerable impact on religious literature. The foregoing study amply shows in each era that Middle Eastern influence continued to act on the Muslim Zone—for example, the pilgrimage, students studying at Makkah and elsewhere, the migration of Hadrami Arabs, and the transfer of Islamic literature to Southeast Asia. These were, of course, not one-time influences but continuing and pervasive, ones that penetrated the religious institutions of Southeast Asia in particular, as well as its religious literature. In fact, the impact of this continual influence was strong enough throughout the entire time frame to induce N. Madjied to refer to Southeast Asian Islam as a "user" of Islam from elsewhere but certainly not an "exporter," as the Middle East was. All of these elements were transferred initially through Arabic, so knowledge of that language was essential. Its influence extended even further by providing a syllabary for local languages, new words and expressions, and a new cultural means for examining Southeast Asia. The third influence came early in history with the importation of a popular literature, but mostly it arrived in Southeast Asian via India.

Asian Influences

It was South Asia that had a considerable impact on Islam in the early years of its existence in Southeast Asia, and much of the message was transferred to the Muslim Zone by Muslim Arabo-Indian traders and propagators. This Arabo-Indian community provided much of the international shipping of the era and favored Muslim-controlled ports in Southeast Asia, thereby prompting non-Muslims to convert for economic advantage, since those traders attracted a large amount of intercourse with local traders when they visited a port. This community was influential until the end of the nineteenth century, although at a lower level of influence than in the earlier centuries of Islamic presence in Southeast Asia. The Arabo-Indian community was not an originator of trade, religion, or literature, but a transferring agent, as it were, from western Asia and India out to the Southeast Asian region. In the formative years of Islam in Southeast Asia, the Chinese also played a role similar to that of the Indians, but it was a short-lived influence, with the major impact seen mostly on the north coast of Java. The popular literature that was transmitted in the formative years of Islam was especially influential, as it was related to Indic tales already familiar to many in Southeast Asia, and its new "Islamic" context was readily accepted as valid as well. On the other side of the coin, however, Chinese and Indians later appeared in the roles of laborers, entrepreneurs, and middlemen in the time of colonial domination and were regarded as superior in talents to the local Southeast Asian populations. This left a negative legacy of suspicion and concern, especially after the creation of independent Southeast Asian nations. Some groups of Muslims—in Thailand, the Philippines, Singapore, and Indochina—have come under control of non-Muslim nation-states with quite different cultures, which have generally been competitive with Muslim culture and often intolerant of Islamic institutions existing in the Muslim populations within those territories.

Western Influences

Western influence has been mostly destructive of Islamic institutions or competitive with them. The sultanate lost its preeminent position in most parts of Southeast Asia as a result of colonial manipulation and interference with the institution. Colonial governments also replaced the sultanate with a Western system of control, and later political systems were adapted from Western culture. Similar developments occurred in the field of education, where general studies were originally introduced by colonial administrations and the study of Islam was not included or maginalized. Because around the same time an urban culture was introduced that demanded general studies and technological knowledge, the public schools proved necessary for good employment prospects. National school systems in the independent nation-states of Southeast Asia followed the lead of colonial education policy and established general and technological courses as the core of learning. Muslim schools concentrating on the Islamic sciences did attempt throughout the twentieth century to upgrade Muslim education and produced several kinds of hybrid educational institutions, but they were assimilated for the most part into the national educational systems. The schools that remained outside those systems continued to teach religious sciences and experienced dwindling enrollments and a shrinking pool of teaching staff. Most important, however, Western economic systems were adopted, especially banking, capital formation, state regulation, and liberal international market policy, all of which displaced more basic systems, and also Muslim economic principles. Some of the Muslim economic institutions, such as the "Islamic bank" and "Islamic poor-tax foundations," have been established as pilot projects or experiments, but economic systems have not abandoned Western principles despite the introduction of Islamic economic institutions. The Western impact on Islamic institutions and life-styles remains highly invasive, probably as much as that of the Middle East.

Ethnicity and Gender

Scholars probably had it right when they stated that the peoples along the coasts of Southeast Asia accepted Islam readily, while those in the interior and the highlands were more resistant to conversion. The discussion con-cerning the sultanate, noted that at the outset of Islamization Muslim rulers were expected to be interested in trade and provide the right laws and insti-tutions for advancing it, which was what coastal peoples were most inter-ested in doing. Strikingly, the Malays, the Tausug, and the Bugis were the three most apparent ethnic groups that fit this interpretation, and they all made Islam an important aspect of their ethnic identity. The Minangs and the Javanese were inland peoples and, though they converted to Islam, they took on the new religion with reservations that gave Islam in those places a different face, somewhat out of kilter with the general impression of Islam prevailing internationally. Still other inland groups, such as the Dayaks and the Bataks, were highly resistant to Islam, and conversion efforts in their areas garnered only limited results.

In general, it can be concluded that there has been an association of certain ethnic groups with Islam, but it has not been an either-or dichot-omy. After all, there are Malays, Bugis, and Tausug who are Christian. Equally, in ethnic groups that are generally not Muslim, such as the Chi-nese, Indians, Dayaks, and Bataks, there are some members who have con-verted to Islam. But history shows that particular ethnic groups have been the carriers of Islamic culture and community institutions in Southeast Asia. We have seen in our discussion on life-cycle events that some cultural differences among varied cultural—that is, ethnic—groups on certain mat-ters persisted. For instance, marriage among the Minangs was historically arranged by the prospective wife's family, while among the Malays it was the prospective husband's family that made the initial contacts. Islam provided the basic infrastructure for the event, with the marriage contract and its blessing of the rite, regardless of the operative ethnic and cultural factors.

Gender has been an important differentiating factor in Southeast Asian Islamic history, and it remained so to the end of the last era. There were women rulers in Southeast Asia in a number of locales, and at least two of them—at Aceh and Japara in the early era—were formidable and noted, but for the most part Islamic society has not viewed women as suited to the role of political leadership. In the same way, with very minor exceptions, women were not much involved in teaching about Islam; women were not leaders in the religious community; and women were not important as intellectuals. The study does show, particularly in its discussions of anthropological institutions, that considerable value was placed on women and that their role in the family was highly respected, not only in matrilineal societies, but in all societies of the region. As the discussion on Javanese customary institutions indicates, the most important marriage in a family was that of the eldest daughter, which suggests the high worth placed on females. Of course, the pattern fits most Muslim societies, where the primary roles are assigned to the male, while the female is expected to fulfill roles in the family and in supporting the male members of the community. The responsibilities of worship for females is the same as that for men, except in public ceremonies, and the same concerns about piety apply to women as to men. The lack of any outstanding public role for Muslim women is certainly apparent in this study, and it is only rarely that we have seen glimpses of the female role indicating that there is a level of significant activity in the sisterhood of the religion.

Reflections

In Southeast Asia, Islam has exhibited great strength and resilience in the process of attaching itself to social institutions that sought accommodation with existent local customs, thus creating a strong hybrid culture capable of withstanding the political disasters that confronted Muslims in the colonial era. Their success suggests that other combinations might be useful and rewarding as well, despite some committed Muslims' insistence that Islamic culture should be unadulterated and that the community should as much as possible eliminate other influences. This attitude misses the great lesson of history—namely, that Islam succeeded in Southeast Asia, and in many other regions, precisely because it retained the essence of its message and became the instrument for entering societies alien to Islam and giving them reinvigorated goals and means of doing things. In Southeast Asia, Islam arrived as Indic civilization was eroding and there was ample evidence that vitality needed to be restored. Islamic institutions did that, but without insisting that purist doctrines, practices, or ways of doing things be adopted wholesale and all else jettisoned. Rather, it seems that Islam provided a significant spiritual component to existing local institutions that brought new levels of strength and identification to these societies by adapting to them and thus forming new cultures. Pietistic reformers might keep this in mind —though they probably will not—lest they lose the very tolerance that allowed their forebears to be successful in the first place.

Modernization has been a major goal of the nation-states of Southeast Asia since the 1950s, and there is no indication that this aspiration will diminish in the near future. It has been charged in the Western press—from a variety of sources—that Muslims have difficulty accepting modern technology, democracy, and contemporary economics. The charge seems spurious for Southeast Asian Muslims, who mostly have embraced modernity easily and effectively. They regard themselves as part of the "East Asian economic miracle," even if the term was not coined for them specifically. In the states where they constitute majorities, they have benefited from the many infrastructure and upgrading projects that have been the hallmark of the era; but it is true that those in states where Muslims constitute minorities they have not profited nearly as well as their non-Muslim counterparts. However, this is a matter of distribution of development funds and projects rather than a reluctance on the part of Muslims to accept modernization. Muslims do hold that there are ethical and moral norms that must be maintained in any drive toward development—these statements often get media attention—but what often is not reported is that Muslims, with reason and intuitively, attempt to make their lives richer and carefully interrelate their religion with the new conditions evolving about them. As one Muslim university science professor stated, "Not everything in science seems to fit with what God's Message says, but that is a matter of human difficulty and at some level the two do mesh. Humans are charged with always striving to find that link." In addition, Muslim politicians have no quarrel with representative government, regarding it as the proper means of representation at the current time. The large number of Muslims involved in representational politics throughout Southeast Asia is impressive. One can hope that this trend will continue and gain strength.

It is probably axiomatic that when controlled by thoughtful and tolerant people Islam is widely beneficial and a force for positive action, but when controlled by those who think narrowly without a wide view of humanity the results are of limited value. In present-day Southeast Asia there are people who fit both categories, and therein lies the problem. Like many other peoples, the Muslims of Southeast Asia face some soul-searching and some community action ahead to overcome narrowness and intolerance for a wider view of the world. Truly, the ethnic divisions and religious differences of Southeast Asia need sensitive treatment and a genuine concern for the status and feelings of both Muslims and non-Muslims. To paraphrase the relatively new adage of "spaceship earth," all the groups within Southeast Asia—Muslim and non-Muslim—are on a common boat (proa) together, and what affects one affects the other; they either survive together or, sadly, suffer in the presence of one another. What they should not do is cause each other suffering. The challenges of the Southeast Asian future call for great tolerance and breadth of vision; and, leaving aside non-Muslims, there are ample indications that many Muslims are moving in another direction. Indeed, Islam may be better than its followers, but its impact in this world is only as good as its followers make it.

Postscript

It is tempting to add a section to the foregoing study that would deal with recent events in Southeast Asia affecting the Muslim Zone. Since the year 2000, economic conditions have been in a state of recovery from the 1997 economic crisis. Politically, al-Qaidah has shown its success in penetrating organizations throughout the zone, instigated "terrorism" at Bali and Jakarta, and flexed its influence in the Philippines, Singapore, and Thailand. Also politically, Indonesia and Malaysia are experiencing regime change, with the more difficult alterations occurring in Indonesia, where Islam has been a large issue in two election campaigns and the choosing of presidents. Further, "independence" movements in southern Thailand and the southern Philippines have resurrected strong "Muslim" calls for separation from non-Muslim states. Indonesia has experienced internal religious quarreling of a serious nature, with demands of Acehnese secessionists, fighting between Muslim Madurese and non-Muslim Dayaks on Kalimantan, and Christian Malukan against Muslim Malukans in the east. Most recently the great tsunami that devastated large coastal sections of the Indian Ocean basin, with Aceh a major disaster area, have opened questions about the religious meaning of the devastation and about the motives of some Christian and Muslim groups supplying relief. All these "new" developments demand historical context and analysis, and while it is tempting to add that analysis to this study, such an examination would undoubtedly be premature. It is obvious that some kind of shift occurred either late in the twentieth century or since then, but the nature of the shift and its probable durability call for full analysis. It may be a new era, but more likely it is short transitional phase. The range of the preceding study indicates that the anthropological, literary, and religious developments taking shape in this contemporary period are still undergoing scrutiny, and no solid conclusions about recent events have yet emerged. This is not to say that studies of contemporary political conditions have no worth, for they do; and fortunately there has been a steady stream of them recently. Rather, it is to conclude that the foregoing study has dealt with long-range macroviews of historical relationships and developments, and that the five years since the end of the period covered here are not adequate to project the study onto the contemporary period. This author, wisely or foolishly, chooses to refrain from attempting that task.

Notes

Introduction
Epigraph. Abdullah and Siddique 1986: 1.
   1. Bergsträsser 1930: 283–294.

1. Muslim Wayfarers
Epigraph. Ibn Mas'udi, cited in Tibbetts 1979: 177.
   1. Chaudhuri 1990: 28–41.
   2. Huzayyin 1942: 143–276.
   3. Hookyaas 1952: 178–184; Braginsky 1993: 22–25.
   4. Labib 1981: 131–155.
   5. British Museum Library, Sloane No. 217.
   6. al-Attas 1969: 11.
   7. Ravaisse 1922: 247–289.
   8. Moquette 1919: 396; Damais 1957: 403–404.
   9. Fatimi 1963: 4–7; Majul 1962: 348–394; al-Attas 1969: 25–32; Johns 1961: 37–49; Drewes 1968: 284–310; Pigeaud and de Graaf 1976: 123; C. C. Berg 1955: 111–142.

2. The Emergence of a Hybrid Muslim Culture
Epigraph. Hamilton 1939: 40.
   1. Barbosa 1967: II, 76–77.
   2. Ibid., 145.
   3. Pyrard 1887–1890: I, 162.
   4. Tate 1971: I, 44.
   5. di Santo Stefano 1857: 7; Barbosa 1967: II, 76.
   6. de Graaf and Pigeaud 1984: 14, 16, 20.
   7. Muljana 1976: 234–236.
   8. Pinto 1614: 64–77; Ibn Batutah 1953: 274; de Graaf and Pigeaud 1974: 141–142.
   9. Saleeby 1963: 42.
   10. Barbosa 1967: II, 75.
   11. de Morga 1962: 308.
   12. R. Jones 1979: 154.
   13. Marsden 1966: 301.
   14. Schrieke 1955: I, 39–41; al-Attas 1969: 1–10; Majul 1962: 394–397.
   15. Pigafetta 1969: 109.
   16. de Gasperis 1986: 52–59.
   17. Pires 1944: 245.
   18. Schrieke 1957: II, 68–69, 271–283.

19. C. C. Brown 1970: 2–6, 13–18; Penth 1969: 6–8.
20. Pinto 1614: 62.
21. Abdurachman 1978: 177–185.
22. Hamilton 1939: 52.
23. Matheson 1985: 220.
24. Ibid., 249–251.
25. Landon 1949: 135–143.
26. Matheson 1985: 216–222.
27. Drewes 1976: 281–285.
28. Carroll 1982: 10.
29. Ibid., 9.
30. Reid 1980 and 1993a: 2: 167.
31. Meilink-Roeloefz 1962: 37.
32. Behrend 1984: 32–34.
33. Kamaruddin 1997: 255.
34. Pigeaud 1967–1970: I, 140, 1423.

3. The Emergence of New Muslim Institutions

Epigraph. Bickmore 1869: 526.
1. H. Geertz 1963: 29–30.
2. Poensen 1886: 7–8.
3. *Encyclopaedie van Nederlandsch Oost-Indië (ENOI)* 1917: II, 192; Sartono 1985: 29.
4. United States Bureau of the Census 1903: I, 48.
5. *ENOI* 1917: I, 462.
6. Ner 1941: 154, 173, 182, 195–196.
7. van Vollenhoven 1918–1931: II, 148–202.
8. Suminto 1985: 92–96.
9. Abdul Patah 1935: 82–84.
10. Vredenbregt 1962: 144–145.
11. Ricklefs 1979: 151–152.
12. Federspiel 2001: 72–74.
13. Yegar 1979: 222–223.
14. Winstedt 1922: 133.
15. Khoo 1974: 170–172.
16. Ner 1941: 159–160, 189, 196.
17. Finley 1908: 22.
18. Kuder 1945: 126.
19. Kumar 1997b: 163–165.
20. Dhofier 1982: 35–36.
21. Dhofier 1995: 22–25.
22. Hurgronje 1929: 222, 225.
23. Dobbin 1983: 132.
24. Hurgronje 1906: II, 117–119.
25. B. W. Andaya 1979: 116–122.
26. Kurzman 2002: 344–354.
27. Sukarno 1969.
28. Ner 1941: 187.

29. Poensen 1886: 51–56.
30. van Bruinessen 1990b: 161–163, 165–167; Hamka 1982: 47–51.
31. Federspiel 2001: 91–108.
32. Skeat 1965: 71–82.
33. Kartini 1920: 165, 233–234.
34. Winstedt 1951: 92–94.
35. Hurgronje 1906: I, 422–430.
36. Ibid., 202–245.
37. Swettenham 1906: 315–316.
38. Abdul Rashid bin Budin 1980: 144–147.
39. Matheson 1989: 160.
40. Drewes 1966: 310–311.
41. Moses 1908: 106.

4. Nation-States and Civil Values

Epigraph. Chandra Muzaffar 1987: 5.
1. United States Central Intelligence Agency 2003.
2. C. Geertz 1964: 5–7; Koentjaraningrat 1985: 316–323.
3. Ratnam 1965: xii, 4; Kaur 2001: xii–xv.
4. Li 1989: 93–95.
5. Thailand National Statistical Office 2002.
6. Gowing 1975: 81–84.
7. Strubbe 1993: 14.
8. Stahr 1997: 266.
9. Palmier 1985: 67; Prijono 1999: 160–168.
10. Cheah 2002: 36, 83–85, 140–143, 220–221.
11. Singh 1991: 153–177.
12. Siddique 1992: 91–92.
13. Singapore, Majlis Ugama Islam 1994: 54–63, 76–77.
14. Li 1989: 169.
15. Mendaki 1993: 43–58.
16. Malay/Muslim Professionals [of] Singapore 1990: 15–21.
17. D. Jones 1987: 25–26.
18. Haemindra 1977: 86–89; Surin 1985: 216–267.
19. Stahr 1997: 262–266.
20. Singapore, Majlis Ugama Islam 1994: 54–77.
21. Nagata 1986: 104–116.
22. Muhammad Kamal 1982: 89–115.
23. Abaza 1999: 201–206.
24. Chandra 1993: 177–181.
25. Jubair 1999: 11–34.
26. Mastura 1984: 183–185, 205–212.
27. van Bruinessen 1990a: 229.
28. Ismail Abd. Rahman 1993: 119–133.
29. Dhofier 1995: 78–83.
30. Horavatich 1994: 811–836.
31. *Waspada,* October 26, 1985, 2.
32. Federspiel 1996: 61–66.

33. *Waspada,* August 11, 1986, 1–2.
34. Zaini 1986: 85–104.
35. Nagata 1986: 85–94.
36. Moore 1981: 121–124, 182–185.
37. Muhaimin 1999: 107–122.
38. van Nieuwenhuijze 1958: 180–183.
39. Lockard 1998: 94–104.
40. Tan Chee 1992: 296–313.
41. Hofstra University Museum 1996: 57–59.

5. Themes of Southeast Asian Islam

Epigraph. Noer 1983: 183.

Glossary

In the text, foreign words are usually rendered in English translation followed by the original term in parentheses. Most of these terms do not require further explanation. Some, however, express important religious or cultural concepts and are further explained in this glossary.

'alim. Scholar. A person learned in the Islamic religious sciences and a primary functionary of the Muslim community.

bayt al-mal. Poor tax administration. A government program to collect the poor tax from Muslims and to distribute the funds to needy Muslims; established in some Islamic states.

berkat. Blessing. The presence of godly power in a shrine or a holy person who forgives sin and assists one to live a peaceful life.

bilal. Caller. The title given to the person at a mosque who announces that one of the five daily worship sessions is about to begin.

bismillah. Opener. The opening phrase of the Qur'an stating that God is merciful and compassionate; also used as a pious exclamation.

dabus. Name of a ceremony in which mystics use music to achieve a trance, during which body parts are pierced by sharp instruments (without apparent injury) to demonstrate the invulnerability of worshipers to pain.

da'i. Propagator of religion. A person who undertakes to promote religion as a revivalist among Muslims or to convert non-Muslims to Islam.

dakwah. Revivalism or intensification of faith; the work of upgrading believers in terms of religious behavior and identification.

dukun. Shaman. On Java, the traditional practitioner of magic, involved mostly with healing. Known in the Malay world as *bomoh.*

dzikir. Remembrance. The repetition of God's name (Allah) in an intoned cadence.

fatwa. Religious opinion. An answer to a religious question on the basis of the examination of Muslim jurisprudence.

fiqh. Law. Jurisprudential teachings formulated by the scholars of a school of thought, such as the Syafi'i. Sometimes confused or identified with the divine law *(shari'ah).*

Gusti. Title on Java for an honored person, or a reference to God.

hadith. Traditions. Narratives that relate what the prophet did or said on specific occasions. In their collected form they constitute an important religious source for Muslims.

hudud. Harsh penalties; laws of death, stoning, and dismemberment for certain heinous acts prescribed by sacred law.

iang yang pertuan. He who is paramount. Malay title for a head of state, somewhat equivalent to sultan.

'Id. The names of two general festivals in Islam. 'Id al-Fitri is celebrated at the end of the fasting month, while 'Id al-Adha is observed as a day of sacrifice during the time of the annual pilgrimage to Makkah.

imam. Leader. The leader of a prayer congregation, or an acknowledged Muslim leader.

Jawi. Malay language in Arabic script.

jihad. Crusade; the act of seeking a higher moral principle; sometimes used in regard to the "holy war."

Ka'aba. The structure at Makkah that is the central feature of the Islamic pilgrimage held annually.

kafir. Disbeliever. A term of disapprobation used for someone hostile to Islam.

kalam. Theology. Name for the body of knowledge dealing with the beliefs of Islam.

keramat. Power; the godly presence or force found in Muslim shrines or in holy men, and that can be harnassed by devotees for use in personal action.

khaek. Outsider or alien. A derogatory term historically used by Thais to label the differentness of Muslims from Thais.

khatib. Sermon giver. Title given to the person who delivers the address to a prayer congregation on Friday or at one of the two 'Id festivals.

kris. Ceremonial sword. There are various forms of these, most looking like a "crooked dagger." Some are held to have magical powers.

Mahdi. Messiah. The hero who will restore Islam to a period of great glory.

Mawlid. Celebration of the anniversary of the prophet Muhammad's birthday, usually including the recitation of a long poem extolling his life and accomplishments.

modin. Secondary prayer leader, on Java.

mubaligh. Propagator. A person devoted to the spread of information about Islam, often to the unconverted.

mufti. Legalist. The official who issues a ruling on a certain matter of religious jurisprudence, often dealing with correct action by believers.

murtadd. Rebrobate. Name for a person who renounces his religion, either directly or through some disdainful action that calls his belief into question.

niyah. Intention. A period of contemplation before prayer or mystical practice during which the worshiper focuses his mind toward worship.

penghulu. Director. Title on Java of the primary religious functionary in a mosque district during the nineteenth century.

perang sabil. Holy war; war undertaken for the protection or furthering of Islam.

pesantren. Islamic boarding school. The classical Muslim school on Java, centering on mastery of religious teachings.

pondok. See *pesantren.*

qadi, kadi. Religious judge. A judge usually trying cases in accordance with Muslim jurisprudence.

Qasidah. Odes in praise of the Prophet Muhammad.

ratib. Litany; an enthusiastic repetition of God's name for purposes of entering a mystical trance.

Ratu Adil. Messiah. Javanese title for the concept of a hero ushering in a new golden age.

Rumi. Malay in Roman script. Malay written in the Western European syllabary. Sometimes called Latijn.

salat. Worship. Formal prayer, usually referring to the five daily prayers required of all believers.

sayyid. Noble. A person descended from Muhammad through his daughter Fatimah.

semangat. Life force. The animist conception of power or life existing in certain animate or inanimate objects that may be harnessed for assisting humans in certain situations.

shahadah. Confession of faith: "There is no God but Allah and Muhammad is the Prophet of Allah."

Shariʾah. Sacred Law. The perfect law of God, generally beyond human comprehension, but still necessarily obeyed.

slametan. Ritual meal. A special meal connected with the animistic past of Southeast Asia and a standard in most rites on Java.

sufi. Mystic. A Muslim devotee using esoteric exercises to move from the world of the senses over to the world of the spirit.

sultan. Ruler. A common title for Islamic rulers throughout the Islamic world prior to 1900.

suluk. Mystic. Another name for a *sufi.*

Tabligh. Information sessions. A session in which important information about the practices and beliefs of Islam are imparted to interested groups of people.

Tafsir. Commentary on the Qurʾan explaining Arabic-language usage and the remarks found in old Muslim sources.

takbir. Magnificat. The recitation or repetition of the term "God is Great," thereby magnifying his greatness.

talkin. Prompting at the graveside. The recitation made at a grave site to inform the deceased about proper belief and behavior.

tasawwuf. Mysticism. The effort to achieve knowledge of God through esoteric exercises.

tasbih. Gloria. The recitation or repetition of the phrase "glory to God."

tawhid. Faith. The belief that all things are unified in and through God, and hence nothing is separate and by itself.

usul al-din. Sources of belief. The techniques and sources for constructing belief patterns in Islam.

usul al-fiqh. Source of jurisprudence. The techniques and sources for arriving at jurisprudential injunctions and their explanation.

wali. Saint; a holy person, usually one who has mastered mystical practice and is believed to be blessed.

Wali Songo, Wali Sangha. The nine fabled propagators of Java who led the drive to convert Java to Islam.

Wujudiyyah. Unitarians. Mystics who held that union with God made them one and the same. This belief was regarded as heretical by Sunni mainstream religious scholars.

zakat. Poor tax; the donating of a portion of one's wealth during Ramadan for assistance to the poor.

Bibliography

Malays often abbreviate the name Mohammed, Muhammad, Moehammed to Muhd., Mohd., etc., and that usage is followed here. To avoid confusion in alphabetization that might result from such variations, all entries beginning with that name are preceded by "Muhammad" in brackets.

Abbreviations

ENOI	*Encyclopaedie van Nederlandsch Oost-Indië* (Encyclopedia of the Netherlands Indies).
KITLV	Koninklijk Instituut voor Taal-, Land- en Volkenkunde (The Royal Institute of Linguistics and Anthropology [Netherlands])
Bijdragen KITLV	Journal of the Royal Institute of Linguistics and Anthropology
KITLV Press	Press of the Royal Institute of Linguistics and Anthropology

Abaza, Mona. 1999. "Intellectuals, Power and Islam in Malaysia: S.N. al-Attas or the Beacon on the Crest of a Hill." In *L'Horizon Nousantarien: Mélanges en homage à Denys Lombard*, vol. 3. *Archipel* 58:189–217.

Abder-Razzak. N.d. "Narrative of the Voyage of Abder-Razzak, Ambassador from Shah Rukh, A.H. 845–A.D. 1442." In *India in the Fifteenth Century*, ed. A. H. Major, 1–49. New York: Hakluyt Society.

Abdul Halim Nasir. 1995. *Seni Bina Masjid di Dunia Melayu Nusantara* (Mosque Architecture in the Malaysian World). Bangi: Penerbit Universiti Kebangsaan Malaysia.

Abdul Patah. 1935. *De medische zijde vaan de bedevaart naar Mekkah* (The Medical Aspects of the Pilgrimage to Makkah). Leiden: Luctor et Emergo.

Abdul Rashid bin Budin. 1980. "Masjid, Surau dan Madrasah di Melaka (Rencana Gambar)" (Mosque, Prayer House, and Islamic School in Melaka). In *Islam di Malaysia,* ed. Khoo Kay Kim, Mohd. Fadzil Othman, and Abdullah Zakaria Ghazali, 138–147. Kuala Lumpur: Persatuan Sejarah Malaysia.

Abdullah, Taufik. 1970. "Some Notes on the Kaba Tjindau Mato: An Example of Minangkabau Traditional Literature." *Indonesia* 9:1–22.

———. 1971. *Schools and Politics: The Kaum Muda Movement in West Sumatra (1927–1933).* Ithaca, NY: Cornell Modern Indonesia Project.

Abdullah, Taufik, and Sharon Siddique, eds. 1986. *Islam and Society in Southeast Asia.* Singapore: Institute of Southeast Asian Studies.

Abdullah al-Qari bin Haji Salleh. 1976. "To' Kenali: His Life and Influence." In *Kelantan,* ed. W. R. Roff, 87–100. Kuala Lumpur: Oxford University Press.

Abdullah bin Alwi Haji Hasan. 1980. "Perundangan dan Pentadbiran Islam Terengganu di Zaman British" (The Islamic Legal and Administrative Systems of

Trengganu in the British Period). *Sarjana: Journal Fakulti Sastera & Sains Sosial* (The Scholar: Journal of the Faculty of the Arts and Social Sciences), Keluran Khas (special publication).

Abdurachman, Parmita. 1978. "Moluccan Responses to the First Intrusions of the West." In *Dynamics of Indonesian History*, ed. Soebadio. Amsterdam: North Holland.

Abha. 1994. *Melur dari Vietnam* (Jasmine from Vietnam). Kuala Lumpur: Dewan Bahasa dan Pustaka.

Aboebakar Atjeh. 1957. *Sejarah Hidup K. H. A. Wahid Hasjim dan Karangan Tersiarnja* (The Biography of K. H. A. Wachid Hasjim and His Collected Writings). Jakarta: Panitya.

Abu Bakar Hamzah. 1989. "Brunei Darussalam: Continuity and Tradition." *Southeast Asian Affairs*, 91–106. Singapore: Institute of Southeast Asian Studies.

Abu Hamid. 1994. *Syekh Yusuf: Seorang Ulama, Sufi dan Pejuang* (Shaykh Yusuf: Cleric, Mystic, and Fighter). Jakarta: Yayasan Obor Indonesia.

Abu Talib Ahmad. 2003. *The Malay-Muslims, Islam and the Rising Sun 1941–1945*. Kuala Lumpur: Malaysian Branch, Royal Asiatic Society.

Ahmad Ibrahim. 1965. *Islamic Law in Malaya*. Ed. Shirle Gordon. Kuala Lumpur: Malaysian Sociological Institute.

Ahmad Ibrahim, Sharon Siddique, and Yasmin Hussain, eds. 1985. *Readings on Islam in Southeast Asia*. Singapore: Institute of Southeast Asian Studies.

Ahmadi, Abdul Rahman al-. 1990. "Bangunan Kuno Masjid Kampung Laut" (Construction Details of the Old Mosque at Kampung Laut). In *Warisan Kelantan* (The Legacy of Kelantan), 9:1–12.

Ahmat b. Adam. 1995. *The Vernacular Press and the Emergence of Modern Indonesian Consciousness (1855–1913)*. Ithaca, NY: Cornell Southeast Asian Program.

Alfian, Ibrahim. 1987. *Perang di Jalan Allah*. (War in the Way of God). Jakarta: Pustaka Sinar Harapan.

Ali, Abdul Mukti. 1975. "Islam in Indonesia." *Handbuch der Orientalistik* (Handbook of Oriental Studies), 3rd part, 2nd Volume, 1st Selection: 55–80. Leiden: E. J. Brill.

———. 1978. *Agama dan Pembangunan di Indonesia* (Religion and Development in Indonesia). Jakarta: Departemen Agama.

Ali, Fachry. 1994. "Masses without Citizenship: Islamic Protest Movements in Nineteenth-Century Java." In *The Late Colonial State in Indonesia*, ed. R. Cribb, 247–260. Leiden: KITLV Press.

Alias Mohamed. 1977–1978. "Kebangkitan Ulamak-Ulamak Kelantan" (The Development of the Kelantan Religious Scholars). *Jernal Sejarah* 15:41–50.

Alves, Jorge M. Dos Santos. 1994. "Princes contre marchands au crépuscule de Pasai (c. 1490–1521) (Rulers Competing with Merchants in the Declining Years of Pasai [ca. 1490–1521]). *Archipel* 47:125–145.

Alwy, Salaman. 1996. "Sejarah Kesultanan Palembang" (History of the Palembang Sultanate). In *Masuk dan Berkembangan Islam di Sumatera Selatan* (Entry and Development of Islam in South Sumatra), ed. K. H. O. [Gadjahnata] Gadjahmata and Sri-Edi Swarsono, 123–173. Jakarta: Penerbit Universitas Indonesia.

Ambary, Hasan Muarif, Hawany Michrob, and John N. Miksic. 1992. *Katalogus Koleksi Data Arkeologi* (Catalog of the Archeological Data Collection). Banten and Jakarta: Yayasan Baluwarti.

Anam, Choirul. 1985. *Pertumbuhan dan Perkembangan Nahdlatul Ulama* (Establishment and Development of the Orthodox Scholars Association). Sala: Jatayu Sala.

Andaya, Barbara Watson. 1975. "The Nature of the State in 18th Century Perak." In *Pre-Colonial State Systems in Southeast Asia,* ed. Anthony Reid and Lance Castles. Kuala Lumpur: Malaysian Branch, Royal Asiatic Society.

———. 1979. *Perak. The Abode of Grace: A Study of an Eighteenth-Century Malay State.* Kuala Lumpur: Oxford University Press.

———. 1997. "Adapting to Political and Economic Change: Palembang in the Late Eighteenth and Early Nineteenth Centuries. In *The Last Stand of Asian Autonomies: Responses to Modernity in the Diverse States of Southeast Asia and Korea, 1750–1900,* ed. Anthony Reid, 187–216. New York: St. Martin's Press.

Andaya, Barbara Watson, and Leonard Y. Andaya. 1982. *A History of Malaysia.* London and Basingstoke: Macmillan.

Andaya, Barbara Watson, and Virginia Matheson. 1979. "Islamic Thought and Malay Tradition (The Writing of Raja bin Haji of Riau)." In *Perceptions of the Past in Southeast Asia,* ed. A. Reid and D. Marr, 108–129. Singapore: Heinemann.

Andaya, Leonard. 1975. "The Structure of Power in 17th Century Johor." In *Pre-Colonial State Systems in Southeast Asia,* ed. Anthony Reid and Lance Castles, 1–11. Kuala Lumpur: Council of the Malaysian Branch, Royal Asiatic Society.

———. 1984. "Kingship-Adat Rivalry and the Role of Islam in South Sulawesi." *Journal of Southeast Asian Studies* 15, 1:22–42.

———. 1993. *The World of Maluku: Eastern Indonesia in the Early Modern Era.* Honolulu: University of Hawai'i Press.

Aqsha, Darul, Dick van der Meij, and Johan Hendrik Meuleman, eds. 1995. *Islam in Indonesia: A Survey of Events and Developments from 1988 to March 1993.* Leiden: Indonesian-Netherlands Cooperation in Islamic Studies.

Arboleya (de) José Garcia. 1851. *Historia del Archipiélago y Sultania de Jolo* (The History of the Archipelago and Sultanate of Jolo). Havana: Imp. De. Sober y Gelada.

Attas, Muhammad Naguib (Syed) al-. 1963. *Some Aspects of Sufism as Understood and Practiced among the Malays.* Ed. Shirle Gordon. Singapore: Malaysian Sociological Research Institute.

———. 1966. *Raniri and the Wujudiyyah of 17th Century Acheh.* Kuala Lumpur: Malayan Branch, Royal Asiatic Society.

———. 1969. *Preliminary Statement on a General Theory of the Islamization of the Malay-Indonesian Archipelago.* Kuala Lumpur: Dewan Bahasa dan Pustaka.

———. 1980. *The Concept of Education in Islam: A Framework for an Islamic Philosophy of Education.* Kuala Lumpur: Muslim Youth Movement of Malaysia.

Azra, Asyumardi. 1988. "The Rise and Decline of the Minangkabau Surau. A Traditional Islamic Institution in West Sumatra during the Dutch Colonial Government." M.A. thesis, Columbia University.

———. 1997. "Education, Law, Mysticism: Constructing Social Realities." In *Islamic Civilization in the Malay World,* ed. Mohd. Taib Osman, 141–196. Kuala Lumpur: Dewan Bahasa dan Pustaka and Istanbul, Research Centre for Islamic History.

———. 1999. *Jaringan Ulama: Timur Tengah dan Kepulauan Nusantara Abad XVII dan*

XVIII (Network of Scholars: The Middle East and the Islands of Nusantara in the 17th and 18th centuries). Bandung: Mizan.

Bailey, Connor, and John N. Miskic. 1989. "The Country of Patani in the Period of Reawakening"—A Chapter from Ibrahim Syukhri's *Sejarah Kerajaaan Melayu Patani.* In *The Muslims of Thailand: Politics of the Malay Speaking South,* ed. Andrew D. W. Forbes. *Southeast Asian Review* 14, 1, 2:151–166.

Ball, John. 1982. *Indonesian Legal History 1602–1848.* Sydney: Oughtershaw Press.

Barbosa, Duarte. 1967 (1812). *The Book of Duarte Barbosa; An account of the countries bordering on the Indian Ocean and their inhabitants. . . .* Ed. Mansel Longworth Dames. 2 vols. Nendelm, Liechtenstein: Kraus Reprint.

Barraclough, Simon. 1986. "Malaysia in 1985: A Question of Management." In *Southeast Asian Affairs 1986,* 185–207. Singapore: Institute of Southeast Asian Studies.

Barros, João de. 1967. *The Book of Duarte Barbosa: An account of the countries bordering on the Indian Ocean and their inhabitants. . . .* Ed. Mansel Longworth Dames. 2 vols. Nendelm, Liechtenstein: Kraus Reprint.

Baudesson, Henri. 1919. *Indochina and Its Primitive Folk.* Translated from the French by E. Appleby Holt. London: Hutchinson.

Beatty, Andrew. 1999. *Varieties of Javanese Religion: An Anthropological Account.* Cambridge: Cambridge University Press.

Beaulieu, Augustin. 1705. "Voyage to the East Indies." In *Navigantium atque Itinerarium Bibliotheca,* ed. John Harris. London. Also 1664–1666. "Journal d'Augustin de Beaulieu." In *Collection des Voyages* (Bibliographical References concerning Navigation), 2 vols., ed. Thèvenot. Paris.

Begbie, Peter James. 1834. *The Malayan Peninsula, Embracing its History, Manners, Custom of the Inhabitants, Politics, Natural History, etc. from its Earliest Times.* Madras: Veperay Mission Press.

Behrend, Timothy E. 1984. "Kraton, Taman, Mesjid: A Brief Survey and Bibliographic Review of Islamic Antiquities in Java." *Indonesian Circle* 35:29–55.

Bellwood, Peter. 1997. *Prehistory of the Indo-Malaysian Archipelago.* Honolulu: University of Hawai'i Press.

Benda, Harry J. 1958. *The Crescent and the Rising Sun: Indonesian Islam under the Japanese Occupation 1942–1945.* The Hague and Bandung: W. Van Hoeve.

Benda-Beckmann, Keebet van. 1984. *The Broken Stairways to Consensus.* Dordrecht: Foris.

Berg, C. C. 1950. "The Islamisation of Jawa." *Studia Islamica* 4:111–142.

Berg, L. W. C. van den. 1886. "Het Modammedaansche godsdienstonderwijs op Java en Madoera on de daarbij gebruikte Arabische boeken" (Muslim Religious Education on Java and Madura and the Use of Arabic Books). *Tijdschrift van het (Koninklijk) Bataviaasch Genootschap van Kunsten en Wetenschappen* (Journal of the Royal Batavian Society of Arts and Letters) 31:519–555.

Bergsträsser, Gotthalf. 1930. "Zur Methode der Fiqh-Forschung" (Toward a Methodology of Muslim Jurisprudential Scholarship). *Islamica* 4:283–294.

Beyer, H. Otley. 1921. *The Non-Christian People of the Philippines.* Manila: Bureau of Printing.

Bickmore, Albert Smith. 1869. *Travels in the East Indian Archipelago.* New York: Appleby.

Black, Ian. 1983. *A Gambling Style of Government: The Establishment of the Chartered Company's Rule in Sabah, 1878–1915*. Kuala Lumpur: Oxford University Press.

Blumberger, J. Th. Petrus. 1931. *De Nationalistische Beweging in Nederlandsch-Indie* (The Nationalist Movement in the Dutch Indies). Haarlem: T. D. Theen Willink & Zoon.

Boland, B. J. 1971. *The Struggle of Islam in Modern Indonesia*. The Hague: Martinus Nijhoff.

Bouchon, Geneviève, and Denys Lombard. 1987. "The Indian Ocean in the Fifteenth Century." In *India and the Indian Ocean 1500–1800*, ed. A. Das Gupta, 46–70. Calcutta: Oxford University Press.

Bousquet, Georges Henri. 1944. *A French View of the Netherlands Indies*. Translation by Philip E. Lilienthal of *La politique musulmane et colonial des Pays-Bas*. New York: Institute of Pacific Relations.

Boxer, C. R. 1969. "A Note on Portuguese Reactions to the Revival of the Red Sea Spice Trade and the Rise of Atjeh, 1540–1600." *Journal of Southeast Asian History* 10, 3:415–428.

Bracciolini, Poggio. N.d. "The Travels of Nicolò Conte in the East in the Fifteenth Century." In *India in the Fifteenth Century*, ed. R. H. Major, 1–39. New York: Burt Franklin for the Hakluyt Society.

Braginsky, V. I. 1993. *The System of Classical Malay Literature*. Leiden: KITLV Press.

Braighlin, G. 1992. *Ideological Innovation under Monarchy: Aspects of Legitimation Activity in Contemporary Brunei*. Amsterdam: VU Press.

Brakel, L. F., and H. Massarik. 1982. "A Note on the Panjunan Mosque in Cirebon." *Archipel* 23:119–131.

Brice, William C. 1981. *An Historical Atlas of Islam*. Leiden: E. J. Brill.

British Museum Library. [17th century.] "Prayers to Mahomet used by the Indian, Javan, Arabians and Persians." In *Medical and Chemical Miscellanies* (binder's title), entry 67. Sloane No. 217.

Brockelmann, Carl. 1996. *Geschichte der arabischen Litteratur* (History of Arabian Literature). 5 vols. Leiden: E. J. Brill.

Brown, C. C., ed. and annot. 1970. *Sejarah Melayu: Malay Annals*. Kuala Lumpur: Oxford University Press.

Brown, Donald E. 1970. *Brunei: The Structure and History of a Bornean Malay Sultanate*. Brunei: Brunei Museum Monograph; also *Brunei Museum Journal* 2, 2:1–239.

———. 1991. "Elites in the Sultanate of Brunei from the 19th Century to the Eve of Independence." *International Seminar on Brunei Malay Sultanate in Nusantara Proceedings*, 2:666–680.

Brueghal, J. de Rovere van. 1856. "Bedingingen over den Staat van Bantam in 1786" (Matters concerning Banten in 1786). *Bijdragen KITLV* 4:110–170.

Bruinessen, Martin van. 1988. "De tarekat in Indonesie, tussen rebellie en aanpassing" (The Mystical Order in Indonesia: Between Rebellion and Accommodation). In *Islam en Politiek in Indonesia*, ed. C. Van Dijk, 69–84. Muidersberg: Dick Coutinho.

———. 1990a. "Kitab Kuning. Books in Arabic Script Used in the Pesantren Milieu." *Bijdragen KITLV* 146:226–269.

———. 1990b. "The Origins and Development of the Naqshabandi Order in Indonesia," *Der Islam.* 67:150–179.

———. 1991. "The Tariqa Khalwatiya in South Celebes." In *Excursies in Celebes,* ed. Harry A. Poeze and Pim Schoorl, 251–269. Leiden: KITLV Press.

———. 1995. "Shari'a Court, Tarekat and Pesantren: Religious Institutions in the Banten Sultanate." *Archipel* 50:165–200.

Brunei Darussalam, Jabatan Muzium Brunei (Brunei Museum Office). 1992. *Sudut Sejarah; Tokoh-tokoh Agama di Brunei Darussalam: Pengalan Ringkas* (The Historical Perspective; Religious Institutions in Brunei Darussalam; The Short Version). [Bandar Seri Begawan]. Bandar Seri Begawan: Muzium Brunei.

———, Jabatan Pusat Sejarah (Central Office of History). 1992. *Islam di Brunei* (Islam in Brunei). Bandar Seri Begawan: Asia Printers.

———, [Kerajaan Negara Brunei Darussalam] Jabatan Kuasa Penerbit (Publications Board). 1984. *Brunei Berdaulat* (Brunei Becomes Sovereign). Singapore: Federal Publications.

Cabaton, Antoine. 1912. "Les Maleis de l'Indochine Française" (The Malay People of French Indo-China). *Revue Indochine Française* I, 1:161–171.

———. 1988. "Orang Cam Islam di Indochina Perancis" (The Muslim Cham People in French Indochina). In *Sejarah dan Kebudayaan Campa* (History and Culture of Champa), ed. Abdul Rahman Al-Ahmadi, 197–242. Kuala Lumpur: Kementarian Kebudayaan dan Pelancongan.

Carey, Peter B. R. 1980a. *The Archive of Yogyakarta.* London: British Academy and Oxford University Press.

———. 1980b. "Aspects of Javanese History in the Nineteenth Century." In *The Development of Indonesian Society,* ed. H. Aveling, 45–105. New York: St. Martin's Press.

Carroll, John S. 1982. "Berunai in the Boxer Codex." *Journal of the Malaysian Branch of the Royal Asiatic Society* 55, 2:1–25.

———. 1986. "Francisco de Sande's Invasion of Brunei in 1578: An Anonymous Spanish Account." *Brunei Museum Journal* 6, 2:47–71.

Chandra Muzaffar. 1987. *Islamic Resurgence in Malaysia.* Petaling Jaya: Fajar Bakti.

———. 1993. "Implementation of Justice in Politics." In *Islam and Justice,* ed. Aidit bin Hj. Ghazali, 183–216. Kuala Lumpur: Institute of Islamic Understanding.

Chandran Jeshurun. 1993. "Malaysia: The Mahathir Supremacy and Vision 2020." *Southeast Asian Affairs* (1993): 203–223. Singapore: Institute of Southeast Asian Studies.

Chang, Hadji Yusuf. 1988. "The Ming Empire, Patron of Islam in China and Southeast Asia." *Journal of the Malaysian Branch of the Royal Asiatic Society* 61, 2:1–44.

Chaudhuri, K. N. 1990. *Asia before Europe: Economy and Civilisation of the Indian Ocean from the Rise of Islam to 1750.* Cambridge: Cambridge University Press.

Chauvel, Richard. 1980. "Ambon's Other Half: Some Preliminary Observations on Ambonese Moslem Society and History." *Review of Indonesian and Malaysian Affairs* 14, 1:40–80.

Cheah Boon Kheng. 1983. *Red Star over Malaya: Resistance and Social Conflict during and after the Japanese Occupation 1941–1946.* Singapore: University of Singapore Press.

———. 2002. *Malaysia: The Making of a Nation.* Singapore: Institute of Southeast Asian Studies.

Che Man, W. K. 1990. *Muslim Separatism. The Moros of Southern Philippines and the Malays of Southern Thailand.* Manila: Ateneo de Manila University Press.

Clammer, John. 1985. *Singapore: Ideology, Society, Culture*. Singapore: Chapmen Publishers.

Cokroaminoto, Umar S. 1924. *Islam dan Sosialisme* (Islam and Socialism). Jakarta: Bulan Bintang.

Colless, B. C. 1969–1979. "Traders of the Pearl. The Mercantile and Missionary Activities of Persian and Armenian Christians in Southeast Asia." *Abr-Nahrain* vols. 1–11.

Crawfurd, J. 1856. *A Descriptive Dictionary of the Indian Islands and Adjacent Countries*. 2 vols. London: Bradbury & Evans.

Crosse, Ralphe. 1612. "Journal on the 'Hoseander.'" In *Voyages of Sir James Lancaster to the East Indies*, ed. Clarence G. Markham. London: Hakluyt Society.

Dahm, Bernhard. 1971. *History of Indonesia in the Twentieth Century*. London: Praeger.

Dalrymple, Alexander. 1808. "Essays on the Sulus." *Oriental Repertory* (London), vol. 1. Also "An Account of Sulu." *The Indian Archipelago* 3, 1:512–531; 545–567.

Damais, Louis Charles. 1957. [1849.] "Études Javanaises. Les tombes musulmanes datée de Trålåyå" (Study of Dating the Javanese Muslim Tombs at Tralaya). *Bulletin de l'École Française d'Extrême Orient* 48, 2:353–415.

Dampier, William. 1705. *Voyages and Descriptions: A Supplement of the Voyage Round the World*. London: Hakluyt Society.

———. 1968. *A New Voyage Round the World*. New York: Dover.

Das Gupta, Ashin K., and M. N. Pearson, eds. 1987. *India and the Indian Ocean 1500–1800*. Calcutta: Oxford University Press.

Day, Clive. 1966. *The Dutch in Java*. Kuala Lumpur: Oxford University Press.

Denny, Frederick M. 1986. *An Introduction to Islam*. New York and London: Macmillan.

Dhofier, Zamakhsyari. 1982. *Tradisi Pesantren: Studi tentang Pandangan Hidup Kyai* (The Islamic Boarding School Tradition: A Study of the Life Styles of the Religious Teacher). Jakarta: Lembaga Penelitian, Pendidikan, dan Penerangan Ekonomi dan Sosial.

———. 1995. *Tradition and Change in Indonesian Islamic Education*. Ed. A. G. Muhaimin. Jakarta: Indonesian Ministry of Religion.

Dijk, P. van. 1983. *Rebellion under the Banner of Islam*. Leiden: KITLV Press.

Diller, A. V. N. 1988. "Islam and Southern Thai Ethnic Relations: in 'The Muslims of Thailand: Historical and Cultural Studies' (ed. Andrew D. W. Forbes)." *South East Asian Review* 13, 1 and 2:155–166.

Di Meglio, Rita Rose. 1970. "Arab Trade with Indonesia and the Malay Peninsula from the 8th to the 16th Century." In *Islam and the Trade* of Asia, ed. D. S. Richards, 105–136. Oxford: Bruno Cassirer.

Djajadiningrat, Hoesein. 1911. "Critische overzicht van de in Maleische werken vervatte gegevens over de Geschiedenis van het Soeltanaat van Atjeh" (Critical Examination of the Malay Manuscripts Dealing with the History of the Sultanate of Aceh). *Bijdragen KITLV* 65:135–265.

Dobbin, Christine. 1983. *Islamic Revivalism in a Changing Peasant Economy: Central Sumatra, 1784–1847*. London: Curzon Press.

Doorenbos, J. 1933. *De Geschriften van Hamzah Pansoeri* (The Writings of Hamzah Fansuri). Leiden: Bateljee and Tempstray.

Drakard, Jane. 1990. *A Malay Frontier: Unity and Duality in a Sumatran Kingdom*. Ithaca, NY: Cornell University Southeast Asian Program.

Drewes, G. W. J. 1954. *Een Javaanse primbon uit de zestiende eeuw* (A Javanese Guide from the 16th Century). Leiden: E. J. Brill.

———. 1966. "The Struggle between Javanism and Islam as Illustrated by the *Serat Dermagandul.*" *Bijdragen KITLV* 122:309–322.

———. 1968. "New Light on the Coming of Islam to Indonesia." *Bijdragen KITLV* 124:433–459. Also 1985. *Readings on Islam in Southeast Asia.* Ed. A. Ibrahim, S. Siddique, and Y. Hussain, 7–19. Singapore: Institute of Southeast Asian Studies.

———. 1969. *The Admonitions of Seh Bari.* The Hague: Martinus Nijhoff.

———. 1971. "The Study of Arabic Grammar in Indonesia." *Acta Orientalia Neerlandica* (Dutch Oriental Records), 61–70. Leiden: E. J. Brill.

———. 1976. "Further Data Concerning ʿAbd al-Samad al-Palimbani." *Bijdragen KITLV* 132:267–292.

———. 1977. *Directions for Travellers on the Mystic Path.* Hague: Martinus Nijhoff.

Eldridge, Philip J. 1995. *Non-Government Organizations and Democratic Participation in Indonesia.* Kuala Lumpur: Oxford University Press.

Ellen, Roy F. 1983. "Social Theory, Ethnography and the Understanding of Practical Islam in South-east Asia." In *Islam in Southeast Asia,* ed. M. B. Hooker, 50–91. Leiden: E. J. Brill.

Encyclopaedie van Nederlandsch Oost-Indië (Encyclopedia of the Netherlands East Indies). 1917–1939. 8 vols. The Hague: Martinus Nijhoff, and Leiden: E. J. Brill.

Enseng Ho. 2002. "Before Parochialization: Diasporic Arabs Cast in Crude Waters." In *Transcending Borders: Arabs, Politics, Trade and Islam in Southeast Asia,* ed. Huub de Jonge and Nico Kaptein, 11–36. Leiden: KITLV Press.

Far East and Australasia 2002. 2002. London: Europa Press.

Fatimi, S. Q. 1963. *Islam Comes to Malaysia,* ed. Shirle Gordon, 29–31, 38–51. Singapore: Malaysian Sociological Research Institute.

Federspiel, Howard M. 1996. "The Structure and Use of Mosques in Indonesian Islam: The Case of Medan, North Sumatra." *Studia Islamika* 3, 3:51–84.

———. 1998. *Indonesia in Transition: Muslim Intellectuals and National Development.* Commack, NY: Nova Science Publishers.

———. 1999. "Muslim Intellectuals in Southeast Asia." *Studia Islamica* 6, 1:41–76.

———. 2001. *Islam and Ideology in the Emerging Indonesian State, 1923–1958.* Leiden: Brill Academic Press.

———. 2002. Contemporary South-East Asian Muslim Intellectuals: An Examination of the Sources for Their Concepts and Intellectual Constructs." In *Islam in the Era of Globalization: Muslim attitudes towards modernity and identity,* ed. Johan Meuleman, 327–350. London: Curzon.

Feith, Herbert. 1963. "Dynamics of Guided Democracy." In *Indonesia,* ed. Ruth T. McVey, 309–410. New Haven, CT: Human Relations Area Files.

Finley, John Park. 1908. "The Development of the District of Zamboanga, Moro Province 1903–1908." Moro Province field report in Warcester Collection, University of Michigan.

Firdaus Haji Abdullah. 1985. *Radical Malay Politics: Its Origin and Early Development.* Petaling Jaya: Pelanduk.

Fischer, T. Th. 1940. *Inleiding tot de Volkenkunde van Nederlands-Indië* (Introduction to the Customs of the Netherlands Indies). Haarlem: De Erven F. Bohn, N.V.

Forbes, Andrew D. W. 1981. "Southern Arabia and the Islamicization of the Central Indian Ocean Archipelagoes." *Archipel* 21:55–92.

Forrest, Thomas. 1969. *Voyage to New Guinea and the Moluccas 1774–1776.* Kuala Lumpur: Oxford University Press, and New York: Hakluyt Society.

Gaffar Peang-Meth. 1974. "Islam—Another Casualty of the Cambodian War." In *Khmer Representation at the United Nations: A Question of Law or of Politics,* ed. Doue Rasy, 251–255. Washington, DC: Embassy of the Khmer Republic.

Gasperis, J. G. de. 1986. "Some Notes on Relations between Central and Local Governments in Ancient Java." In *Southeast Asia in the 9th to 14th Centuries,* ed. D. G. Marr and A. C. Milner, 49–64. Singapore: Institute of Southeast Asian Studies.

Geertz, Clifford. 1964. *The Religion of Java.* Glencoe, IL: Free Press.

Geertz, Hildred. 1963. "Indonesian Cultures and Communities." In *Indonesia,* ed. Ruth T. McVey, 24–96. New Haven, CT: Human Relations Area Files.

George, T. J. S. 1980. *Revolt in Mindanao: The Rise of Islam in Philippine Politics.* Kuala Lumpur: Oxford Unversity Press.

Girardet, Nikolaus. 1983. *Descriptive Catalogue of the Javanese Manuscripts and Printed Books in the Main Libraries of Surakarta and Yogyakarta.* Wiesbaden: Franz Steiner, 1983.

Gomez, Liborio. 1917. "Mohammedan Medical Practice in Cotabato Province." *Philippine Journal of Science* 12:261–280.

Gonzalez, Francisco L. 2000. "Sultans of a Violent Land." In *Rebels, Warlords and Ulama,* ed. Kristina Gaerlan and Mara Stankovitch, 85–144. Quezon City: Institute for Popular Democracy.

Gowing, Peter. 1967. *Mandate in Moroland: The American Government and Muslim Filipinos 1899–1920.* Quezon City: New Day Publishers.

———. 1975. "The Muslims in the Philippines." In *Handbuch der Orientalistik,* 81–116. Leiden: E. J. Brill.

Gowing, Peter, and Robert D. McAmis, eds. 1974. *The Muslim Filipinos: Their History, Society and Contemporary Problems.* Manila: Solidaridad Publishing House.

Graaf, H. J. de. 1958. *De regering van Sultan Agung, Vorst von Mataram 1615–1645 en zijn voorganger Panembahan Sedang-Krapjak 1601–13* (The Reign of Sultan Agung, the Ruler of Mataram 1615–1645 and his Predecessor Panembahan Sedang-Krapjak 1601–1613). The Hague: Martinus Nijhoff.

Graaf, H. J. de, and Th. G. Th. Pigeaud. 1974. *De eerste moslimsche vorstendommen op Java. Studien over de staatkundige geschiedenis van de 15de en 16e eeuv* (The First Muslim Principalities on Java. Studies of the Political History of the 15th and 16th Centuries). The Hague: Martinus Nijhoff.

———. 1984. *Chinese Muslims in Java in the 15th and 16th Centuries.* Melbourne: Ruskin Press.

Guillot, Claude, with Hasan M. Ambary and Jacques Dumercay. 1990. *The Sultanate of Banten.* Jakarta: Gramedia.

Gullick, J. M. 1958. *Indigenous Political Systems of Western Malaya.* London and New York: Athlone Press and Humanities Press.

———. 1990. *Malay Society in the Nineteenth Century.* Singapore: Oxford University Press.

———. 1992. *Rulers and Residents: Influence and Power in the Malay Sates 1870–1920.* Singapore: Oxford University Press.

Gunning, J. G. H. 1881. *Een Javaansch geschrift uit de 16de eeuw handelende over den Mohommedaanschen godsdienst* (A Javanese Writing from the 16th Century concerning the Islamic Religion). Leiden: E. J. Brill.

Gutierrez, Eric. 1999. "Religion and Politics in Muslim Mindanao." In *Rebels, Warlords and Ulama,* ed. Kristina Gaerlan and Mara Stankovitch, 145–162. Manila: Institute for Popular Democracy.

Haar, Berend ter. 1962. *Adat Law in Indonesia.* A partial translation by A. Arthur Schiller and E. Adamson Hoebel of the 1939 *Beginselen en stetsel van het Adatrecht.* (Groningen: J. B. Wolters). New York: Institute of Pacific Relations, and Jakarta, Bhratara.

Hadi, Amirul. 2003. *Islam and State in Sumatra: A Study of Seventeenth Century Aceh.* Leiden: Brill Academic Press.

Haemindra, Nantawan. 1976–1977. "The Problem of the Thai-Muslims in the Four Southern Provinces of Thailand." *Journal of Southeast Asian Studies* 7, 2:197–225; 8, 1:85–105.

Hall, Kenneth R. 1992. "Economic History of Early Southeast Asia." In *Cambridge History of Southeast Asia,* ed. Nicholas Tarling, 183–275. Cambridge: Cambridge University Press.

Hamilton, A. 1939. *A New Account of the East Indies.* 2 vols. London: A. Betlesworth and Hitch.

Hamka, Dr. [Haji Abdulmalik Karim Amrullah]. 1982. *Ajahku: Riwajat hidup Dr. H. Abd. Karim Amrullah dan Perdjuangan Kaum Agama di Sumatera* (My Father: Biography of Dr. H. Abd. Karim Amrullah and the Struggle of the Religious Group in Sumatra). Jakarta: Penerbit Umminda.

Harrisson, Tom. 1970. *The Malays of Southwest Sarawak before Malaysia: A Socio-Ecological Survey.* East Lansing: Michigan State University Press.

Hasan Madmarn. 1999. *The Pondok and Madrasah in Patani.* Bangi: Penerbit Universiti Kebangsaan Malaysia.

Hasymy, A., ed. 1989. *Sejarah Masuk dan Berkembangnya Islam di Indonesia* (The History of the Entry and Development of Islam in Indonesia). Bandung: Al-Maarif.

Hefner, Robert W. 2001. "Multiculturalism and Citizenship in Malaysia, Singapore, and Indonesia." In *The Politics of Multiculturalism,* ed. Robert W. Hefner. Honolulu: University of Hawai'i Press.

Hill, A. H. 1960. "Hikajat Raja-Raja Pasai" (The Royal Chronicles of Pasai). *Journal of the Malayan Branch Royal Asiatic Society* 33, 2:3–125.

Hitchcock, Michael. 1996. *Islam and Identity in Eastern Indonesia.* Hull: University of Hull Press.

———. 1997. "Indonesia in Miniature." In *Images of Malay-Indonesian Identity,* ed. Michael Hitchcock and Victor T. King, 227–235. Kuala Lumpur: Oxford University Press.

Hodgson, Marshall G. S. 1958–1959. *The Venture of Islam.* 3 vols. Chicago: University of Chicago Press.

Hofstra University Museum. 1996. *Inscription as Art in the World of Islam—Unity in Diversity.* Hempstead, NY.

Holt, P. M., Ann K. S. Lambton, and Bernard Lewis, eds. 1970. *The Cambridge History of Islam,* 4 vols. Cambridge: Cambridge University Press.

Hooker, M. B. 1976. *The Personal Laws of Malaysia: An Introduction*. Kuala Lumpur: Oxford University Press.

———, ed. 1983. *Islam in Southeast Asia*. Leiden: E. J. Brill.

———. 2000. *Indonesian Islam: Social Change through Contemporary fatawa*. Honolulu: University of Hawai'i Press, and London: Allen & Unwin.

Hooker, Virginia Matheson. 2000. *Writing a New Society: Social Change through the Novel in Malaya*. Honolulu: University of Hawai'i Press. *See also* Matheson, Virginia.

Hooykaas, C. 1952. *Literatuur in Maleis en Indonesisch* (Literature in Malay and Indonesian). Groningen: J. B. Wolters; and Kuala Lumpur: Oxford University Press.

Horvatich, Patricia. 1994. "Ways of Knowing Islam." *American Ethnologist* 21, 4:811–826.

Hurgronje, C. Snouck. 1906. *The Achehnese*. Trans. R. J. Wilkinson and A. W. S. O'Sullivan. 2 vols. London: Luzac, Leiden: E. J. Brill.

———. 1929. "Het Moehammedanisme" (Islam). In *Nederlands Indië*, ed. D. G. Stibbe and A. Colijn, 1:210–233. Amsterdam: Elsevier.

———. 1931. *Mekka in the Latter Part of the 19th Century. Daily Life, Customs and Learning. The Moslims of the East Indian Archipelago*, ed. J. H. Monahan. Leiden: E. J. Brill.

Hussin Mutalib. 1997. "Islamic Malay Polity in Southeast Asia." In *Islamic Civilization in the Malay World*, ed. Mohd. Taib Osman, 1–48. Kuala Lumpur: Dewan Bahasa dan Pustaka, and Istanbul: Research Centre for Islamic History.

Huzayyin, S. A. 1942. *Arabia and the Far East, their commercial and cultural relations in Graeco-Roman and Irano-Arabian times*. Cairo: Société Royale de Géographie d'Egypte.

Ibn Batutah. 1953. *Travels*, 10:228–230. Trans. by C. Defremery and B. Sanuinetti (of *Voyages d'Ibn Batoutah*. Paris, 1893). Cambridge: Hakluyt Society.

Ibrahim bin Abu Bakar. 1994. *Islamic Modernism: The Life and Thought of Sayyid Syekh Al-Hadi 1867–1934*. Kuala Lumpur: University of Malaya Press.

Ileto, Reynolda C. 1971. *Magindanao, 1860–1888; The Career of Dato Uto of Buayan*. Ithaca, NY: Southeast Asia Program, Cornell University.

Ismail Abd. Rahman. 1993. *Pendidikan Islam Malaysia* (Islamic Education in Malaysia). Banggi: Penerbit Universiti Kebangsaan Malaysia.

Ismail Hamid. 1987. *Politik Sastra Islam: Kassim Ahmad [dan] Shahnon Ahmad* (Islamic Literary Politics: Kassim Ahmad and Shahnon Ahmad). Kuala Lumpur: Dewan Bahasa dan Pustaka.

———. 1997. "Kitab Jawi: Intellectualizing Literary Tradition." In *Islamic Civilization in the Malay World*, ed. Mohd. Taib Osman, 197–244. Kuala Lumpur: Dewan Bahasa dan Pustaka, and Istanbul: Research Centre for Islamic History.

Jacobs, Hubert Th. Th., ed. and annot. 1971. *A Treatise on the Moluccas* (c. 1544) [translation of Galvao, *Historia dos Maluccas*]. Rome: Jesuit Historical Institute, and St. Louis, MO: St. Louis University Press.

Jaspan, M. A. 1970. "Recent Developments among the Cham of Indo-China: The Revival of Champa." *Journal Royal Central Asian Society* 57, 1:170–176.

Jesudason, James V. 1995. "Malaysia: A Year Full of Sound and Fury, Signifying... Something?" In *Southeast Asian Affairs 1995*, 199–219. Singapore: Institute of Southeast Asian Studies.

Johns, Anthony H. 1955. "Aspects of Sufi Thought in India and Indonesia in the

First Half of the 17th Century." *Journal of the Malayan Branch of the Royal Asiatic Society* 25:1.

———. 1957. "Malay Sufism as Illustrated in an Anonymous Collection of 17th Century Tracts." *Journal of the Malaysian Branch of the Royal Asiatic Society* 1:78, 130; 2:5–111.

———. 1958. *Rantjak Dilabueh: A Minangkabau Kaba: A Specimen of the Traditional Literature of Central Sumatra.* Ithaca, NY: Southeast Asia Program, Cornell University.

———. 1961. "Muslim Mystics and Historical Writing." In *Historians of South East Asia,* ed. D. G. E. Hall, 37–49. London: Macmillan.

———. 1967. "From Buddhism to Islam: An Interpretation of the Javanese Literature of the Transition." *Comparative Studies in Society and History* 9:40–50.

Jones, David M. 1987. *Political Development in Pacific Asia.* Cambridge: Polity Press.

Jones, Russell. 1979. "Ten Conversion Myths from Indonesia." In *Conversion to Islam,* ed. Nehemia Levitzion, 131–158. New York: Holmes & Meier.

Jonge, Huub de, and Nico Kaptein. 2002. "The Arab Presence in Southeast Asia." In *Transcending Borders: Arabs, Politics, Trade and Islam in Southeast Asia,* ed. Huub de Jonge and Nico Kaptein, 1–10. Leiden: KITLV Press.

Josselin de Jong, P. E. 1952. *Minangkabau and Negri Sembilan.* The Hague: Martinus Nijhoff.

Jubair, Salah. 1999. *Bangsamoro: A Round of Endless Tyranny.* Kuala Lumpur: I. Q. Marin Shd. Bhd.

Juynboll, A. W. T. 1881. "Een Moslimsche Catechismus in het Arabisch met eene Javaansche interlineaire vertaling in pegonschrift" (An Islamic Catechism in Arabic with an Interlinear Javanese Translation Using Arabic Script). *Bijdragen KITLV* 29:215–231.

———. 1882. Kleine bijdragen over den Islam op Java" (Short Report concerning Islam on Java). *Bijdragen KITLV* 30:262–296, 422–427.

Juynboll, Th. W. 1930. *Handleiding tot de kennis De Mohammedaaansche Wet volgens de leer der Sjafi'itische School* (Guide to Understanding Islamic Law of the Shafi'ite School). Leiden: E. J. Brill.

Kamaruddin Mohd. Ali. 1997. "Architecture: Unity of the Sacred and the Profane." In *Islamic Civilization in the Malay World,* ed. Mohd. Taib Osman, 245–278. Kuala Lumpur: Dewan Bahasa dan Pustaka, and Istanbul: Research Centre for Islamic History.

Kaptein, Nico. 1997. "Sayyid Uthman on the Legal Validity of Documentary Evidence." *Bijdragen KITLV* 153, 1:85–102.

Kartini, Adjeng. 1920. *Letters of a Javanese Princess.* New York: Alfred Knopf.

Kartomi, Margaret J. 1993. "Revival of Feudal Music, Dance, and Ritual in the Former 'Spice Islands' of Ternate and Tidore." In *Culture and Society in New Order Indonesia,* ed. Virginia Matheson Hooker, 48–69. Kuala Lumpur: Oxford University Press.

———. 1998. "Sumatra." In *Garland Encyclopedia of World Music: Southeast Asia,* ed. Terry E. Miller and Sean William, 598–629. New York and London: Garland Publishing Company.

Kathirithamby-Wells, J. 1986. "Royal Authority and the Orang Kaya in the Western Archipelago, circa 1500–1800." *Journal of Southeast Asian Studies* 17, 2:256–267.

————. 1990. "Banten: A West Indian Port and Polity during the Sixteenth and Seventeenth Centuries." In *The Southeast Asian Port and Polity,* ed. J. Kathirithamby-Wells and J. Villiers, 107–125. Singapore: Singapore University Press.

————. 1993. "Hulu-Hilir Unity and Conflict: Malay Statecraft in East Sumatra before the Mid-Nineteenth Century." *Archipel* 45:77–96.

Kauer, Amarjit. 2001. *Historical Dictionary of Malaysia.* Lanham, MD, and London: The Scarecrow Press.

Ken Yeang. 1992. *The Architecture of Malaysia.* Amsterdam/Kuala Lumpur: Pepin Press.

Keyzer, Salomo. 1871. *De bedevaart der inlanders naar Mekka* (The Pilgrimage of the Indonesian People to Makkah). Leiden: Gualth, Kolff.

Khoo Kay Kim. 1974. "Malay Society, 1874–1920's." *Journal of Southeast Asian Studies* 5, 2:179–198; also in *Malay Society: Transformation and Democratisation,* 83–156. Petaling Jaya: Pelanduk.

Kiefer, Thomas M. 1990. *The Tausug: Violence and Law in a Philippine Moslem Society.* New York: Holt, Rinehart & Winston.

Klinkert, H. A. 1867. "Verhaal eener Pelgrimsreis van Singapoera naar Mekah door Abdoellah bin Abdil Kadir Moensji" (Narration of a Pilgrimage Journey by Abdoellah bin Abdil Kadir Moensji). *Bijdragen KITLV* 15:336, 348–408.

Kobkua Suwannathat-Pian. 1988. *Thai–Malay Relations: Traditional Intra-regional Relations from the Seventeenth to the Early Twentieth Centuries.* Kuala Lumpur: Oxford University Press.

Koentjaraningrat. 1985. *Javanese Culture.* Singapore: Oxford University Press.

Kratoska, Paul H. 1995. *Malaya and Singapore during the Japanese Occupation.* Singapore: University of Singapore Press.

Kuder, Edward. 1945. "The Moros in the Philipppines." *The Far Eastern Quarterly* 4, 2:119–116.

Kuder, Edward, with Pete Martin. 1945. "The Philippines Never Surrendered." *Saturday Evening Post,* no. 217 (February 10), 9–11, 61–63; no. 218 (February 17), 22–23, 82–83, 85; no. 219 (February 24), 22–23, 90; no. 220 (March 3), 20, 81–83; no. 221 (March 10), 20, 50, 52, 56.

Kuenig, J. 1988. "Development in Four Societies over the Sixteenth to Eighteenth Centuries." In *The Development of Indonesian Society,* ed. H. Aveling, 1–44. New York: St. Martin's Press.

Kumar, Ann. 1997a. "Java: A Self-Critical Examination of the Nation and Its History." In *The Last Stand of Asian Autonomies: Responses to Modernity in the Diverse States of Southeast Asia and Korea, 1750–1900,* ed. Anthony Reid, 321–344. New York: St. Martin's Press.

————. 1997b. *Java and Modern Europe: Ambiguous Encounters.* London: Curzon.

Kuntowijoyo. 1991. *Paradigma Islam: Interpretasi untuk Aksi* (Islamic Paradigm: An Interpretation for Action). Bandung: Mizan.

————. 1994. "Between Mosque and Market: The Muslim Community in Quiapo, Metro Manila." *Studia Islamika* 1, 3:25–72.

Kurian, George Thomas. 1990. *Encyclopedia of the Third World.* New York: Facts on File.

Kurzman, Charles, ed. 2002. *Modernist Islam 1840–1940.* New York: Oxford University Press.

Laarhoven, Ruurdje. 1989. *The Maguindanao Sultanate in the 17th Century: Triumph of Moro Diplomacy.* Quezon City: New Day Publishers.

Labib, Subhi J. 1981. "Die islamische Expansion und das Piratenwesen im Indischen Ozean" (Islamic Expansion and Piracy in the Indian Ocean). *Der Islam* 58: 147–167.

Laksono, P. M. 1986. *Tradition in Javanese Social Structure, Kingdom and Countryside: Changes in the Javanese Conceptual Model.* Yogyakarta: Gadjah Mada University Press.

Lamant, P.-L. 1995. "Orang Melayu di Kemboja Menghadapi Sistem Politik Protektorat Perancis" (The Malay People in Cambodia Confronting the Political System of the French Protectorate). In *Dunia Melayu dan Dunia Indocina* (The Malay World and the Indo-China World), ed. Tan Sri Ismail Hussein, Prof. P.-B. Lafant, and Dr. Po Dharma, 123–136. Kuala Lumpur: Dewan Bahasa dan Pustaka.

Lancaster, Sir James. 1867. *The Voyages of Sir James Lancaster in the East Indies.* Ed. Clements R. Markham. New York: Burt Franklin.

Landon, Kenneth. 1949. *Southeast Asia: Crossroads of Religion.* Chicago: University of Chicago Press.

Leclerc, Jacques. 1997. "Jakarta in Sukarno's Image." In *Images of Malay-Indonesian Identity*, ed. Michael Hitchcock and Victor T. King, 203–208. Kuala Lumpur: Oxford University Press.

Leirissa, R. Z. 2000. "The Bugis-Makassarese in the Port Towns: Ambon and Ternate through the Nineteenth Century." In *Authority and Enterprise among the Peoples of South Sulawesi*, ed. Roger Tol, Kees van Dijk, and Greg Acciaoli, 241–255. Leiden: KITLV Press.

Leur, J. C. Van. 1955. *Indonesian Trade and Society: Essays in Asian Social and Economic History.* Bandung: Sumur Bandung.

Lev, Daniel S. 1972. *Islamic Courts in Indonesia: A Study in the Political Bases of Legal Institutions.* Berkeley: University of California Press.

Li, Tania. 1989. *Malays in Singapore: Culture, Economy, and Ideology.* Singapore: Oxford University Press.

Liaw Yock Fang. 1976. *The Undang-Undang Melaka* (The Laws of Melaka). The Hague: Martinus Nijhoff; also 1983 (summary). *Melaka: The Transformation of a Malay Capital*, ed. K. S. Sandhu and P. Wheatley, 181–194. Kuala Lumpur: Oxford University Press.

Liddle, R. William. 1996. "Media Dakwah Scripturalism: One Form of Islamic Political Thought and Action in New Order Indonesia." In R. William Liddle, *Leadership and Culture in Indonesian Politics.* St. Leonard's, N.S.W., Australia: Allen & Unwin.

Lockard, Craig A. 1987. *From Kampung to City: A Social History of Kuching, Malaysia 1820–1970.* London: George Harrap.

———. 1998. *Dance of Life: Popular Music and Politics in Southeast Asia.* Honolulu: University of Hawai'i Press.

Loeb, Edwin M. 1935. *Sumatra: Its History and People.* Vienna: Verlag des Instituts für Volkenkunde der Universität Wien.

Loire-de Hauteclocque, Ghislaine. 1991. "The Institutions of the Magindanao." Part 6 of *General History of the Philippines.* Manila: Historical Conservation Society. Translation of *À la recherche de l'Islam Philippin: La communaute Maranao.* Paris: Éditions l'Harmattan, 1989.

Low, Hugh. 1848. *Sarawak: Its Inhabitants and Productions.* Petaling Jaya: Delta.

Low, James. 1849. "A Translation of the Keddah Annals Termed Morong Maha-wangsa." *The Indian Archipelago* 3, 1:1–23, 90–101, 162–181, 253–270, 314–336, 468–488.

Mackeen, A. M. M. 1969. *Contemporary Islamic Legal Organization in Malaya.* New Haven, CT: Yale University Southeast Asia Studies.

Madale, Abdullah T. 1997. *The Maranaws: Dwellers of the Lake.* Manila: The Rex Book Store.

Majul, Cesar Adib. 1962. "Theories on the Introduction and Expansion of Islam in Malaysia." *International Association of Historians of Asia Second Biennial Conference Proceedings, October 6–9, 1962,* 339–398. Taipei, Taiwan.

———. 1999. *Muslims in the Philippines.* Silliman, Quezon City: University of the Philippines Press.

Mak Phoen. 1999. "Masyarakat Cam" (Cham Society). In *Dunia Melayu dan Dunia Indocina* (The Malay World and the Indo-China World), ed. Tan S. A. Ismail, P.-B. Lafant, and Po Darma. Kuala Lumpur: Dewan Bahasa dan Pustaka.

Malay/Muslim Professionals of Singapore. 1990. *Forging a Vision: Prospects, Challenges and Directions . . . in 21st Century Singapore.* Singapore.

Manguin, Pierre Yves. 1985. "The Introduction of Islam into Champa." *Journal of the Malayan Branch of the Royal Asiatic Society* 51, 1:1–28.

Mani, A. 1992. "Aspects of Identity and Change among Tamil Muslims in Singapore." *Journal of the Institute of Muslim Minority Affairs* 13, 2:337–357.

Marrison, G. E. 1954. "Persian Influences in Malay Life (1260–1650)." *Journal of the Malayan Branch of the Royal Asiatic Society* 28, 1:52–69, 169.

Marsden, William. 1966. *The History of Sumatra.* Kuala Lumpur: Oxford University Press.

Mastura, Michael O. 1984. *Muslim Filipino Experience: A Collection of Essays.* Manila: Ministry of Muslim Affairs.

Matheson, Virginia. *See also* Hooker, Virginia Matheson.

Matheson, Virginia. 1989. "Pulau Penyengat: Nineteenth Century Islamic Centre of Riau." *Archipel* 37:153–172.

Matheson, Virginia, and Barbara Watson Andaya. 1985. *The Precious Gift (Tuhfat al-Nafis) by Raja Ali Haji Ibn Ahmad.* Kuala Lumpur: Oxford University Press.

Matheson, Virginia, and M. B. Hooker. 1988. "Jawi Literature in Patani: The Maintenance of an Islamic Tradition." *Journal of the Malayan Branch of the Royal Asiatic Society* 61, 1:1–86.

Mawardi, Ahmad Imam. 2003. "The Political Backdrop of the Enactment of the Compilation of Islamic Laws in Indonesia." In *Shari'a and Politics in Modern Indonesia,* ed. Arskal Salim and Azyumardi Azra, 125–147. Singapore: Institute of Southeast Asian Studies.

McArthur, M. S. H. 1987. *Report on Brunei in 1904.* Athens: Ohio University Center for International Studies.

McDonnell, Mary Bryne. 1990. "Patterns of Muslim Pilgrimage from Malaysia 1885–1995." In *Muslim Travellers,* ed. D. E. Eichelman and J. Piscatori, 111–129. London: Routledge.

McKenna, Thomas M. 1998. *Muslim Rulers and Rebels: Everyday Politics and Armed Separatism in the Southern Philippines.* Berkeley: University of California Press.

McKinlay, William E. W. 1903. "A Brief Summary of Historical Accounts respecting the Spanish Military Operations against the Moros from the year 1578 to 1898." Manila: U.S. Army Division of the Philippines.

Means, Gordon P. 1982. "Malaysia: Islam in a Pluralistic Society." In *Religion and Societies: Asia and the Middle East,* ed. Caro Calderola, 445–459. Berlin: Mouten.

Mednick, Melvin. 1974. "Sultans and Mayors: The Relation of a National to an Indigenous Political System. In *The Muslim Filipinos,* ed. Peter G. Gowing and Robert D. McAmis, 225–229. Manila: Solidaridad Publishing House.

Meilink-Roeloefz, M. A. P. 1962. *Asian Trade and European Influence in the Indonesian Archipelago between 1500 and about 1630.* The Hague: Martinus Nijhoff.

———. 1970. "Trade and Islam in the Malay-Indonesian Archipelago Prior to the Arrival of the Europeans." In *Islam and the Trade of Asia,* ed. D. S. Richards, 137–158. Oxford: Bruno Cassirer.

Mellema, R. L. 1947. *De Islam in Indonesie (in het bijzonder op Java)* (Islam in Indonesia, Particularly on Java). Amsterdam: Druk de Bussy.

Mendaki. 1993. *Making the Difference: Ten Years of Mendaki.* Singapore.

Menon, K. U. 1987. "Brunei Darussalam in 1986: In Search of the Political Kingdom." In *Southeast Asian Affairs 1987,* 85–101. Singapore: Institute of Southeast Asian Studies.

Miller, Terry E., and Sean Williams, eds. 1998. *The Garland Encyclopedia of World Music: Southeast Asia.* New York and London: Garland Publishing Company.

Minhaji, Akh. 1997. "Ahmad Hassan and Islamic Legal Reform in Indonesia (1887–1958)." Ph.D. diss., McGill University, Montreal.

Mintz, Jeanne S. 1965. *Muhammad, Marx and Marhaen: The Roots of Indonesian Socialism.* London: Pall Mall Press.

Mobini-Kesheh, Natalie. 1999. *The Hadrami Awakening: Community and Identity in the Netherlands East Indies, 1900–1942.* Ithaca, NY: Southeast Asian Program of Cornell University.

Moertono, Soemarsaid. 1968. State and *Statecraft in Old Java: A Study of the Later Mataram Period. 16th to 19th Centuries.* Ithaca, NY: Cornell Modern Indonesia Project.

Mohammad. *See* Muhammad.

Moore, Ruth Laura Perry. 1981. "Women and Warriors: Defending Islam in the Southern Philippines." Ph.D. diss., University of California, San Diego.

Moquette, J. P. 1919. "De oudste Mohammedaansche Enscriptie op Java, n.m. de Grafsteen te Leran" (The Oldest Muslim Inscription on Java, i.e., the Grave Marker at Leran). *Handelingen eerste Congress voor de Taal-, Land- en Volkenkunde van Java* (Proceedings of the first Congress of the Royal Institute of Linguistics and Anthropology), 391–399. Weltereden.

Morga, Antonio de. 1962. "The Philippine Islands." Translation of *Sucesos de las Islas Filipinas* by Encarnación Alzona. Manila: José Rizal Centennial Commission.

Moses, Edith. 1908. *Unofficial Letters of an Official's Wife.* New York: Appleton & Co.

Mudzhar, Mohammad Atho. 1993. *Fatwa-Fatwa Majelis Ulama Indonesia.* Translation by Soedarso Soekarno (of "Fatwas of the Council of Indonesian 'Ulama': A Study of Islamic Legal Thought in Indonesia, 1975–1988" Los Angeles: UCLA, 1990). Jakarta: Indonesia Netherlands Cooperation in Islamic Studies.

Muhaimin, A. G. 1999. "The Morphology of Adat: The Celebration of Islamic Holy Days in the North Coast of Java." *Studia Islamika* 6, 3:101–130.

Muhammad Bukhari Lubis. 1983. *Qasidahs in Honor of the Prophet.* Banggi: Penerbitan Universiti Kebangsaan Malaysia.

[Muhammad] Mohammed Idwar Saleh. 1975. "Agrarian Radicalism and Movements of Native Insurrection in South Kalimantan. *Archipel* 9:135–153.

[Muhammad] Mohamed Jani Naim. 1980. "Sekolah Agama Rakyat si Sabak Bernam Hingga 1945" (The Popular Religious School of Si Sabak Bernam since 1945). In *Islam di Malaysia*, ed. Khoo Kay Kim, Mohd. Fadzil Othman, and Abdullah Zakaria Ghazali, 52–61. Kuala Lumpur: Persatuan Sejarah Malaysia.

Muhammad Kamal Hassan. 1982. *Muslim Intellectual Responses to "New Order" Modernization in Indonesia*. Kuala Lumpur: Dewan Bahasa dan Pustaka.

[Muhammad] Mohd. Taib bin Osman. 1972. "Patterns of Supernatural Premises Underlying the Institution of the Bomoh in Malay Culture." *Bijdragen KITLV* 128:219–234.

———. 1989. *Masyarakat Melayu: Struktur, Organisasi dan Manifestasi* (Malay Society: Structure, Organization and Manifestation). Kuala Lumpur: Dewan Bahasa dan Pustaka.

[Muhammad] Mohamed Tajuddin Haji Mohamad Rasdi. 1998. *The Mosque as a Community Development Centre: Programme and Architectural Design. Guidelines for Contemporary Societies.* Johor Darul Ta'zim, University Teknologi Malaysia.

Mulder, J. A. Niels. 1983. "Aliran-Kebatinan as an Expression of the Javanese Worldview." *Journal of Southeast Asian Studies* 1, 2:105–114.

Muljana, Slamet. 1976. *A Story of Majapahit*. Singapore: University of Singapore Press.

Mundy, Peter. 1919. *Travels in Europe and Asia, 1608–1667*. Ed. Lt. Col. Sir Richard Carnac Temple. 2 vols. Cambridge: Hakluyt Society.

Nagata, Judith. 1986. *The Reflowering of Malaysian Islam*. Vancouver: University of British Columbia Press.

Nakula. 1989. "Keturunan Melayu di Kamboja dan Vietnam" (Malay Descendants in Cambodia and Vietnam). *Warisan Kelantan* (Heritage of Kelantan) 8:6–41.

Nathan, K. S. 1995. "Vision 2020 and Malaysian Foreign Policy: Strategic Evolution and the Mahathir Impact." In *Southeast Asian Affairs 1995*, 220–240. Singapore: Institute of Southeast Asian Studies.

Ner, M. 1941. "Les Musulmans de l'Indochine Française" (The Muslims of French Indochina). *Bulletin de l'École Française d'Extrême Orient* 41:151–200.

Newbold, T. J. 1971. *British Settlements in the Straits of Malacca*. 2 vols. Kuala Lumpur: Oxford University Press.

Nicholl, Robert. 1977. "Relations between Brunei and Manila." *Brunei Museum Journal* 4, 1:128–176.

Nieman, George Karel. 1861. *Inleiding tot de kennis van den Islam, ook met betrekking tot den Indischen Archipel* (Introduction to the Principles of Islam, with Reference to the Indonesian Archipelago). Rotterdam: M. Wiit & Zonen.

Nieuwenhuijze, C. A. O. van. 1958. *Aspects of Islam in Post-Colonial Indonesia*. The Hague and Bandung: W. Van Hoeve.

Nitibaskara, Ronny. 1993. "Observations on the Practice of Sorcery in Java. In *Understanding Witchcraft and Sorcery in Southeast Asia*, ed. C. W. Watson and Roy Ellen. Honolulu: University of Hawai'i Press.

Noer, Deliar. 1978. *Administration of Islam in Indonesia*. Ithaca, NY: Cornell Modern Indonesia Project.

———. 1982. *Gerakan Moderen Islam di Indonesia 1900–1942* (The Modern Muslim Movement in Indonesia 1900–1942). Jakarta: Lembaga Penelitian, Pendidikan, dan Penerangan Ekonomi dan Sosial.

————. 1987. *Partai Islam di Pentas Nasional, 1945–1965* (Muslim Political Parties on the National Stage). Jakarta: Pustaka Utama Grafiti.

Noorduyn, Jacobus. 1989. "Makassar and the Islamization of Bima." *Bijdragen KITLV* 143:312–341.

————. 2000. "The Wajorese Merchants' Community in Makassar." In *Authority and Enterprise among the Peoples of South Sulawesi*, ed. Roger Tol, Kees van Dijk, and Greg Accialioli, 95–120. Leiden: KITLV Press.

Okuma Memorial Social Sciences Research Institute. 1959. *Indonesia ni Okeru Nihon Gunsei no Kenkyu* (Research on the Japanese Military Administration in Indonesia). Tokyo: Kinokuniya Shotan. Translated into English as *Japanese Military Administration in Indonesia*. Washington, DC: Joint Publications Research Service, 1963.

Omar Farouk. 1988. "The Muslims of Southeast Asia: An Overview." In *Islamic Banking in Southeast Asia*, ed. Mohamed Ariff, 5–33. Singapore: Institute of Southeast Asian Studies.

O'Neill, Hugh. 1993. "Islamic Architecture under the New Order." In *Culture and Society in New Order Indonesia*, ed. Virigina Matheson Hooker, 151–165. Kuala Lumpur: Oxford University Press.

Ongkili, James P. 1959. "Pre-Western Brunei, Sarawak and Sabah." *Sarawak Museum Journal* 20:40–41, 1–20.

Oroso, Sixto Y. 1923. *The Sulu Archipelago and Its People*. New York: World Book Company.

Osman-Rani, H. 1992. "Towards a Fully-Developed Malaysia: Vision and Challenges." In *Southeast Asian Affairs 1992*, 202–217. Singapore: Institute of Southeast Asian Studies.

Palmier, Leslie H. 1985. *Understanding Indonesia*. Brookfield, VT: Gower Publishing Company.

Panitia Seminar Sejarah Masuknja Islam di Indonesia (Organizing Committee for the Seminar on the History of the Entry of Islam to Indonesia). 1963. *Sejarah Masuknja Islam ke Indonesia* (The Entry of Islam in Indonesia). Medan.

Peacock, James L. 1978a. *Purifying the Faith: The Muhammadijah Movement in Indonesian Islam*. Menlo Park, CA: Benjamin Cummings.

————. 1978b. *Muslim Puritans: Reformed Psychology in Southeast Asian Islam*. Berkeley: University of California Press.

Peletz, Michael G. 1993. "Knowledge, Power and Personal Misfortune in a Malay Context." In *Understanding Witchcraft and Sorcery in Southeast Asia*, ed. C. W. Watson and Roy Ellen, 149–179. Honolulu: University of Hawai'i Press.

Pelras, Christian. 1975. "Introduction à la Littérature Bugis" (Introduction to the Literature of the Bugis). *Archipel* 10:239–267.

————. 2001. "Religion, Tradition, and the Dynamics of Islamization in South Sulawesi." In *The Propagation of Islam in the Indonesian-Malay Archipelago*, ed. and annot. Alijah Gordon, 209–250. Kuala Lumpur: Malaysian Sociological Research Institute.

Pelzer, Karl J. 1948. *Pioneer Land Settlement in the Asian Tropics*. New York: American Geographical Society.

Penth, Hans. 1969. *Hikajat Atjeh: Die Erzahlung von der Abkunft und den Jugend Jahren des Sultan Iskandar Muda von Atjeh (Sumatra)* (The Aceh Chronicles: The Saga of the Descent and Youthful Years of Sultan Iskandar Muda of Aceh). Wiesbaden: Otto Harrassowitz.

Philippines Office of Muslim Affairs. 1988. *Muslim Development: Two Years under the Aquino Administration*. Manila.

Philippines Statistical Office. 2003. *2000 Census*. Manila [Philippine Government website].

Pigafetta, A. 1969 (1905). *First Voyage around the World* (J. A. Robertson's version). Reprint. Manila: Filipiana Book Guild.

Pigeaud, Th. G. Th. 1960–1963. *Java in the Fourteenth Century: A Study in Cultural History. The Nagara-Kertagama by Rakowi Prapanca of Majapahit, 1365 A.D.* 5 vols. The Hague: Martinus Nijhoff.

———. 1967–1970. *The Literature of Java*. 3 vols. Leiden: E. J. Brill.

Pigeaud, Th. G. Th., and H. J. de Graaf. 1976. *Islamic States in Java 1500–1700: A Summary, Bibliography and Index*. The Hague: Martinus Nijhoff.

Pijnappel, J. 1872. "Over de kennis die de Arabieren voor de komst der Portugeezen van den Indischen Archipel bezatten" (Regarding the Knowledge of the Arabs about the Indonesian Archipelago before the Arrival of the Portuguese). *Bijdragen KITLV* 19:135–158.

Pijper, G. F. 1977. *Studien over de Geschiedenis van Indonesia 1900–1950* (Studies of the History of Indonesia 1900–1950). Leiden: E. J. Brill.

Pinto, Fernão Mendes. 1614. *Peregrinacao* (The Peregrination). 4 vols. Lisbon.

Pires, Tome. 1944. *The Suma Oriental of Tome Pires: An Account of the East, from the Red Sea to Japan, Written in Malacca and India in 1512–1515*. Trans. and ed. Armando Cortesão. 2 vols. London: Hakluyt Society.

Poensen, C. 1886. *Brieven over den Islam uit de binnenland van Java* (Letters concerning Islam from the Interior of Java). Leiden: E. J. Brill.

Prijono, Onny S. 1999. "Education: Access, Quality, and Relevance." In *Indonesia: The Challenge of Change*, ed. Richard W. Baker et al., 159–178. Singapore: Institute of Southeast Asian Studies.

Pyrard, François. 1887–1890. *The Voyage of François Pyrard of Laval to the East Indies, the Maldives, the Molucas and Brazil*. Ed. Albert Grey and H. C. P. Bell. London: Hakluyt Society.

Rahmat [Hadijah Binti]. 1991. "Sastera dan Manusia Melayu Baru" (Literature and Modern Malay). In *Dinamika Budaya* (Cultural Dynamics), ed. Nadwah Sastera, 175–212. Singapore: Majlis Pusat Pertubuhan–Pertubuhan Budaya Melayu.

Raja Fuziah Raja Tun Uda and Abdul Rahman Al-Ahmadi. 1997. "Malay Arts and Crafts: Islamic Inspiration in Creativity." In *Islamic Civilization in the Malay World*, ed. Mohd. Taib Osman, 279–352. Kuala Lumpur: Dewan Bahasa dan Pustaka, and Istanbul: Research Centre for Islamic History.

Ramage, Douglas. 1994. *Politics in Indonesia: Democracy, Islam and Ideology of Tolerance*. London: Routledge.

Ratnam, K. J. 1965. *Communalism and Political Process in Malaysia*. Kuala Lumpur: University of Malaya Press.

Ravaisse, P. 1922. "Deux Inscriptions Coufiques du Campa" (Two Sufi Inscriptions of Champa). *Journal Asiatiques* 11, 20:247–289.

Reid, Anthony. 1969a. *The Contest for North Sumatra: Atjeh, the Netherlands and Britain 1858–1898*. Kuala Lumpur: Oxford University Press.

———. 1969b. "Sixteenth Century Turkish Influence in Western Indonesia." *Journal of Southeast Asian History* 10, 3:395–414.

———. 1975. "Trade and the Problem of Royal Power in Acheh." In *Pre-Colonial State Systems in Southeast Asia,* ed. Anthony Reid and Lance Castles, 45–55. Kuala Lumpur: Council of the Malaysian Branch of the Royal Asiatic Society.

———. 1980 and 1993a. *Southeast Asia in the Age of Commerce.* 2 vols. New Haven, CT: Yale University Press.

———. 1993b. "Kings, Kadis and Charisma in the 17th Century Archipelago." In *The Making of an Islamic Political Discourse in Southeast Asia,* ed. Anthony Reid. Clayton, Victoria: Monash University.

Reid, Anthony, and Lance Castles, eds. 1975. *Pre-Colonial State Systems in Southeast Asia.* Kuala Lumpur: Council of the Malaysian Branch of the Royal Asiatic Society.

Reischauer, Edwin O., and John K. Fairbank. 1960. *East Asia: The Great Tradition.* Boston: Houghton Mifflin Company.

Reischauer, Edwin O., and Albert M. Craig. 1965. *East Asia: The Great Transformation.* Boston: Houghton Mifflin Company.

Remmelink, Willem. 1994. *The Chinese War and the Collapse of the Javanese State 1725–1743.* Leiden: KITLV Press.

Ricklefs, M. C. 1979. "Six Centuries of Islamization on Java." In *Conversion to Islam,* ed. Nehemia Levitzion, 11–23. New York: Holmes & Meier.

———. 1981. *A History of Modern Indonesia.* Bloomington: University of Indiana Press.

———. 1993. *War, Culture and Economy in Java, 1677–1726: Asian and European Imperialism in the Early Kartasura Period.* Sydney: Asian Studies Association of Australia and Allen & Unwin.

———. 1998. *The Seen and Unseen Worlds in Java, 1726–1749.* Honolulu: University of Hawai'i Press

Riddell, Peter. 2001. *Islam and the Malay-Indonesian World: Transmission and Response.* Honolulu: University of Hawai'i Press.

Rinkes, D. A. 1911. *De Heiligen van Java* (The Saints of Java). 6 vols. Batavia: Albrecht. Also *The Nine Saints of Java.* 1996. Trans. H. M. Froger and ed. Alijah Gordon. Kuala Lumpur: Malaysian Sociological Research Institute.

Rixhon, Gerard. 1998. "The Parang Sabil Epic of the Tausug Revisited: Exploring Various Levels of Discourse." Paper presented at the Third Conference on Philippine Studies, Aix-en-Provence, 1998.

Robison, Francis. 1982. *Atlas of the Islamic World since 1500.* Oxford: Equinox Books.

Roff, William R. 1967. *The Origins of Malay Nationalism.* New Haven, CT: Yale University Press.

———. 1970. "Southeast Asian Islam in the Nineteenth Century." In *Cambridge History of Islam,* ed. P. M. Holt, Ann K. S. Lambton, and Bernard Lewis, vol. 2, pt. A, 155–181. Cambridge: Cambridge University Press.

Saber, Mamitua Desarip, and Abdullah T. Madale, eds. 1975. *The Maranao.* Manila: Solidaridad Publishing House.

Sabihah Osman. 1986. "Malay–Muslim Political Participation in Sarawak and Sabah 1841–1951." *Sabah Society Journal* 8, 2:290–295.

Salam, Solichin. 1963. *Sekitar Wali Sanga* (The Milieu of the Nine Propagators). Kudus: Menara Kudus.

Salamat Muljana. 1976. *A Story of Majapahit.* Singapore: Singapore University Press.

Saleeby, Najeeb M. 1963 (1907). *The History of Sulu.* Manila: Filipiana Book Guild.

———. 1974. "History of Maguindanao." In *The Muslim Filipinos,* ed. Peter G. Gowing and Robert D. McAmis. Manila: Solidaridad Publishing House.

Saleh, Fauzon. 2001. *Modern Trends in Islamic Theological Discourse in Twentieth Century Indonesia.* Leiden: Brill Academic Press.

Sanib Said. 1989. "Malays under the Brooke Regime 1841–1941: The Beginnings of Socio-Political Alienation of the Race." *Sarawak Museum Journal* 40:87–106.

Santo Stefano, Hieronimo di. 1857. "The Journey of Hieronimo di Santo Stefano, a Genoese." In *India in the Fifteenth Century,* ed. R. H. Major. London: Hakluyt Society.

Sar Desai, D. R. 1994. *Southeast Asia: Past and Present.* 3rd ed. Boulder, CO: Westview Press.

Sartono, Kartodirdjo. 1985. "The Peasants' Revolt of Banten in 1888: The Religious Revival." In *Readings on Islam in Southeast Asia,* ed. A. Ibrahim, S. Siddique, and Y. Hussain, 103–110. Singapore: Institute of Southeast Asian Studies.

Saunders, Graham. 1994. *A History of Brunei.* Kuala Lumpur: Oxford University Press.

Schrieke, B. J. O. 1955 and 1957. *Indonesian Sociological Studies.* 2 vols. The Hague: W. Van Hoeve.

Scupin, Raymond. 1980. "Islamic Reform in Thailand." *Journal of the Siam Society* 68, 1:55–71.

———. 1988. "Cham Muslims in Thailand." In "The Muslims of Thailand: Historical and Cultural Studies," ed. Andrew D. W. Forbes. In *The South East Asian Review* 13, 1:31–46.

Seda-Poulin, Maria Luisa. 1993. "Islamization and Legal Reform in Malaysia: The *Hudud* Controversy of 1992." In *Southeast Asian Affairs 1993,* 224–242. Singapore: Institute of Southeast Asian Studies.

Serudin, Mohammed Zain bin Hadji. 1992. *Brunei Darussalam: Persepsi, Sejarah dan Masyarakatnya* (Brunei Darussalam: Perspective, History and Its Society). Brunei: Azza Publishers.

Shahril Talib. 1990. "The Port and Polity of Terengganu during the Eighteenth and Nineteenth Centuries: Realizing Its Potential." In *The Southeast Asian Port and Polity: Rise and Demise,* ed. J. Kathirithamby-Wells and J. Villiers, 213–230. Singapore: Singapore University Press.

Shantakumar, G. 1993. "The Indian Population of Singapore: Some Implications of Development." In *Indian Communities in Southeast Asia,* ed. K. S. Sandhu and A. Mani, 867–910. Singapore: Institute of Southeast Asian Studies.

Sharom Ahmat. 1984. *Tradition and Change in a Malay State: A Study of the Economic and Political Development of Kedah, 1878–1923.* Kuala Lumpur: Malaysian Branch of the Royal Asiatic Society.

Siddique, Sharon. 1985. "Negara Brunei Darussalam: A New Nation but an Ancient Country." In *Southeast Asian Affairs 1985,* 99–110. Singapore: Institute of Southeast Asian Studies.

———. 1992. "Brunei Darussalam 1991: The Non-Secular State." In *Southeast Asian Affairs 1992,* 91–100. Singapore: Institute of Southeast Asian Studies.

Singapore, Majlis Ugama Islam (Islamic Council). 1994. *Muslims in Singapore: A Shared Vision.* Singapore: Times Editions.

Singh, D. S. Ranjit. 1991. *Brunei 1939–1983: The Politics of Political Survival.* Singapore: Oxford University Press.

Sjamsuddin, Nazaruddin. 1985. *The Republican Revolt: A Study of the Acehnese Rebellion.* Singapore: Institute of Southeast Asian Studies.

Skeat, Walter William. 1965. *Malay Magic: An Introduction to the Folklore and Popular Religion of the Malay Peninsula.* London: Frank Cass.

Soebardi, S. 1969. "Raden Ngabehi Jasadipura I, Court Poet of Surakarta: His Life and Works." *Indonesia* 8:81–102.

———. 1971. "Santri-Religious Elements as Reflected in the Book of Tjentini." *Bijdragen KITLV* 127:331–349.

Spat, C. 1925. *De Islam en zijn beteekenis voor Nederlandsch-Indie* (Islam and Its Meaning in the Netherlands Indies). Breda: de Koninklijke Militaire Academie.

Spruitt, Ruud. 1995. *The Land of the Sultans; An Illustrated History of Malaysia.* Amsterdam: The Pepin Press.

Stahr, Volker S. 1997. *Südostasien und der Islam: Kulturraum zwischen Kommerz und Koran* (Southeast Asia and Islam: Culture Space between Commerce and the Qur'an). Darmstadt: Primus.

Steinberg, David J., ed. 1987. In *Search of Southeast Asia.* Honolulu: University of Hawai'i Press.

Strubbe, Bill. 1993. "The People Persist." *Aramco World* 444, 2:10–15.

Stutterheim, William Frederik. 1935. *De Islam en zijn komst in de archipel culturgeschichte van Indonesië* (Islam and Its Arrival in the Indonesian Cultural Zone). Gröningen: J. B. Wolters.

Sukarno. 1969. *Nationalism, Islam and Marxism.* Trans. Karel H. Warouw and Peter D. Weldon, with an introduction by Ruth T. McVey. Ithaca, NY: Cornell Modern Indonesia Project.

Sumalyo, Yulianto. 2000. *Arsitektur Mesjid dan Monumen Sejarah Muslim* (Mosque Architecture and Historical Muslim Monuments). Yogyakarta: Gadjah Mada University Press.

Suminto, Aqib. 1985. *Politik Islam Hindia Belanda* (The Islamic Policy of the Dutch Indies Administration). Jakarta: Lembaga Penelitian, Pendidikan, dan Penerangan Ekomomi dan Sosial.

Suradi Parjo. 1991. "Sejarah dan Pencapaian Hadiah Sastera Melayu Singapore" (History and Competition of the Malay Literature Prize of Singapore). In *Dinamika Budaya,* ed. Nadwah Sastera, 133–174. Singapore: Majlis Pusat Pertubuhan-Pertubuhan Budaya Melayu.

Surin Pitsuwarn. 1985. *Islam and Malay Nationalism: A Case Study of the Malay Muslims of Southern Thailand.* Bangkok: Thommasat University.

Sutherland, Heather. 1989. "Eastern Emporium and Company Town: Trade and Society in Eighteenth Century Makassar." In *Brides of the Sea: Port Cities of Asia from the 16th to 20th Centuries,* ed. Frank Broeze, 97–128. Honolulu: University of Hawai'i Press.

Sutton, R. Anderson, Endo Suanda, and Sean Williams. 1998. "Java." In *Garland Encyclopedia of World Music: Southeast Asia,* ed. Terry E. Miller and Sean Williams, 630–728. New York and London: Garland Publishing Company.

Swettenham, Frank. 1906. *British Malaya: An Account of the Origin and Progress of British Influence in Malaya.* London: Allen & Unwin.

Tamano, Mamintal A. 1974. "Problems of the Muslims: A National Concern." In *The Muslim Filipinos,* ed. Peter G. Gowing and Robert D. McAmis, 259–270. Manila: Solidaridad Publishing House.

Tan, Samuel Kong. 1993. *Internationalization of the Bangsamoro Struggle*. Dilliman: University of the Philippines Press.

Tan Chee Khaun. 1992. *Lukisan Pelukis–Pelukis Perintis daripada Koleksi Persendirian —Paintings of the Pioneer Artists from Private Collections*. Pulau Pinang: Lembaga Muzium Negeri.

Tarling, Nicholas. 1978. *Sulu and Sabah: A Study of British Policy towards the Philippines and North Borneo from the Late Eighteenth Century*. Kuala Lumpur: Oxford University Press.

———, ed. 1992. *The Cambridge History of Southeast Asia*. 2 vols. Cambridge: Cambridge University Press.

Tate, D. J. M. 1971. *The Making of Southeast Asia*. 2 vols. London: Oxford University Press.

Taussaint, Auguste. 1961. *History of the Indian Ocean*. Chicago: University of Chicago Press.

Taylor, Keith W. 1992. "The Early Kingdoms." In *The Cambridge History of Southeast Asia*, ed. Nicholas Tarling, 1:137–182. Cambridge: Cambridge University Press.

Teeuw, A. 1970. *Hikayat Patani—Story of Patani*. 2 vols. The Hague: Martinus Nijhoff.

Thailand National Statistical Office. 2002 ["Census Website"].

Thomas, M. Ladd. 1989. "Thai Muslim Separatism in Southern Thailand." In "The Muslims of Thailand: Politics of the Malay-Speaking South," ed. Andrew D. W. Forbes. *The South East Asian Review* 14, 1 and 2:19–32.

Thomaz, Luis Filipe Ferreira Reis. 1994. "The Malay Sultanate of Melaka." In *Southeast Asia in the Early Modern Era: Trade, Power, and Belief*, ed. Anthony Reid, 69–90. Ithaca, NY, and London: Cornell University Press.

Tibbetts, G. R. 1975. "Early Muslim Traders in South-East Asia." *Journal of the Malayan Branch of the Royal Asiatic Society* 30:1, 1–4

———. 1979. *A Study of the Arabic Texts Containing Material on South-East Asia*. Leiden and London: E. J. Brill.

Uka Tjandrasasmita. 1984. "Jaman Pertumbuhan dan Perkembangan Kerajaan-Kerajaan Islam di Indonesia" (The Era of the Rise and Development of Islamic Kingdoms in Indonesia). In *Sejarah Nasional Indonesia* (National History of Indonesia), ed. Marwati Djoened Poesponegoro and Nugroho Notosusanto, vol. 3. Jakarta: Balai Pustaka.

United States Bureau of the Census. 1903. "Remarks on the Moro Population." *Census of the Philippine Islands*, vol. 3. Taken under the direction of the Philippine Commission.

United States Central Intelligence Agency. 2003. *CIA Factbook*. Website report.

Valentijn, François. 1724–1726. *Oud en nieuw Oost-Indien* (Old and New East Indies). 5 vols. Dordrecht: J. Van Braam.

Van der Veur, Paul W. 1986. "The Difference between Mecca and Digul." Introduction and annotation to a text by Mohamad Amanoe. *Journal of Southeast Asian Studies* 17, 2:268–281.

Van Leur, J. C. *See* Leur, J. C. Van.

Vaughn, J. D. 1858. "Notes on the Malays of Pinang and Province Wellesley." *The Indian Archipelago* 2, 2:115–175.

Villiers, John. 1985. *East of Malacca*. Bangkok: Calousie Gulbenkian Foundation.

———. 1990. "Makassar: The Rise and Fall of an East Indonesian Maritime Trading

State, 1510–1669." In *The Southeast Asian Port and Polity*, ed. J. Kathirithamby-Wells and J. Villiers, 143–159. Singapore: Singapore University Press.

———. 1995. "Cash-Crop Economy and State Formation in the Spice Islands in the Fifteenth and Sixteenth Centuries." In *The Southeast Asian Port and Polity*, ed. J. Kathirithamby-Wells and J. Villiers, 83–105. Singapore: Singapore University Press.

Voll, John Obert. 1982. *Islam: Continuity and Change in the Modern World.* Boulder, CO: Westview Press.

Vollenhoven, C. van. 1918–1931. *Het Adatrcht van Nederlandsch-Indie.* 4 vols. Leiden: E. J. Brill.

Von der Mehden, Fred R. 1963. *Religion and Nationalism in Southeast Asia.* Madison: University of Wisconsin.

———. 1993. *Two Worlds of Islam: Interaction between Southeast Asia and the Middle East.* Gainesville: University of Florida Press.

Voorhoeve, P. 1951. "Van en Over Nuruddin ar-Raniri" (Concerning al-Raniri). *Bijdragen KITLV* 107:353–358.

———. 1959. "Over Nuruddin ar-Raniri" (Concerning Nuruddin al-Raniri). *Bijdragen KITLV* 115:90–91.

Vredenbregt, J. 1962. "The Haddj. Some of Its Features and Functions in Indonesia." *Bijdragen KITLV* 118:91–154.

———. 1973. "Dabus in West Java." *Bijdragen KITLV* 129:301–319.

Warren, James Francis. 1981. *The Sulu Zone 1768–1898. The Dynamics of External Trade, Slavery and Ethnicity in the Transformation of a Southeast Asian Maritime State.* Singapore: Singapore University Press.

———. 2002. *Iranun and Balangingi: Globalization, Maritime Raiding and the Birth of Ethnicity.* Quezon City: New Day Publishers.

Waspada. 1986–1990. Medan.

Weatherbee, Donald E. 1985. "The Pancasila State." In *Southeast Asian Affairs 1985*, 133–151. Singapore: Institute of Southeast Asian Studies.

Wheatley, Paul. 1961. *The Golden Khersonese: Studies in the Historical Geography of the Malayan Peninsula before A.D. 1500.* Kuala Lumpur: University of Malaya Press.

Wilkinson, R. J. 1925. "Life and Customs." *Papers on Malay Subjects.* 2 parts in 2 vols. Kuala Lumpur: F.M.S. Government Press.

———. 1935. "The Malacca Sultanate." *Journal of the Malayan Branch of the Royal Asiatic Society* 13, 2:22–67.

Williams, Michael C. 1990. *Sickle and Crescent: The Communist Revolt of 1926 in Banten.* Ithaca, NY: Cornell Modern Indonesia Project.

Wilson, H. E. 1989. "Imperialism and Islam: The Impact of 'Modernisation' on the Malay Muslims of South Thailand." In *The Muslims of Thailand: Politics of the Malay-Speaking South* [ed. Andrew D. W. Forbes] in *The South East Asian Review* 14:1 and 2:53–72.

———. 1992. "Tengku Mahmud Mahyiddeen and the Dilemma of Partisan Duality." *Journal of Southeast Asian Studies* 23, 1:37–59.

Winstedt, R. O. 1922. *Malaya and Its History.* New York: Hutchinson's University Library.

———. 1938. "The Chronicles of Pasai." *Journal of the Malayan Branch of the Royal Asiatic Society* 16, 2:24–30.

———. 1951. *The Malay Magician Being Shaman, Saiva and Sufi.* London: Routledge & Kegan Paul.

———. 1969. *A History of Classical Malay Literature.* New York: Oxford University Press.

Winzeler, Robert L. 1974. "The Social Organization of Islam in Kelantan." In *Kelantan,* ed. W. R. Roff, 259–271. Kuala Lumpur: Oxford University Press.

———. 1983. "The Development of British Colonial Scholarly Interpretations of Malay Islam." *Crossroads* 1, 3:65–81.

Woodward, Mark E. 1989. *Islam in Java: Normative Piety and Mysticism in the Sultanate of Yogyakarta.* Tucson: University of Arizona Press.

———, ed. 1996. *Toward a New Paradigm.* Tempe: Arizona State University Program in International Studies.

Yegar, Moshe. 1979. *Islam and Islamic Institutions in British Malaya 1874–1917. Policies and Implementation.* Jerusalem: Magnes Press. Also "The Development of Islamic Institutional Structure in Malaya, 1874–1941." In *Islam in Asia,* ed. Raphael Israeli and Anthony Johns, 2:190–205. Jersualem: Magnes Press.

Yousuf, Ghulam Sardar. 1994. *Dictionary of the Traditional Southeast Asian Theatre.* Kuala Lumpur: Oxford University Press.

Yunus, Abdul Rahman. 1995. *Posisi Tasuwuf dalam Sistem Kekuasaan di Kesultanan Buton pada Abad Ke-19* (The Place of Mysticism in the Political System of the Buton Sultanate in the 19th Century). Jakarta: Indonesia–Netherlands Cooperation in Islamic Studies.

Yunus, Mahmud. 1957 and 1960. *Sejarah Pendidikan Islam di Indonesia* (The History of Islamic Education in Indonesia). Jakarta: Mutiara.

Zainal Abidin, Andi. 1974. "The I La Galigo Epic Cycle of South Celebes and Its Diffusion." *Indonesia* 17:161–169.

Zainal Kling. 1976. "Life-cycle and the Socialization of Values among Rural Malays in Sarawak." *Sarawak Museum Journal* 24, 45:1–35.

Zaini, Syahminan. 1986. *Isi Pokok Ajaran al-Qur°an* (Principles of the *Qur°an*). Jakarta: Kalam Mulia.

Zaleha Syed Hassan (Sharifah) and Sven Cenderroth. 1997. *Managing Marital Disputes in Malaysia. Islamic Mediators and Conflict Resolution in the Syariah Courts.* London: Curzon.

Zen, A. Muhaimin. 1985. *Tata Cara/Problemika Menghafal AlQur-an dan Petunjuk-Petunjuk* (The Custom of Memorizing the *Qur°an* and Guidance for that Activity). Jakarta: Al Husna.

Zuhri, Saifuddin. 1981. *Sejarah Kebangkitan Islam dan Perkembanannya di Indonesia* (History of the Establishment of Islam and Its Development in Indonesia). Bandung: Al Maarif.

Zuraidah Ibrahim. 1994. *Muslims in Singapore: A Shared Vision.* Singapore: Times Editions.

Index

About the Author

HOWARD FEDERSPIEL received a Ph.D. in Islamic Studies from McGill University in Montreal. He served in the U.S. State Department as an analyst of Southeast Asian political affairs and was field director for higher education development projects in Indonesia. He has been a Fulbright Scholar in Indonesia (1996) and has traveled extensively throughout the Southeast Asian region. His publications include studies of Muslim intellectuals and militant Islamic organizations. His most recent work is *Islam in the Emerging Indonesian State* (2002). He is presently professor of political science at Ohio State University.

Production Notes for
FEDERSPIEL / SULTANS, SHAMANS, AND SAINTS

Cover and interior designed by University of Hawaiʻi Press
production staff in New Baskerville and Antique Olive

Composition by Josie Herr

Printing and binding by The Maple-Vail Book
Manufacturing Group

Printed on 60 lb. Glatfelter Offset B18, 420 ppi